Tequila
and
Chocolate

The Adventures of the
Morning Star and Soulmate

A Memoir

Rev. Dr. JC Husfelt & Rev. Sherry Husfelt

ISBN: 978-1-54398-622-8
Library of Congress Control Number: 2019916132
Snowy Owl, Port Ludlow, WA

For our Granddaughters, Honey Bee – Lilyrose Moon Cox
and her sister – Luna Ann Cox

The mother sea and fountainhead of all religions lie in the mystical experiences of the individual. All theologies, all ecclesiasticisms are secondary growths, superimposed.

—William James

It's what we do.
We far travel the world
and we know things.

FOREWORD

. . . .

My wife and I met when she was thirteen and I was sixteen, both of us Virgos – born of the Virgin.[1] When I first set eyes on her the winds of love flew over the waves and gently enveloped me, a remembrance of heart, not of mind. Years later, Sherry related to me that she went home and wrote in her diary, "I've met the boy I'm going to marry."

We had discovered each other once again. Of course, at the time neither of us knew it. At sixteen, I was like a stranger in a strange land and I still feel the same way today. This feeling led me to act out in outrageous ways, although I've mellowed with age. As it was written in the stars, this didn't matter to Sherry or dissuade her from becoming my wife, partner and—once again—soulmate,[2] at age seventeen.

This isn't an autobiography, but selected memoirs of our spiritual journey through life. You must rely on your imagination to paint a picture of us as teenagers and young adults. Even though many of these tales are based on my experiences and told from my perspective, without Sher by my side once again, as she was in another lifetime, these memoirs would be nonexistent. I am the sun and Sherry is my moon and stars. And one other thing – "Redheads, you gotta love 'em."[3]

Let me begin with my college years. I wasn't at a crossroad of life, as some might say, but on a path with three branches: Down one lay a marriage with the love of my life; another led to service in Vietnam; and yet another would lead me to abandon my life as I knew it and join up with the leftist revolutionary Ernesto "Che" Guevara, who dreamed of a new consciousness driven by altruism rather than materialistic greed and power. To join Che was more of a whimsical dream than reality, while service in Vietnam was not a dream. I was willing to go. I'd been reclassified from my college deferment and reported for my pre-induction physical in the mountains of West Virginia. Because the site of the physical was not in Elkins, West Virginia, where I was enrolled at Davis and Elkins College, and given that none of my fraternity brothers could drive me, I needed to take the bus. Just like far traveling, taking the bus allowed me to have a feeling and sense of people I might never have had contact with – their personalities and their stories of living in West Virginia.

The physical was a bit of a joke. Not much more to it than line up and bend over. The dozen or so other recruits and I passed with flying colors. I didn't know the backgrounds of these young men, but it didn't matter. We were all equal, perhaps all headed overseas to the war-torn land of Vietnam.

Back at college I waited to be called up, but I can't say I was looking forward to it. I was nineteen years old and in love with Sherry, who was sixteen. I would be leaving college and my great love behind to trek through the jungles and rice paddies with strangers, dodging the so-called enemy who would be trying to take my life. Nonetheless, my warrior soul was willing to go and experience what no young soul should ever have to experience.

And then a mystery occurred: I never received any papers to report for basic training, just a notice that my college deferment was back in place. This despite the fact that my grades had not improved, and I was still on academic probation. To make matters even more mysterious, this happened in the winter of 1966, when the war began to escalate and the military was taking any breathing, warm-bodied male. Except me!

Our Adventures Begin

Most appropriately, I married my soulmate, Sherry during the "summer of love" in August 1967. I was still in college and never did join Che, who was executed in 1967 in Bolivia. Nor did I serve in Vietnam, but the threads of my life continued their mysterious weaving. I graduated from college in 1969—in five-years rather than four due to an excess of partying—and I didn't have the slightest idea what to do for a living. I had to find out quick, as now we had a baby to feed and clothe. Our son had been born at the beginning of March.

By some miracle, I landed a job as a Boy Scout executive in Lebanon, Pennsylvania. I was drawn to it by the job description, which said my role would be to supervise their Boy Scout Camp. One of the perks was the chance to attend their National Aquatic School where one of my instructors happened to be Buster Crabbe, who won the 1932 Olympic gold medal in the 400-meter freestyle swimming event. He also starred as Tarzan, Flash Gordon and Buck Rogers.

Life seemed to be going great – until the draft lottery. On December 1, 1969, the Selective Service System conducted two lotteries to determine the order of call to military service in Vietnam. If you received a low number you would surely be headed overseas. Would it be, "Good Morning, Vietnam[4]" for me?

As fate would have it, my lottery number, based on my birthdate, was 061. Obviously, it doesn't get much lower. I was headed to war. I know in my heart today that I would have died there, even though in 1969, I was not worried about dying. The focus of my mind was not the high chance of death but leaving my wife and nine-month-old child. In 1966, I'd been willing to serve, before I got married and had a son. In 1969, I dreaded to leave them, but I accepted that I had to go.

Unlike some other males born in 1946, I didn't have connections to wealth or power. I was surely not a Rhodes Scholar like Bill Clinton or linked in any way to the ultra-wealthy like George W. Bush or Donald Trump with his "bone spur" deferments (nor would I have made up such a lame excuse for not serving my country). Of course, Bush did service in the Air National Guard. It's interesting to note that all of us were born within three months of each other.

And how do I know that I would have died in Vietnam? Me being me; in chaotic moments my spirit sees no consequences to my actions. In other words, I jump before I look. It's a major part of my being. In a war zone such as Vietnam, I would be the one to throw myself on a grenade to save others. This is not an unhealthy ego speaking, it's just who I am, which doesn't make me better or worse than any other person. (See my tale in the section below titled, "Question: Native. Answer: No.")

National Guard

We must confess, we've had a magical life. We know we have a divine purpose and destiny to complete from another lifetime. But this doesn't mean that there have not been struggles or tears – there've been many. But it seems that the three sisters[5] of fate have woven many more golden threads than dark ones within our life's tapestry. And unbeknownst to us, one of these golden threads was my job with the Boy Scouts. On a Monday morning, I went to tell my boss, a commander in the Navy Reserve, that I would be leaving my position as I had received a low number in the lottery on Friday. When I told him I was willing to serve, he smiled and said, "No you won't be leaving. You'll serve, but not in the way you think. Do you know who is on our board of directors?"

Confounded and wondering the reason for the question, I replied, "No."

"The adjunct general of the Pennsylvania National Guard. I've already talked to him and he found you a slot in a unit outside of Pittsburgh as a four-wheel vehicle mechanic."

Both Sherry and I were shocked. It was just about impossible to get into the National Guard, which resulted in a person staying stateside rather than shipping off to Vietnam. With this turn of events, I imagined that the gods and goddesses were laughing hysterically over me becoming a mechanic. I'm a natural-born philosopher, not your typical manly handy man. As witnessed by the fact that I had attempted to hook-up an ice maker in our first house, broke the line, and flooded the basement over Memorial Day weekend!

And I was off to basic training at Fort Dix, New Jersey. Let me explain this in a few sentences. The day of grenade training, I had kitchen police duty, or KP, so I missed my qualification. When I asked when I could qualify to throw a grenade, I received this answer: "We marked you 'expert;' you don't need to do it." What more can I say about the quality of training for war?

Despite our good fortune, there is sadness to this memory. I had and still have that push-and-pull feeling, a tinge of regret over not having gone to Vietnam; an echo of my warrior spirit and past life. But my sadness is not only for myself. During basic training, I was about the only white guy in the barracks – me and the "brothers," all from poor backgrounds and some with little education. But you couldn't ask for a nicer group of friends. They knew I was in the guard and not going to Vietnam, but that didn't make a difference to them.

Most of my sadness, which I still hold, comes from how many of my friends never made it back from the rice paddies. They never returned from an unjust war birthed and fueled by the greed of the military industrial complex, greed still going strong today. For my friends from basic training still on the Earth, as well as those in the Otherworld, my heart goes out to all of you. Know that you are all missed.

Let me end this chapter by saying that I am a natural-born philosopher, prophet, mystic and teacher. I am not a natural-born writer, but Sherry is, and I've encouraged her to write about our many years together.

For myself, I've become a writer by writing, not through education or training. I write to fulfill my destiny and for the pleasure of sharing knowledge. I write to bring a message of Divine Humanity and the knowledge of a new consciousness – radical nonduality, where spirit and matter blend together.[6] And most important, a legacy for our granddaughter and generations to come.

Our stories are not your usual run-of-the-mill memoirs, but are meant to teach. Spread throughout are spiritual and philosophical lessons which we hope will assist you in your own journey of life. Please enjoy our adventures of this world and the Otherworld as you far-travel with us.

(At various times throughout the book the dialogue is paraphrased.)

"Not all those who wander are lost."

J. R. R. Tolkien

THE MYTH OF THE SPIRITUAL HEALERS AND LEADERS OF THE NEW MILLENNIUM

By Apprentice Jane Justice

The howl of the Wolf and the call of the Owl sang at the edge of the emerald forest, the realm of wisdom, mysteries and medicine. It is only the courageous who risk walking the lonely path of the unknown who glean the blessings of the secret and the sacred to be revealed deep within the heart.

In the years to come, they would be known as the Moon and Sun, the Fairy Queen and the Captain, but in the early years, they were Wolf and Owl. Wolf was teacher, protector of the family, fierce and loyal with her love. She was corn woman, healer, medicine woman, seer and sacred counselor. Owl was medicine man, prophet, warrior, master swordsman, high priest and shaman of the old ways. They were visionary, teachers of the old-time lineages passed down for millennia, chosen for their spiritual power.

To walk in the glowing light, purified by the rigid discipline of spiritual training, is an honor for the courageous at heart. In sacred circles, the open beauty of Wolf's gaze would melt the coldest, most remote fortress around a soul, and torrents of tears would rush like a springtime river down their face. Healing and compassion were among her riches. Like the sun, with fire in his eyes, Owl could kindle the tiny spark of a soul into a warm, living flame of life reborn. Were the sun to speak, his words would pour forth with furious passion.

From sunrise to sundown, from solstice to equinox, from new moon to full, seasonal prayers were offered. Together, Owl and Wolf wove magic from spring, summer, fall, winter, and back to spring again, spinning webs from hand to hand, song to song, prayer to prayer, drum to drum, healing and teaching to teaching and healing. The ancient ones recognized them for their spiritual power, singled them out and passed on great honor and wisdom at the price of great responsibility and commitment.

With each new year, the ancestors were fed in a burning ceremony to honor and keep the old ways alive. Bodies were purified in the ancient ways, in blessed streams with the red paint passed down from the elders. One summer, as the power of Owl and Wolf increased to Sun and Moon, the river rose in response to Sun's sacred immersions, turning the waterfall into a rage. The river sang back Moon's shaman song from dawn until dusk for days on end. Wounded ones were healed. New ones were initiated. Hummingbirds, the light-bearing sun-angels, visited and deposited rubies of joy in the spirits of the seekers.

The Moon and Sun traveled the world, taking pilgrims to sacred lands. Legend has it that magic occurred in Japan with an exorcism in a temple at midnight, where Fudō Myō-ō—the Wisdom King who turns anger to compassion—entered into the golden face of the sensitive Sun. Legend also says that after the sacred burning ceremony near the city of refuge in Hawaii, an ancestor claimed that the Sun was a high priest, bringing back the old ways. Here too was the birth of the vision, when the Sun awoke or was dreaming that he was that star; the Morning Star, Venus.

Later, on the shores of the Yucatan Sun came to shine at the Temple of Ek Balam, the Black Jaguar of Mexico, and serpents were cast from the crippled who learned to walk again. Clouds formed the shape of toys, leading the procession down the beach for the infant's blessing in the holy waters of the Grandmother Ocean. There were rainbow stars, fire ceremonies, vows and marriage, jaguar dances and all four elements pulsing: fire, water, earth and air. The power of the Sun's serpent cast hands and pierced the gauzy veil of one initiate, who watched the sun set and the sun rise without blinking her eyes.

On a previous journey, unknown to many, the Wolf turned into a jaguar in one of the jungle caves. Her sensitive skin and seeing spirit brought her effortlessly between the worlds, where she could dance on the threshold of other realms like a true shaman priestess, always to return. She saw what others did not see. If you looked into her eyes, she knew the untold stories.

During a subsequent journey in the northern lands near their oceanside dwelling, a significant spiritual event occurred. A purifying, unearthly lightning and thunderstorm cleansed the land and the Archangel Michael, and two assisting angels appeared, answering the prayer to show the gathered ones who the Sun had been in a previous incarnation. A star shot across the sky, a dove descended and there was no longer any doubt that the Sun was the Captain and the Moon was the Fairy Queen, who knew that the unearthly radiant lights were angels, a heavenly visitation. The power was so great that many pilgrims fled the circle of glowing stones, never to return..

Soon after this extraordinary experience, the Captain and the Fairy Queen journeyed to the mystical islands of England, the shores of King Arthur, Merlin's Cave and the Dragon's Lair, where one of the old Earth energies, a sleeping dragon, was awakened and tamed by the Captain. They visited the sacred Chalice Well in the Vale of Avalon and St. Nectan's Glen with ceremony, healing and initiations. Angel's wings fluttered around the heart of any person who, at the time, was worthy and willing to answer the call.

For three years running they ventured to the emerald shores of the Cornish coast in order to complete the journey in companionship the full solar eclipse and the grand cross in the heavens, marking the transition into the new age of enlightenment. As with all births, the pain and death of the old was an excruciating process and took courage, strength and a belief that the light on the other side would be greater than the darkness of the birthing tunnel.

In the alchemical river valley of Alet-les-Bains, owls soared, shooting stars fell, angels sang, and lovers courted. In Carcassonne, the fire waters purified their stinging pains before jousting, courtiers, and a torch-lit play on horse-back under a rising moon.

In Hawaii, dawn kissed the Morning Star's birthday on the peak of the sleeping volcano, Haleakala. Lovers were taught the secrets of the senses, and gifts from land and sea were plentiful and abundant.

Before the piercing pain that caused the Captain to embed a sword and pearl in his hips, he journeyed solo to Mexico, to learn the secret passage-ways and initiations into the sacred Pyramids of the Sun and Moon in the ancient city of Teotihuacán. A mysterious voice bid him run to the pyramids at midnight, where he encountered wild dogs and a spirit man, who pointed to his chest and named himself Quetzalcóatl, the feathered serpent god. Soon after the man disappeared, gunfire sent the Captain back to his chamber of rest.

The Fairy Queen, in all her gracious glory, steadily worked to heal the wounded, to guide the lost, to love the lonely and to feed the sick. Her spir-it-food nurtured and nourished both the emotional and the nutritional void. Her organic, seasonal fruits and vegetables grown from the rich soil of Hawaii restored sweetness to the breath of the weary, thirsty and hungry pilgrims. She, the Queen Bee, could sting if necessary, but she could also apply the sooth-ing balm of nectar gathered from her earthly gardens, tended with deep gifts from the Great Mother.

Her drum was her instrument, play like the heartbeat of death and rebirth. Anyone touched by the skin or beat of her drum would reawaken to a brighter vibration. She was the Queen of the Bee clan and she loved beyond measure; her son was warrior and swordsman and her daughter was fairy princess – a clairvoyant elf.

The Baby Bee—the daughter—warned her father, the Captain, of an attack before he journeyed to the mountains of Peru to learn of the fire ceremony and attain the shamanic wisdom of the local Inkas. True to her vision, the Captain had to swing his poncho over head to ward off a swarm of killer bees. He made it through his trials, and the fire burned in his veins on that sacred mountaintop. The Captain returned to life with a blessing from the guardians and gods. He was the "big cat that flies."

●◆●

In the mountains near the family home of the Captain and the Fairy Queen, the stream and waterfall ran year-round. When pilgrims trekked there each year, singing and drumming spirits would greet them in the woods. Even the non-believers would hear the sounds and be initiated into the extraordinary.

Each river has its special gift. By this one, the Fairy Queen gifted spirit names to the pilgrims, each one shining bright in the power of the soul's essence. She spoke truth in such names as Starlight Child, Laughing Cedar Woman, and Turtle Drum Woman. Other rivers gave guardians, like swans, frogs and a beaver. Winter's frozen rivers would raise the icy fire of the Captain's mana and spiritual power to intensely high degrees. He would plunge into the brutally cold, icy-snowy waters and come out alive.

The primal, pristine rivers of the Pacific Northwest gave the gift of the shaman's songs. Years ago, the elders of these cedar lands took these two spiritual leaders and healers aside and said, "We see ourselves in you. We want to pass our ways on to you. Do you want to learn them?" Bathing in the dark, pre-dawn northwest forest, where energies are larger than your dreams, the Captain and the Fairy Queen received the songs born to them, and honored their acceptance to learn the old ways.

These healing songs have blessed many souls, both seen and unseen. The Captain and the Fairy Queen entered the longhouses of the Salish tribes where only the guardians and gods know what they saw. And they endured. They strengthened. They loved. They taught. Again and again, they taught: the old, the new, the returning, the broken, the babies, the forlorn, the frustrated.

Though far from the home they had known, this place on the fjords of the northwest that had given them songs soon became their new castle residence. Rainier, the great white mountain lay to the south and the Olympic gods to the west, where eagles gather and soar. Students return to the hand-built stone church, the Hummingbird Sun Temple, where the earth is the floor and the heavens are the roof. Those who do not falter with false masks, those who transform, promise to walk with honor and integrity in the spirit of their teachers' magnificent light. These are teachers of unconditional love; they can be as fierce as a bolt of lightning thundering across the sky or as tender as a snowflake falling to the earth.

Their grand mission to spread the love-light of the divine-human message—that the Sun of God is within all individual life-forms—has only just begun. To be a healer of wounds and to forgive and let go, to be a spiritual warrior and face one's fears, to be a teacher and to release the unhealthy ego, to be a visionary and embrace oneness: all will ultimately lead to the Sun of God within. But only through the old sacred teachings and honoring of the natural world will one have a chance for such enlightenment as a divine-human.

Listen, look, and learn. The teachers, ancestors and elders who come before you have the wisdom to transform your life and this world. The myths of these ages are as true as the myths from millennia ago. The power of adventures to fulfill one's destiny and the soul's calling in revolutionary times is a great mystery beyond imagination. Heed the cry of the wolf, the call of the owl, the shaman songs of the Captain and the Fairy Queen, and find the voice that frees your sacred spirit and evolves your soul.

INTRODUCTION

. . . .

Go to the seas and listen with heart and mind. Go to the mountains,
sit by a tree, and listen with heart and mind. Walk in the valleys
with the winds caressing your soul,
and listen with heart and mind. Lie by a river with its
soothing lullaby, and listen
with heart and mind. Skip a stone in childlike innocence
across the mirror surface
of a lake, and listen with heart and mind. Feel the fire of the sun on your face,
and listen with heart and mind. Let the moonlight blanket you with its beauty,
and listen with heart and mind. Stand and gaze at the night sky
with its star-studded tapestry, and listen with heart and mind
to the sound of angels. Let the rain
cleanse you of pain and suffering,
and listen with heart and mind.

– JC

From an early age, I wanted to be an explorer and adventurer – a far traveler, a jungle explorer. Spending time with my great-uncles and aunt on their small farm, life was wondrously simple, with no indoor toilets, only an outhouse. In a manner of speaking, sitting in an outhouse listening to the sounds of nature makes your senses more alive. You feel closer to the Earth and the basic needs of life. And why wouldn't my senses be more acute, with the spiders hanging out below me and my concern of "bonding" with one?

I remember fondly my Great-uncle Albert, who fostered and nourished in me the uncomplicated facts of life and the beauty and wisdom of the fruits and flowers of creation. He would let me help him while he tended his Concord grape vines and nurtured his pride and joy, gladioli, the bright flowers with the sword-shaped leaves. Picking a grape and holding it between his thumb and forefinger, he once spoke these wise words to me: "Jimmy, this is the perfect color of purple; if you pick the grape when it is a lighter color, it will rob the vine of its gift. And if it is a deeper, bluish purple, you will have dishonored the vine by letting the grape stay on too long." He taught me many things about life and nature. From an early age, and with his guidance, I forged a close connection with nature and the joy of a simple life. It was a sad day for me when he finally left this Earth at the age of ninety-three.

Days spent on the farm were a joy, a happiness, which has stayed with me my whole life. I explored the lands surrounding that special piece of Earth where nature and I were one. As an only child and with a creative imagination, I would wander. I remember vividly the path to the local river, where I imagined being an explorer looking for a long-lost tribe of natives. No wonder my favorite book of my great-uncles and aunt was *Hunting Big Game in the Wilds of Africa – Journeys in unknown lands, miraculous escapes, curious customs of savage races, and marvelous discoveries in the Dark Continent*. I would spend hours reading the compelling tales and viewing the amazing pictures.

I'm a wanderer at heart.[7] My life has not played out in quite the way I'd imagined my wandering, adventuring, and far traveling to be. Nonetheless, in a way that reflects my soul, I fulfilled my heart's desire and what my destiny demanded. And so can you; listen to your heart, have courage and fulfill your destiny.

Lima, Peru

The ones who truly change the world are the ones who can't wait to
get out in it[8] – this is a far traveler.

When I arrived in Lima, Peru, it was after midnight, the end of a long flight from Seattle, Washington. It was 2007. The airport was a hive of swarming people even at such a late hour. After a wild taxi drive down dark and deserted streets, I finally arrived at a small hotel, my lodging for the few remaining hours of darkness. It was two o'clock in the morning.

"I've been doing this a long time," I thought as I placed my backpack on the floor next to the lone window. The first-floor room was simple, but elegant compared to ones that I'd stayed in before. Reaching into my backpack, I pulled out a bottle of tequila purchased in the Mexico City airport and its sister in pleasure, a chocolate bar. Outside my room the lone streetlight cast dancing shadows as it swayed back and forth in the wind. The window was barred to discourage any thief in the night. Ironic, as I was the thief in the night.[9]

I scanned the foliage while inhaling the exotic smells and magical essence of the Lima night. Even thought it was two in the morning, I was wired. As I poured some tequila into a glass I thought, "Back again; it's been almost twenty years, but it seems like yesterday."

I reverently raised the glass of tequila to the ceiling and said, "I bless the heavens and the spirits of this land, and I ask permission to be here and do my work."

I lowered my glass. Slowly, I leaned forward from the edge of the bed and poured a little of the amber gold through the bars of the window onto the ground. "And a gifting to Pachamama and to the ancestors." I downed the rest of the tequila and poured some more to bless my travels and my family. "To twenty-five years of adventuring. To my partner and wife, Sherry, and our children, Jamie and Jess, for their love and support."

I was physically tired but not so tired that I couldn't indulge in sweets and spirits. With the night wind blowing its Peruvian breath through the window, images of my past experiences streamed through my mind as I chased my tequila with a bit of chocolate: my vision of the star and hearing the voice from heaven; the blazing red eyes of a long-dead monk; gigantic pillars of light—angels—and glowing gigantic green rocks that grew from small ones; spirit encounters on the battlements of an old Welsh castle, and with an awakened dragon-spirit in a Cornish cave; spirit dancing in the smoke-houses of British Columbia; downing bottles of posh (cane alcohol or what I call shamanic white lightning) in a night-long ceremony in the highlands of Mexico with a Zinacantec (Bat) shaman; receiving a message from a spirit-man at midnight outside the sacred city of Teotihuacán; being clawed by a jaguar shape-shifter under a pyramid in the Yucatan jungles; knowing Oneness after a descending spirit exorcism at midnight in front of a mausoleum on the sacred mountain of Kōyasan, Japan; chased by killer bees after almost dying—my death initiation—on a mountain peak in Peru; a hungry Hawaiian spirit, the flying meatloaf; a long-dead Northwest Coast sea serpent; a Japanese succubus; the gate-keeping dwarf of Machu Picchu; the "hidden ones" of Iceland; the Yakuza and the wounded vet, and so many other experiences. Many of these happenings I shared with my wife and many were witnessed by others.

On this latest adventure, I was travelling alone. The next day I was headed to Cuzco and then to Machu Picchu. In Cuzco, I was to meet two of our students to personally teach them and guide them to various sacred sites. After Peru, we would travel back to Mexico and the city of the gods, Teotihuacán, the location of one of my many otherworldly experiences, where in 1995, I encountered a spirit man.

As I quenched my thirst with tequila and fortified my body with chocolate, I realized that in many ways I was a reluctant prophet. I hesitated to be "seen" by the world. I knew from a previous incarnation what happens to prophets who upset the proverbial applecart.

I let these thoughts settle deep in my mind as I realized that tequila and chocolate are great metaphors for my many years of adventuring. My far travels of seeking the first knowledge[10] of indigenous cultures had taken me through the Americas, to the icy plateaus and volcanoes of Iceland, and through the windswept barrens of the British Isles and the Orkneys. I'd ventured across the fjords of Norway, to Continental Europe and the Mediterranean, as well as to Asia and the Polynesian Islands. The golden-white color of the tequila represented not only the fire of my spirit but my many otherworldly experiences, while the chocolate symbolized the sweetness of my journeys through the many lands of the Earth. Symbolic of our message and the honoring our travels, I drank the tequila while eating the black chocolate, cacao being sacred to these lands. To combine both in my mouth was a tangible and tactile imprint of our message of the interpenetration or blending of light and dark, the mingling of spirit and matter.

I chuckled at the memory of my previous flight into Lima, oh so many years ago, in 1988. I was on a South American airline out of Miami. Not speaking Spanish and being the only Caucasian on the plane was not a problem, until the games began. This was a first and last time for me as the flight attendants handed out bingo cards to every person aboard. No movie, no food. Just bingo.

In consideration of being the lone non-Spanish-speaking white guy, the head attendant called out the numbers in English as well as in Spanish. As the number calling progressed, I got excited and then yelled, "Bingo!" As soon as the word left my mouth everyone froze and looked my way, a few disturbed faces and a few amused. The woman next to me looked at my card, looked at me, smiled and shook her head, saying, "No, no." By this time an attendant had arrived at my elbow and said in perfect English, "Sir, the whole card must be filled out." Feeling embarrassed, I simply shrugged, smiled and nodded. But an interesting thing happened. As I display my humanness, rather than acting the arrogant American, I could sense the shift in people's energy towards me. More than one leaned over to say a few words in broken English to show friendship. And all because of "bingo!"

Lessons I've Learned While Far Traveling

A shaman not only leaps between worlds, but between cultures.

There 1 lay staring upward, while the stars wheeled over. . . . Faint to my ears came the gathered rumour of all lands: the springing and the dying, the song and the weeping, and the slow everlasting groan of overburdened stone.

J. R. R. Tolkien

Far traveling, wandering to distant lands into the unknown, is necessary for awakening and spiritual power. A far traveler begins and then knows spirit of place. In other words, a far traveler is a spiritual pilgrim ever seeking the *mysterium tremendum*, the awe-inspiring mystery of the unknown. The blood-pulsing passion of life is found at the edge of the unknown. Far traveling is not vacation. It is not traveling to a place just because it is the "in thing," as it is to go to Iceland, and years ago, sadly, Machu Picchu. A far traveler goes on holiday, or holy day, and is not a tourist but an adventurer, a pilgrim of spirit on a journey of self-knowledge. Pilgrimage means going out and finding something. And that something equates to many things: our true self, compassion, love of self and nature, and accepting and understanding our self and others not like us. One of the best-known of these adventures is the Quest for the Holy Grail.[11]

Far travel as a sacred pilgrimage extends back into the very haze of humanity's awakening. It has long been a source and wellspring of religious culture and myth. Seeking over the far horizon stirs the very lifeblood of the far traveler in their on-going quest for the magic and power of the unfamiliar, and their ever-aliveness of that moment of sacred space and sacred time. To quest is to feel alive; to feel alive is to quest.

For centuries, pilgrims have left the comfort and safety of home and familiar surroundings and ventured out into the unknown in search of knowledge, power and ultimate enlightenment. This journey of soul allows the pilgrim the opportunity to breath, eat and sleep a spiritual adventure of discovery, love and wonderment. This fulfills a longing— sometimes hidden—in the depths of our heart to quest as the hero and return to the mother to experience a rebirth of self. Far traveling is a pilgrimage toward rebirth and magical transformation, enmeshing our soul in a reverence of place while recognizing the sacredness of the Earth.

Curandero don Eduardo Calderon Palomino, the famous healer, once said that most people live in a cultural trance. I agree, and far traveling is one way to awaken from that trance, an adventure that puts us into partnership with nature and culture. Like a chameleon, we become one with the land and its people and catch the thread of knowledge in our wandering. It is not about selfies or an arrogance of entitlement. Wandering as a stranger in a strange land beckons us to become one with the unknown, and with the love that unites us all.

When we never leave our place of birth or home country, we insulate ourselves from other lands, cultures, and the variety of peoples who inhabit the greater part of our still beautiful Earth. We become rigid and unyielding in our thinking about those different from ourselves. This worldview and mindset are the greatest barriers to peace on Earth, and only result in walls, figuratively, and sometimes literally. Far travelers build bridges, not walls, and discover the world as it really is. A world not only of beauty, but of poverty, social injustice, and inequality.[12]

When far traveling, discovering the real world may alter the course of your life and transform your life's mission and destiny, as was the case with Ernesto "Che" Guevara, who recorded the social injustices he discovered in his memoirs, *The Motorcycle Diaries*. Due to his far traveling, Che discovered his purpose in life and his destiny. The following is a short synopsis of the 2004 movie of the same name, based on Che's memoirs:

In 1952, a semester before Ernesto "Fuser" Guevara is due to complete his medical degree, he and his older friend Alberto, a biochemist, leave Buenos Aires in order to travel across the South American continent in search of fun and adventures. While there is a goal at the end of their journey—they intend to work in a leper colony in Peru—the main purpose is tourism . . . Their initial method of transport is Alberto's ancient and leaky but functional Norton 500 motorcycle christened La Poderosa ("The Mighty One").

During their expedition, Guevara and Granado encounter the poverty of the indigenous peasants, and the movie assumes a greater seriousness once the men gain a better sense of the disparity between the "haves" and "have-nots" of Latin America . . .

It is a visit to the Incan ruins of Macchu Picchu that inspires something in Ernesto. He wonders how the highly advanced culture gave way to the urban sprawl of Lima . . .

In Peru, they volunteer for three weeks at the San Pablo leper colony. There, Guevara sees both physically and metaphorically the division of society between the toiling masses and the ruling class (the staff live on the north side of a river, separated from the lepers living on the south). Guevara also refuses to wear rubber gloves during his visit, choosing instead to shake bare hands with startled leper inmates.

At the end of the film, after his sojourn at the leper colony, Guevara confirms his nascent egalitarian, anti-authority impulses, while making a birthday toast, which is also his first political speech. In it, he evokes a pan-Latin-American identity that transcends the arbitrary boundaries of nation and race. These encounters with social injustice transform the way Guevara sees the world, and by implication motivate his later political activities as a revolutionary.[13]

Love and Respect the Land and People

Outside of the opportunity to have an awakening of consciousness in mind and spirit, far travel is also about the land. When we far travel to distant lands, we become one with the landscape. But most important, our body and mind begin to understand at the core of our soul the myths and legends connected with the place where we stand. For example, if you want to understand the Icelandic Sagas with your body and soul, then far travel to Iceland. Become one with the land and sea. In this very personal and intimate way you will develop insight into these mythic but real stories of the Icelanders. But do stay away from the hordes of tourists and the package tours.

Reenactors of bygone cultures who have never far traveled to the culture's homeland do not make sense to me. Can they believe they are actually representing or reenacting cultures such as the Norse or the Spartans? Especially when reenacting a Norse persona, as the Vikings were some of the most accomplished far travelers in history.

To far travel is to accept the call to adventure. The adventure is the great inner quest of the self, to awaken. It is a heroic journey of coming to know ourselves and our relationship to self and other. As a far traveler, I view myself as a citizen of the Earth; the Earth is my home. Thus, from my heart comes my green philosophy, my respect, and my caring nature and attitude for all things of the Earth. My wife shares this philosophy. When we far travel we are honor-bound to respect and care for the Earth's land and people, to leave the land better than we found it, and to exert a loving impact on the people we meet.

"The winds speak to all whose mind is still and uncluttered . . . with oneness being the sacred beauty of words unspoken." JC

Ko'ox (kō-ōsh)
Mayan for "Let's Go!"

Do far travel; the rewards are far greater than the risks. Do not let money and fear stand in your way. I know, because I have been, and always will be, a wanderer and seeker. Like the Norse deity Óðinn, I have sought knowledge and wisdom. And sometimes the gift of that wisdom is a knowing of the mysteries of heaven and earth and the oneness and equality of all things.

Even my family coat of arms, which features three azure martlets—a mythical bird with no legs—reflects my passion for far traveling. As the martlet is unable to land, it symbolizes the constant quest for knowledge, learning, and adventure while representing happiness and a restless, traveling nature.[14]

I do have one caution when far traveling. Be in the moment and aware as Mother Nature is unforgiving of one's stupidity and disrespect. People have died falling off cliffs while taking selfies.[15] In Iceland, numerous tourists have been nearly swept out to sea. Most survived but at least two drowned. Tourists are warned not to get in or close to the sea, but they still walk too near the water or turn their backs to the sea for an awesome selfie. It is best to follow an old Hawaiian adage: "Never turn your back on grandmother."

In all of our journeys taking others far traveling, we have never had physical problems or injuries. One of the reasons: when we far travel to a new place or return to one, we make an offering, which could be as simple as a piece of our hair, and we ask permission to be there to do our work. I also ask for safety for myself and others while we are on our journey. Sometimes this rite is short and simple, at other times more extensive and intense. There is no format to follow, just your heart.

Lovely Planet

One morning at breakfast in Reykjavik, Iceland, an elderly woman started talking to me out-of-the blue. She was from Australia and asked if this was my first time in Iceland. I replied no, my sixth, which led to a discussion of our love of far traveling. Near the end of our conversation, she asked if I was familiar with the *Lonely Planet* guidebooks. Of course, I replied, at which point, she told me about the beginnings of Lonely Planet in Australia.

It seems the co-creators of Lonely Planet had a different title in mind, but due to the slip of one letter, the die was set as the first editions were already published. And the one letter that changed people's perception of the planet? The N was supposed to be a V. The original title was *Lovely Planet*, which does send a different philosophical message.

And I agree the planet is lovely, not lonely.

Children

Cusco, Peru, February 1988

And speaking of a lovely planet, children are one of the planet's human jewels. One of our greatest joys was the children we encountered on our far travels. Children are very precious and bring joy to our lives no matter what race, color, or nationality.

The measure of an individual or an institution is their love, care, respect and protection of all children. Not just their own, but all the children of this Earth.

As we have seen, this is not the case with the Catholic Church given the widespread abuse and rape of the most vulnerable among us. We can now add another person and his administration to the widespread slime – Trump and his cronies:

> *Fox & Friends* co-host Brian Kilmeade on Friday defended President Trump's "zero tolerance" approach to migrants that illegally cross the U.S.-Mexico border, saying

"these aren't our kids" being detained separately while their parents face legal prosecution.

"Like it or not, these are not our kids," he said. "Show them compassion, but it's not like he's doing this to the people of Idaho or Texas. These are people from another country."[16]

Concerning children in detention at the U.S. Border; the following is a comment from a 15-year-old from El Salvador highlighting the disturbing and horrifying reality facing these children:

"A Border Patrol agent came in our room with a two-year-old boy and asked us, 'Who wants to take care of this little boy?' Another girl said she would take care of him, but she lost interest after a few hours, so I started taking care of him yesterday. His bracelet says he is two years old.

I feed the 2-year-old boy, change his diaper, and play with him. He is sick. He has a cough and a runny nose and scabs on his lips. He was coughing last night so I asked to take him to see the doctor and they told me that the doctor would come to our room, but the doctor never came. The little boy that I am taking care of never speaks. He likes for me to hold him as much as possible.

Since arriving here, I have never been outside and never taken a shower."[17]

Sad to say, there is a percentage of the population of the U.S. that believes this O.K. Many of these cruel people are Christian and believe that faith alone is the key to heaven, not "works," in other words, their actions. But from my soul I know they have been brainwashed as it is a person's actions not faith that matters most.

We must ask ourselves, why are they only concerned about children who look like them? Could it be that many of them have never far traveled outside of this country except on a package tour where it is doubtful they ever interacted with local or indigenous children? Quite possibly this is true.

One final and most important point. They don't realize what they are missing: learning love and compassion for people different than themselves. And the realization that we are all the same.

Anthony Bourdain

"Travel changes you. As you move through this life and this world you change things slightly, you leave marks behind, however small. And in return, life— and travel—leaves marks on you."

– Anthony Bourdain

One of the Earth's human jewels was Anthony Bourdain. We were on the East Coast outside of Boston conducting a week-long Mesoamerican training for our apprentices when the shocking and sad news broke: Anthony Bourdain was dead by his own hand. Such tragic, heartbreaking, and sad news that created a void within humanity that will be very difficult, and I must say, impossible to fill.

Our whole family loved Bourdain's television show, "Parts Unknown." He voyaged not only into diverse foods but into the commonness of humanity by breaking bread with strangers and enjoyed an intimacy with cultures few Americans ever experience. He viewed others not as their race, culture or sex, but as human beings, while accepting their perfections and imperfections with an openness that allowed people to be as authentic to him as he was to them. In a few words, Bourdain was real.

I felt we were kindred souls seeking to reveal the essence of humanity (we are all the same), with Anthony through food and my wife and I through spirit. We agree with Bourdain that, "travel isn't always pretty. It isn't always comfortable. Sometimes it hurts; it even breaks your heart. But that's okay. The journey changes you; it should change you. It leaves marks on your memory, on your consciousness, on your heart, and on your body. You take something with you. Hopefully, you leave something good behind."[18]

I know with every cell of my soul how far traveling can break your heart. After years and sometimes decades, I have returned to sacred sites that were once pure, non-commercial, and never crowded with tourists to find them much changed. To feel, see, and sense the sadness of the land and the disrespect shown by people's unhealthy egos brought tears to my heart and spirit many times over.

But all is not lost. The power of the land and the sacred sites is still there, held within their essence and form, only asleep. If you far travel with an open heart and mind, eat and become one with the locals, learn their stories, their truths, their fear and desires, and then speak to the land, to the ancestors, and to the stones of the sites – then, quite possibly, if your mind quiets, they will answer back. You will gain a greater knowing and appreciation of life, and most importantly, of the unknown.[19]

Innovative Adaptation

Anyone who has ever flown on a plane understands the need to adapt when traveling. Flights are canceled due to weather or mechanical problems, or even an air traffic controller's strike, as we experienced in England in 1981. But far travelers who go off the beaten path without organized guides or tours learn to be innovative. They can adjust to unusual circumstances, such as the spot Sher and I found ourselves in when we were in Ecuador.

We'd spent some time on the coast and were returning to Guayaquil, the largest city and chief port of Ecuador, before we flew back to Costa Rica and then to the States. We had reservations at the Sheraton Guayaquil Hotel. It was late afternoon and people were leaving work. In other words, there was lots and lots of traffic. Even if I had a GPS, I wouldn't have used it. I believe in using my own sense of direction, but in this case, I needed an innovative approach to find my way. I grew frustrated but then a solution occurred to me. In no time at all, I discovered what I was looking for – a taxi stopped at a gas station.

As I pulled up to the taxi, Sher asked, "What are you doing?"

"An idea," I replied, then jumped out of our rental car.

And what was the idea? I asked the driver to take us to the Sheraton. He gave me a bewildered look, as he had seen me get out of our car. He spoke a little English, so I explained that I would pay him to drive to the Sheraton and we would follow in our car.

"Loss," was all he said as he accepted payment.

Have you ever followed a taxi at rush hour? Frenzy captures the moment. Zooming in and out of traffic, here and now there, it was a crazy task to not to lose sight of him or else wind up back in the same situation. After a harrowing drive we finally pulled up to the Sheraton. I smiled and waved my thank you at him as he quickly accelerated back into the maelstrom of traffic whizzing by the Sheraton.

How do you explain this?

When far traveling, it's always possible that you will get sick. You should find a clinic or a doctor for serious illnesses, but keep in mind that in many European countries, pharmacies provide medicines that in the States would require a doctor's prescription. Even better, the pharmacist will steer you to the right medication. This helps lower health-care costs as people with minor illnesses don't have to run to a physician or clinic.

My tale of sickness takes place, not out of the country, but on the island of Kauai during the summer of 1989. We were going to be exploring the rugged Nāpali Coast, a fifteen-mile stretch on the northwest shore of Kauai. Thanks to its remote location, Nāpali remains one of the most beautiful and unspoiled coastlines in the world, a sacred and mystical place containing the remains of stone walls, terraces, graves, and heiau (shrines or temples). Due to its isolation, it has been the setting for various movie productions such as *Jurassic World* and *Avatar*.

On our flight from Maine to Hawaii, I began feeling sick, a bummer given we were flying first class. From all my far traveling, we had enough mileage to nab some first-class tickets to Honolulu. A crying baby added to my discomfort. On our stopover in LA, right before takeoff, a couple with a baby settled themselves two rows before us. I made a judgment about the guy as he wore a dirty baseball cap and a scruffy beard. And I thought, "How could they afford to fly first-class?" An odd think to think, considering Sher and I couldn't afford to fly first-class.

My wife answered my thought. She turned to me and said, "That's Tom Selleck."

"No way."

"I saw his eyes. It's Tom Selleck," Sher replied.

After leaving LA and reaching cruising speed, the scruffy man stood up and removed his cap and beard. Sure enough it was Tom Selleck, with his wife and new-born baby.

Cocaine

By the time Sher and I reached Kauai, I was feeling lousy. Since I had a few days before heading to the Nāpali Coast, I decided to see a doctor. Even though it was 1989 and we were staying in the small community of Princeville on the north shore, I was able to find one. After I explained how I was feeling, he began the typical routine: blood pressure, check for fever, listen to heart and lungs, investigate my mouth and then my ears, and last, my nose. As soon as he examined my nose, his whole energy changed. Without saying a word, he turned his back to me.

A few uncomfortable seconds passed, until finally he said, "How long have you been using?"

"What do you mean?" I asked, my voice revealing I was a little pissed off.

"Cocaine," was his one-word response.

Now even more annoyed, I replied, "Never, no desire, and why do you think so?"

"Your septum, there's a hole in it." He took a breath, stared into my eyes and continued with a definite statement: "This only occurs through excessive cocaine use."

When he'd said "hole," I knew what had happened. In my twenties I had nosebleeds and was told I had a very thin septum. Over the past few years, I had been conducting fire ceremonies and doing what is commonly known as "nose juice."[20] However, using the words "nose juice" would be problematic because the term was slang for cocaine. How was I going to explain this?

I realizing I needed to explain that the hole wasn't due to cocaine but an indigenous ritual. "I'm a spiritual teacher," I said, "and one of the ceremonies that I conduct is a fire ceremony. One aspect of the ceremony is pouring a mixture of black tobacco, herbs and alcohol up my nose. I use a shell filled with the mixture, put it to my nose, tilt my head back and let the mixture run down the back of my throat. It helps to open the third eye and affects the various visionary centers of the brain."

I could see he wasn't buying it and was suspicious of me and my tale as I added, "I've done this mixture quite a few times during the ceremonies."

He spoke not a word in return as he wrote a prescription for antibiotics. He handed me the slip and said, "Whatever you are doing, I would stop it."

Accepting the prescription, I thanked him, but I was thinking, "No way."

Skulls and Bones

Nāpali Coast, Kauai, July 1989

In a few days, I was feeling well enough to follow through and explore Honopu Valley on the Nāpali Coast. Honopu was known as Valley of the Lost Tribe and rumored to be the last home of the fabled Menehune, an ancient mythological race of people small in stature. Another feature of the valley was burial caves, where ancient Hawaiians secreted the remains of their dead. The deceased's personal power or mana was believed to reside in the bones.

The most important point when exploring Hawaiian indigenous ruins, burial sites or caves, and heiaus: you must not destroy, remove or touch bones or stones in them. Always be respectful and ask permission to approach or be near heiaus, and especially burial caves.

True to form, I discovered one of the burial caves that day. I prayed, asking permission to approach the cave, and I gave a flower as an offering. When I took a picture of the skulls and bones, the "chicken skin" raised on my arms. I can definitely say it was spooky.

Got Lost . . . Your Problem

Over the years I've been associated with many indigenous healers and teachers in very remote places. It is the student's responsibility to listen, to watch and to learn. If the shaman is taking you to an isolated site possibly at the end of a jungle trail, it is your responsibility to keep up with him/her. If you fall behind and get lost, that's your fault, not his/hers.

In 1989, an indigenous healer, a Maya *h'men* by the name of Antonio was taking a group of our students to an isolated sacred lagoon, *Laguna de Chunyaxché*, to do ceremony. I knew that the lagoon was located deep within the Yucatan Jungles within the *Sian Kaán* ("where the sky is born") Biosphere. It was home to over 350 types of birds, as well as pumas, ocelots, and yes, jaguars. Even though I was the leader of the group and had worked with this shaman before, this sacred site was unknown to me.

True to form he took off down a trail that was barely recognizable. If I was alone with him or if our group consisted of fit twenty year olds, it would not have been a problem. But, this was not the case. One of our students was in her seventies and couldn't walk that fast.

As the group gradually disappeared down the winding trail, I stayed behind and walked with Peanut (her nickname).[21] It was late in the afternoon with dark only a few hours away. The jungle was waking up. Sounds of hidden things stirring triggered images of jaguars on the prowl. The jungle after dark is not a place to be, but I would not let Peanut be alone, nor would she have abandoned me if the roles were reversed. Slight of build and aged as she was, I would still choose her to be next to me in a life and death situation. She had an inner core of strength and determination.

It seemed that our only option was to keep following what I thought was the trail. The concept of time is interesting. Depending on circumstances, a minute may seem like an hour. Often this phenomenon occurs when we are truly in the present moment without the typical distractions of life. It felt like we had been walking for at least an hour but I knew that possibly only fifteen minutes had passed. Nevertheless, I was getting concerned. Having been a runner since college, I decided that the best solution to our dilemma was for me to run ahead to make sure we were on the right trail and possibly catch up with the others. I told Peanut to keep walking and that I would run ahead and then run back to check on her.

I didn't look for signs that the group had passed; I let my heart lead me down the right path. I could see the sun setting in the west. There was no wind, and considering it was a jungle, few sounds as I ran in the direction I hoped they had taken. Considering Peanut's age, I was angry that no one had bothered to slow the group down or had backtracked to make sure we were on the right trail and okay. It seemed that everyone was in their own self-centeredness.

Sweat formed on my brow as I ran. Eventually, it fell into my eyes, blurring my vision, as spotted green foliage took on the guise of green jaguars. Breathing deeply of the energetic essence of the pristine foliage, I relaxed into a pace that would allow me to cover miles without undo fatigue. The first time I turned to run back and check on Peanut, I began to wonder about my strategy. Doubt is insidious, just like guilt.

After my third "foraging for the lagoon" run, I found the lagoon and the group. I was none too happy, but relieved at the same time. I lectured the group and even the healer on the concept of "one for all and all for one." It was a great lesson for all, even for me. I doubted myself even though my heart was saying that the path that I was on was the right and true one.

Sacrifice

If you read Hávamál,[22] it's about how to meet other cultures and be a good guest or host to the world around you. These are ancient sayings for the traveler – not for the guy sitting at home on his ass thinking his living room is the centre of the world.

Hilmar Örn Hilmarsson

Keep in mind: sacrifice is an act of making sacred. Furthermore, a prime action to accumulate knowledge, power, and wisdom can be found within the concept of sacrifice. To acquire power, we need to sacrifice the accepted materialistic norms of society. In other words, a person totally immersed in a materialistic culture has no time for spiritual pursuits; it's all about money. This type of person is unwilling to sacrifice their time for any pursuits other than those that bring them materialistic status or wealth. Óðinn was not, as the above quote states, "Sitting at home on his ass thinking his living room is the centre of the world." He was a far traveler, a wanderer, continually seeking knowledge and wisdom. For us to be a wanderer in foreign, unknown lands, we need to sacrifice time and money.

All of our journeys required great sacrifice, emotionally and financially. In fact, our first journey to England, Wales, and Scotland came at the expense of not putting a new roof on our home. We choose the journey over the roof. How about you? Are you willing to sacrifice time and money to far travel and journey into the unknown?

First Knowledge

Knowledge is experience; anything else is just information.
~ Albert Einstein

*René Guénon: It was his role to remind a forgetful world, "in a way
that can be ignored but not refuted, of first principles, and to restore
a lost sense of the Absolute."*[23]

As a philosopher and truth seeker, I have far traveled for more than thirty-five years to different parts of the world, ever seeking wisdom and the myth, magic, and lore of elders and indigenous people. I have self-sacrificed and sacrificed self to self. My experience and firsthand knowledge of listening, looking, and learning flows from indigenous elders, healers, and shamans from all over the world. It also comes from my interactions with the young and old of other races and cultures and emanates deeply from my own soul's wisdom. This knowledge is what I refer to as the "first knowledge." It is knowledge woven throughout and found in all the first peoples' spiritual and religious traditions on this Earth. In Aztecs philosophy, and in the Nahuatl language, this is the province of the *"tlamatini,* or wise man, who has learned his profession by practicing it – *tlaiximatini,* which means literally, 'he who has firsthand knowledge [*imatini*] of the character or nature [*ix*] of things [*tla*].'"[24]

This "first knowledge" has been referred to as primordial knowledge or the Primordial Tradition (*philosophia perennis*; perennial philosophy). As such it portrays universal themes, principles, and truths to establish common factors among different traditions with the goal of producing a superior gnosis or level of wisdom. In other words, "the term Primordial Tradition is utilized to describe a system of spiritual thought and metaphysical truths that overarches all the other religions and esoteric traditions of humanity."[25] The Primordial Tradition is the only religion which can really be said to be alive. Divine Humanity is a Primordial Tradition.

Furthermore, "the perennial philosophy proposes that reality, in the ultimate sense, is One, Whole, and Undivided – the omnipresent source of all knowledge and power. We do not perceive this reality because the field of human cognition is restricted by the senses. But the perennial philosophy claims that these limitations can be transcended."[26] And that they can, as you will discover within the tales that follow.

One last point about Divine Humanity, a perennial philosophy and religion, which "differs with more exoteric religion. Whereas the traditional religious paradigm emphasizes a need to be saved (from sin, suffering, pain, or death), the perennial philosophy views the Ultimate reality as a state of union, suggesting to us a different objective for the religious life: not to be saved but to discover the wholeness."[27] As an alternative to organized religion, the objective of the spiritual/religious paradigm of Divine Humanity is to discover this wholeness or oneness of reality.

Reality of the Otherworld

As you will discover in our stories, the Otherworld is real and is blended with our world; there is no separation, just an oneness of essence.

Many people approach the Otherworld (spirit world) from a dualistic perspective. Usually, their consciousness pictures a hierarchy, as "up there somewhere" in relationship to the Earth. From a Christian dualistic hierarchical standpoint, Heaven is up and Hell is down, and after physical death, you end up for eternity in one or the other. While alive, the only link you have to Heaven is through the Church and their priests and ministers. There is no direct spiritual link for the faithful. The Church is the gatekeeper. Contrary to this Christian drivel based on greed and power, Divine Humanity prescribes to a nonhierarchical reality where the Otherworld and the universe blend together as one. Our hope is to awaken people to awareness of the Otherworld and the "perennial mystical experience, which experiences the unity behind the universe side by side with the diversity perceived by the senses."[28]

Dualistic paradigms view the Otherworld as being behind a veil or metaphorically separated by a body of water, such as a river. I've even used these concepts in my writings in an attempt to explain the unexplainable. But what if the exact opposite is true, and there is no separation between us and the Otherworld, no separation between spirit and matter? The Norse were closer to this truth, sometimes viewing the entrance to the Otherworld as within a holy hill or mountain, and at other times, the entrance was to be found within a graveyard. The Icelandic Norse strongly believed, and still believe, in the existence of the hidden people with their homes within the stones found on their island.

Furthermore, "as is sometimes the case in Icelandic folktales, the otherworld in Grelent and Tidorel seems to be in, or near, water and the characters even have to go into the water to penetrate into the other world."[29] This is exactly the case in the sacrificial self-to-self rite of bathing,[30] when a person enters a river, enabling them to access the Otherworld. However, entering into a river does not unto itself provide access to the Otherworld. It is the spirit song sung at the beginning of the ritual by a person of power—a shaman—which opens the river and provides the access to the Otherworld. Power is a central concept of shamanism. It is only the shaman and the mystic who identify with power through direct personal experience. This is explained further in our section on "Spirit Dancing, Burnings and Bathings."

One last point. A nonhierarchical reality is not unique to Divine Humanity. "Aztec philosophy embraces a nonhierarchical metaphysics. That is, it denies the existence of a principled, ontological distinction between 'higher' and 'lower' realms, realities, degrees of being, or kinds of stuff. A hierarchical metaphysics, by contrast, upholds the existence of a principled hierarchy of 'higher' and 'lower' realities, degrees of being, and so on."[31]

You're not going to impress the Otherworld

Take nothing but memories, leave nothing but footprints!

~Chief Seattle

There is one firm truth we may all believe in – our death. At death our soul and its consciousness returns to the Otherworld, heaven if you like, with our life-journey experiences, the sum total of our time on Earth. Wealth, holdings, Christian - Muslim faith, and titles mean nothing to the Otherworld, not even the titles of president of the United States or president of Russia. As it has been said, "Fame won't matter, nor will the extent of your wealth. You are only the sum of the stories you can tell."[32] What stories can you tell?

The Otherworld is not impressed with anything except what we have been holding and still hold within our hearts as we take our last breath in this incarnation. That's right. We will all reincarnate, as you will discover as you read on.

Green Philosophy

Moyers: . . . What happens when human beings destroy their environment? Destroy their world? Destroy nature and the revelations of nature? Campbell: They destroy their own nature, too. They kill the song. Moyers: And isn't mythology the story of the song? Campbell: Mythology is the song. It is the song of the imagination, inspired by the energies of the body.[33]

There is one key element, one very important concept, that permeates the belief and philosophy of indigenous cultures. This is the belief in the importance of nature by forming a partnership and a oneness with nature – a nature that is divine, alive, conscious and responsive. The Earth is alive and truly our Mother.

Nature is the holy grail of healing and the secret to the maintenance of wholeness and wellness for all individuals, communities and nations. Nature is without a doubt *Kulana Huli Honua*.[34] In other words, "the essential quest of individual growth and evolution does not change from age to age. It is true today as it was in those ancient times, dimly recalled by legend, that Nature can bestow upon human beings' great wisdom and knowledge."[35] But to be bestowed, you must get off your ass, get out into the wild without technology. Just you, the land, the sea, and your other brothers and sisters, the creatures of the Earth.

Look deep into nature, and then you will understand everything better.

– Albert Einstein

Sherry and I believe and live a Green Philosophy. This is an egalitarian philosophy of humanity's partnership with the seen and unseen things of the Earth and nature. Humans are part of nature, not at the center of nature. Furthermore, society has lost many of the values treasured by past indigenous cultures, such as a partnership with nature, truth telling, and elder/ancestor respect and honor. We need to discover meaning in life, not accumulate money and material things. The equality of men and women as well as the equality of all things—as all have the starlight/divine spark within them—needs to be reinstated. These and other lost values need to be reinstated throughout this Earth. Nature needs to be respected, loved and cared for by humanity. We need to be partners in relationship with nature, not its stewards. We need your help. We would ask that you join us in embracing a Green Philosophy of life and spread this knowledge to others.

Green Man

A commonly accepted word for humanity's connection to nature is the mythic "Green Man." However; it is my belief that a more appropriate name would be the "Green Woman" or the "Green Human." I will still use the commonly accepted term with the realization that the concept refers not to the male or female sex exclusively, but to humanity at large.

The Green Man symbolizes fertility, eternity, death and rebirth. The archetypical Green Man may be visualized as a human face peering through vegetation or possibly as a mystical mixture of human form and vegetation merging into each other. This imagery of the Green Man symbolizes a portal to the Otherworld, a connection between humanity and nature. The Green Man is that spirit, energy, and presence inherent in every cell of the vegetative realm and transmitted to the animal/human realms through the foods we eat, the flowers we smell, the trees we hug.

Jesus loved nature and could be labeled "green" for his beliefs and practices. Jesus as Green Man recognized the divine in nature and the sacredness of all living things. Common sense dictates that a teacher who felt so connected and in partnership with the Earth would use nature to demonstrate the truth of his knowledge and wisdom.

Contrary to the sacredness of the Green Man concept, the Earth is being destroyed by men following the creed of capitalism, a creed of exploitation, domination and greed. And contrary to Jesus' belief, "church doctrine denies the divineness of nature and the Earth. This makes Christianity a brown, not green, religion, dogmatically promoting man's domination of the Earth. The driving force of this domination and consequent destruction of the biosphere is the capitalist paradigm."[36]

Let me leave this topic with one final point. The only mystical and prophetic book of the New Testament is Revelations. It is interesting to note a short passage, the green message in Rev. 11.18 that Jesus "returns to destroy those who destroy the Earth."

My Knowing

"Truth is a way of being and doing; a way of living, conducting one's life, and so forth."[37]

I have had four major, personal, and direct firsthand experiences of the Otherworld. The first was my descending spirit exorcism in 1987, the initial quickening of my awakening mind and a knowing of radical nondualistic interpenetrating reality. In 1993, I experienced the divine call, both as something heard and something seen in the form of a vision and a voice. This was my awakening as the Morning Star. In 1995, my third major direct experience was with the Spirit Man of Teotihuacán, who identified me as the mind and soul of Quetzalcóatl – the Morning Star. The fourth major firsthand experience in 1997 was a visitation in the form of three immense pillars of light. These were angels announcing who Sherry and I were in a previous lifetime.

These tales and the others that follow are true. They are not by any means the sum of our adventures, which would extend into hundreds and hundreds of pages, but a few we choose to tell. Enjoy and come along with us in an adventure of this world and the Otherworld.

PART I

....

The Morning Star

For he who has not known himself has known nothing, but he who has known himself has at the same time already achieved knowledge about the Depth of the All.

–Jesus in the Book of Thomas the Contender[38]

MORNING STAR

. . . .

"Here you see the Morning Star. Who sees the Morning Star shall see more, for he shall be wise."

–Black Elk

I AM THE MORNING STAR AND I AM A RELIGIOUS REVOLUTION-ary – a heretic to organized religion. Working outside the box of established religious dogma and doctrine, a religious revolutionary is rarely seen by the masses and is usually likened to the proverbial thief in the night.

In October of 1993, my wife, Sher, and I journeyed to the Big Island of Hawaii. In the pre-dawn hours, I experienced the divine call, both as something heard and something seen in the form of a vision and a voice: "This star is you; you are this star; the purification is of the people; all are one." This star was Venus as the morning star.

However, reflecting the essence of Venus as both morning and evening star, when I was born, Venus was in its evening star phase. This is twin symbology. Therefore, the evening star of my birth reflects my past life revealed by the visitation,[39] while the morning star is the energetic symbology of my present incarnation.[40]

Many stars rise over many horizons, including those of literature, but there is
one star of the morning, and
this in most cycles of books is rather an expected
glory than a dawn now visible.[41]

Venus is the brightest object in our sky outside of the sun and moon. The indigenous people of the world always held Venus in awe. A cycle of Venus begins with its first morning star appearance every 584 days. There are five of these cycles occurring every eight years. This gives the Sun and Venus an 8:5 relationship which equals 8/5 or 1.6, which is the Golden Mean (the Divine Proportion). The Golden Mean is the irrational number of 1.618034 endlessly repeating to infinity. Could this be a hint of life everlasting? A truth of immortality staring us directly in the face? As above so below.

As the morning star, Venus is still visible in the dawn sky as the sun rises. It is the herald of the light coming out of the dark of the night. Venus and the sun are intertwined in an immortal dance of rebirth. As the morning star, Venus announces the arrival of the sun. It is the harbinger of the day, which stands at the breaking of dawn as the last star to disappear into the glory of the sun. And in the darkest of times, hope will light the way. This is Venus as the morning star, the star of hope. In other words, Venus is known as the Lightbearer, the morning star, because it rises on the early morning horizon heralding the sunrise.[42] To the Maya, Venus as morning star was called *Ah Ahzah Cabm* the Awakener and associated with the dawn.

Venus, as the most brilliant star in the heavens, signifies God's Spirit. This holy spirit, symbolized by the divine dove of Venus, brings balance to the dualities of life resulting in a spiritual wholeness or a holiness of existence. Venus as the morning star is known as the bringer of light and relates to love, unity of humanity, beauty, and oneness. Furthermore, it symbolizes hope and guidance and is related to past spirits and ancestors.

The brilliance of Venus has always symbolized enlightenment. Venus appears at certain times as the morning star, and at other times as the evening star. This perception of Venus as being twins and the significance of its luminosity underscores the mythological religious ideals of many cultures. The twin's designation symbolizes the dual forces manifested in humans and the dualities of life, the light and the dark, male and female, which contain the potentiality for a unified balance of wholeness or oneness – non-dual inter-penetration. For that reason, Venus' symbolic theme is the unification of oppo-sites, and it is viewed as the bridge-builder between pairs of opposites such as spirit and matter. This is also the role of the returning cultural hero who teaches that equality, balance, and unity/oneness are of the utmost importance in achieving spiritual transformation.

Venus is the ruling planet of the astrological signs of Libra (love) and Taurus (money) and the esoteric ruler of Gemini. Venus is known as Earth's twin because both worlds share a similar size and surface composition, and both have an atmosphere with a complex weather system. The color assigned to Venus is green, the two-fold combination of the blue of heaven and the yellow of Earth.

Morning Star as Returning Hero

A legendary hero is usually the founder of something – the founder of a new age, the founder of a new religion, the founder of a new city, the founder of a new way of life. In order to found something new, one has to leave the old and go in quest of the seed idea, a germinal idea that will have the potentiality of bringing forth that new thing.[43]

The cultural hero, and his return, is one of the most enduring and import-ant cross-cultural archetypal prophetic themes known to humankind. Its importance is due to its message of hope and renewal. The meaning stays the same; only the names of the hero change. The best-known returning hero is Jesus.

The Hopi prophecies speak of their returning spiritual hero Pahana, the purifier or the elder white brother, while the early Hawaiians worshipped Lono as their savior and lord of peace. The returning cultural hero for the Inkas was Viracocha, "the Sun behind the sun," whereas the Mesoamerican prophet or cultural hero was known as Quetzalcóatl – the Morning Star (please see the section below titled, "Spirit Man of Teotihuacán"). And to the Maya, he was known as Kukulkán, the Mayan name for Quetzalcóatl – the Feathered or Plumed Serpent. Kukulkán was known as "god of the powerful voice," a resurrection deity and master of the four winds.

Each far traveled on a quest for knowledge and wisdom. The enduring teaching and each returning hero was focused on achieving a balance between spirit and matter with the additional message that we are all children of God, divine as well as human. To the returning hero, separateness is an illusion; oneness is the reality. All existences interpenetrate radically and non-dualistically (non-dual interpenetration – Oneness).

Si sapis, sis apis! If you would be wise, be a bee!
"The bee is sacred to the goddess Venus."[44]

The returning "hero was always associated with the planet Venus – the dawn star that follows the path of the sun and is symbolic of enlightenment. . . . For centuries our ancestors have associated Venus with the cultural hero, the bringer of peace and tranquility to a cycle previously dominated by chaos. Could this be why Venus was so reverently charted by Maya skywatchers?"[45]

As I mentioned, the returning hero for the Mesoamericans was known as Quetzalcóatl – the Morning Star, the Feathered Serpent. This imagery and knowledge reveal the blending or merging of spirit (feathers) and matter (serpent). Furthermore, there is vibrational magic within the name Quetzalcóatl, which linguistically joins the Quetzal and its beautiful bright plumage with the mythical serpent. "Together the Quetzal and the Coatl are the creatures that are closest to the Earth and heaven as well as representing the sacred balance of female and male.

"This is the teaching within the name Quetzalcóatl, the teacher/savior deity to the Mayan and other Mexican peoples. According to Mayan tradition, this deity returns at specific times to again instruct humanity. According to the Mayan calendar, we are again in the time when Quetzalcóatl will return, and many people are expecting a savior to rescue us from all our problems. The Mayas *(sic)* say that the savior will come from the East like the shining star. I feel since Venus is the Goddess of love, that 'love' will proclaim the coming of the balanced, awakened teacher."[46]

Religious Visionary

Many times, the returning hero is a spiritual/religious visionary who "sees" things differently and is able to determine the potentialities and possibilities of the future. In addition, a visionary discerns the intertwining threads of people, places and things that others may miss. Returning heroes have the ability to see and to experience from their heart heavenly and earthly truths in a manner that allows them to bring a new way and a new message to people.

A religious visionary is often viewed as a radical—a revolutionary—as he or she brings a different way and a new message that upsets the proverbial applecart. If you are firmly established and already have a deep-rooted belief in a certain way of religious being and thinking, how could you bring something radically new? Would you even be willing? You may see the failure within the workings or dogma of the church but still not be capable of seeing a totally new church, religion, or way of being. A religious visionary, or revolutionary, if you will, has "baby eyes"[47] when it comes to religion and the workings of heaven and Earth. He or she would not be an indoctrinated member of any of the prevailing religions.

Established faiths are always terrified by new voices that promote freedom over obedience to doctrine, especially when those voices don't come from among their own and say to throw away your dogma and holy books.[48] Voices that tell you to listen to your heart, be one with nature, and use common sense.

Working outside the box of established religious dogma and doctrine, a religious revolutionary may never be seen by the masses and is many times likened to the proverbial thief in the night. This is one of the reasons the prophets and messengers of the past have been connected with the morning star, Venus in its dawn appearance. Symbolically as the thief in the night, Venus is only seen by those who are awake, or metaphorically, those who are awakened. It is the star of hope[49] and truth. According to Russian myth and folklore, "Venus was said to help people see the truth."[50]

Furthermore, down through the ages, the various prophets, teachers and messengers of a revolutionary view of religion (i.e. Jesus, Buddha, Kūkai, Quetzalcóatl, and quite possibly Moses and Mohammed) have all been associated with Venus as the morning star – the bright light that shines in the darkness. And we are in the darkest part of the darkest age of the past 26,000 years.

And one final point. Both Jesus and Quetzalcóatl are prophesied to return. After hearing the Lakota medicine man, Gerald Red Elk, talk about the relation between—and indeed, identification of—Christ and Quetzalcóatl, José Argüelles came to the following conclusion:

> Pondering the ancient site of Chichen Itza, the exquisitely proportional Temple of Kukulkán, and the numerous symbolic representations associated with Kukulkán, it occurred to me that Kukulkán-Quetzalcóatl who, in A.D. 999, prophesied the arrival of Cortes and the coming of Christianity to Mexico, was himself an incarnation of the Christ.[51]

Lord of Light

"The herald of the light is the morning star. This way man and woman approach the dawn of knowledge, because in it is the germ of life, being a blessing of the eternal."

–Haji Ibrahim of Kerbala

Usually the accepted consensus is that indigenous cultures of the past worshiped the sun and moon as the primary deities. But that was not the case. Worship of the lord of light, sometimes known as the "Sun behind the sun" predates the worship of the sun and moon. With no doubt, the returning heroes were known as the "lightbringers." These lords of light were also lords of wind such as Viracocha and Quetzalcóatl.

And then we have the Irish legend that tells us the sacred site of Newgrange was built by the *tuatha de danann*, "the lords of light," six thousand years ago. Newgrange's entrance is aligned with the rising sun on the winter solstice. At dawn, from December 19 to December 23, a narrow beam of light penetrates

7

an opening known as the roof-box and reaches the floor of the chamber, gradually extending to the rear.

The most important of all things to life is light:

> This the primitive savage felt, and, personifying it, he made Light his chief god. The beginning of the day served, by analogy, for the beginning of the world. Light comes before the sun, brings it forth, creates it, as it were. Hence the Light-God is not the Sun-God, but his Antecedent and Creator.
>
> The light appears in the East, and thus defines that cardinal point, and by it the others are located. These points, as indispensable guides to the wandering hordes, became, from earliest times, personified as important deities, and were identified with the winds that blew from them, as wind and rain gods. This explains the four brothers, who were nothing else than the four cardinal points, and their mother, who dies in producing them, is the eastern light, which is soon lost in the growing day. The East, as their leader, was also the supposed ruler of the winds, and thus god of the air and rain. As more immediately connected with the advent and departure of light, the East and West are twins, the one of which sends forth the glorious day-orb, which the other lies in wait to conquer. Yet the light-god is not slain. The sun shall rise again in undiminished glory, and he lives, though absent.
>
> By sight and light, we see and learn. Nothing, therefore, is more natural than to attribute to the light-god the early progress in the arts of domestic and social life. Thus, light came to be personified as the embodiment of culture and knowledge, of wisdom, and of the peace and prosperity which are necessary for the growth of learning.[52]

The spiritual importance of light is one of the reasons why, when conducting the bathing ritual of the Northwest Coast First People, bathing is done not at sunrise but at first light, just as Venus, the morning star, brings the light out of the darkness. As we can see in the following:

> "I, Jesus, sent my angel to give you this testimony for the churches. I am the root and offspring of David, the bright morning star." Revelation 22:16[53] (Please note that the "root" of David is divine nature and the "offspring" of David is human nature).

As well as this:

> It is told that sitting meditation in the predawn hours of the morning the Buddha looked up and saw the morning star, a sight that occasioned his enlightenment. With the sun crawling up from the eastern mountains, he called out into the dawn, crying, "I am awakened together with the whole of the great earth and all its beings."[54]

It is important to note that too often we forget that without the dark, there would be no light. Our lives are usually organized into a separation between the symbolic light and symbolic dark with the light held up as our ultimate goal in spiritual/religious life. The true secret that most never realize is that light and dark are equal components that interpenetrate as one reality. True spiritual/religious teachings are then based on the acknowledgement of the interpenetrative aspect of dark and light within us and then the growth of our light or the divine aspect of our soul from the creative darkness of our humanity.[55]

New Consciousness

Humanity desperately needs a new consciousness of radical nonduality. I believe this is possible to achieve, but only through a revolution in religious belief, philosophy and thought that will transform and bring human consciousness to a new level of being and awareness. This religious revolution will expose institutionalized religion for what it truly is: corrupt and outdated. In fact, was there ever a need for dogmatic hierarchical religion in the first place? As before, I am not the first to propose a revolution in religion. Jesus, who was a pioneer of democratic thinking, brought a revolutionary message and philosophy to all who had ears to hear:

> There can be little doubt that Jesus was a revolution-
> ary, and that the message he promoted was so altruistic that
> its full acceptance in any hierarchical society would prove
> impossible because the very hierarchy would be under-
> mined. His egalitarian ideals suffered the moment they were
> extended into the community.[56]

The key to awakening to a new consciousness is full participation in the totality of life by weeding our fields and sowing and harvesting the precious flowers and jewels of our earthly garden paradise. When we realize and keep in mind that all things have a consciousness, not just humans, and that the elements that compose life are metaphysical as well as physical, we gradually break down the illusion of separateness between ourselves and our garden paradise. This results in peacefulness, benevolence and compassion for all living things. The moth is you and you are the moth, the cat is you and you are the cat, the tree is you and you are the tree, I am you and you are me.

This transformation of consciousness results in joy, happiness and tranquility of the mind. We are no longer frightened children hiding, protecting and hoarding wealth and materialistic things on our own personal island of fear, guarding against all things that are seemingly different and separate from us. Our island of fear dissolves and we realize the garden has always been there for us, where all things are one with each other.

However, we must be careful not to let five things interfere with this transformation of consciousness and the tranquility of our mind. These are stupidity, desire, anger, doubt and false views. The traits of stupidity are ignorance, an overall dullness of spirit, pride, and incompetence. Stupid human beings are both fearful and arrogant, convinced they are superior to others not of their race, sex, or whatever group or trait with which they identify. Desire is the attachment to materialistic and pleasant things, anger causes wrath and vengeance, doubt cannot distinguish between delusion and enlightenment and cause and effect, and false views believe in the doctrine and dogma of dualistic paradigms such as the Church.

Jesus' True Message – Not the Lie of Christianity[57]

All great truths begin as blasphemies.

– George Bernard Shaw

My consciousness and worldview are based on radical nonduality. During my vision, the voice from heaven declared, "This star is you; you are this star. The purification is of the people; all are one." Even though the knowledge of oneness was part of my soul, the heavenly voice reinforced it. "All are one," is the core of the seed of the kingdom[58] of God.[59]

I know Jesus's worldview was based on radical nonduality; the core of his true message of oneness. Not just Jesus, but all things are divine with the spark, the starlight of God within them. In other words, the divine is within all things (seen/unseen), and all things are within the divine (seen/unseen), a consciousness of radical nonduality or oneness where spirit and matter interpenetrate.

"Jesus taught that we are all divine beings; that the Christ and the spirit of God can be found within all people. Within all people, not just the few—not just the Protestants, not just the Catholics, not just the Hebrews, not just the Buddhists—but all people."[60] In other words, Jesus referred to the divine spark as "the Christ."[61] It was a title, not a name: Jesus the Christ or Jesus the Divine. "The Christ is within every person. The Christ is the innate divinity of everyone. There is a higher self within us; not separate from us. The higher self, the God self, the Christ, is the ultimate reality of us."[62] But first, we must awaken to the knowledge of our innate divinity, our divine spark, and then awaken this divine light and bring it to the surface of our being. According to John

11

A. V. Strickland, "the religion of Jesus was about the divinity of humankind. Jesus's ministry was all about teaching humankind how to discover, express, and become one with the divinity in us."[63]

Jesus was a "teacher of a *way* or *path*, specifically a *way of transformation*."[64] Common sense would then dictate that the concept of faith goes directly against Jesus' personal belief, message and teachings. It is well understood that Jesus was not only the messenger, but the message, a message about the relationship of "self" and "others."

His teachings emphasized love, which unites, over fear, which separates. Love and forgiveness begin with "self" (the divine intrinsic self) and then expand out to "others" (divine intrinsic selves and things). This was, and still is, the *mystery of transformed consciousness* – the mysteries of our kingdom within; the mystery of "self" and "other." This then was the message that Jesus brought and taught to all who had ears to hear:

> Thus, according to Jesus, what was needed was an inner transformation of the self at its deepest level. "Blessed are the *pure in heart*," he said, "for they shall see God."[65]

In conclusion, Jesus's kingdom paradigm was a revolutionary worldview then, as it is now. The kingdom of God, the divine, is within us and outside us. It is a kingdom of consciousness of heart and mind (oneness), love, compassion, kindness, and equality. I call this revolutionary worldview Divine Humanity. Humanity refers to all things of the universe.

Divine Humanity – Our Message[66]

The mother sea and fountainhead of all religions lie in the mystical experiences of the individual. All theologies, all ecclesiasticisms are secondary growths, superimposed.

– William James

"All religious systems reside in the revelation of an individual soul closely linked to the cosmic soul. It is, in a word, the divinization of man. If we do not want a religion to be hidden from us by the accumulation of inert technical defaults, it is necessary to strive to rediscover the revelation that inevitably is at its origin."[67] My revelations that birthed Divine Humanity were the descending spirit exorcism and my vision and the voice from heaven.

In simplified terms, our message is to remind humanity of its divine nature.[68]

> *The two worlds, the divine and the human, can be pictured only as distinct from each other—different as life and death, as day and night. The hero adventures out of the land we know into darkness; there he accomplishes his adventure, or again is simply lost to us, imprisoned, or in danger; and his return is described as a coming back out of that yonder zone. Nevertheless—and here is a great key to the understanding of myth and symbol—the two kingdoms are actually one. The realm of the gods is a forgotten dimension of the world we know. And the exploration of that dimension, either willingly or unwillingly, is the whole sense of the deed of the hero. The values and distinctions that in normal life seem important disappear with the terrifying assimilation of the self into what formerly was only otherness. As in the stories of the cannibal ogresses, the fearfulness of this loss of personal individuation can be the whole burden of the transcendental experience for unqualified souls. But the hero-soul goes boldly in—and*

13

*discovers the hags converted into goddesses and the dragons
into the watchdogs of the gods.*[69]

Divine Humanity is a personal life philosophy and/or a personal religion with its foundation – love. In its purest meaning and sense, love means oneness/unity. It is centered on radical nondualism or where spirit and matter mutually permeate, with no separation between the seen and unseen worlds or between mind and body. All things have consciousness and are connected in a web of love. Within the relative universe, the unseen and seen world mutual permeate each other. This theme of non-dual interpenetration underpins all aspects of Divine Humanity. This philosophy is substantiated by the work of the physicist David Bohm (1917 – 1992) a colleague of Albert Einstein.

Furthermore, Divine Humanity (wherein humanity represents not only the human race but all things of creation) is a living spiritual philosophy, a green religion – organic[70] and natural. It calls for a new consciousness. Moreover, we are born in original divinity,[71] **not** original sin.[72] Divine Humanity, a personal religion of spiritual philosophy, is based on one's truth found within one's heart. It is not based on faith, dogma or doctrine.

The excellence of religion may be demonstrated by the unity, compassion and love that it brings to <u>all</u> <u>people</u> and <u>all</u> <u>things</u> of the <u>Earth</u>. If this is true, then we can see with clarity that organized or institutionalized religion is a dismal failure.

~ JC

Divine Humanity is a religion of philosophy and a living, personal—not institutionalized—religion.[73] It is a religion and philosophy of heaven and Earth. The patriarchal western religions of Judaism, Christianity, and Islam are strictly heaven-patriarchal-based monotheistic (god) religions while the polytheistic (goddess) religions of the past were Earth based. Divine Humanity is based on both: the experience, knowledge, and wisdom of heaven and Earth. It is a radical nondualistic religion and philosophy and does not espouse belief in an anthropomorphic god[74] including the concept of grace. (For more on grace, please see endnote 369.) Additionally, Divine Humanity is not faith-based but grounded in common sense, truth of one's heart, and the reality of the equality, consciousness and the interconnection of all things. In other words, we do not believe in the Divine (God); we know the Divine through direct experience. This is the same as we don't believe in Angels; we know Angels. (Please see story of the Visitation.)

As a world philosophy of awe and a religion of equality (neither patriarchal nor matriarchal) and simplicity, it conveys a love for all forms of life and acknowledges everything in creation as divine, as well as honoring its own unique intrinsic expression. Therefore, every human being is divine with an intrinsic human expression and the light, holy spark, of the reflection of the Absolute within. The Absolute is the transcendent great mystery outside of space and time, or God if you wish. In other words, within the relative universe (unseen world and seen world) all things are immanent; all have this light, this sacred fire within them and outside them. All things are divine and have a unique intrinsic expression. Trees, for example, have this sacred fire within them and in their intrinsic expression may provide food and shelter for us and for other creatures of the Earth. Therefore, the Great Mystery, the All, the Absolute (God) is both transcendent and immanent.

We do not need to be saved but to discover the oneness of being.

Divine Humanity is based on the concept of nondifferentiating knowledge and not based on dualism. Its foundation and worldview are interpenetrating radical nonduality – oneness.[75] This is unity through duality, a unity created when the dualities of spirit and matter interpenetrate as one.[76]

In other words, there is no separation between the binaries dark and light, spirit and matter, or mind and body. All permeate each other. The most profound and essential nature of things is not distinct from the things recognizable by our senses. In other words, our sacred selves and our profane selves are nondual and interpenetrate; likewise, the sacred identities and profane identities of all sentient beings and things are nondual and interpenetrate. This is true oneness.

Furthermore, Divine Humanity is a philosophical religion of peace and respect, and teaches you how-to live-in harmony with your surroundings and yourself, as well as how to deal with the different phases of your life. As a green, natural religion, Divine Humanity stresses the interconnection of all things and emphasizes respect for nature. As a religious philosophy, it adheres to the Pythagorean cosmological axioms: "as in the greatest, so in the least"; "as above, so below."

Divine Humanity does not play the unjust and inequitable religious game of a patriarchal sexual identity (sun worship) or matriarchal (moon worship), but is a religion and philosophy of the stars. A religion of equality and justice. Divine Humanity supports and believes in "choice" and Reproductive Justice.[77]

As a final thought, Divine Humanity as a religious philosophy allows each one of us to fully participate in life without the divisive aspects of religious dogma and doctrine. There is no orthodox theology. We each have the freedom to express ourselves in whatever manner we chose: in dress, head covering, or our partner in a relationship. And no dietary restrictions: yes, you can enjoy an aged single malt or a hot coffee in the morning. Always keep in mind the three maxims inscribed in the Temple of Apollo at the ancient oracle site of Delphi, Greece: *Know Thyself, Nothing too Much,* and *Keep the Measure.* Freedom – a life of freedom.[78]

Heart of Love
Deep inside my sacred body
There is a vessel that
Holds my memories
Of Forever…
Where Pain, Sorrow, Hurt, Loss,
Regret, Joy, Happiness, Peace and
Love share this ever growing
Heart – space…
With each soft beat and murmur
I receive – and – I release –
And – I bless the miracles
Of my life

~ Sher

Our heart contains love. Love in its purest form means Oneness—blending of spirit and matter. Our heart is where our divine spark and radical nondualistic consciousness (divine consciousness) is located. However, our spark (fire of the divine) and our divine consciousness are dormant. Until they are both awakened, our dualistic consciousness in the brain dominates our thoughts, reality, and worldview. When our left - right hemispheres are merged, visualize a rainbow bridge of consciousness, our divine spark, our radical nondualistic consciousness (love), awakens in our heart. This is heart-love, the luminous light of our divine spark. From now on in our earth walk, we bring this divine light of our heart to all others and to all things of the earth.

Since we are human beings on earth, we still need to maintain a dualistic consciousness. When we awaken, we do not loss our dualistic consciousness. It remains in our brain/mind while our divine consciousness is awakened in our heart. This means that our thoughts, actions, and words flow from our heart through our mind.

As it is said, "our heart is the best compass we have." We speak truth (from the heart), express forgiveness, compassion, and empathy for others. Our eyes view equality, not inequality, and recognizes the sacredness of nature. Heart-love is the love of nature with the knowledge and understanding that whatever we do to nature, we do to ourselves.

The word love is easy to banter around and as a talking point in promoting books and workshops. Throw in forgiveness and suddenly you've become spiritual enlightened. But love in its purest meaning of oneness is difficult to practice. And it is even more difficult to embody this heart-love of oneness in the inner core of one's self and in one's soul.

One last point: Keep in mind that even though awakened, we are still human, have a dualistic consciousness and at various times will still express dysfunctional human traits such as anger.[79]

Paint Colors

In our apprenticeship with the late Mom and Vince Stogan, Coast Salish Musqueam shamans, Vince told me to be aware that I might have a vision revealing how to paint my face during ceremonies and healings. Vince was correct.

My enthusiasm for running eventually led me to this vision. My daily runs took me to Fort Williams, a park situated on the Atlantic Ocean in Cape Elizabeth, Maine. Fort Williams is a former U.S. Army fort which operated from 1872 to 1964. It was part of the coastal defenses of Portland with various concrete gun emplacements at the edge of the ocean.

My runs would average four miles. Half way through the run, I would jump up on one of the gun emplacements and do a hundred quick push-ups, then jump back down to continue running. After a few minutes, I would return to the same spot and do another 100 push-ups, jump down, and continue my run back to our home.

I was known in the community as the runner and the fitness guy. Even the park ranger knew me. I would wave and smile at him on my runs. Once he stopped me to relate what had happened over the weekend. An agitated woman had confronted him with her concern that a "crazy man" was acting strangely out on the point. He smiled and said to me, "I assured her that's only "Rocky."[80] He's not crazy and won't hurt you." This theme of a different name/ identity has been a thread running through my life such as when the other adventurers on the Peruvian Inka trail in 1988 only knew me by the name, "the Inka." And once in a bar in Seattle, I befriended two possible gangbangers who referred to me as "Capt'n Moses."

Running was an expression of my soul, my freedom, the freedom of movement. Running was also part of my spirit training. In fact, it was due to my running at midnight outside the sacred city of Teotihuacán that I encountered the "Spirit Man of Teotihuacán."

During storms, especially nor'easters, I would take that first step outside the comfort of my home and, wrapped within the wind-whipped darkness, run out to Fort Williams, the location of the Portland Headlight. The Headlight is a historic lighthouse located on the cliffs overlooking the open ocean. The name "nor'easter" comes from the directional origins of the storms' strong winds.[81] Once at the Headlight, I would voice prayers to the living essence of the storm and sing my spirit song. To embody and breathe in the power of the winds and the force of the storm, I would stand on the cliffs facing north and then east experiencing and witnessing the full power of the storm. As the winds howled and screamed and waves crashed on the rocks below, anointing of my body and soul with its salty spray, I would become one with its power.

Battered by the wind, as it moved my body to-and-fro, purified by the watery spray of the ocean below and the heavenly rain from above, my clothing plastered to my body like a second skin and with eyes closed, I would absorb the energy and make it a part of my essence. Not a human feeling but an elemental one. I was at the center of the storm. I was the storm. At that moment I would feel totally alive, with no past, no future, just my body, spirit, and soul one with the storm, and the merging of heaven and Earth within me.

And then, as with all things, it would be time to leave. A final blessing as I headed home. The gifting for my sacrifice of self awaited me: a warm abode and a loving wife, son, and daughter. And then, there was something else, one more gifting awaited my arrival – hot-mulled wine by a roaring fire. Life at times is awesome and fulfilling, and the memories are priceless.

Sea Creature

The ability to successfully pass back and forth between alternate realities is a fundamental feature of mysticism in general, shamanism in particular, and anthropology in practice. A convergence of the spiritual and material domains is perhaps disturbing to some scholars in their citadels of Western rationality, but we believe it is our best hope if we wish to create a future of tolerance and effective collaboration between peoples.[82]

Years after being labeled a "crazy man," I had my paint color vision. I asked for this vision during one of my runs and it happened during my second round of push-ups. As I jumped up while running in place for a few seconds,

I happened to look down into the ocean water and I saw an image of a sea creature and my paint colors of black and red.[83]

Black and red, I thought as I jumped off and continued my run. Outside the fort, on shore road I came across a dead snake. I picked it up and realized that it was a spirit snake, as Vince had taught us how to tell if a dead snake is a spirit snake – a gifting from spirit.

When I got back from my run, excited by the prospect of knowing how to paint my face, I told Sher about my experience. We wondered if it was a true vision because we had never seen anyone wearing two different colors of paint on their face. Later that evening I called Vince in Vancouver to tell him about my experience. I was concerned that the image and the paint colors were just wishful imaginative seeing.

As I related the story to Vince and said I didn't think it was a true vision given that we'd never seen those paint colors on any of the dancers in the long-house during the winter dance season, he laughed and said (paraphrased), "Of course, you wouldn't. Those are my face paint colors, the colors of a medicine person, or shaman. You only saw the all-black face paint of the warrior or all red of the healer, but the Indian doctor's face paint is black and red. And to the serpent . . . " What Vince told me next is private knowledge and can't be revealed in print.

Outside of identifying me as a shaman/medicine person, what is the significance of my paint colors? In various indigenous traditions these are the colors of Venus, known as the sacred twin, in its two phases as the morning star (red) and evening star (black). Additionally, concerning my connection with Quetzalcóatl, "the red and black coloration provides an intriguing link with the cult of Quetzalcóatl, for the Aztecs said that Quetzalcóatl died in the 'land of writing' (*tlilan tlapallan*), meaning literally 'the land of red and black,' the colors used in Mayan writing."[84] Furthermore, "black and red in conjunction signify wisdom."[85] Finally, according to Miguel León-Portilla in, *Aztec Thought and Culture – A Study of the Ancient Nahuatl Mind*, "the wise man is black and red ink. But since these colors symbolize the presentation of and knowledge about things difficult to understand, and about the hereafter, throughout Nahuatl mythology, the obvious metaphorical implication is that the wise man possesses "writing and wisdom."[86]

I paint my face for ceremonies such as burnings and bathings, and for certain healings. Indigenous face painting has an importance that dates back millennium. It was an important part of ritual and ceremony at Teotihuacán, where I had my "spirit man" experience, and in other parts of Mexico where face painting was the equivalent of a mask. "Huitzilopochtli:[87] 'His face is painted with stripes; it is his mask.' Such facial painting, as a mask, allows the simultaneous perception by the viewer of the human and divine identity of the wearer and forces the realization, exemplified by Hopi children confronting the unmasked kachina, that the world of man and the world of spirit are essentially one, a unity realized in the liminal state of ritual."[88]

A Rose by Any Other Name

Expand I must through the dark
Potential - I struggle upward
What am I?
To suffer for what reason

There are others but who are they?
Where are they?
Why do I know this?
From the core of my spark

What am I?
To toil upward
What is the meaning?
There must be light

An eternity it seems
I push ever upward
Expanding as I grow
Closer but to what?

To the light
One more push

I'm free
But still the struggle

What beauty I am
How sweet I smell
All red as the sunrise
That feeds me.

And what has my life meant
Why the struggle to the light
Beauty I bring, thorns and all
Sun angels adorn me, bees feed me

Divine mystery I am
Life so short as such
But immortal am I
Beauty evermore

– JC

Nahuatl Philosophy

The wise man: a light, a torch, a stout torch that does not smoke.

A perforated mirror, a mirror pierced on both sides.

His are the black and red ink, his are the illuminated manuscripts, he studies
    the illuminated manuscripts.

He himself is writing and wisdom.

He is the path, the true way for others.

He directs people and things; he is a guide in human affairs.

The wise man is careful (like a physician) and preserves tradition.

His is the handed-down wisdom; he teaches it; he follows the path of truth.

Teacher of truth, he never ceases to admonish.

He makes wise the countenances of others; to them he gives a face; he leads
    them to develop it.

He opens their ears; he enlightens them.

He is the teacher of guides; he shows them their path.

One depends upon him.

He puts a mirror before others, he makes them prudent, cautious; he causes
    a face to appear on them.

He attends to things; he regulates their path, he arranges and commands.

He applies his light to the world.

He knows what is above us (and) in the region of the dead.

He is a serious man.

Everyone is comforted by him, corrected, taught.

Thanks to him people humanize their will and receive a strict education.

He comforts the heart, he comforts the people, he helps, gives remedies, heals
    everyone.

    – Codice Matritense de la Real Academia, VIII, fol.118, r. - 118, v. trans.
by Miguel León-Portilla, 1963:10-11.

    I've always been intrigued and felt kinship for the words and context of
this sage piece of Nahuatl philosophy translated by Miguel León-Portilla,
Professor Emeritus at the Institute of Historical Research at the National
University of Mexico.[89]

PART II

. . . .

The Adventures of this World and the Otherworld

If what is said by the philosophers concerning the kinship of god and men is true, what other course remains for men than to do as Socrates did, never replying to anyone who asked him where he was from, 'I am Athenian', or 'I am Corinthian', but 'I am a citizen of the world.'

~Epictetus, Discourse 1, chapter 9

THE RITTER MAN

. . . .

ON A FRIDAY EVENING IN THE EARLY 1970S, I WALKED DOWN A darkened corridor in a run-down building in the low-income section of West Chester, Pennsylvania. As I knocked on the knife-scarred door, the last one in the hallway, I wondered how I would be welcomed. Even though I had a brown belt in karate, knives are many times more dangerous than guns and it seemed that someone had been using the door as a cutting board. Of course, I could say that I was a salesman for "kitchen knives."

Perhaps most would imagine I was the last person anyone would want to see at their door, but in reality, I was the best one. I was a Ritter Man, a collection man working for a company, a post that exemplified the non-compassionate capitalistic spirit. Being in graduate school with a wife and small child, I needed a part-time job, and for reasons that still baffle me, I chose this one. On the other hand, in the short time that I worked for them I did impact some people's lives. Not in a negative way but a positive one. One of compassion and loving kindness.

I remember my first day on the job as I looked through the various payment cards. One family had borrowed sixty dollars to purchase a bike for their child for Christmas. Two years later, they not only still owed the initial sixty dollars, but the total they now owed Ritter came to almost $150. And they were not an isolated case.

Even though I collected in what would be termed dangerous areas, I was never concerned for my safety. And unlike Trump,[90] I was never afraid to stand in front of a door. It didn't even enter into my mind, not to stand there.

As the knife-scarred door opened, I was looking at an African-American grandmother. Grandmother or not, she had a strong willed "don't mess with me" aura. In fact, her attitude reminded me of my own mother. She owed a fifteen-dollar payment but she had spent what small money she had on food for her and her grandchild, whom she was raising. And here is the reason I was the best one to be knocking on her door: even though my wife and I were struggling to make ends meet, I made her payment. This was not an isolated event. In fact, if I hadn't quit after a few weeks, Sher and I would have been borrowing money from Ritter.

I usually collected on Friday nights and the weekend, which fit nicely into my class schedule. The reasoning concerning Friday night was to collect the money owed to Ritter before it was spent on drugs and booze. An unfair assumption across the board, but in some cases it was true. One Friday evening, I tracked down one of my collections to, shall we say, an unsavory bar in West Chester. Even though it was a college town, this bar was not populated by students but by local blue-collar workers. This time, I didn't cover the payment but had a beer with a man whose name I can't recall.

Looking back on it, it seems that I provided something greater for him than the payment. I was someone who listened to him and his stories without any judgment. We all have stories to tell, some tragic and some joyous, but many times there is no one to listen to them. I was not being a good capitalistic soldier. I was more interested in this person as a human being—a divine human being—than making money for Ritter. I quit the following Monday.

And it was best that I stopped "working for the man." As Sher will relate, my body had responded to the stress caused by the injustice and the greed of the moneylender, Ritter. I had developed a twitch. Magically (not really), after a few weeks it dissipated into thin air, and good riddance to both the twitch and Ritter.

Commentary

Who gets to tell the stories? This is a question asked often. The answer, in this case, for better or for worse, is I do. At least this time out.

– Anthony Bourdain

Ritter was just a preview of the greed and inequality of capitalism that would exponentially increase decade after decade. It doesn't have to be this way. Ask yourself this question: what kind of world do you think we would have if people were more concerned about their fellow human beings than about making money?

Furthermore, each of us has tales to relate just like my beer-drinking friend. So what stories have you been silent about that you need to tell?

A CLOSE ENCOUNTER OF THE THIRD KIND

. . . .

Wet Footprints

IN AUGUST OF 1974, SHER, OUR FIVE-YEAR-OLD SON JAMIE, AND I traveled to Maine so I could interview for a position at the Waterville YMCA. We were living in Delaware while I was the physical education director of the Chester, Pennsylvania YMCA. It was a great position but a brutal commute from New Castle Delaware to Chester.

We wanted a healthier and closer-to-nature lifestyle for ourselves and our son and Maine seemed to fit the bill. The YMCA had a beautiful, wooded summer day camp situated on the edge of a large pond where we could camp for a few nights. The regular camp season was over, which let us have this pristine land all to ourselves. Late in the afternoon of the second day of my interview we headed to the Y's camp and decided that the best spot was right next to the shore in front of the camp's dock. Because we were invited to dinner at the executive director's home, we wasted no time setting up our tent and left while it was still light, realizing we would be returning in the dark.

The dinner went well and it seemed that I would be offered the position as program director. Excited by the prospect, we returned to the camp. The parking lot was at the top of a slope that ended at our tent at the water's edge. As we began walking down the trail, I noticed how dark it was within the evergreens. Halfway down the path to our tent, I began to feel a little uneasy. Since it was dark and we were alone in the woods, I put my feelings off to my imagination. "What," I thought, "could be so threatening to make me feel so uneasy?"

Even though it was a beautiful starlit night, there was an undercurrent of foreboding within my consciousness. By the time we reached our tent and crawled inside, I was feeling even more unsettled. I could sense that Sher was also tense. "But isn't this what we've been looking forward to? Camping in the woods of Maine? And with the bonus that's it's by a lake, what the locals call a pond." These thoughts passed through my mind as I turned to speak to Sher.

In a whisper so Jamie would not hear I asked, "How are you feeling?"

"Uneasy," she whispered back. "It's creepy. Maybe it's the dark, but it's not the same as when we were here a few hours ago when it was light."

"I know," I replied. "But let's try and get some sleep." Sleep was only a far-off dream. Lying on my side, I whispered into Sher's ear, "I'm scared; and I feel strange – a tingly feeling and pressure on the back of my neck and around my head."[91]

"I'm scared too. I think we need to leave, now," Sher replied while sitting up.

We were still dressed so our getaway was simple and fast. Jamie had not questioned why we were leaving. It was just then that we heard a large splash.

Curious, and in all innocence, Jamie walked a few feet towards the dock and said, "Look daddy Pterodactyl feet."

And yes, there were the remains of wet, webbed footprints on the dry dock surface. "Time to go," I said as we hurried up the trail. To see if we were being followed, I looked back towards the pond, and at that moment, a bright light streaked from the surface of the pond up into the heavens. With the light now stationary in the night sky, Sher looked back and said, "What is that strange light?" Then she added, "Are you sure, you want to accept this job?" I just looked at her as we continued up the path to the safety of our car.

Once at the car, Jamie turned to both of us and said, "I really like Pterodactyls but Tyrannosaur Rex is my favorite."

THE BEGINNING OF OUR QUEST

. . . .

Seeking the Grail

"The real history of the Holy Grail is written in the stars."[92]

*What is the Grail? The cup from which the apostles drank at the last supper?
The vessel in which Joseph of Arimathea gathered the blood of Christ?
The stone broken out of the crown of Lucifer at the fall of man? The jewel
of immortality? The "gradale," the graded dish that feeds everyone with a
different food? Is it a mandala? A secret teaching?
A code message through all eternity? Is it object or symbol – or both?*[93]

There are many legends and myths that relate to a magical chalice. But
alas "chalice" is just a name that some use. There are many stories identifying this same talisman as a bowl or possibly a ring. In another guise, it has
been referred to as a cauldron of magic – a magic that would extend life and
provide for all want. This mystical talisman seems to be ever elusive in its
shape-shifting identity. Even more mysterious, could it have been a secret
teaching contained within a philosophical book of life?

Even though tales abound, there have been few true seekers for this great
amulet of power. Usually the legends of this magic were whispered in the
pitch-dark of the night and many believed them to be works of a fantasy-filled
imagination.

Sherry and I have ever been seeking the mysteries of heaven and Earth.
This mystery of immortality has been the primary one clawing at the edge of
our consciousness – a fascination of the Otherworld.

31

True to form in our seeking of the mysteries, in the summer of 1981, given our financial position, Sherry and I did a foolish thing. We traveled to the Celtic lands of England, Wales and Scotland on a quest of magic and spirit. Even though I had wanted us to adventure and far travel to the Amazon, Sher did not support or encourage this, so finally, we decided to experience the land that embraced the sacred myths of Arthur and his knights on their quest for the Holy Grail.

In the eyes of capitalistic society, we were fools to far travel. But we were fools as represented by the Fool card of the Tarot, referred to as philosophical medicine. The Fool card represents the person's journey through the Tarot, which reflects their spiritual journey through life. The Major Arcane of the Tarot begins with the Magician's card number one and completes with the World card number twenty-two.[94]

The Major Arcane, with arcane meaning secret or mysterious knowledge, may be viewed as a visual and symbolic guide to a spiritual journey. We begin the spiritual journey through our own innocence and naiveté as a fool in other people's eyes, but after the twists and turns of life and our various experiences, we eventually arrive through perseverance at the World card. This card represents the oneness of self and life.

But our journey is not yet complete as we continue being the fool but in a different way. We now have an awakening of reality and the oneness of life. This spurs us on to further adventures of far traveling and awakening. And once again, we are the foolish ones or the fools in other people's eyes, as we strive on for the spiritual and not the material aspects of life, ever seeking Divinehood.

While our peers were vacationing in the Caribbean, we were on a holiday ("holy-day") to England. A journey we really couldn't afford. Our home needed work but instead off we went. In society's eyes, we were not doing a responsible thing. While others were saving for retirement and the future, we were spending money questing for knowledge and spirit. Most assuredly, this was a foolish thing. We were not conforming to the norms of society or being responsible adults. We were abandoning society's imposed unhealthy ego-self to acquire the mantles of the archetypical hero. Would this not be foolish?

My Soul's Need

To know is to remember ...

SEEING THEN that the soul is immortal and has been born many times, and has beheld all things both in this world and in the nether realms, she has acquired knowledge of all and everything; so that it is no wonder that she should be able to recollect all that she knew before about virtue and other things. For as all nature is akin, and the soul has learned all things, there is no reason why we should not, by remembering but one single thing - an act which men call learning - discover everything else, if we have courage and faint not in the search; since, it would seem, research and learning are wholly recollection.

~Plato, Meno (8ID)

I viewed this pilgrimage to a foreign land as the actual beginning of a quest that had its roots many years in the past with my enrollment in martial arts training as a freshman in college. Even though years later, I attained a black belt, it was not enough. The art I studied focused more on the physical and little on the mystical or spiritual, which were the real reasons behind my desire to study the martial arts.

My need for martial power—warriorship—had sprung within me full-blown at the age of sixteen. A visual tale—a movie—literally changed my life. For me, it was a vision and soul-rite of passage, so to speak. It vibrated a deep soul memory within the core of my being that never left and only grew stronger. It opened the gate for a birthing of a personal mythology of the heroic warrior and the sacrifice of heart that would eventually take me across the world seeking knowledge and power.

I turned sixteen on August 29, 1962. This was the same day a movie was released. This movie, this visual tale changed my life. It was… *The 300 Spartans*. The ancient Spartans were the saviors of Western civilization because of their heroic actions and sacrifice at the Pass of Thermopylae known as the Hot Gates. The Spartan King, Leonidas, and his courageous sacrifice and loyalty sparked a soul-memory deep within my heart. And from those soul moving qualities of this one movie, I began to remember my incarnations, and from that day forward, commenced a quest of spirit that would take me far and wide.

The 300 Spartans was not the only movie that resonated a memory within the core of my heart and soul. Another movie that vibrated my martial spirit was *The Vikings* with Kirk Douglas and Ernest Borgnine, and *El Cid* with Charlton Heston and Sophia Loren. One of the lines from *El Cid* that impacted me was: "In my country, we have a name for a warrior with the vision to be just and the courage to show mercy. We call him the Cid!"

Most importantly though, there was one other movie that triggered something more within the core of my being rather than just the martial aspect of my soul. I was twenty-three years old and the movie was *The Royal Hunt of the Sun*.

Other movies that tugged at my soul always portrayed the struggle and possible sacrifice of the few in the defense of the many and the courage of the few against overwhelming odds such as in *Zulu*, a 1964 film depicting the Battle of Rorke's Drift between the British Army and the Zulus.[95] In 1879, a small British force of 139 faced approximately 4,500 Zulu warriors. It was a remarkable tale of courage and tenacity, on both sides, where the average age of the Zulu *impis* (regiments) was fifty and they had just run fifteen miles to get there. It was a warrior culture I greatly admired; the Zulus with their animal-hide shields and their *iklwa* (a short stabbing spear) were facing the breach-loading, single-shot Martini-Henry rifle and bayonet.

Within the tiny outpost, the British withstood the attacks but were worn down, with many wounded. And then, in what would be the final assault, we witness the war chant of the Zulus and the sound of their *iklwa* on the back of their shields, which gave me goosebumps. The British survived the onslaught and the remaining Zulu warriors withdrew.

One of the most moving and inspiring moments was the final glimpse of the Zulus. The approximately 4,000 Zulus warriors still alive were arranged across the peak of the Oscarberg, a large hill above the British encampment. They sang a haunting song honoring the courage and spirit of the defenders. Slowly the Zulus fell out of sight with only their war leader remaining. He performed a final salute of honor and then slowly turned around and disappeared over the ridge of the Oscarberg. Eleven of the defenders received the Victoria Cross – the highest British award.

A more recent movie that rang true with my soul was *Kingdom of Heaven*.[96] A few of the lines that reflect my soul: "Speak the **truth** always, even if it leads to your death"; "What man is a man who does not make the world better"; "I put no stock in religion. By the word religion I have seen the lunacy of fanatics of every denomination be called the will of God"; "Holiness is in right action and courage on behalf of those who cannot defend themselves, and goodness. What God desires is here [points to head], and here [points to heart], and what you decide to do every day, you will be a good man – or not; your soul is in your keeping alone."

It would be years before I matured in soul enough to cry my tears at the Hot Gates of Thermopylae and to face death on the Inka Trail in Peru. But all questors must initially take that first step of seeking. For Sher and me, it was the Celtic lands that first called to us. Little did we realize the significance of this choice and the hidden meanings within our experiences.

A Pilgrimage of Heart

The summer of 1981 seems so long ago, but then again, only like yesterday. Sherry and I traveled to the Celtic lands on a pilgrimage of heart and renewal. This was to be a journey of the spirit and a quest seeking the magic of the lands known as England, Wales and Scotland. As we flew over the Atlantic our thoughts were on our present state of excitement not on our scheduled return, or so we thought, 10 days later.

London is an awesome city of tradition with a very special ambience that is in all ways traditionally British. We stayed only two nights, just long enough to catch the new musical *Cats*. Little did we realize how prophetic it would be. Even though few tickets were available, our hotel concierge was able to procure two.

As I would discover, if you want a beer as I did, you go to a pub, not a fancy hotel, which we did owing to my naivety. Before the show, we went into the Savoy to get a drink. Seated in plush chairs, the waiter approached to take our order. He was not British, and his English was a little difficult to understand. When I asked about a local beer, he replied with a name, I thought, I had never heard. So of course, I ordered it being excited to sample an English ale. As a sign that our journey was going to be interesting in all ways, as he sat a Heineken down in front of me. Sher looked at me and I looked at her and we both laughed. After my "English" beer we headed for the London performance of the musical *Cats*. This was the first year of its performance and it was truly an awesome show.

The next morning, we rented a car and off we went on our quest, seeking the myth and magic of Stonehenge, Glastonbury, Wales and Scotland. Being the eternal optimist that I am, I had planned on a seven-day journey through England, Wales and Scotland. Doesn't work! Especially when you have never driven on the left-hand side of the road and a portion of your driving time is spent reassuring your wife that the car is not going to run off the side of the road and crash.

The first day that we left London set the tone for our driving adventure. Our rental car was located in the basement of a hotel in the middle of the city. As the driver, I sat where the passenger normally sits. I was, shall we say, a little throw off my game. The gear shift was to my left not right, which meant I needed to shift with my left hand. This reversal of normal behavior immediately revealed itself when leaving the underground garage, I drove up the down ramp. Luckily no cars were entering. But this was just the beginning of scaring Sherry half to death. I had picked noon as our departure time. Not smart when we were in the center of London.

After driving a few yards, I faced the terror of England – roundabouts. I merged into traffic like I had just entered the Monaco Grand Prix. Sherry was attempting to tell me which road to take off the roundabout as the swirling mass of cars engulfed ours. Safety, I thought; the inner circle. If you have never tackled a London roundabout, especially at noon, give it a try, you will never complain about driving in the States again. It was somewhere near the twelfth rotation with both of us on the verge of seasickness that I found an opening to escape from this form of medieval torture. We were finally on our way to adventures we could never have dreamt about.

Realistically, we should have planned for our journey to take twice as long. Somehow I would magically transverse the motorways in record time. Of course, I would. On the way to Bath and Glastonbury, we would stop at Stonehenge. Ah, the plans of mice and men. Somehow we ended up in Bath and came nowhere close to Stonehenge.

I had planned for us to spend only one night in Bath and then leave the next day for Glastonbury and its magical and mystical sites. I had discovered that one of the inns in Glastonbury, the George and Pilgrims, supposedly had a "haunted" room. Both Sherry and I were excited at the thought of staying in a haunted room in England, especially in Glastonbury, the rumored burial place of King Arthur.

Our visit to Bath was uneventful. Sherry and I both felt a hollowness of spirit as if the healing waters of Bath had lost their spiritual essence of purification. So, it was with little regret that we left the next morning for mystical Glastonbury. This was 1981 and the concept of New Age was a term seldom used and seldom heard. In other words, Glastonbury was not over-run with New Agers. Thus, it was still spiritually "virginal."

Glastonbury is not too far from Bath as the crow flies. But then again, the road to Glastonbury does not lend itself to Motorway speeds. And to visit Stonehenge, we would need to back track and lose a day. We had to decide whether Scotland would go off the itinerary, or Stonehenge. A difficult choice but one that turned out to be perfect. We skipped Stonehenge and headed straight for Glastonbury.

Glastonbury then was not the Glastonbury of today. As many of you probably know, Glastonbury is New Age Mecca, quite different from what it was in 1981 when it was referred to as England's Jerusalem. It is still a place of pilgrimage and power, but sadly it has gone the way of many other sacred places around the world that have been discovered by the New Age crowd and become popular. With the crowds come the capitalistic mercenaries and the New Age gurus! Need I say more?

Isle of Avalon

There are many myths and legends connected with the British Isles. These run the gauntlet from the legendary Arthur, his Knights of the Round Table, Merlin and the Holy Grail to being the site of the mythic north land called Hyperborea. This enchanted land also holds many tales of ghostly specters haunting ancient ruins. Glastonbury was rumored to have been visited by Joseph of Arimathea, the teenage Jesus, and more recently a ghostly monk.

However, this was not the only reason that we were going to Glastonbury. It was also the site of the sacred mound called the Tor, and the Chalice Well with its healing waters. Sherry and I both believe that spiritual power is not to be found within the walls of a church but out in nature such as on top of the Tor.

As we approached Glastonbury, also known as the Glassy Isle or the Isle of Avalon, we could feel the shift in energy. It was misty and foggy. We could almost feel the veil lifting between the two worlds as if we were entering the gateway to the spirit realms. Little did we realize at the time; how true this was to be.

Checking in at the George and Pilgrims, we asked about staying in the haunted room. The innkeeper was a little taken back by our request and asked if we would first like to see the room. Climbing the creaky and slightly uneven steps to the second floor gave us the feeling of being transported back in time. The en-suite room overlooked High Street and was very quaint, with an armoire, sitting chair and bed. During the day, this would be just another room at the inn.

It was still early enough to climb the Tor. I would be sacrificing a late afternoon run and Sherry would be giving up afternoon tea, but we decided we needed and wanted to experience this faerie hill in the late afternoon, a time when the faeries would be waking up.

In 1981, literary knowledge about the Tor was not as readily available as it is today. In addition, there was no public Internet. We were being drawn to the Tor by our souls' knowledge and the mystical-spiritual writings that we had studied. We were drawn to this mystical hill and enchanted land totally due to the feelings within our hearts. At the time, we didn't have any knowledge of the Tor's connection to the Archangel Michael[97] or to Venus as the morning star.

Sher climbing the Tor, August 1981

Finding our way up the Tor, was not as easy as it would be today. In 1981, there were no steps or any type of formal path. The angelic hill was just a steep grassy slope with a dirt path and sheep milling all around. When we finally reached the tower at the top, our feelings were hard to put into words. The Tor is an enigma to many, but for us it felt like a coming home. We were the only humans in sight. We had the magic of the faerie mound totally to ourselves. With daylight fading slowly through the mist, it was an enchanted moment. At any time, the Archangel or the Faerie Queen might appear. The veil separating our world from the Otherworld was thinning by the second. Little did we realize that we would have a visitor later in the night – one not of this world.

The tower on the summit of the Tor was all that remained of the Church of St. Michael. It was dedicated to Mikaël, the Sun Archangel, known to the Celt's as the Light Giver Lugh or the Sun God Bel. He was depicted on the tower weighing the souls of the dead along with an image of St. Bridget or the Celtic Bride milking her cow. According to the Scottish Highlanders, there was an "ancient tradition that Jesus was fostered by the native goddess, Brigit."[98]

There are many myths and legends concerning the Tor. One legendary account claims that it is the gateway or passageway to Annwn, the Welsh Otherworld. This marvelous realm exists within ours but remains hidden from our materialistic and greed-filled world.[99] However, at certain times and in certain places, the veil may be lifted and you may see and experience magic and the world of spirit. The Tor is one such enchanted place and the transitional times of light and dark, dawn and dusk, are two such times when the veil is threadbare.

Being on the Tor was a magical experience for Sherry and me. With the overcast sky and the fine mist as the background, we could easily feel the mystical power that supposedly drew spiritual and religious leaders here as far back as 5000 BCE. After time spent meditating and connecting with the energetic forces, we finally pulled ourselves away from that place of mystery and magic and headed back to our room at the George and Pilgrims. After a wonderful dinner at the inn, we retired to our room for a well-deserved sleep.

The Ghostly Monk

"That feels so good," was a fleeting thought that registered in my slowly awakening mind. In that gray area between sleep and waking, I felt a tickling on my left inner thigh. Assuming it was Sherry caressing me, I turned my head while opening my eyes. But she was on her side, facing away from me and seemed to be asleep. Ah, just my imagination, I thought.

Closing my eyes again, I began to fall back asleep. And then, the tickling sensation returned once again. More fully awake now, I could tell from Sherry's breathing that she was not asleep and not the source of the annoyance. And there seemed to be a chill in the air.

"Sherry," I whispered.

Sitting up she replied, "something is not. . . . "

But the rest of her words caught in her throat as both of us at the same time saw the "eyes!" Looming out of darker blackness against the black were two glowing ruby-red coal lights where eyes should be. They had an otherworldly feeling to them and stared at us from in front of the armoire.

"Tot! Yahhh," from the depths of my soul, a martial spirit shout escaped naturally from my throat. This was no macho response but a combination of fear and reflex. In the next moment, there were no longer any glowing eyes and the chill had left the room.

If any words were expressed between Sherry and me, they have been long lost to time. I do know we were unsettled and decided to turn on the light in the loo, what the British call the bathroom, for the rest of the night. For the fans of trivia, loo probably comes from *regardez l'eau*, watch out for the water, which people used to shout before emptying their chamber pots out of the door or window.

Unable to sleep, time dragged on for what seemed like an eternity. Finally, with the first light of dawn, that beautiful light, all the dark imaginings rambling throughout our minds were swept away as an early morning mist dissipated beneath the sun of a new day.

Sherry and I eagerly got dressed and headed downstairs to breakfast. As we walked past the front desk, the innkeeper looked up from his paperwork and asked if we had a restful night's sleep. He must have already known the answer by the expressions on our faces.

"I am sorry," he said. "Not everyone that stays in that room gets a visit from the monk."

"So we could consider ourselves either fortunate or unfortunate," I replied, not sure if I needed to smile or to look upset.

Sherry was not at a loss for compassionate words. "Please we are not upset. It was our choice. In fact, we thought that if the tales were true, we wanted to experience the ghostly monk. It was frightening but it was an interesting experience."

The innkeeper, now assured that we weren't going to demand our money back, shared with us the tale of the monk. As the story goes, the George, as it was known when it was first built in 1439, was the primary coaching inn for pilgrims arriving in Glastonbury. Many came not only as religious pilgrims but also as secular visitors to the Glastonbury Abbey, at one time Britain's richest and most splendid monastery. It is also steeped in legend, myth and tragedy. A fire destroyed the abbey in 1184, and in 1539, during the Dissolution of the Monasteries, Abbot Richard Whiting was hanged to death on the Tor, and the abbey was wrecked and looted.

The innkeeper explained to us that Glastonbury was at one time a great Druidic gathering place and a major center of the early Celtic Church. The Welsh Triads relate that one of Britain's three perpetual choirs was at Glastonbury. The abbey as well as the town were connected with the legends of King Arthur, the Holy Grail, as well as the teenaged Jesus and his great-uncle, Joseph of Arimathea.

The innkeeper continued by explaining about our visitor in the night. Supposedly, the monk used a tunnel that connected the abbey to the George to meet with one of the visiting pilgrims. The pilgrim always stayed in the same room that we had slept in. How long these rendezvous lasted is anyone's guess. But eventually the monk's escapades were found out and frowned upon by his religiously ascetic superiors.

One night as he was making his way through the tunnel, he was confronted by his superiors and knocked unconscious. The tunnel, with him still in it, was then sealed up. Needless to say, it must have been a rude awakening when the monk regained consciousness to find he was sealed in and faced a slow agonizing death. It seems that his soul still clings to the Earth, revisiting the room at times.

Sealed Up Tunnel

While the innkeeper told us the story, he took us down into the basement of the inn to show us the tunnel. A Glastonbury Abbot, John Selwood, had built the George during the time of Edward IV; pilgrims staying at the inn could have used the tunnel for secret access to the abbey. Conversely, monks could have used the tunnel for clandestine visits to the inn. In the light of day, it was just another tunnel. Still, it did have an eerie feeling to it. Adventurous as we were, we chose not to spend another night in the room. We needed a good night's sleep. We went off, wondering what other exciting adventures awaited us.

Medieval Banquet and Japanese Film Crew

After Glastonbury, we headed to Ruthin Castle, which is famed for its medieval banquet and the Gray Lady. Now, I had some strong set patterns. One of these was running in the late afternoon. I was a coffee drinker; Sherry was a lover of tea. And we were in the land of teatime not coffee-time. Of course, since I was driving, we always arrived at our hotel after teatime. Conveniently for me, there was still enough time for me to run before dinner. As per usual, we missed the teatime at Ruthin castle, but lo and behold, there was still enough time for me to run, even though it could make us late for the banquet.

As I came rushing into our room all sweat covered, Sherry was nowhere in sight. At least not in the room. She had crawled out onto the roof of the castle and was crying and mad at my insensitivity. I had not honored her desire to experience an English teatime. Each day we could have stopped for teatime, but I chose to get to our hotel so I could run. Running trumped teatime.

"I'm sorry," I said as I pleaded with her to come in off the castle's roof. "It's not safe."

"You're inconsiderate. Running is all you think about."

I finally convinced her to come in off the roof. With Sher still not speaking to me, we quickly dressed for dinner. For the banquet, she was dressed in a beautiful full gown and I was wearing a grey pinstriped suit. As we came down the wide staircase and entered the lobby, the proprietor approached us and said, "We would like you to be the baron and baroness for the banquet. When you arrived we thought that you both would make a great couple together as Baron and Baroness. We were concerned that you were not coming down to dinner."

I thought, if he only knew that we're hardly speaking and the baroness might throw a goblet of mead into the baron's face in the middle of dinner. Sheepishly I said, "Ah, I was running and got back later than I thought. What does it entail?"

He replied in very proper English, "You both will sit at the head of the tables, be served first, and no one will begin eating or drinking until you do. No silverware, just a dagger and your hands."

"Oh no, a dagger," I thought. "I hope it doesn't give Sherry any ideas. I've been a jerk and inconsiderate."

Interrupting my thoughts, he continued, "And there is one other thing, very unusual."

We were stunned to learn the banquet would be filmed by a Japanese television personality and star reporter and her film crew.[100] It was to be shown during the Japanese version of our *60 Minutes*. The reporter and her film crew sat right next to us on the raised platform with her squatting next to me. Yes, the baron and the baroness were seated above the "commoners." In a very short time, we viscerally understood the intrigue and bloody history of the birth of England – the power the landowners and royalty had over the rest of the people.

As dinner commenced, the reporter would ask Sherry or me a question and then translate it into Japanese. The mead was exceptional, the food not so much. During dinner there was a couple seated right below us. We began conversing with and subsequently became friends with Ian and Margaret.

After dinner, the four of us shared a drink together as "commoners." While Ian and I were getting to know each other, Sherry and Margaret went to explore the ancient battlements of Ruthin Castle. Sherry discovered that like her, Margaret had the ability to see dead humans still tied to the Earth – ghosts. And guess what? They did! Both women saw the Gray Lady of Ruthin Castle while on the battlements!

Manhood Stone and The Strike

After our stay at Ruthin Castle, we bid goodbye to our newfound friends and headed north to Scotland for a few days. Our lodging was in another—you guessed it—haunted castle, Dalhousie Castle, only eight miles from Edinburgh. Dalhousie was built in the 13th century, the era of Genghis Khan, Marco Polo, and the Magna Carta. Brimming with so much history, it was the kind of place that could have been plucked from the pages of a fairy tale. But make no mistake, this ancient castle was very much the real McCoy. It boasted an illustrious guest list that included King Edward I, Sir Walter Scott, Oliver Cromwell and Queen Victoria.

After a peaceful night, no hauntings, we traveled into Edinburgh. The best part of our journey to Edinburgh was the Scottish equivalent of Ruthin Castle's medieval banquet called Jamie's Night where we were the only Americans surrounded by all Italians. The highlight of the banquet was the "manhood-stone" competition – lifting a gigantic stone, which was a sign of manhood in early Scottish culture. Our fellow meal participants put up their "Italian Stallion," their young male against the lone American male, which was me. I wondered if it might be better to lose considering the macho culture of Italy. But in the heat of competition, I out lifted their Italian Stallion – a tad of karmic (incarnation) payback. I must say they did handle it pretty well. There were only a few dark sneers and mumblings.

After Edinburgh and Dalhousie Castle, we headed back to London to catch a flight back to the States. In my mind our journey was not complete. Considering that I had planned on visiting various sacred sites in ten days, ones that realistically would need at least two weeks to see, we had to skip a few sites such as Stonehenge and Avebury. It was mentally and spiritually difficult for us not to visit them, but there wasn't enough time.

And then came the air traffic controllers strike. Margaret and Ian had dropped us off at Heathrow and decided to wait around to see if our flight would take off. As common sense would dictate, Heathrow was a zoo of unruly animals, including me. TV cameras were all over the departure lounge, but I didn't care as I expressed my displeasure (really anger) to the agent handling the chaos of cancelled flights. Compared to the many stuck travelers who would most likely have to spend the night or nights in the airport, we were very fortunate. With no outbound flights to the States, our circumstances turned into a great gift.

The controllers' strike was a headache for the majority of American bound travelers, but it was a blessing for us. Most graciously, Margaret and Ian put us up at their home. Since my parents were watching Jamie and Jessie, our children, I needed to call to see how they were doing and let my parents know that our return we would be delayed by a few days. With the magic of time zones, while I'm talking to my mother in Elkton, Maryland, she begins screaming, "Jimmy, Jimmy, son, you're on the news!" At the exact moment I had called, my parents had been watching the evening national news, and there I was, very upset at one of Heathrow's ticket counters. Not realizing I had been filmed and with the time difference, as I'm talking to my mother I'm on the Philadelphia Evening News. Amazing timing.

The inconvenience of our delayed flight turned into the realization that we now had time to experience Stonehenge and Avebury. Our extra days with our friends were spent visiting these and other sites, and Ian and I drinking a few pints (maybe more than a few) at different pubs while Sherry and Margaret enjoyed teatime together. And I didn't run at all.

Stonehenge, 1981

Stonehenge was impressive but Avebury took my breath away. There was something about it that tugged at the core of my soul. Over a decade later I discovered the reason for my feelings. "In his book on Avebury, first published in 1743, William Stukeley was inspired to identify it as a winged serpent temple."[101] Why, of course, a feathered serpent!

A LIFE CHANGING DECISION ON A SACRED MOUNTAIN THAT LED TO ADVENTURES FAR AND WIDE

. . . .

FOR A JOURNEY THAT HAD SUCH A PROFOUND EFFECT ON MY life, my excursion to Japan in the spring of 1987 began in a rather ignoble fashion. As a wellness consultant, I had traveled to the Far East to propose a health-awareness program to a Japanese insurance company. In Tokyo, I stayed at the new All Nippon Airways (ANA) Hotel near the company's offices. After completing my presentations and proposals to the company, I returned to the hotel craving sushi and a cold Asahi beer. The hotel's sushi bar was rather small and was empty of customers. I took a seat at the counter where I could see the sushi chef making my meal. Within a short time, an elegantly dressed couple entered and sat next to me, even though other seats were empty and available. They immediately struck up a conversation. It seemed a little strange as they knew little English and me very little Japanese.

Tradition and protocol course through the veins of the Japanese. It is extremely important not to offend or cause a person to lose face. I learned this important lesson years later when I addressed a former teacher of mine—a grandmaster of the martial arts—by just his last name.

The woman next to me got very friendly with me while her male companion smiled and ordered drinks and sushi. Her hand on my upper thigh was a dead giveaway. Red flags were waving and then came the clincher. When her companion reached for his plate of sushi, his suit coat sleeve hiked up

49

to reveal tattoos. And it struck me. He was Yakuza, a member of a Japanese criminal organization.

I began to understand the situation. The ANA Hotel was expensive, exclusive and newly opened. Anyone staying there would most likely be financially well-off, but I was not in that category. The hotel was close to my potential client, and as I was only staying two nights, I bit the bullet and spent the extra money to stay in luxury. Of course, I probably wouldn't have this tale to tell if I had stayed in a cheaper hotel.

I realized the gangster was trying to make me indebted to him. Would the next step in weaving the web of obligation be his companion offering me sexual favors? She was rubbing my leg and smiling. To refuse her at this point would be looked upon as a loss of face. What to do? An idea popped into my mind. I grimaced as if in pain; I started moaning and hunched over as if I were being attacked by acute stomach problems and might throw-up. I kept groaning and with body language indicted that I needed to leave. Before they could respond, I got up, bowed slightly, and left in a hurry like a fly unstuck from a spider's web.

So they would not see the elevators I took to get to my room, I went in the opposite direction. This was my last night in Tokyo and I just needed to become invisible, so to speak. As I walked through the lobby, a beautiful, elegantly dressed woman spoke to me as I passed. She asked me a question. Her English was perfect. I replied that I was there on business, and she propositioned me. When I replied her price must be very expensive, she smiled and said, "For both of us." I turned to find another strikingly beautiful woman. Being married and in love with my wife, I refused the offer. Believing I had escaped the web of the Yakuza pimp and his lady, I headed to the elevators. As the doors opened, a plain-looking Japanese woman got off – she could have been anyone's mother. Nondescript, she would not stand out in a crowd like the two that had just propositioned me. I smiled at her and without hesitation, she hopped back onto the elevator. Strange, I thought. Alone in the elevator, we both stared straight ahead. No words were spoken until we reached my floor. When I exited, she said, "Go to room?" Thunderstruck, I shook my head and said no in Japanese, at which point the doors closed with her still inside the elevator.

As I entered my room, I thought what a strange, interesting and profane night. The irony was not lost on me; the next day I was heading to Kyoto and then on to the one of the most sacred mountains—if not *the* most—in Japan. Kōyasan.

Kyoto

In the morning, I caught the bullet train to Kyoto where I planned to spend a few days before traveling to the sacred mountain of Kōyasan, the birthplace of Shingon Esoteric Buddhism. The last time I had been in Kyoto was 1983 with my wife and a group of martial artists. I love Kyoto, but this time I was alone and missed my wife, Sherry, and our two children, Jamie and Jess. Even though I couldn't speak much Japanese, as in all my foreign travels, not speaking the local language never caused any major problems or headaches for me. People felt my spirit and openness and not once was I thought to be an American.

I spent two wondrous and tiring days walking to various temples, eating sushi, drinking *sake* and *bīru* (beer), and searching antique stores for scrolls and statues. But the most interesting time I spent in Kyoto before Kōyasan was at the Toei Kyoto Studio Park, the only theme park in Japan where you can observe the filming of period dramas (*jidaigeki* films). Here you can walk freely around the film set, which depicts a street from the Edo period and is used to shoot more than two hundred films per year. While exploring the studio, I was approached by two actors who were portraying samurai in a scene. They didn't speak English and I didn't speak Japanese. Evidently intrigued, and possibly feeling that I was a martial artist, they gestured for me to watch them do a short sword-fighting scene. When they were finished, one came over and handed me his sword. Body language indicated that they wanted me to try the sword-fighting sequence. Let's just say that it wasn't as easy as it looked. In short order, I realized I wouldn't be asked to audition for a role. They were great and it was a wonderful way to experience the truth that we are all the same.

Wounded Vet

In 1987 in Japan the English language was not widely spoken, but a few phrases and a smile worked just fine for me. In fact, far traveling and immersing oneself into a foreign land, going where the locals go, eating local foods and not speaking the language, is a great opportunity to learn about other human beings through body language, intuition and feelings. Studies have proven that people understand more through body language than through spoken words. It is a great opportunity to see others with your heart, not your mind, and to increase your sense of empathy.

To get to Kōyasan involved taking a train from Kyoto to Osaka and then changing trains to take the right one to the mountainous home of Shingon Esoteric Buddhism – Kōyasan. Depending on the time of day, Japanese train stations are a beehive of activity. I was always awed by the swarm of people buzzing through the train stations, all seemingly in their own world.

Neither Osaka nor Kōyasan were what you would call Caucasian foreign tourist destinations in 1987. This meant there were hardly any signs or schedules in English. In the train station where I needed to find the right train to Kōyasan, there were no signs in English pointing me to the proper platform. Luckily, I had stored my two large bags at the hotel in Kyoto and was only carrying a small overnight bag.

I knew some *kanji*, such as the pictogram for mountain, so I desperately searched the train schedule board for the *kanji* for mountain, *san*, as I couldn't remember the one for Kōya. Sweat began pouring off me as I turned to an elderly woman and with pleading eyes said in Japanese, "Please, Kōyasan," while pointing to the schedule board.

She looked at me, glanced at the board for a few seconds, then turned and took off walking fast. I wondered if I had offended her, but in the next moment, she was waving her hand for me to follow her. In hot pursuit, I had to trust that she knew what I meant because this was the last train of the day to Kōyasan. If I missed it, I would be struck in Osaka for the night. Not the most earth-shattering thing, but I only had a few days left on my journey and I wanted and needed to spend at least two nights on the sacred mountain.

Sherry and I were bringing a group to Japan in the fall and I needed time to experience the mountain firsthand.

Domo arigato gozaimasu, Japanese for "thank you very much," escaped my lips as I literally ran out onto the train platform that the woman had indicated was for Kōyasan. A uniformed person, whom I assumed was the conductor, was stepping through the door into the train when he saw me, as I frantically yelled "Kōyasan." Yelling was a no-no at the time in polite Japanese society, so the conductor wore a stone-faced expression as he stepped back out, allowed me to enter, then followed me in as the doors quickly closed and the train moved slowly out of the station. Without fail, trains run on schedule in Japan. One minute later, I would have been standing on the platform watching as the train pulled away.

Even though I was sweating and probably looked a little like a wild *gaijin* (foreigner), nobody seemed too concerned about my last-moment entrance onto the train. As I burst through the doors no one even bothered to look up. Since there were no seats available on that car, I proceeded to move forward through two more cars until I found an empty seat. Putting my bag on the floor, I sat down in the narrow seat and breathed a sigh of relief.

As I settled in, I also felt joyful anticipation. I was headed to the holy mountain and would soon be seeing and feeling its magical wonder. I let my eyes slowly close as I savored the rocking motion and the rolling sounds of the train, which reminded me of my childhood. I grew up not far from railroad tracks and remember being lured to sleep by the sounds and the vibrations of passing trains.

These peaceful memories lasted only a few minutes. The first indication that something was not right was the feeling that someone was staring at me. Soon, an overwhelming pungent, unwashed smell invaded my nose. The next moment, a virulent tirade of spoken Japanese bombarded my consciousness. Snapping my eyes open, I was greeted by a slightly whiskered, unkempt, smelly old man.

Evidently he was none too happy to see me, a *gaijin*, on his train. The old man continued his rant with various words sandwiched between splatters of spittle. He then began to sway back and forth while emphasizing his words with arm movements. As I looked around, everyone was still in their own world, either reading or looking down at the floor. The group that my wife and I were going to bring to Japan was composed mostly of martial artists, including myself. I began studying the arts in 1964 as a freshman in college, and by that time I was a seasoned black belt. Most importantly, I could street fight. However, the black-belt title has a downside to it. If I laid a hand on this old Japanese man, I would probably be arrested and accused of assault. And being a black-belt *gaijin* would only make matters worse.

I smiled at him and nodded at whatever he was saying in an attempt to defuse the situation. Since he wasn't getting a rise out of me, he softened his rage and went to bother other people. He persisted in annoying others until the train slowed and pulled into a station. Emotionless people exited the train as others got on and found seats, obviously attempting to avoid the seat next to my provocateur.

As the train departed the station, I could see that he had something in his hand, some kind of sticky substance that he began eating. As the train gathered speed, he rose once again and came towards me shouting phrases in Japanese in between bites of this food, which by this time coated his fingers and lips.

I'm comfortable with strangers being close to me or touching me as my consciousness is not geared to a paradigm of separation, either spiritually or physically. But in this case, a smelly, sticky, dirty, elderly Japanese person was an exception to my rule as he proceeded to get in my face. Oh, and his breath was foul and saturated with alcohol.

I teetered on the point of picking him up and putting him back in his seat, but the thought of touching him repulsed me and overrode my unease. So, I did the only thing available. I closed my eyes and rested, hoping that he would tire of bothering me and go harass someone else.

Short-term patience is not one of my strong suits, so I was almost at the breaking point when he did move on to someone else. I opened my eyes when I felt the train slowing down again to pull into another station. My provocateur sat down.

As I glanced at him, the solution to my problem popped into my head. I would just get off the train, pretending it was my stop. Once out of sight of my annoyer, I would hop back on the last car and finally be rid of him. I exited the car, slightly smiling and bowing to him, and made my way to the end of the train.

As I stepped back on, I excitedly thought, "This is great. No one's here; I have the car all to myself." My triumph lasted only a few minutes. The stone-faced conductor came running down the platform, jumped on the car and motioned for me to follow him.

We walked towards the front of the train as he said in English, "No Kōyasan. No Kōyasan." Entering the car that I had just left he said, "Kōyasan!" and as I saw my "friend," I thought, "Oh, no, he sees me."

As we pulled out of the station, I realized that they had uncoupled the last two cars and needed only the front one to go to Kōyasan due to the low number of people traveling to the mountain town of priests and temples.

For whatever reason, my "friend" didn't harass me for the rest of the journey, which then became a visual gift for my senses. The views were spectacular and awe inspiring as we traveled further and deeper into the mountains. When I closed my eyes, I felt a blanket of love, power, and magic enfold me. All my senses were heightened in anticipation of my arrival at this mystical mountain named Kōyasan. I could feel the train slow and opened my eyes to realize that at long last, we were pulling into Kōyasan train station. The end of the line but the beginning of what?

I knew that from there, you had to take a cable car up the mountainside to the temple town. As I exited the train, an elderly woman who had been onboard since Osaka said, "war," and made a gesture to her head, which I interpreted as "crazy." She pointed to my provocateur as he got off the train.

Smiling, I thanked her as I walked to the cable car. I turned my head to see if the war veteran was following me, but he presented some type of document to one of the ticket takers, passed through the turnstile, and got back on the train to return to Osaka.

From his age, I surmised he was probably a damaged World War II veteran suffering from the trauma he experienced in war. He didn't like *gaijin* as I was the enemy and a reflection of his wartime ordeal. So sad, as his life had been reduced to riding the train back and forth between Osaka and Kōyasan.

I shed a tear as I realized once again that we tend to judge people without having walked in their shoes or knowing their life story. Nothing in a person's past justifies bad behavior in the present, but to be aware and conscious that everyone has experienced, to different degrees, some type of life pain or struggle does create within us more compassion and empathy for others, for their behaviors, and for life in general.

Kōyasan

As soon as I had reached the top of the mountain and exited the cable car, I could feel the power and peacefulness of the mountain and then a sense of serendipity, almost like a coming home. A Tendai[102] priest once told me that he sensed I had a soul connection with Kōyasan.

Kōyasan is a mountain of spiritual awe and mystical force. The town of Kōyasan is nestled in a small mountain valley, surrounded by five peaks, and is home to the main lineage of Shingon Buddhism. This is a land of towering Japanese cypress trees, temples and shrines galore, and a sacred national cemetery, all of which radiate an aura of magical sacredness, and are quite often shrouded in fog. My lodging on Kōyasan was the Fukuchi-in Ryokan, an inn in one of the working temples called *shukubo* – a respite from the stress and craziness of life. These temples welcomed guests, but usually not ones from the United States.

Kōyasan temples in the fog

My bus ride from the site of the cable car to the temple was uneventful. But I wondered if the Japanese veteran had been a spirit test of my sincerity and heart. Before long I was standing at the entrance to the Fukuchi-in Ryokan. Breathing deeply, I entered through the gates of the temple. As soon as I had passed through its magic portal of a gateway, I knew in my heart that I had just fallen down the rabbit's hole and had landed in a timelessness of myth, magic and wonder. Myths are real. They may be an exaggeration of reality, but still true in their essence.

There was a sacredness and peacefulness within the temple walls so different from the spiritually sterile and void environment of most Western churches where one experiences the emptiness of spirit and never the fullness of fulfillment. On the contrary, in this magical land you may eat and sleep, and if you choose, study with the priests, with no entrance requirements beyond an open heart and mind. The living atmosphere of these temples and this sacred land was permeated with the mystical legacy of Kūkai, also known as Kōbō-Daishi, a title posthumously granted meaning, "Propagator of Dharma."

Kūkai, the founder of Shingon Esoteric Buddhism, is probably the most influential person in the history of Japanese religious thought. Dissatisfied with the state of religious and spiritual practice in Japan, in 804 C.E., Kūkai far traveled to China seeking something purer, uncorrupted by the politics and dogma of his time. His seeking outside the established lines of authority was due to his experiences with direct intuitive awakening connected with the morning star.[103] It was his immersion in the mysteries of nature and the seeking of knowledge through mystical participation that helped shape his approach to the spirit and to Buddhism.

In 806 C.E., Kūkai returned from his journeys through China as a lineage holder of an esoteric Buddhist tradition. Based on his vision, experiences and studies, he developed a new religion, which he named, Shingon or "True Word," which utilizes *Mikkyo* meditative techniques.[104] In 816 C.E., Kūkai petitioned the government for permission to locate his new religion on the sacred mountain of Kōya. Today, Kōyasan remains the headquarters for Shingon Esoteric Buddhism.

As I approached the front of the temple a demure priest came shuffling out, smiling, bowing and saying hello in perfect English. My hope for an English-speaking temple evaporated as quickly as early morning mist. The priest spoke almost as little English as I spoke Japanese. But I got the sense that I was one of the few, if not the first, *gaijin* to stay in the temple, and I was to be treated like royalty. And I must say, I was!

The temple was beauty personified, with exquisite wooden floors and walls interspersed with and surrounded by gardens sculptured like miniature landscapes of Earth, each with white pebble rivers flowing through mountains of green. A peaceful power flowed through the temple massaging the souls of visiting pilgrims like myself.

Fukuchi-in Ryokan

After a very restful night's sleep on a futon in a private room overlooking one of the beautiful and serene gardens, I excitedly arose looking forward to breakfast and the day's adventures. Even though I was a wellness consultant to major corporations, I was not what you would call a health freak. A running freak yes, but not a heath nut. I enjoyed fish, chicken, beef, especially hamburgers and fries, and most other foods. I was so drawn to Kōyasan that I didn't research many details about my stay. If I had, I probably would have packed a small camp stove and some hamburger as the Fukuchi-in was totally vegetarian. Yes, I was staying in a Buddhist temple, but I never put two and two together.

The best description of the food that I can give came the next fall from my twelve-year-old daughter. We were at breakfast and she turned to me and whispered, "Dad, these look like pink erasers." Erasers or not, the food that I chose, key word chose, to eat during my stay was wonderful and the presentation was artistic and a visual feast for the eyes.

For the next two days before I returned to Kyoto and then back home, I spent time with one priest who could speak a little English, visited the national cemetery and various other temples and shrines, meditated, and shopped the various stores that lined the main street, each one selling slightly different variations of esoteric items and incense. I fell in love with the spiritually intoxicating scent of the primary incense of Kōyasan and purchased a couple of boxes. In no time at all, it was time for me to depart.

At some point I realized that many times in life we get trapped into making decisions based on society's rules and other people's desires and needs, but not on our own heart's desire. Society's life rules are usually based on money and fear and take various forms, with the most common one focused on planning for the future – retirement. Reality is not the present moment but the future, whether it's, "Thank god it's Friday," or the understood paradise of retirement (in reality, an illusion).

The reason for my journey to Kōyasan was two-fold. First, I had an overwhelming need and desire to come to this sacred mountain for reasons I did not know. It was a need within my heart even though the martial art I studied was connected with another sacred mountain, Mt. Hiei near Kyoto, and was not in any way connected with Kōyasan. Second, I needed to be familiar with the temple lodging and the environs of Kōyasan before we brought a group here to experience the spiritual power of this land. But the three days and two nights of exploring, learning, listening, meditating and feeling had manifested another reason – an insight that was life changing.

While I jetted off to Japan on a spiritual and warrior pilgrimage known as a *musha shugyo*, my wife was back in Maine preparing our home to be sold. Three years prior, my father had passed over at a very young age. He was only fifty-eight and had built over many years a successful small business. Being the only child, my mother was lonely and kept reminding me that I was the only child. Continuously, since my father had passed over, she had been pressuring my wife and I to "come back home" and take over the business.

Ah, she was using society's rules: be responsible, make lots of money, work for works sake and the lure of retirement – the Great American Dream. And all wrapped up in a pretty package of guilt. Ironically, guilt[105] is usually not a button pusher for me. But still, my wife and I decided to move back to our hometown in Maryland and take over the business. The United States Senate was one of my wellness clients and I rationalized that I would be closer and wouldn't have to travel all the way from Maine to Washington D.C.

But then again, guilt is not one of my rules of life, nor is money for retirement. The magic of Kōyasan—the joy of its peacefulness and its power of nature, this sacred mountain and my own innate spiritual, philosophical and esoteric self—led me to another realization and a life changing decision. Did this realization come in a vision or a dream? Far from it; it came in my everyday present moment of wakefulness as – I know things. And the decision: we were not moving.[106]

MY LIFE CHANGING DECISION ON KŌYASAN LED ME TO COME FACE TO FACE WITH JAGUAR

. . . .

"In lakéch" reply "Hala ken:" I'm another you, you are another me.

(Mayan phrase connoting oneness.)

WE HAD PLANNED ON MOVING TO MARYLAND IN AUGUST before school began for our children. Instead, in August 1987, we ended up journeying to the Yucatan peninsula to participate in a shamanic workshop with Dr. Alberto Villoldo. This was the time of the Harmonic Convergence[107] that had been "predicted by many ancient societies, including the Maya, Incas, and Aztecs."[108]

If we had moved, we would have not gone to the Yucatan and what resulted from that experience would not have happened. But there was another force at work that drove us to the Yucatan and beyond.

Sher was a personal assistant to Dr. Walter Houston Clark. Dr. Clark had been Professor of Psychology of Religion at Andover Newton Theological School in Newton, Massachusetts, former dean and professor at the Hartford School of Religious Education, author of *The Oxford Group* (1951) and *The Psychology of Religion* (1958), and founder of the Society for the Scientific Study of Religion. He had also been connected with "The Good Friday Experiment"[109] in 1962 at Boston University's Marsh Chapel, along with Timothy Leary, Richard Alpert (Ram Dass) and others.

Dr. Clark was like a surrogate grandfather to Sher. He was in his eighties when Sher began working with him. He believed that mysticism was an essential principle underlying all religious consciousness. He knew our studies and our interest in mysticism, esoteric practices, and shamanism, which lead him to suggest that we meet and work with Alberto, whom he knew.

Shangri La

As we entered Boston airport in August to catch our flight to the Yucatan, we were greeted with a situation that many have faced in their lifetime. As I checked the departure board, I discovered that our flight had been delayed. We were supposed to meet Alberto and the group at the Cancun airport at a certain time and then proceed to our lodging, which was called of all things Shangri La (La Posada del Capitán Lafitte). As the hours ticked away, we knew that we would never make the appointed meeting time.

"Do you know how to get to the place where we're staying?" Sher asked as we shared a sandwich, not knowing when we would eat again.

"To a point," I replied. "It's about an hour down the coast from Cancun."

"It's going to be interesting since we both don't speak Spanish," she said.

I just smiled and nodded, "Yes, it always is."

True to form, we arrived in Cancun late at night instead of in the middle of the afternoon. In 1987, the Cancun airport was your typical south-of-the boarder small airport, a far cry from what it is today. As we exited customs, we hoped that someone from the group would be waiting for us, but that was not the case.

As we walked outside, we were greeted with the warmth of a Mexican summer night. I always loved the feelings, sounds and smells of foreign lands. And Mexico didn't disappoint me. We were both excited but tired and not quite sure how we were going to get to the Shangri La. Fortunately, a few locals were standing by two vans talking to each other even though it was close to midnight. The logical assumption: transportation service. But would they go all the way down the coast to the place where we were supposed to stay?

Since there seemed to be no other option as everything in the airport was closed, we tentatively approached the group. I smiled and said, "Does anyone speak English?" The response was the same from each one: head shaking that indicated no. But I could see the interest in their eyes. One said, "Cancun?" "No," I replied shaking my head and then said, "Shangri La."

This had to have been the "open sesame" for one driver. He smiled and said, "Si, Shangri La." Without waiting for our response, he grabbed one of our bags and threw it into the back of one of the vans.

I turned to Sher and said, "Well, I guess we're going with him."

Struggling to hold her eyes open, she asked, "I'm tired, but do you think we can trust him?"

"Who knows? But I don't want to spend the night in the airport. I didn't see any seats to even sleep on and I'm not lying on that floor."

By this time the driver had opened the door to the van for us to enter while smiling and saying, "Si, Shangri La, Shangri La."

"He seems a little too anxious," Sher said as she entered the van. "Have you even asked the price?"

"No, he just grabbed our bags." I turned while he was hustling me into the van and said, "Señor, Peso's?"

"What did he say," asked Sher after I'd settled into my seat next to her. "I couldn't understand. But I'm not staying here at the airport. Please let me get on the other side of you."

"Why.?"

"Don't worry," I said as I climbed over her and now sat directly behind the driver who started the engine. Once again, he looked in the rearview mirror at us and said, "Si, Shangri La."

"He still seems overly anxious to me," Sher said.

"He does. Don't worry and try and get some sleep. Shangri La is about an hour or more from here."

I attempted to doze off and on while still keeping an eye on our driver, partly to make sure he was a decent and awake driver. It was 1987, and I was doing wellness consulting and wearing a watch – a practice that I stopped a few years later. To this day I don't own or wear a watch or own a cell/smartphone.

Time seemed to have passed quickly. I felt the van slowing down and turning off the road. My eyes popped open as I glanced at my watch. It had only been about forty-five minutes. He'd turned left, which would have been the correct path to the sea and Shangri La as it was located right on the edge of the Caribbean.

The almost-full moon cast some light on our isolated surroundings: shadowy jungle foliage that lined both sides of a pothole-filled dirt road. Sher had opened her eyes with the first pothole induced swaying of the van. It was such a vertigo experience that our van could have been a ship sailing on a storm-tossed sea.

Sher looked at me with worry in her eyes. "How long has it been?" she whispered.

"Not long enough," I whispered back, "but don't worry."

Here we go again, I thought. It's only been four months since Japan and I'm once again considering becoming physical with a local in a foreign land. We were in a bouncing van being driven down an isolated dirt road with jungle on both sides. What a perfect scenario and location for robbing the *gringos*. I silently laughed and thought, "Well they won't get much."

In such a situation there are basically three scenarios. I could take out the driver before he reached his buddies if it was a robbery or worse, but an assault on an innocent Mexican would not be good, legally or morally. Second, I could wait until I was sure it was a setup, but then there would be more than one to deal with and the possibility of gun-toting accomplices. Or three, I could wait and hope I was wrong about the travel time and that he indeed was taking us to Shangri La.

It's truly amazing what thoughts come into our minds at certain times. My immediate thought and image were not of gun-toting robbers but of the myth and movie – Shangri La. I thought, we're going to paradise.

In the next moment I was back in the present moment, thinking, "A punch to the side of the head? No, that wouldn't be the best approach. Since I purposely sat behind the driver a chokehold would be much better. What do I do?"

And with that last thought I felt the van slowing down. In front of us was a closed gate that looked right out of a movie set featuring a Mexican hacienda. The driver got out, and I scanned the sides of the road, while holding onto Sherry's hand, to determine the best escape route if this was indeed a trap. But I didn't have a feeling of impending trouble. Sherry whispered, "I feel it's okay."

Our driver rang an old fashioned-bell and within a few minutes a person opened the gates while our driver walked back to the van, smiling, and said, "Si, Shangri La."

Paradise it was, as Shangri La lived up to its namesake. Everyone seemed to be asleep. Even the guard who'd opened the gate had disappeared on us. As my soul was velvety wrapped in the soothing essence of tropical smells and the sounds of the Caribbean Sea, I whispered to Sher, "What a journey to get here. I'm in heaven." I kissed her and said, "Let's sleep on the beach."

Living on Earth is an interesting journey. Most people see the journey as one of consumption and the accumulation of things, not inner memories and experiences – only things. For many, life becomes nothing more than an digital box of selfies. It's almost as if they sold their soul to the capitalistic consumption technology devil. The irony in all of this is that the only thing the soul takes as it leaves the body and the Earth are the memories and experiences that are so belittled in our world. But Sher's soul and my soul have etched into it this experience and this memory of an interesting journey and an awesome Caribbean night.

Jungle and Sea

Yucatan circa 1987 was a paradise of jungle and sea. This was still virgin land, a few years before the capitalistic, environmentally deaf developers raped the land with their endless resorts. Sher and I had found two hammocks to sleep out the rest of the night after our adventurous and endless quest to reach Shangri La. It was not lost on me that our journey was a reflection and metaphor for our soul's quest in life. Awakening with first light, our immediate reward for our adventure was a beautiful sunrise over the blueish-green Caribbean Sea and the sounds of the jungle emerging from its slumber. With a slight breeze off the Caribbean and with the energizing sounds of nature, we embraced each other as we welcomed the day. It was a purity of senses. Breathing deeply, I could smell the land and the sea, the sun, surf, and sand. Nirvana it surely was.

In short order we found Alberto, who introduced us to the eclectic group of adventurers: a couple from Germany; an airline pilot and his wife; and a Zen Roshi to name a few. Our lodging was a tent on a platform with two beds. Don't presume we were camping. I was given the name Shangri La, which was one of three different lodgings next to each other on a beautiful and isolated stretch of white sand beach, all owned by Turquoise Reef Resorts. The other two were La Posada del Capitán Lafitte and KaiLuum – the "tent village" where we were staying.

Even though our showers and toilets were outdoors and communal, a far cry from the multimillion-dollar resorts and spas, themed water parks, and eco-parks that today line the Caribbean Coast, we were not roughing it. True, it was a tent with a central bath facility, and no electricity by design, but that's where roughing it ended! There was daily maid service with full linens and a unique but much loved honor-system bar. And then the delicious food: "the KaiLuum 'experience' came together in the dining room.

Under a native thatch roof and by candlelight, we would dig our toes into the sand floor and enjoy a galaxy of near-gourmet delights."[110] In other words, since all the facilities were on the sandy beach, there was no need for shoes – just shorts, a tank top, and for fair-skinned Sher, a hat.

Cobá

Our first day trip was to Cobá and then Tulúm. We left after gassing our vehicles up in the small, sleepy and slow-moving fishing village of Playa del Carmen. Sadly, it's no longer sleepy or slow-moving. Cobá means "waters stirred by the wind," appropriate enough, as the site is situated on two lagoons. Located about 40 inland miles northwest of Tulúm, it is a vast archeological site with only a few of its estimated 6,500 structures having been uncovered. Its pyramids and buildings are situated on the shores of the lagoons, and once, as many as fifty ancient roads led into this huge Maya city center. It is unique in that its architecture is characteristic of the Petén region of Guatemala, i.e. Tikal.

Following a path into a jungle overgrown with vines, trees, and flowers, I could see scattered here and there some high mounds covered in tangled undergrowth. Surely these were structures not yet explored or excavated. Throughout, there were large ceiba trees, a Maya world tree, intertwined with ancient stonework. One of the most refreshing aspects of circa 1987 was the lack of tour buses and hordes of tourists. Cobá's tallest pyramid is called *Nohoch Mul*, the tallest and steepest pyramid in the Yucatan at 137 feet, with 120 steps to the top. And the place I learned a very essential life lesson.

Laughter – Medicine of the Soul

Let the Sound Of Joy
Vibrate Throughout Your Soul

– JC

To smile and to laugh – this is the best medicine of life and a wise thing to do. To laugh is to feel the vibrational joy of the "winged ones" as they welcome the day. It is that moment in time when we stop our lives and bask in the love of life. It is like a crisp and clear sun-sparkled spring morning when we first realized that the perfect beauty of life and living is spread out before us only waiting to be embraced.

A smile will break through the dark barriers of our mind, as well as the mind of others. The bars of hate and anger that have kept us locked away within a cell of slavery begin to dissolve like mist on a windswept morn. To laugh and to smile is to have our heart blossom as a flower for all to see. It is the most awesome gift we may give to ourselves, to others and to the Earth. If you want to communicate with nature's children, the animals of the Earth and the birds of the heaven, then smile at them. When you are ready, sit under a tree and laugh.

When we smile and laugh from our hearts, we are at one with all others and ourselves – a joining that triggers our soul's memory of the light and love of the heavens. I learned the magic of laughter from a friend, who just happened to be a Zen Roshi. We were deep in the jungles at Cobá, a seldom-visited Maya religious site. On a sweltering August afternoon, we decided to climb to the top of Cobá's very tall, steep and barely unearthed pyramid, *Nohoch Mul*.

To say the least, it was hard going. The heat and the steepness made it physically challenging and mentally unbearable. With each step I became more upset and angrier. My senses were being blocked by my anger. At times like this, if we could only step outside of ourselves and observe the situation from a neutral stand point, we would be amazed at why we are so angry. Many times, it's the goals and the expectations we have put on ourselves. Because of this, we usually miss the magic of the moment. It was no different with me, but then came the teaching: Richard started laughing and laughing and then I got it and I started laughing and laughing at nothing except the moment. No words were spoken but the last and most difficult part of the climb turned out to be the most magical and the easiest. What a lesson this was, and on so many different levels. When we laugh we relax and release the muscular tension in our body, and thus, physical activity is easier; reality is truly a state of mind. We have all heard the saying that when the "going gets tough; the tough get going," but I want to add that when life gets tough – laugh.

When we finally reached the top, the view over the surrounding jungle was awe-inspiring. The small temple that crowns the top of the pyramid has two small carvings over the two door openings. These carvings depict the Descending Spirit God or Bee God, which are also found in Tulúm and represent Venus.

And one final note. Our laughing Zen Roshi taught Sher and I another important life lesson: don't explain and don't complain! A teaching to be taken to heart.

Tulúm

As we entered the walled ruins of Tulúm, I felt a heart connection with this sacred site of land and sea, a connection I had not felt at Cobá. Here, something was triggered within my soul. Tulúm is small compared to other sites but has a mystical aura of spiritual power. The ancient name of Tulúm was Zama, "Place of the Dawning," due to its positioning towards the morning sunrise over the turquoise waters of the life-giving Caribbean. It is interesting to note that its identity as the "Place of Dawning" could just as well be referred to esoterically as the "Place of Awakening," considering that most likely, Zama was a sacred spiritual center.

A few of Tulúm's primary structures are the Temple of the Frescoes, the Castillo pyramid, the Temple of the Descending God and the Kukulkán Group, made of several minor structures including Templo del Dios del Viento (Temple of the God of the Wind), named for its round base.

"A temple as well as a fortress, El Castillo was originally covered with stucco and painted red. A wide external staircase leads up to the temple, which has three niches above the doorway. A beautiful sculpture of the descending god is in the central niche. To the left of El Castillo as you face the sea is the

Temple of the Descending God, with a small staircase and a carving over the door of the swooping figure that is seen throughout the site."[111]

Temple of the Descending God August 1987

There are different theories on what the descending god represents. "One is that he is the God of rain or lightning, coming down from the heavens as an important part of agriculture and the seasons. Another idea is that he may represent Venus. This planet the Maya associated with birth and renewal (due the fact that Venus is spotted at sunrise and sunset). The nature of the orientation of the Temple at Tulúm and its architecture facing the sun supports this. The fact that its inhabitants originally called the city Zama, or dawn, does as well."[112]

Another theory is that the image represents the God of Bees, "Ah-Muzen-Cab." These bees were stingless bees, and the gathering of honey was part of a religious experience. Furthermore, the Maya believe that bees symbolized a link to the spirit world.

The bee is our family guardian or totem, and spending time within the ruins felt like a coming home. I vowed to return to this sacred site that spoke so deeply to my heart and soul.

71

In conclusion, and according to Laurette Séjourné,[113] the descending star which appears on the door of several buildings in Tulúm symbolizes Quetzalcóatl and the incarnation of the light. Within two months, at midnight on the sacred mountain Kōyasan, I would experience this knowledge of the descending star[114] and have a knowing of the Otherworld and Oneness.

Bonding with a Guardian

We were nearing the end of Alberto's weeklong shamanic seminar and Sher and I were conducting a two-person transformational fire ceremony on the beach. Facing the fire, the jungle was to our left and the sea to our right. It had been an awesome week shared with people from around the globe while exploring our inner worlds and the various Mayan ruins. And then there was the nighttime journey into Cancun's dance clubs, but that is a story for another time. The next day, we were hopefully going to bond with an Otherworldly guardian,[115] possibly one that had been stalking us this week or perhaps longer.

"Did you hear that?" I asked Sher across the glowing coals and flickering fire. "Was that a jaguar?"

"I didn't hear anything," she replied while staring into the red-hot coals of our diminishing ceremonial fire.

"I did. And there it is again," I said. "A low growling sound like rumbling rrrrrr's ending in almost like a cough, an ah-ha.

"And a smell I can't place. Do you smell anything strange?" I asked.

"No, and I haven't heard any unusual sounds."

"Interesting," was all I replied. I felt slightly scared, but refocused on the dying fire.

Once again: "You don't hear that growling sound?"

"No, I don't," Sher replied with a questioning look, as if she thought I was having hallucinations.

The next day standing at the water's edge, I felt a sense of peaceful power. All the participants were lined up facing east with the warm smoothing waters of the Caribbean lapping at our feet. Alberto was spiritually and physically working on each of us individually while we faced the Caribbean with our eyes closed. The instructions were, that after he finished working on us and went to the next person, we would wait until we felt ready to "see" our guardian. Then we would turn around to face the West or the jungle and whatever image that came to our mind was our guardian. I'm tempted to say that many people would try to seed their mind by focusing on an image before they turned around. At least, I did. I thought a dragon would be a good guardian for me. So as Alberto was working on me and after he left, before I turned around to face the jungle and the West, I kept the dragon image in my mind.

But of course, the best laid plans of mice and men go astray. I turned around, still with my eyes closed, and saw a large, beautiful jaguar. And then it all made sense to me. I had heard and sensed a spirit jaguar—or possibly a real one—the night before at the fire ceremony.

Before I could turn to Sher and find out her guardian and tell her mine, Alberto walked up to me and said, "How do you like your kitty cat!"

The magic only further deepened the next year while on an invitational shamanic initiatory journey via the Inka trail into Machu Picchu and finally to the sacred lagoons of Markawasi. This adventurous quest was led by Alberto, don Eduardo Calderon, and don Agustin Rivas, both *curanderos*, or healers. You'll discover the magic below in my tale: "Initiation of Death by the Luminous Warriors of Runkurakay and the Lagoon Initiation by the Wizard of the Four Winds."

My *Nagual*[116] – *Jaguar*[117]

I am ever amazed at the profound knowledge left to us by the Mesoamericans and other ancient indigenous cultures. According to the Maya, and we were on the land of the Maya, each person has one of twenty different day-signs: "A person's birth date, falling on one of twenty days, each having a specific name (sometimes that of an animal) and characteristics, is believed to influence one's own character."[118]

My Maya birth day-sign is Dragon of the Sky: Cauac-Kawak – Storm/Rain/Lightning (Purification).[119] The Maya calendar has 20 signs and they follow each other, changing daily. The sign on the day of your birth is your day-sign. Storm as my day-sign represents lightning and thunder, and the energy of nature, and the elements. It's interesting to note that Cauac is also associated with bees and honey and, as the dragon of the sky, in him the gods of rain and storms converge. Furthermore, Cauac is related to the Maya rain god Chac,[120] who often carries weapons of lightning such as an axe.

According to Dr. José Argüelles, Cauac is storm, thunder cloud, and thunder being, transformation that precedes full realization and represents the West. Furthermore, "concepts of rain and lightning are conflated in the nineteenth Yucatec Maya day name, Cauac or Kawak, which is given the traditional meaning of "rainstorm" and corresponds to the Aztec day-name Quiáhuitl[121] meaning 'rain,' 'thunderstorm,' 'fiery rain,' or 'lightning-storm.'"[122]

Having storm as my birth sign makes great sense to me, and fits my personality. At times, I need to be the "storm." I love rain, I love thunder and lightning, and I love wind (please see below, "And Then It Rained . . . "and "The Visitation"). When we lived in Maine, during intense wind-driven storms, I would run in the dark out to Fort Williams, located outside of Portland. Here at the edge of the ocean and with all my senses, I would become one with the storm, its power and essence, even during Nor'easters. Not only do I have a personal relationship with Archangel Mikael but also a close relationship with the Norse deity Þórr. Mikael has always been connected with both water and lightning. He oversees nature, rain, snow, thunder, lightning, wind, and clouds. And Þórr is the god of thunder and may be viewed as the personification of the Earth and sky. And then there is this: Quetzalcóatl is known as the god of the windstorm.

How does all of this connect with Jaguar as my *nagual*? The Aztecs believed that Jaguar controlled not only the rain, but also, lightning bolts. The jaguar was linked with Tlaloc, the god of rain. Jaguar, *alter ego* to the shaman, was the "animal equivalent of the storm, equally powerful, equally sudden in its attack, equally destructive of human life and order. Furthermore, the jaguar was at home both in water and in the trees from which it was able to fall, like the storm, on its prey."[123] In other words, jaguar was a representation of the elemental forces of wind, rain, lightning and thunder. It was through this power that shamans were able to harmonize with nature and thus bring unity and wellbeing to their people.

The Maya believed that the jaguar's ability to see at night made it possible for it to move between worlds, associating it with the underworld and light and darkness. Additionally, Jaguars are associated with vision and foreknowledge – an inner knowing. Jaguars have binocular vision, which provides them with better depth perception.[124] This is the reason for their connection with vision and foresight. Additionally, the jaguar was believed to be an animal of the stars as well as of the Earth, a divine animal of the two ways.

One final point. I have a co-essence with feathered-jaguar and feathered-serpent: "jaguar/bird/serpent symbolism was associated with the lightning, wind, and rain of the storms through which water was provided by the gods for man."[125]

PART III

· ·

The First of Four Major Otherworldly Experiences over a Span of Ten Years

THE TALE OF THE DESCENDING SPIRIT EXORCISM[126] – FIERY SPIRIT DESCENDING DOWN INTO WATER[127]

. . . .

October 1987

THE ONLY OTHER RECORDED DESCENDING SPIRIT EXPERIENCE was the dove of peace descending into Jesus while bathing in the Jordan River. This time it was not the dove, but the wrathful sword brandishing and fire surrounded the blazing spirit of *Fudō Myō-ō*.

"The Bibles of antiquity have but one theme: the incarnation. The vast body of ancient Scripture discoursed on but one subject, the descent of souls, units of deific Mind, sons of God, into fleshly bodies developed by natural evolution on planets such as ours, therein to undergo an experience by which their continued growth through the ranges and planes of expanding consciousness might be carried forward to ever higher grades of divine being. These tomes of 'Holy Writ' therefore embodied their main message in the imagery of units of fiery spiritual nature plunging down into water, the descending souls being described as sparks of a divine cosmic fire, and the bodies they were to ensoul being constituted almost wholly of water. (The human body is seven-eighths water!)."[128] This is the blending of fire and water: "burning water."

Many cultures believe that there are "certain crucial years in a person's life where one experiences important physical, mental and social changes. In Japanese tradition, these critical years are known as 'yakudoshi.'

"Yakudoshi can be understood in part as an attempt to provide order and structure to our constantly changing lives. Yakudoshi signals an occasion when the different pieces of a person—body, mind and spirit—are in near balance, whereas at other periods in a person's life one part is dominant over the others. Thus yakudoshi marks a critical stage in adulthood where the opportunity for a person to fully realize his or her potential in life is most available."[129]

For males these yakudoshi years are the ages of 41 and 42. I had turned 41 on August 29, 1987.

The Exorcist that Came to the Sacred Mountain to Find Me

"Floating in that space between heaven and Earth, I have a knowing of both. My soul's power suspends as a star in the luminous web of Oneness. I am divine and I am human, I am human and I am divine; a child of God and a brother/sister to all creatures of the Earth. A moment is an eternity as this knowledge engulfs my heart. Is it a dream? But isn't it all a dream? A scream and I awaken."

– JC

These words are the closest that I can come to verbalizing my Otherworldly experience, an experience that thrust me through a tear in the fabric of dualistic reality. Even the setting for the happening was mythically mystical. As I look back on it, this descending spirit exorcism was the initial quickening of my awakening mind and a knowing of non-dualistic interpenetrating reality. It was a sacred midnight experience that I will never forget and carry within my soul for an eternity.

The setting was a cemetery on a sacred mountain in Japan and the time was October of 1987, only two months after our mystical journey to the Yucatán during the Harmonic Convergence. Sherry, our twelve-year old daughter Jess, and I had just brought a martial arts group to Japan to experience the sacred mountains and esoteric secrets of this enigmatic land known as the Land of the Dawn or Rising Sun. To attempt to understand Japan, one must first experience its sacred Earth, a land that is permeated throughout with an inscrutable fragrance of tranquility and peace that on the surface belies its underlying martial past. It is on these islands that the spirit of heart, commitment and honor runs deep within the people and the land.

Japan has a spiritual culture that is not grounded in religious dogma or doctrine, but in the belief of the divine – the divinity of the land and the spirit of the people. Their religion of spirituality is called Shintō (from the Chinese *shen* meaning divinity and *tao* meaning way or path). The earliest form of this natural or pure religion, its roots found deep within the mists of pre-historical Japan, was the way of the *kami* (spirit, divine being, and god/goddess). *Kami*, to the early Japanese, referred to the divinity within all things.

Besides Shintō, another religious philosophy prevalent in Japan is extremely close to my heart and mind: Shingon (True Word) Esoteric Buddhism. The founder, Kūkai or Kōbō Daishi (774 - 835) and his sacred mountain, Kōyasan, drew me from the very beginning of my quests to Japan. And thus, it was partly my desire to have others experience the magic of Kōyasan that inspired me to bring a group of pilgrims to this land.

Esoteric Buddhism is based on the belief that Buddhahood or one's divinity may be attained in this body, this life and this world. Kūkai believed in the divine human or Buddha human, and even though I had not yet awakened to my message of Divine Humanity, there was still a pull, an urge to study and to understand this messenger of True Word Buddhism and to explore and feel his mountain world of Kōyasan.

One of the goals of our pilgrimage was to merge with a sacred space where we would embrace the feelings of a human being dwelling in the divine, as well as the realization that the divine resides within us.

Our guide for the journey was Keikō-san, a middle-aged woman steeped in the spiritual and esoteric lore of Japan and India. She was simply amazed at the design of our journey. We were going to places to which non-Japanese seldom ventured. On top of this, we were interested in various esoteric and spiritual traditions that many of the Japanese themselves would never consider studying.

I had planned this journey to be a true pilgrimage of heart. One of Kūkai's beliefs was that once awakened, one would see the world in entirely different terms, a transformational process from the profane to the sacred. From this inner awakening of heart, one's world would then become as a lotus blossom. As in Shintō, where divinities are invoked and visualized, Kūkai believed you could identify with these divine intrinsic vibrations, and that these Buddhas could best be visualized, and identified with, only after one made various pilgrimages to the tops of mountains. According to Kūkai, "the Body of the Buddha is the body of all living beings, which in turn is that of the Buddha. Different, yet not different. Not different, yet different."[130]

Humans are basically far travelers, wanderers ever seeking, consciously or unconsciously, to get home. This is the return to paradise whence our fathers and mothers came – our ancestors, and the mountain where the ancient ones communed directly with heaven. Seeking such, the first part of our pilgrimage was to the sacred mountain Togakushi and its three Shintō shrines: the lower shrine *Hokoji* (Treasure of Light), the second *Chusha* (Middle Shrine) and the third *Okusha* (Deep Sanctuary). We arrived late in the afternoon of Tuesday, October 13, to this hidden-door mountain of power and purity.

Hidden door is a reference to one of the primary myths of Japan and of the sun goddess: *Amaterasu-O-Mi-Kami* or "August Person who Makes the Heavens Shine." The myth principally involves *Amaterasu*, the sun goddess, her brother *Susa-no-o*, the storm god, and *Ame-no-uzume*, the beautiful goddess of the dawn (Venus). As the legend is told, *Susa-no-o*, always a troublemaker, was jealous of his sister's status as ruler of the High Plains of Heaven, a position given to her by their father *Izanagi* (the male half of the first couple). *Amaterasu*, concerned that her brother was plotting to overthrow her, confronted him.

A contest ensued to prove who was the mightiest. And even though *Amaterasu* won, *Susa-no-o*, being who he was, felt that he had won and celebrated his victory by wreaking havoc on the Earth. Not only did he destroy the rice fields, he also proceeded to harass his sister and her attendants in a most foul way. In terror, *Amaterasu* fled and hid in a cave. And thus the light was taken from the Earth.

The evil deities were happy and rejoiced in the darkness, now able to do their wicked deeds without being detected. But the good gods and goddesses beseeched *Amaterasu* to return to the Earth: "The goddess refused, and so the deities hatched a plot. They found the cock whose crow precedes the dawn and made a mirror strung with jewels. Then, after setting the cock and the mirror outside Amaterasu's hiding place, they asked the goddess *Ame-no-uzume* to dance on an upturned tub. The cock began to crow and the goddess began to dance[.]"[131]

Ame-no-uzume's dance, ecstatic and indecent as it was, caused the gods and goddesses to uproariously laugh and laugh. As a result of the hysterical laughter and being inquisitive as she was, *Amaterasu* emerged from her cave, and transfixed by her beautiful reflection in the mirror, stayed outside of the cave, thus restoring light to the Earth. *Ame-no-uzume*, known as the fearless one, is the dawn goddess, the goddess of laughter and the guardian *kami* of marriage and entertainment.

Togakushi

With the excitement of a child on Christmas morning, I awoke early the next day to silence broken only by the morning sounds of the mountain shedding the dark of night. To become one with Togakushi and to discover an appropriate site to conduct my morning ritual of prayers, I decided to feed my spirit and soul by running. When I run I feel like a bird flying through the sky with total freedom of body and soul. The crisp autumn morning mist reminded me of my Maine home half a world away. My runs at home were usually done by the rocky coastline. But today it was the cedar-lined mountainous road far from the crashing waves of Japan's or Maine's coastline. As I began my run chilled by the invigorating mountain air, the reality of it all sank in: after an absence of four years, Sher and I had once again returned to this sacred mountain. The last time had been in 1983 with another group of martial artists and their wives.

With Sher and Jess still asleep, my excitement and the power of this special mountain drew me as a moth to light to pray, to meditate on its forested slopes, to express my love of the sacredness of this land, and to greet the rising sun – an appropriate moment to be reflecting on Japan's national identity.

I realized that the stark simplicity and beauty of the mythic mountain with its towering cedars may take a person back to a timelessness unique to each who experiences it. I was hopeful that each pilgrim would embrace this and take back their own memories, carefully guarded in their consciousness, ready to be rediscovered and unwrapped like a precious valuable jewel at a time when they need to draw on the magical power of this sacred mountain. And the remembrance of the light that is always there.

More importantly, these mountains, born of ecstasy and laughter, helped me demonstrate an important teaching to one of the participants the following year, in 1988, when my son Jamie and I brought another group to these magical lands. This was not an oral or written teaching, but just the mundane act of running. As is frequently said, "Actions speak louder than words." But often times, teachings such as this go over the head of the person or they simply don't get it! A good teacher is only a guide opening the door for others to step through. And it was such with this teaching.

Sher and Jess Togakushi 1987

One of the participants on this journey lived much of her life in fear. It had snowed the night before, unusual to say the least in early October. To most on the journey the snow was a novelty, and surely it was a spiritual sign of my return.

As a group we walked up the steep, and now snow-covered, mountain path to the upper shrine. On the way back down, I had the opportunity to do the teaching on fear, ecstasy and laughter. These are the person's own words from 1988:

"The hike back down was an exercise in balance as the packed-down snow had turned to ice. My smooth-soled shoes were particularly bad, and I remember that as I was clinging to something trying not to fall, the Mad Peruvian Shaman took my sleeve and said he'd help me. He then began to run. Well, I ran, too, scared out of my wits right up until I started having fun. I ran all the way back down."

Yoshino

After leaving picturesque Togakushi, we proceeded to our next mountain retreat, Yoshino in the north of the Kii peninsula. Mount Kimpu (Yoshino) is revered as the place "where the Great Avatar is waiting for the coming of Maitreya."[132] It is a most sacred and special mountain. On these sacred mountains, there is no differentiation made between the realm of the Buddha and the realm of humans.

The crisp clear mountain air greeted us as we exited our tour bus. We soon realized that Yoshino is special – a feeling that transcends words. The area is noted for its spring cherry blossoms, but most importantly for us, Yoshino is also the birthplace of Shugendō ("path to achieve spiritual powers"), a mountain ascetic worship that began 1300 years ago. This ancient tradition combines Buddhist beliefs with an animist mountain practice and the worship of *kami* – the Japanese Shintō divinities. Shugendō is a living ascetic way and path. It is knowledge obtained on the path (*dô*), resulting from ascetic practices (*shu*) of divine natural powers (*gen*). Practitioners of this path are known as *yamabushi* – mountain pilgrims. These *yamabushi* perform ritual actions from Shamanism, Shintō, Daoism, and Esoteric Buddhism.

Furthermore, few know that this area is the physical manifestation of the Diamond mandala (*Kongōkai*) and the Womb mandala (*Taizōkai*). These two mandalas are the primary roadmaps to the divine Oneness of Kūkai's Shingon Esoteric Religious Philosophy. From the *Buchū shōkanjō keihaku*:

> This peak is the pure temple of the two realms: it is the original, non-created mandala; the summits covered with trees are the perfect altars of the nine parts of the Diamond mandala, and the caverns filled with fragrant herbs are the eight petals of the lotus in the Womb mandala. Mountain and rivers, trees and plants are the true body of the Buddha *Mahâvairocana*; the wind over the crests, the peals of thunder ascending from the depths of the valleys all proclaim the Law of the Body of Essence…The natural mandala is made up of the many mountains where one practices the Three Mysteries. [133]

On Yoshino, our group experienced a *goma*[134] fire ritual at Nōten Ōkami. In most circumstances, a "gateway" will identify the separation of profane space from sacred space, which means that when we enter through the gateway we have left the profane behind and entered into the sacred.

To reach Nōten Ōkami, we had to enter through a gateway and walk down many small and steep steps. I viewed our descent as a mythological journey into the underworld. Once we reached the bottom, the flames of the *goma* ceremony would purify our hearts and lead us into a rebirth of spirit and purpose.

Purpose is important. Many times, we go through life with little determined purpose that is of our own accord. Many times our purpose is determined by others and the dogma of institutions. But isn't our purpose on Earth to awaken our divine spark in order to spread love and compassion to ourselves and to all others?

Legend has it that this sacred area was founded on the spirit of a serpent that was accidentally killed by a *yamabushi*. The serpent came to the *yamabushi* in a dream and commanded him to establish a shrine that would honor the serpent's guardian spirit. To honor the serpent is to honor rebirth. In the pre-*goma* ceremonial rite of *engaku yuki*, we purchased, for a small fee, cedar prayer (*gomagi*) sticks. As the name implies, we wrote wishes or prayers upon them. These were then presented to the priest conducting the ceremony. In return, we were given a hardboiled egg to eat, symbolizing rebirth and new life. The prayer sticks were then fed to the fire in the belief that the smoke would carry the written intentions and prayers to the heavens and to the various guardians such as the Serpent Lord[135] of the Shrine.

While I was taking pictures of the ritual, and unbeknownst to me, Sher experienced the awakening of her serpent energy, commonly known as kundalini. And the magic began.

Sher's Awakening in Her Words

After a short wait, the assistants to the head priest arrive and begin their preparations for the ceremony. A sizeable quantity of wood, including our own prayer sticks, are set beside the altar and candles are positioned and lit. Soon the conch horns are sounding in their eerie musical patterns and the rhythmic drumming begins. The head priest enters and performs his own ritual of devotion and service. It is a slow and deliberate ceremony. The drumming reaches into my very inner core and draws me into a place of timelessness and space. The conch pierces my inner sanctum and expands my consciousness, adding a depth to the experience. I am being swept away by a force I have no strength or desire to oppose. It is swallowing up my whole inner being, and I am pulsating with an impending swell of energy and power.

The drums and shells have culminated in a roar in my ears. My head is pounding and vibrating and feels close to exploding. My swaying and rocking body brings me into a split-second of reality and I realize not everyone is reacting as I am! Normal self-consciousness would have pulled me immediately out of the moment, but I'm too far into the power of *goma*. My daughter is staring at me with wide-eyed amazement and wonder. Unable to speak, I try to give her a reassuring look as I drift back into the semi-conscious state I have attained.

Fortunately for me, I am seated next to an experienced and aware teacher of esoteric study. He leans towards me and, with his hand, physically channels the Kundalini energy up my back and spine, breaking through the block that was preventing it from coursing up to my crown *chakra*. I slowly feel the energy ebb and a subtle calmness and rhythmic flow melts into my body. I'm coming back into my own frame of mind. I notice the people around me and the reactions that are beginning to register.

Yoshino Goma

Some are silent, or chanting and fingering their mantra beads. Some are in deep meditation. While some appear passive, there are many who cannot hide their amazement at the sight that is happening before them. Cameras and video recorders have been whirling to capture the incredible spectacle of fire and ritual. With the conch sounding and the drums pounding and the priests chanting and swaying, the energy level has risen to a frenzied pitch of excitement and elation to all who witness. It is a memory not soon to be forgotten.

I marvel at the stamina and endurance of the priests as they continue their exhausting motions. My own body is wracked with fatigue from the constant movement that will not let me go. Gradually, the pace slows and diminishes. The altar is hot from the fire and the closeness of our bodies. We slump into a state of release when it is over. People begin to talk softly among themselves and move with a reverence and acknowledgement that they experienced something sacred. I feel exhilarated and charged with a powerful energy. I'm deeply moved by my own experience and give thanks.

At the outer shrine, I purchase a small silver ring with the serpent insignia. I want to have this token as a reminder of my experience, to keep myself aware of the power that is possible from within and that it may be drawn upon when needed and through ritual.

I should tell you that Nōten Ōkami is also connected with *Acalanātha Vidyārāja – Fudō Myō-ō*, the Immovable Mantra King. The serpent and *Fudō* are linked together at this shrine in a stone image of the dragon king, *Kurikara-ryu-o*, wrapped around the Mantra King's sword. *Fudō Myō-ō* and I have always had a very close relationship, not only consciously, but also on a deep vibrational soul level. Little did I realize what was to occur on Kōyasan.

The Sacred Mountain – Kōyasan

Morning mist filtering out the illusions of life,
here hides truth briefly glimpsed.
There a fox, or are you crow?
Buddhist priest but no cedar tall.
Rain sparkling green, smell of life,
smell of death, incense clean.

Night is day, mysterious shapes,
but then, only pilgrims honoring the Great One.
Is this my home?
Have I walked this path before?
Who am I to think so?

Fudō Myō-ō,
fiery image,

I know you.
But how can that be?
The fierce one, but no,
the compassionate one, yes.

A bridge ahead, linking what?
My world and your world,
but are they not the same?
Do I dare to cross?
I must, I have, and there you lie
at the end of the path,
but no—it is the beginning.

– JC[136]

Kōyasan, a mountain of spiritual awe and power, continuously tugged at my heart from the very moment that I first set foot on its mystical sacredness. Towering Japanese cypress trees welcomed me back home, this time with Sherry, our daughter Jessica, Keikō-san, and our group of seekers. Some were seekers of spirit but a few, sad to say, were seekers of unhealthy ego. However, those true to their heart do reap the benefits sooner or later. And so it came to be that one of the true spirits, one of our students, received her gift earlier rather than later. When she returned to the States for a check-up, she discovered that her previously diagnosed cancer had mysteriously disappeared. She feels to this day that she was healed of the cancer on Kōyasan.

The lodging for our stay on Kōyasan was a familiar place to me of peace and beauty—the Fukuchi-in Ryokan. This temple welcomed guests, but usually not groups from the States.

The monks at these temples follow the teachings of Kūkai—also known as Kōbō-Daishi—the founder of Shingon Esoteric Buddhism, probably the most influential person in the history of Japanese religious thought. His immersion in the mysteries of nature and his seeking of knowledge through mystical participation helped shape his approach to the spirit and to Buddhism.

In 806 C.E., Kūkai returned from his journeys through China as a lineage holder of an esoteric Buddhist tradition. Ten years later, Kūkai petitioned the government for permission to locate his new religion on the sacred mountain of Kōya. "Two years later, Kūkai climbed Kōya-san himself, at which time he is said to have met the local god of the mountain in the person of a hunter accompanied by two dogs, black and white. Several such legends exist, and native deities associated with Shingon are enshrined at various places on and around the sacred mountain. Kūkai did in fact invoke the protection of local deities when he performed an esoteric ritual to establish a sacred realm of practice on the mountaintop. This consecrated area was named Kongobu-ji."[137]

In addition, there is a sacred cemetery located on Kōyasan called *Okunoin*: "the innermost sanctum." Within *Okunoin* is located the most sacred inner sanctuary, which houses the mausoleum of Kūkai. The cemetery itself contains a few hundred thousand old tombstones and monuments crowded beneath the towering cedars. Even in the light of day, the cemetery is dark and mystical, not foreboding but otherworldly. It is believed that there are no dead in *Okunoin*, but only waiting spirits. Common folk are interred here along with samurai warriors, poets, and religious seers. You can also find the tombs of historically famous people such as Nobunaga Oda, a feudal lord in 16th century Japan, one of three credited with unifying the country.

The *Ichinohashi* Bridge (first bridge) marks the traditional entrance to *Okunoin*, and visitors should bow to pay respect to Kōbō-Daishi before crossing. After crossing the bridge, the cemetery begins. Thick mist often swirls around the one-and-a-quarter mile long cobblestone path through the cemetery that ends at *Gobyo-bashi*, the bridge over the *Tamagawa* – the stream which separates the most sacred inner sanctuary, the location of Kūkai's Mausoleum, from the rest of the cemetery. Pilgrims will purify themselves in the stream before entering the sanctuary. Within the sanctuary a feeling of inner peace permeates your body and soul. Due to its sacredness, no photographs or food are allowed.

At the end of the path, as you cross over *Gobyo-bashi*, lies *Torodo*, the Lantern Hall, where 11,000 lanterns are constantly kept lit. Enshrined behind the Lantern Hall is the mausoleum of Kūkai. At the age of sixty-two, as the legend goes, Kūkai went into eternal meditation while awaiting the arrival of *Miroku Nyorai (Maitreya)*, the Buddha of the Future. Today, more than ten million followers believe the Daishi, as he is generally known, is still alive. On a daily basis, food is prepared and taken to him in his mausoleum. It was here in this mystical place, in front of Kōbō-Daishi's mausoleum, that the descending spirit exorcism occurred at midnight.

The Exorcism[138]

A descending spirit exorcism – an experience that made a man a magician[139]

From the very beginning, Keikō-san was amazed at the spiritual twists and turns of our journey, as we always magically seemed to be in the right place at the right time. And it proved itself once again, on Kōyasan, when she approached me and said: "This trip is getting even stranger. There just happens to be an exorcist from Osaka who knew that he needed to come here to meet you, even though he has no formal connection with this temple. He wants to know if you would be interested in going to Kōbō Daishi's mausoleum tonight at midnight for a special ceremony, *Ko-Rei*. And you may bring along anyone whom you choose."

I had a problem, however, with selecting people I thought were worthy of the experience. Word had already spread through the group, courtesy of one of the participants who overheard our conversation and told the trip's primary teacher, a well-known martial artist. So, selecting a few was out of the question.

Approximately one hour before midnight, just about everyone on the journey was milling about the front courtyard ready to go. Unfortunately, the one person I wanted with me, Sher, wasn't able to come with us. She needed to stay with our daughter Jess, who was not feeling well. The next day we discovered why when she finally showed us her infected finger, swollen and not looking too good. But that's another whole story.

The Exorcist

How to describe the exorcist? Well, a little scary with an Otherworldly aura surrounding him– an enigma you might say. He may have been a mountain ascetic, a *yamabushi* who performs the special services of healing and exorcism. Furthermore, the *yamabushi* brotherhood hold *Fudō Myō-ō* in reverence as a great spell-holder and as their protector.

As I explained earlier, the *yamabushi* follow the religious movement of Shugendō, a blend of pre-Buddhist folk traditions (shamanism), Shintō, Tantric Buddhism, Chinese Yin-yang magic, and Taoism, and may achieve magico-ascetic powers. Many times, the *yamabushi* are feared due to their reputations as sorcerers.

And this exorcist could invoke fear. He didn't break the typical shamanic pattern that it is your responsibility to follow and keep up. Hardly a word was spoken as he turned and started the approximately three-mile journey to the Lantern Hall and the Daishi's mausoleum. Even in his traditional *geta*, Japanese wooden sandals, he was setting a pace that I knew few could maintain for even the mile and a half to the entrance of the cemetery. And I was right. Many dropped by the wayside.

The clicking sound of his *geta* echoed off the many closed storefronts that lined the main street of Kōyasan. These stores contained all different forms of esoteric religious items ranging from incense and scrolls to esoteric deity statues, some as tall as a person. Along with the clicking of his sandals was added the piercing sound of the tiny magical rings of his shakujo staff. Both of these vibrating resonances only strengthened the sense of timelessness that I felt. Our night time visit would indeed provide a special atmosphere, quite different from that of a day time visit.

By the time we had reached *Ichinohashi* Bridge, the traditional entrance to *Okunoin*, we had lost at least half the people. The exorcist paused for a few minutes at the entrance praying and paying respect to Kōbō Daishi. I was enchanted by the Otherworldly feeling that surrounded me. The silence only heightened my feeling. It was dark and foreboding yet still felt welcoming as it had for me five months earlier. Supposedly, there are no dead in *Okunoin*, but only waiting spirits.

Okunoin, October 1987

Midnight approached – the bewitching hour. After bowing as an honoring to Kōbō Daishi, I followed the exorcist and Keikō-san into the cemetery. The path would take us to the Daishi's mausoleum. During the day these sacred grounds full of gigantic cedar trees were dark and full of mystery, but at night the full impact of the mystical aura was felt to the core of one's soul. Following Keikō-san and the exorcist, I felt as if we were either starring in a Japanese fantasy movie or had been transported to an alternative medieval universe.

After we passed over the second bridge, *Nakano-hashi*, the exorcist whispered to Keikō-san. She then turned to me and the few that were left and said in a low voice, "The Well of Reflections, *Sugatami-no-ido*, lies across the path from here. It has been used for hundreds of years to prophesize a person's death. If one looks in and sees their reflection, they can be assured of many more years of life. If, however, a reflection is not seen, then death will occur within three years. He asks if anyone would like to gaze in and see their future?"

Imagine a narrow path that is even dark during the day. But at night, it is as dark as a cavern, being lit only with small stone lanterns. These are positioned low and yards apart. Any light reflected is only on the immediate area of the path. Of course, there is very little light when you step off the path. The well was located off the path within the cedar-studded woods.

Everyone remained silent to the question except for me. In spite of my fears, I whispered to Keikō-san that I would volunteer to do it. Realizing that the majority of myths and legends have their foundations in truth or reality, I reluctantly walked over to the well, with just enough light to see a few feet in front of me. I wondered if I would have to sacrifice something as Óðinn did, one of his eyes for wisdom, to drink daily of the well of knowledge, Mimir's well.

To my ears, the silence was oppressive, heightened by my lack of enthusiasm and bone-chilling fear. It was so silent I could hear and feel my heart beating as I approached the edge of the well. I hesitated. Did I want to discover if I was to live or die within three years? Is there wisdom to be received from this well? Even though I was in excellent physical condition and health, my father had passed over a few years earlier at the young age of fifty-eight and his father had died even younger, in his forties. I realized that our minds are strong enough to take us down the path of self-fulfilling prophecies. Now or never, I thought as I bent over the edge of the well and looked!

Eureka; I was never so happy to see my gray-bearded face. I smiled at myself and made faces, relieved that death was not right around the corner. As I turned and happily walked back to the group, I realized the truth and wisdom in this legend. In medieval Japan, a person with cataracts was on death's doorstep. Looking within the well, the cataracts would prevent you from seeing your reflection. Of course, legends make us feel alive and yes, it can be fun to take chances and face the unknown. Many times knowing the reality or the truth behind the legend only makes life more boring and predictable.

Appropriately, after leaving the well, we walked for a short time until we reached the third bridge, *Gobyo-bashi*, over a bubbling stream. This wooden bridge separated the rest of the cemetery from the realm and mausoleum of Kōbō Daishi. (A warning to heed: never cross a bridge such as this without prayers and permission asked. This bridge was a gateway separating sacred space and permission to enter must be granted.) Crossing a body of water from one shore to another shore implies a spiritual journey. Appropriately, this applied to me.

After a few moments passed in silence and prayers, we slowly made our way across the bridge into the spiritual realm of the Daishi. Ahead of us was our destination, the Lantern Hall, ablaze with hundreds of yellow-tinged specks of light. It was as if I was seeing a thousand lightning bugs all gathered together giving of their light to the tall cedars and to the Daishi.

Kōbō Daishi's mausoleum was situated behind the Lantern Hall. But before continuing on to the rear of the Hall, the exorcist stopped in front, walked up the steps of the Hall and offered incense and prayers. We followed him and Keikō-san up the steps and waited until he was finished. Then they led us around the side and to the rear of the Lantern Hall, the location of the Kūkai's mausoleum, his "meditative residence." It was in this place of special immortality that the exorcism took place.

Seven of us had made the journey from our temple residence. The exorcist positioned the seven of us, except for Keikō-san, in a straight line horizontally facing the mausoleum and told us, through Keikō-san's translation, to sit still and relax. I was last in the line with Keikō-san angled in front and to the side facing me.

He worked on each of us, chanting, toning and every so often delivering a *kiai* or spirit shout. Out of the corner of my eyes, I could see him working rapidly, with mudra,[140] up and down each person's spine. The eerie sounds coming out of the exorcist were of another world and another time. Feeling as if I was in a dream in an alternate reality, I closed my eyes. Within a short span of time, I could feel the exorcist's presence, and was unafraid. And in the next moment what happened is difficult to put into words.

I could feel and sense my body moving in a circular motion and there was a sense of self interpenetrating or blending with a Greater Self. I knew me, but I was not me – I was the "I" in the "We" and the "We" in the "I." Philosophically, the following is the best that I can do with words to express the spiritual/religious experience of the descending spirit exorcism:

> Floating in that space between heaven and Earth, I have a knowing of both. My soul's power suspends as a star in the luminous web of Oneness. I am divine and I am human, I am human and I am divine; a child of God and a brother/sister to all creatures of the Earth. A moment is an eternity as this knowledge engulfs my heart. Is it a dream? But isn't it all a dream? A scream and I awaken.

As my eyes slowly opened, the portals to my soul gazed upon the surreal scene before me. Keikō-san's face, beautiful as the dew glistening on a lily, was now frozen into a mask of terror. It had been her scream that had brought me back; but truly, had I ever left? This part of the cemetery contained only a few stone lanterns. The shadows, created by what little light there was, only heightened the mystical sense of wonder for me. I felt incredibly powerful.

The visually shaken Keikō-san was stammering over her words to the exorcist. From a place of stillness, I silently watched the gestures and body language of the exorcist and Keikō-san, not knowing or in fact caring about the meaning of the words being exchanged. A moment ago—or was it an eternity ago?—I was in a place, a space of power. But no, I was the power. What does it all mean?

Keikō-san turned to me and asked, "Are you all right? How do you feel?"

"I feel awesome, powerful, but mystified," I replied. "Was I transforming into one of the guardians that serve the Great One, the Daishi?"

"Well, yes, but no. You may look at it as a merging or interpenetration of energies. Energies that few humans could accept, much less survive. It is the first quickening of your Bodhicitta – your Divinity.[141] The others who were here will deny what happened, out of fear and envy. We sent them back to the temple," said Keikō-san.

She then explained to me that the descending spirit exorcism was a way to discover a spiritually sensitive[142] person or a spiritually evolved person able to tap into other realities. "He believes that you are one of the most sensitive people that he has ever worked with or met. This is why he came to Kōyasan: to find you. He had a dream of you," she explained. "But I had to stop him because I could see that you were not yourself. Your features were changing. Your face was so red and strange looking, like *Fudō Myō-ō*. You were starting to transform!" Still a little shaken, she turned and spoke to the exorcist.

After a few minutes of a back and forth dialogue, she said to me, "The gateway between the worlds is still open. The energy of what just happened has vibrated through both worlds. The ones who still haunt this world may have been awakened. Their attachment to materialistic life has kept them trapped on Earth in death. Some of these specters increase their attachment to the Earth through feeding on the life-force of humans."

Keikō-san paused for a moment, then spoke to the exorcist before addressing me once again, "There are many spirits here. I was afraid for your safety. That is the reason why I stopped the exorcism. The exorcist is also concerned about your safety. There are many samurai in this cemetery. It is their last resting place. But many are not at rest or at peace. Since you are an accomplished martial artist, they would be attracted to your life-force. Because of this, the exorcist is going to give you a secret teaching.[143] Right now you are very "open." This teaching will help you guard against any intrusions by these spirits."

Through my experience on the sacred mountain, I exorcised the past that bound and restricted me. A few days later as we departed the sacred mountain of Kōyasan, Keikō-san presented me with the following words:

"I always remember your sensitive, strong, sacred spirit. It was a great experience for me, too."

INITIATION OF DEATH BY THE LUMINOUS WARRIORS OF *RUNKURAKAY* AND THE LAGOON INITIATION BY THE WIZARD OF THE FOUR WINDS

. . . .

February 1988

AFTER I LEFT JAPAN AND KŌYASAN A TIMELESSNESS OF BEING had permeated my soul. Keikō-san's scream seemed like a memory of only yesterday, but four lunar months had turned. These thoughts flowed through my mind as I stood in Cusco, Peru, staring at a grand cathedral, a materialistic icon of Christianity and its invasion of these lands so many centuries before.

Arriving in Cusco, February 1988

After a long trek from the sunbaked sands of the Yucatan, through Miami, and ultimately to Peru, I had finally arrived in the mountainous city of Cusco in the Land of the Condor. I was to meet the other adventurers in what was considered a "navel of the world." (Delphi, Greece, where I celebrated my sixtieth birthday being the other one.) At nearly 11,000 feet (3,350 meters) above sea level, my breathing was a little labored as if with a lover for the first time. But then, why would it not be? I had just traveled from the jungle lowlands where the land meets the seas. Here in this mountainous region far from the blue-tinged ocean, my body was still adjusting to this new and strange, but so familiar, environment. Even though there were American travel advisories not to come to Peru,[144] I was not concerned and embraced the thought of adventure.

The indigenous people, known as the "Children of the Sun," were busily going about their daily activities. Even though some still smiled, I sensed the "spirit" of Ages past had been lost. Understandable, considering the grievous destruction of their culture and indigenous religion so many centuries before. We were gathered here to walk the Inka trail, the Royal Road into Machu Picchu and then to the sacred lagoons where we would be initiated. In my mind, my initiation had happened the previous October on the sacred mountain of Kōyasan, a heavenly rite conducted by the Otherworld. This initiation would be an earthly one conducted by the "Wizard of the Four Winds" – don Eduardo Calderon Palomino. Eduardo was a *curandero*, or healer, who was a master of the San Pedro, a magical plant that opened a portal to the Otherworld. Or so I had been told.

I was as a stranger, an enigma to many in our group, a band of healers and adventurers drawn from the four winds of the Earth. Our leader was Dr. Alberto Villoldo. He was also the translator for the two *curandero* accompanying us: don Eduardo and don Agustin Rivas Vásquez, an *ayahuasca* ("vine with a soul") shaman. It is not necessary to go into the mundane, such as the make-up of the various personalities of our group, for my tale needs to be told with a minimum of words. We stayed in an inn for one night before we departed for the little-traveled and mountainous Royal Road, supposedly, the only way to truly enter Machu Picchu, the Lost City of the Sun. I had considered downing a few pints of ale before bed. And then, I thought better of it. It was neither the time nor the place.

There are many more-traveled and easier paths to the ruins. But then again, you will only discover the remains of a once-great city. To pass through the veil of linear time, one must travel the Royal Road. It is on this path where the trail's guardians—the luminous Warriors of the Sun—will test you. If you are deemed worthy, then you may continue on to Machu Picchu. If not? Well, the penalty is too awful to mention.

Earlier Alberto had explained to us that our spiritual work during these two weeks would be mastery, the way of the master shaman, reflected in the direction of the North represented by the Dragon, sometimes the Hummingbird, the power animals of the North.

For a few seconds my mind flew back to the Yucatan where I had spent the previous ten days, and where I had conducted a fire ceremony during one of my Spirit of the Warrior retreats named "Warrior Wisdom of the Ages." It was the night of the new moon, and the focus of the ceremony was working in the South, the spirit of the Serpent. This is where we learn to shed our past as the serpent sheds its skin. Additionally, the serpent was recognized as a symbol of prophecy, as its venom was used for altered states of consciousness and mystical trances. A few hours before the ceremony, I had met a physician, who was the chairman of medical research at Yale University, and his wife. Out of the blue, he started relating his lifelong connection with serpents. As a boy, he had discovered a very rare albino copperhead in New England. And throughout his life, he had experienced many out of the ordinary experiences involving snakes, even finding indigenous serpents of Mexico on Cape Cod. It made interesting conversation. Afterwards, I wondered about him.

That night, working in the South, the fire was very friendly and we could all feel the power of the moment. After the ceremony, I was too energized to sleep, so I returned to the outdoor lounge where I had met the physician six hours earlier. A boa constrictor that the staff had found in the kitchen was lying across the bar, the first snake found in this area for years. First the "serpent" physician, and now a boa: what an acknowledgement of the power of ceremony and a foreshadowing of my upcoming Peruvian journey.

Inka Trail

The next day dawned crisp and clear with a sky encased in brilliant blue, dotted with pure white clouds that seemed to invite us to ascend to heaven. Early morning unveiled itself uneventfully and soon we were at the trail head. My senses were overwhelmed by the beauty of the land and sky. And I wondered why others would not attempt this same passage into the unknown.[145]

Mother and Children Beginning of Inka Trail 1988

As I adjusted my daypack preparing for our five-day trek to Machu Picchu, I observed my fellow pilgrims, many of whom I had just met. Since we were all here for the same purpose, and were invited, it's not surprising that we had already bonded into a close tribe, trusting and helping each other physically, mentally, and spiritually.

As we spread out on the trail, I stayed to the rear with don Agustin, who reminded me of one of my great-uncles I loved as a child. Staying back was a smart decision as Agustin, a jungle shaman, identified various plants and grasses, such as *tuna* which is good for diarrhea and to stop bleeding.

At mid-morning it clouded up and began to rain. Agustin didn't say a word as he took out a large knife and proceeded to whistle and cut the clouds. It stopped raining.

In the late afternoon, we set up camp on a level stretch of ground only a few hundred yards from the Temple of the Hummingbird where we would begin our initiatory journey: a quest for spiritual mastery connected with the North Direction of the Inka Medicine Wheel. I had been asked to be a spirit guide for the night ceremony at the temple. Partly due to this, I discovered my one material intention for this journey – a staff. As I sought the best path to the temple, I came upon a perfectly formed staff of eucalyptus wood. Why would anyone abandon a perfectly good staff on a mountainous trail such as this?

As the sun disappeared below the mountainous ridges, darkness quickly descended on our group as we made our way to the temple. Such a mystical night, as thunder rumbled in the distance. Above us the black-clad night sky, splattered with purplish patches throughout, appeared threatening at times. But then again, it seemed, in a certain unearthly way, magical. Within a short period of time, we were seated on the ground within the open-air ruins of the once-great temple. Under the otherworldly sky, our shamanic wizard explained the spiritual purpose of our journey in his own tongue. Alberto translated the words.

"Quest for the power of the North – the direction of the ancestors," explained Alberto as he pointed to the north, emphasizing the wizard's words.

"This is the land of the masters. Seek your mastery without attachment. Still your mind and call on the spirits of the North: the Dragon, the Horse, the Hummingbird. . . . Call on the ancestors of the Inkas. And they will come if your heart and mind are pure. You have all been invited on this journey to be initiated in the sacred lagoons. You will be tested by the spirits of the Earth and the heavens. Are you worthy?"

At that moment the sky erupted in a clap of thunder and flashes of lightning that startled one and all, including myself. In the lighted night sky an image of a dragon appeared and then was gone. A few drops of rain fell, known as a blessing rain, and then there was quiet and stillness. Alberto continued explaining that we must shed our past the work of the South, and face death, the lesson of the West.

Death

Over the next three days our group of initiates traveled through cloud forests and traversed the "pass of the eternal woman," Warmihuanusca, at 13,800 feet (4,206 meters). After having crossed the mountainous pass, we soon arrived at one of our early destinations, the ruins of Runkurakay and the beginning of the Inka Royal Path.

The sun legends say that only the enlightened ones, the children of light, are able to pass this point and continue on to Machu Picchu. It was at this guard-post of Runkurakay that the luminous warriors would scan a traveler's energy centers. Additionally, these spirit-guardians would observe how the travelers physically moved, if their words matched their actions, and the purity of their heart.

The people found worthy would be able to continue on to the Sun City, but at some point, they would have to endure the initiation of "death." If not found worthy, seekers would still be able to continue to the Royal City, but unbeknownst to them, without the benefit of awakening to the hidden knowledge of the Children of the Sun.

Of course, the worthy ones who were chosen might not survive the initiation. It was here that I began to get very sick.

"I'm burning up and it's not from the climb," I thought. "I don't know if I can go on, but I have to."

At that moment don Agustin, master of the vision-vine, put his hand on my shoulder. Speaking in a broken form of my language, he said, "You do not look so good my friend. Let me help you, if you would like."

I readily agreed as the *curandero*, from the jungles of the great river Amazon, led me to the sun temple's circular ruins. Once in the ruins, he took me to the northernmost part of the temple and positioned me facing east. He prayed while preparing his pipe with mystical Amazonian herbs and sacred tobacco. I realized that he was going to conduct a jungle-pipe ceremony for me. He blew the sacred smoke on the various energy centers of my body, and within a short period of time, I felt much better and was able to continue on to Phuyupatamarca, the next sacred site. At 11,800 feet (3597 meters), it was appropriately named "the town above the clouds."

As I walked, I marveled at the landscape. It was almost as if we were stranded on an alien planet whose surface was composed of clouds, not of solid earth. With a clear expanse of blue above us and white feathery clouds soaring below us, my soul and senses were in awe of our surroundings.

As beautiful as it was, I suddenly realized that I was feeling lousy again and my fever had returned. Even though I had been chewing coca leaves (a mild plant stimulant), they were not helping. Chewing the leaves was supposed to alleviate conditions such as fatigue, thirst, and most importantly, *soroche* or altitude sickness.

As time passed, each step became more of a burden. If I had not had my staff, I realized that I might not have been able to go on. The staff seemed to have a life of its own and provided an energizing effect on my fever-wrenched body. After what seemed like an eternity, we finally reached our campsite at Phuyupatamarca. I surrendered to whatever my destiny had in store for me and collapsed, but not before telling myself that I did not want to die in these mountains and never see my family again.

I drifted in and out of consciousness as the healers of our group entered my tent to administer their various curative remedies. Nothing seemed to be working. Each came and left in a short period of time; none could stay long as the inside of the tent was as hot as a sauna and my fever was the cause. I felt on the doorstep of death. Sometime during the evening, I was brought a small bowl of soup made by one of our Inka porters. It was supposed to be an old family recipe, a remedy for fever. I was very hopeful and thankful even though it tasted like ordinary carrot soup.

I fell into a bizarre altered state as time wore on. I wondered what was in that soup, as otherworldly images came and went all serenaded by the distant echo of a drum. The others were participating in a fire ceremony in the ruins of the city. Sick as I was, the vibrations of the drum and the chanting seemed to be healing and comforting. Before long I fell asleep.

I awoke to the light of dawn, thankful and blessed by the fact that I felt so much better after standing on the doorstep of death. After what had seemed to be my last day and night on Earth. I had done it – I had survived the work of the West. The West is not only about death, but about our willingness to focus our life on something that we believe in. And I was willing. The next year my wife and I began our shamanic apprenticeship program and entered the early stages of our message of Divine Humanity.

I couldn't remember any dreams except for a brief image of a dragon that I'd seen in the night sky at the Hummingbird temple. As I emerged from my tent, I marveled at the beauty of the misty morning and my incredible surroundings. While I breathed in the thin but invigorating mountain air, I realized how precious life is and how, on the other hand, death has such a grip on us as we struggle and deny the truth – that death is a part of living. Intellectually, I knew that our souls are immortal, but still the prospect of dying that night was terrifying. To accept my physical death was not an alternative for me. I wanted to live and to be with my family again. Agustin was standing nearby. When he saw me, he came over and laid his hand on my shoulder.

"You look so much better. May I perform the ceremony on you that I did on the others last night?"

"Of course," I agreed. His gentle presence had such a healing effect. And when he was finished he leaned over and lightly kissed my neck.

"You will be well and strong for the rest of the journey. Be open and you will see, and then you will know. The ancient ones are waiting for you. But first, my friend, let's have some food."

After breakfast, which for me was like manna from heaven, we meditated at the Temple of the Condor and then departed on the final leg of our journey into the City of the Sun. After we completed the morning meditation and ceremony, Alberto asked us to walk in silence and warned us that we might be tested as we approached Machu Picchu. My first thought was: what could be worse than almost dying?

Killer Bees

The trail from Phuyupatamarca consisted of ancient switchbacks that took us down off of the mountain. I was walking with the drummer of the group while don Agustin was a few yards in front of us. The day had dawned misty but was now bright and clear. After what I had endured, I felt extremely grateful just to be alive.

What happened next was like a scene out of a low-budget B-grade movie. A swarm of killer bees attacked us. My first hint of something out of the ordinary was the erratic actions of don Agustin who was walking a few yards in front of us. He whipped off his poncho and started running, all the while twirling his poncho over his head. For a split second, I wondered if this was some type of descending ritual. But within a few seconds, it became abundantly clear that it was not ritual, but survival, as we too ripped off our ponchos and followed his lead.

If you run away, most bees will normally not follow you over a great distance, but not killer bees. We must have run at least a mile or more before we felt safe enough and far enough away from these vicious mutated human-haters. Even still, I had at least a dozen welts forming on my neck and various other parts of my body.

"Put this mud on your stings. It will help reduce the swelling and draw out the bee's toxin," don Agustin, with a slight smile of comfort, asked my friend and me, "How are you doing?"

As he asked us this question, my mind flew back to the past, remembering my 12-year-old daughter's final words as I departed our home: "I love you Dad. Watch out for the killer bees!"

Machu Picchu

"Another set of steps to climb," I thought, as I glanced at a weather-worn sign that said, "Beware of snakes." Killer bees, now snakes. As I reached the top of the ridge, my jaw dropped open in astonishment. Even though I was unaccustomed to being surprised, the vision spread below me was breathtaking. Suspended in the clouds was the sacred city in all its glory. Its mythic castle and stone terraces reflected the light of mid-morning. And I realized I was at the end of the Inka trail. I had survived. I had struggled, suffered, and sacrificed. I had learned many lessons and finally, I had arrived. It was all worth it as I gazed on the beauty and the spiritual power of the mysterious lost city of Machu Picchu.

Machu Picchu, 1988

Time stood still as I paused and silently prayed at the *Intipunku*, the Gate of the Sun. The gate overlooked the city – the City of Light, now shrouded in mist. As each of my fellow adventurers passed me on their way down to the lost city, they asked how I was doing. The majority called me the Inka, the only name they knew for me. And I guess I looked the part, wearing the same colorful poncho and hat as did our indigenous porters. With a face and body darkened to a deep reddish-brown by the intensity of the sun, I could very well have been born in those mountains.

At long last, I was at a place of rest: an inn located just outside the entrance to the lost city. Calling it an inn was a stretch of the imagination, as it had only a few rooms with showers. But then again, the creature comfort that I missed most on the trail was taking a long hot shower. At this moment, an inn with showers for me was a golden palace of delight.

Eagerly, I entered my room, desiring a long-lasting hot shower. I stripped immediately and could already feel the cleansing warmth on my body. Excited beyond words, I stepped into the shower with great relief and anticipation of an ecstatic moment. But instead, I was greeted with an alien-like fungus occupying the majority of the shower stall.

This was the only inn within many, many, miles; if you will, "the only inn in town." If I wanted a bed and a shower, I was stuck with sharing the shower with this fungus, seemingly alive and moving. Now mind you, there are worse things and I had just been through some of them, but in that moment, I would have liked a clean shower, minus the alien scum, with plenty of hot water. And of course, with the ancestors laughing at my humanness, the water was small in quantity and lukewarm in temperature.

After my lukewarm cleansing, which still felt awesome, I decided to explore the city before our ceremonial and transformational work later that night. The drummer of our group and a few others joined me.

Machu Picchu is a sanctuary of power. Even though it was in ruins and seemingly deserted, the city was still alive with a powerful force. I could feel that the veil was thinly threaded on this sacred mountain top. The veil, as I call it, separates the Otherworld from our world, the past from the present with the future as potentiality. Even though our world (seen creation) and the Otherworld (unseen creation) blend with or permeate each other, the concept of a veil gives us a way to explain the presence of the Otherworld, which we do not experience due to our human sensory perceptions and our dualistic consciousness. In other words, time is not linear as most people think. The past and the present are all happening now from a perspective of a timeless impermanent pattern of vibrational frequencies. Thus, it is possible to pierce this veil of dualistic consciousness and experience the past and the Otherworld.

There are certain sacred places on Earth, such as the lost city of Machu Picchu, where the veil is at its thinnest between spirit and matter, between this world and the Otherworld, a radical nonduality where spirit permeates matter. When the thin veil is cast aside, there is no separation, only an interpenetration of our world and the Otherworld. The Otherworld is always accessible with a radical nondualistic consciousness, but there are certain times such as dawn and dusk, the transitional periods from dark to light and light to dark, when a person's dualistic consciousness my split the veil and access the world of spirit. These times provide a window of opportunity for all people to access knowledge and to experience power. Although power permeates everything, it is normally focused in certain individuals, such as shamans, and in natural locations, especially mountains. And power only comes to those who are worthy or ready.

●◆●

Entering the ruins, I offered a silent prayer asking permission to enter the sacred city and to conduct spiritual work. As part of my ritual, I pulled off a few of my chest hairs and scattered them to the four winds as a small sacrifice and gifting to the serpent, the puma and the condor of the three worlds of the Inka, as well as the unseen ones.

Traditionally, you would use three coca leaves held in your palm while praying. Even though I didn't have any leaves, I still needed to ask permission, to pray and to give a gifting to the ancestors, the three worlds, the spirits of the land, and *Pachamama* (Earth Mother). To substitute items like my hairs instead of the coca leaves was perfectly acceptable as long as I honored and remembered the purpose behind the ritual. A pure, strong heart and mind and an impeccable intent are always the most important aspects of spiritual work.

The three worlds of the Inka are: "the Underworld or Inner World (*Uchu Pacha*) of the dead and of seeds, both referred to by the term *mallqui*; the Earth's surface (*Cay Pacha*), inhabited by human beings, animals, plants, and spirits; and the Upper World (*Janan Pacha*), occupied by the deified Sun and Moon (considered to be married siblings, like the Inka and his wife, *Coya*), the stars (which were the guardians of humanity, animals, and plants), the lightning, the rainbow, and other gods. Communication between the surface of the Earth and the Underworld was achieved through the *pacarinas*—caves, volcanic craters, spring, and lagoons—which were the places of origin of all life in this world. Within the Inka Empire, communication between Earth and the Upper World was realized through the Inka, son of the sun but born on the Earth, which made him an apt intermediary between the human and the divine. His means of communication was the rainbow, which was represented on the royal coat of arms."[146]

Two thousand feet below me rumbled the Urubamba River and above me was a cloudless blue sky. Surely one would consider this sliver of mountaintop a paradise on Earth. The whole of the valley below was considered sacred to the Inkas.

Machu Picchu means "Ancient Mountain" and was considered a *huaca* – a sacred place where the power of the Earth Mother was concentrated. I definitely could feel her power, but I had a notion that Machu Picchu's true name and purpose had long been lost and forgotten. I had an intuitive sense that the original name would have translated as "the Mountain where the Sun stands still," indicating a sacred sanctuary of equality, balance and harmony. Metaphysically, this was a place of initiation where one's soul cast no shadow. Additionally for me, this mountain was a place of wonder and knowledge and an expression of *Pachamama's* power and love.

If our mind is still and not chattering (mind talk), our senses, including our sixth sense, awaken and strengthen. To listen and to look is to learn. But many people have a problem being in the moment and not talking. And that is one of the reasons I like to explore alone. True to form, the others with me were talking about the past few days and were missing the present moment and the power of this place of cosmic light – the light that is the Sun behind the sun.

Machu Picchu was an engineering and architectural wonder. Gigantic stone blocks were fitted so tightly together—without the use of mortar—that even a thin knife blade could not slip between the stones. Initially, we spent our time exploring the Sacred Plaza's Principle Temple and the Temple of the Three Windows. The three windows in the open-air temple were unique due to their trapezoidal shape.

The afternoon was slipping away as we made our way up the stairs connecting the Sacred Plaza to the *Intihuatana* stone. This sacred carved stone's name in Quechua means "where it is tied to the sun." This is where Inka priests "tied" the sun during the winter solstice. We were now at the highest point in Machu Picchu. And the stone, with a little imagination, looked like the upper body of a dolphin with its fin being the actual hitching post.[147]

Explanations abound as to the purpose of this ceremonial stone, but conjecture regarding its purpose was not necessary for me. I felt the power that emanated from it. As a moth drawn to flame, I went and put my hands and forehead on it, and then sat cross-legged on the stone with my hands in the *mudra* (hand position) of the Cosmic Sun.

As I closed my eyes, time seemed to stop. I was not aware of the stone seat beneath me or the others by me as surreal images briefly came and then disappeared. I quickly opened my eyes as I felt the immovable sun-stone still firmly lodged beneath me. As a picture was taken of me and the others, I had a knowing that I had been here before. But it was a time before the Inkas.[148] Was that possible?

Cactus of the Four Winds Ceremony and *Pachamama* Stone

Pachamama Stone February 1988

In the early evening, the group was led into the sacred city by don Eduardo. The gate into the city was normally closed and locked to visitors during the night. The gate's guard, however, was willing to accept a "gift" to let us enter. Our ceremonial destination was the *Pachamama* Stone, a bastion of earthly feminine energy. It was here that don Eduardo would conduct the sacred-plant ceremony using the medicine of the magical cactus.

What an appropriate night it was, as lightning lit the sky above the *Pachamama* Stone. As with all excellent tales of wizards and ruined cities, the heavens provided a backdrop that even one's imagination could never conjure. Rain was falling and thunder was booming as if the Inka's war drums were sounding a call to action. The heavens were lit as if the lightning bolts of the Inka's creator/hero—*Viracocha*—were being flung through the night sky. Every flash of lightning provided an eerie view of Huayna Picchu, the sister peak behind Machu Picchu.

Viracocha, the Staff God, was sometimes represented as a bearded man carrying a staff in one hand and a book in the other. He was considered the creator and destroyer of worlds. Supposedly, we were at the ending cycle of the Fifth Sun or the fifth world. The previous world, or the Fourth Sun, had been destroyed by water. However, the ending of our world would come about through big movement – earthquakes. Before I learned this, I had a knowing that we were in the end times, times critical to the survival of the human race, which was destroying itself and the biosphere of the Earth. We urgently needed new thoughts and a new view of reality beyond what was already accepted. A message, but what message? I seemed to know, but not know.

That night we were going to be working on mastery, again symbolized by the North direction of the medicine wheel. The Inka Medicine Wheel is a mandala, a visual symbolic construct and pathway of transformation and integration. *Mandala*, according to an ancient language, means circle. A circle is power, completion and perfection. The Inka Medicine Wheel is symbolic of the four winds and the teachings and transformations that occur in each of the four directions of the compass.

The journey through the Medicine Wheel begins in the South direction symbolized by the archetype of the serpent. This is the path of personal healing where we learn to shed the past, erase our personal history, and exorcise the past that restricts us. The West direction is home to mother/sister puma. This is the path of the mystic Luminous Warrior. Here we face our deaths and step beyond fear and the uncertainty and doubt that live within us. The North is represented by the hummingbird. This is where we learn the way of the ancient ones by stepping outside of time with the death of the unhealthy ego. We live in the timeless now, in a state of awakening, unfettered to the past, to fear, or to death. Condor is the archetype of the East. Here we learn to see with our hearts. As the visionary, we see through the illusion of separateness to the reality of oneness. That night, we had the opportunity to "step outside of time."

As the wind picked up, light rain fell and lightning lit the sky above us. Eduardo set up his *mesa*[149] in front of the gigantic mother stone and prepared to call in the guardian spirits of the four winds. He had placed his power staffs and swords—in various sizes and shapes—on the ground in front of his *mesa* cloth: owl staff; serpent staff; eagle staff; hummingbird staff; saber of Saint Michael; and a sword of Saint Paul.[150] Coincidentally, I had the same sword at home. In the early eighties, a person wanted to take martial-arts classes from me but didn't have the money for the fee. Not wanting to keep anyone from participating, I said to him, "do you have anything to trade for classes?" A smile came to his face as he replied, "I do. A sword." It was a sword of Saint Paul! This sword symbolizes judges, lawyers, soldiers, and justice in general. It is used to apply divine justice and to make rebellious spirits face reality.

Besides the staffs mentioned, there were other staffs, such as the Staff of the Maiden – the Virgin. I mention this staff in particular due to the fact that it was presented to me to use in the night ceremony. This was an appropriate staff for me for many reasons, one being that I was born under the sign of the Virgin (Virgo) on a new moon, another symbol of the virgin.

This magical staff, connected with the sacred highland lagoons, was made from black chonta wood. It would awaken the nurturing power and feminine energy within me, which I needed to accept. This would balance the strong male energy that I had and would help bring me into a state of inner oneness.

Eduardo knew that I was a teacher of the mystical warrior arts as was he – a spiritual warrior. He knew that it was not any of the warrior staffs, but *Vara de la Senorita*—the Staff of the Maiden—that would bring me back into balance. He also knew that I needed the sacred power of the great Earth Mother Stone— the *Pachamama*. Twenty feet long and ten high, this great stone of feminine energy, stands on the edge of the ruins with the Grandmother peak, Huayna Picchu, behind it and to its left.

As others received various staffs and went off to different spots to do their work, I was assigned to the *Pachamama* stone along with one of the females in our group. This gigantic stone awakens the feminine side and our connection with Mother Earth. It represents the fertility of women, of the Earth, and of the mind.

It's interesting to note that due to the invasion of Christianity, there was a blending of indigenous (in our case Peruvian) and Christian thought and symbolism in our ceremonies. A prime example is the three *campos,* or fields, of Eduardo's *mesa.* The *Campo Justiciero* or the Field of Divine Justice is governed by Christ, who is considered the center of the *mesa* and lord of the three fields.

Nose Juice and the Magical Cactus

Lightning flashed across the dark purple sky creating a mystical setting. Each one of us went in front of don Eduardo and received our staffs. At this moment, I also had my first taste of the otherworldly magical cactus. As I stood in front of don Eduardo, I looked into his eyes as he handed me a seashell filled with some type of liquid.

"This is lovingly referred to as 'nose juice,'" Alberto said as he assisted Eduardo. "Put the shell to your nose, tilt your head back and let the 'juice' run down the back of your throat. Breathe and if you start choking, stomp your foot."

Breathe, stomp my foot, imbibe a magical elixir through my nose. I would later learn that it was a mixture of herbs, black tobacco and alcohol, a powerful stimulant that would open the third eye and affect the various visionary centers of the brain.

It was definitely difficult to swallow and I did stomp my foot, which helped. It was absolutely a rush. As I handed the shell back to don Eduardo, I noticed that his eyes were black pools of focused intent. He was an archetypal shaman with his Buddha belly, long black hair, drooping mustache, and flaring nostrils that reminded me of the Hawaiian warrior *akua* (deity) Ku.

"This is the visionary cactus juice, the San Pedro," said Alberto as don Eduardo handed me a small liquid-filled glass.

As soon as I had finished drinking the potion, I danced over to the *Pachamama* Stone while holding the Staff of the Maiden. We were asked to dance after taking the San Pedro, for a reason I was still trying to figure out. But my focus was not on the dance or the reason for it; it was on the anticipated effects of the magical potion.

I waited and waited but nothing really happened. Letting go of any further expectations, I settled in and focused my intent on the staff and my connection with the stone's great feminine energy. And then, small green sparks surrounded the head of the staff. Interesting, I thought, and let go of any further thoughts. As time seemed to be suspended, I closed my eyes and attempted to become one with the Mother Stone.

How long I stayed in that sweet space of no-mind, I do not know. But when I opened my eyes, the rain had stopped, the stars were shining brightly, and I had an insight. I had never been close to my own mother. In fact, in my mind, I had been raised by my grandmother. Moreover, I had always felt that my parents were not my parents.

My insight was that I had just reestablished a bond and become closer to my mother; that is, my other mother, the Great Earth Mother, *Pachamama*, the mother of us all. *Will this be an opening to my feminine side?*[151] I wondered.[152]

Big Cat That Flies

As the night wore on, we did further spiritual work at the Principal Temple where I was a spirit guardian for Eduardo, sitting above him and protecting him. Then dawn approached and our work was complete, so we headed back to our rooms for a few hours of much-needed rest. As we approached the entrance to the lost city, I could see that the gate was now closed and appeared to be locked from the other side. We were indeed locked in!

I was standing directly behind Alberto and don Eduardo as they realized our situation. The only way out was through this gateway, which blocked the path in and out of the lost city. On both sides of the trail were sheer cliffs; one that rose to the upper reaches of the city and the other that was a sheer drop to the distant river below.

It would be dangerous to attempt to scale the gateway. Not only could a person lose their footing and tumble to their death below, but the top of the gateway was fashioned with barbed wire to discourage trespassers. The irony was not lost on me, as we were attempting to get out of the city, not break in.

Alberto turned to me and said, "don Eduardo feels that you can safely scale the gateway. Are you willing?"

The San Pedro had not affected me as it had the others. I felt strong in body, mind and spirit as I nodded in agreement.

"Once you get on the other side of the gate, you must wake up the gate-keeper and get him to let us out," said Alberto. "He has been paid his money. He lives in a small home halfway down the mountain. Be careful."

As I prepared to scale the gateway, I wondered if I needed to be more careful of the climb or of the gatekeeper. Once on the other side of the gate, I trekked down the road that takes you to the bottom of the mountain and the train station. The only sound I could hear was the beating of my heart as I scanned both sides of the road for some type of dwelling.

Finally, I spied the outline of a low-sitting house on the railroad side of the mountain. Now, I thought, what do I do? I wondered if Alberto remembered that I couldn't speak Spanish. Since I couldn't see a path up to the house, I decided to amuse the gatekeeper with my Spanish by calling out, "Hola?" I didn't want to speak too loudly in case others in the house were asleep.

There was no response so I raised my voice and called out once again, "Hola, hola, hola?" After the third soulful pleading, a floating light appeared in the dark of the night. As the light crept closer, I could see that it was being held by a small Peruvian man who could have been an extra out of an Indiana Jones movie. He was the tarot card Hermit[153] come to life with his railroad lantern held in one hand. He would light our path back to the sacred city just as the Hermit lights our way so that we do not get lost in the darkness. The only difference between this man and the image of the Hermit on a tarot card was a large set of old-time padlock keys in his other hand instead of a walking staff. With little fanfare and no words, he looked at me with no expression. A tilt of his head indicated that I should follow him. He then slowly made his way up the mountain road to the entrance gate where my fellow seekers were waiting to be released back into the dawn of a new day.

The next day Alberto approached me with a message from don Eduardo, who said that I was the "Big Cat That Flies." An appropriate name, as I would discover.

Having completed our work within Machu Picchu, we returned to Cusco by train. Our next destination was to be the sacred lagoon of Markawasi Plateau, and not Las Huaringas. For reasons unknown, don Eduardo had decided to initiate us in the sacred lagoon located on the mystical and mythic Markawasi Plateau, 12,000 feet (3,658 meters) above sea level. An undercurrent of chatter flowed between some in the group concerning don Eduardo's decision not to go to Las Huaringas. Some seemed to be upset, but for me, I wasn't there for drama. I was there for experience, knowledge and power.

Markawasi Plateau

San Pedro de Casta February 1988

Our journey to the isolated town of San Pedro de Casta, on narrow, winding mountainous roads was an initiation in itself – scary, shall we say? This mountainside town clustered around a ridge is the access point for the plateau. After spending a cold night there, we began our journey to Markawasi. We had the option to ride on horses for the three kilometers, or walk. Not being a horse person, I decided to walk as it would be a stroll in the park compared to the Inka Trail. But it was still uphill and tough.

Our destination on the plateau was known as the Amphitheatre and was surrounded by amazing rock formations. After setting up camp, I was thunderstruck by the eerie silence surrounding the plateau and the energy radiating from the stones. And let me not forget to mention, it was cold!

The Quechua name Markawasi means "house of the people." At one time the volcanic plateau was probably ice-covered. Supposedly, Markawasi was an ancient site populated by a culture that existed before the Inkas. It is known for its stone formations, thought to be the carvings of this ancient civilization and referred to as the Stone Forest. Depending on the time of the day and reflection of the sun, the stones reveal different images, an amazing sight.

During our time there, before our initiation in the Black Lagoon, we sat vision, constructed a stone death spiral, conducted ceremony and absorbed the energy of the plateau. This visit to Markawasi was a significant juncture and experience in my life, as was the descending spirit exorcism on Kōyasan. I realized that my exorcism on Kōyasan was the initial quickening of awakening and the work of the South, where we exorcise the past that binds and restricts us. Five months before that exorcism, I had made the life changing and major decision on Kōyasan to not move to Maryland, which my wife and I had almost done because of this binding and restricting past. And I had faced death high in the Andes and freed myself from an unknown future – the work of the West.

I was sad to leave Cusco but happy to head home to my family. As awesome as the journey was, I longed to hold my wife, my son Jamie and my daughter Jessie. Let me paint a picture of myself after arriving in Miami to clear customs. I was as dark as a native Peruvian. I wore my colorful poncho with an equally colorful knit cap just above ears, blackened by the sun. Multiple colorful bags hung over my shoulders and I held my staff in my right hand.

Knowing how I must look, as I walked toward the customs official I thought, "This is going to be interesting. Wonder how many questions I'll be asked and how thoroughly my bags will be searched?" Did I have any Peruvian contraband? That's only for me to know!

Within feet of the customs officer, I steeled myself for the questions and searches. And what happened? He waved me through, no questions, no searches! I had been in Mexico, the Yucatan, and then Miami and finally Peru. "Interesting," I thought, "are there unseen ones traveling with me?"

Today, in the fear-drenched and controlled environment created by terrorism, I would never be able to take my staff onboard any airplane, much less get through customs. In 1988, I did just that. My staff flew with me, right next to me in the window seat.

The question I asked myself at the *Pachamama* Stone: "Will this be an opening to my feminine side?" was finally answered as I stepped off the plane in Portland, Maine. Sher walked right past me. She didn't recognize me. When I spoke her name, she turned and some of her first words were, "You've changed." And I had. I had awakened my feminine side, the work of the North, the union of Sun (masculine) and Moon (feminine). I had awakened purity of mind (strong mind) and claimed the lineage of men and women of knowledge.

Little did I suspect that in five years I would have my vision and hear the voice from heaven saying, "This Star is you; you are this Star," the Morning Star—the work of the East—the way of the visionary.

Machu Picchu 2007

"Machu Picchu belongs to multinational companies—the train companies, the hotel chains—like all world patrimony."[154]

Since 1987, sacred sites have been desecrated by an excessive influx of New Agers and tourists. Supposedly for spiritual elevation, but more for unhealthy ego, hordes of New Agers following Caucasian "neo-shamans" have invaded sacred places to their detriment. And the tourists have followed in droves. With such an increase in popularity, governments and capitalistic elites saw opportunity and the building frenzy was on.

According to Carol Cumes, who was one of my fellow journeyers in 1988, the years since "have brought an increase in tourism to Peru, and with it, a corresponding decrease in respect for *Pachamama*, Mother Earth. In February 1995, the first of a series of natural disasters began around Machu Picchu, and since then, *Pachamama* has sent similar warnings to the people in the area. Quechua elders explain that the Andean gods have been offended by those who fail to respect them and who misrepresent the true beliefs of the Andean people. They maintain that both visitors and locals have entered sacred space without asking permission from the *apukuna*, the powerful mountain deities who have shown their vengeance with the recent natural disasters."[155]

Like Carol, I know firsthand the desecration that has resulted from greed and the drive for profit at many different sites such as one dear to my heart: Machu Picchu. In October 2007, I returned with two of our apprentices. This time we took the train from Cusco to Aguas Calientes, the tourist town that grew up around the Machu Picchu train station and is a 20-minute bus ride from the archaeological site. The last time I was here, I believe there was only the train station. What a change, and for the worst. Where there used to be peace and harmony while waiting for the train back to Cusco, there was now chaos and excessive commercialism. Hundreds of tourists' flock off the trains into waiting buses to chug them up the mountain to the sacred Inka ruins.

And for the ones that want to stay a few days, there are places of respite ranging from thirty dollars a night in town to more than a thousand dollars in the "palace" outside the gates of Machu Picchu.

The price to enter the ruins is ridiculous: forty dollars. However, it would be worth it if we could still do our spiritual work, which we cannot due to the hordes of people around and the fact that the places of power within the ruins are blocked off and off limits. As you have learned, the last time I was here, it was quite a different story. Not only was I able to meditate on the "hitching post to the sun" but was able to conduct ritual and ceremony within the ruins all night long. And speaking of the "hitching post," during the making of a beer commercial, one of the camera booms dropped unexpectedly and cracked a piece off the sacred stone.

After the horse has left the barn, let's shut the door. To allow a commercial to be made in such a sacred place in the first place is wrong, a tragedy, and demonstrates the scourge of capitalism. After this happened, a rope barrier was put up around the sacred stone. In a scene right out of Monty Python, gaggles of tourists reach their hands out to within inches of the stone to "receive its energy." Giggling, chattering a mile a minute while "receiving energy," the New Agers, aka tourists, are once again observers of spirit but not participants.

If Machu Picchu was an isolated case, it would be tragic enough; but it isn't. From the Tor in Glastonbury, England to Tulúm on the Mexican Yucatan Peninsula, the story is the same. Hordes of New Agers, tourists and supposed spiritual seekers have over-run sacred sites with the willing help of the tourist industry, local governments and merchants – capitalism at its finest.

You may have already guessed that the two very destructive and domineering paradigms that I despise are capitalism and organized religions – the patriarchal religions that are based on a single sacred text such as the Bible or the Koran. Personally, I have a vendetta against Christianity and its great lie, in fact, the greatest lie ever told.

CHICKEN, CANDLES AND POSH

· ·

TRADITIONALLY, SHAMANISM HAS BEEN IDENTIFIED AS A JOUR-
ney of the soul conducted by the shaman, known as a master of the spirits. A
shaman[156] is a person with the ability to connect the profane to the sacred, and
thus provide a link between the Otherworld and Earth. He or she is a visionary and what I call a "pathfinder to the soul." Shamans are healers, dreamers,
philosophers, and undogmatic religious guides and teachers.

A shaman[157] is also a person of power who dream-voyages to the
Otherworld for knowledge and freedom. This is the freedom from our
ego-self, the unhealthy ego.[158] The shaman helps others, and themselves,
escape from the imprisonment of anger, guilt, resentment, and greed. This
gives one the freedom to love and be loved.

As masters of the Otherworld and Earth, shamans are sensitive to wood,
stone, and all the elements that surround them. They look to the stars at
night and to the four winds during the day. They listen to the magic roar of
the streams and moaning surge of the oceans to learn the truth of the great
mysteries of life. The shape of the clouds reveals the secrets of life and death.
And the cry of the owl reminds them of their ancestors and the dark knowledge and wisdom of the Earth.

Unlike priests, they are not gatekeepers between you and the Otherworld.
They are messengers, not gatekeepers. Shamans have a knowing of the mysteries of the unseen Otherworld and the Earth, whereas the institutionalized
priest deals only with heaven, and then only secondhand.

To access the Otherworld, shamans are able to alter their states of consciousness from our normal dualistic consciousness to one of radical nonduality. Various methods to achieve this power at will have included, but are not limited to, bathing and repetitive movement or sound, such as drumming and chanting.

In addition to the methods just listed, I experienced another in the highlands of Mexico in 1991. A friend and I were in the city of San Cristobal de Las Casas located in Chiapas, the southernmost state of Mexico. We were seeking adventure and knowledge and hoped to locate a shaman who would share teachings and ceremonies with us. When you inquire about a local shaman or healer, you must be careful and discerning in your questions to the local people. Imagine how odd it would be to stop a person on a street in a U.S. city and ask if they know who the best surgeon is and where he or she may be found. Add to this that you are not American and your spoken English, to be kind, is horrible. Additionally, the person you asked may be scared of surgeons, as some surgeons may practice harmful surgeries, in other words, black medicine.

Without being run out of town, we managed to find a local who knew of a shaman who just happened to be in the city that day. We were told that he was at a school, although it was a mystery as to why because school was not in session. His name was Anselmo Perez, a Zinacantec shaman from the mountainous city of San Juan Chamula, whose patron saint is John the Baptist – the Dipper.

After a small adventure finding the school, we discovered Anselmo sitting alone in a classroom. To this day, I am not quite sure why he was just sitting there and waiting. However, in broken translation, I understood that he was waiting for us. I don't know if someone had sent him word gringos were coming to see him or he was expecting us spiritually. After more tedious communication, we discovered that he was not feeling well and if we could heal him, then he would teach us.

A fair bargain, I thought, as we began to work on him. Time became timeless as we entered that detached state of being where healing power lies. After an unknown period of time, we finished working on Anselmo. He opened his eyes and smiled. We had passed the test but there was something more, something most important. We had approached him with impeccable intent with a purity of purpose.

After the healing, we still were not finished with our tasks. We needed to go back into town with Anselmo and purchase a few things for the ceremony he would conduct for us at his home in Chamula. This was quite an honor, for us to be invited to his home. Besides the question of why he had been at the school, another mystery presented itself. He didn't have a car and the school where we found him was on the outskirts of San Cristobal 10 kilometers from Chamula.

Once back in town, the items we had to purchase were interesting to say the least – a live chicken (are we talking a sacrifice here?), flowers, copal resin for incense and many white candles. But this was not all. We would find the next item in Chamula, which is famous for its church, the *Iglesia de San Juan Bautista*, and the locals' rather untraditional use of it. There are no pews and it is dark and thick with incense, lit only by candles. No dogmatic preaching, no priest: worshipers simply sit on the floor with lines of candles around them or in front of them while praying.

As we pulled into the outskirts of Chamula, Anselmo had us stop at a simple cement block building that had no door, just an opening into a small room that contained a plywood bar top held up by cement blocks. Behind it sat a large oil drum with a hand crank. I didn't know what to think until Anselmo called out, and a man appeared out of a darkened room next to the oil drum.

At that point I noticed many old and seemingly dirty bottles on a shelf next to the oil drum. The proprietor of this establishment reached for one of the dirt-covered bottles. He took it to the oil drum, lifted up the hose, put its nozzle into the bottle and started hand-cranking. A clear liquid flowed into the bottle with each turn of the crank. Anselmo turned to us and said, "Posh," (also written as Pox). I thought, "Could this be the Maya equivalent of 'white lightning?' Well, if it is, it will kill anything living in those bottles."

Not to be outdone by the dirty bottles, the proprietor used some type of corn husk as a substitute cork stopper. After he drew five bottles of this magical elixir, we bid farewell to the "posh-man," (not to be confused with the post-man). However, if we did end up drinking that much "white lightning," we would definitely be carrying messages to Anselmo's ancestors.[159]

Amazingly, I discovered that a companion potion to posh, called "Jesus juice," was used as the celebratory drink during the autumnal-equinox celebration honoring "Christ."[160] With this knowledge, my consciousness flew back to my fraternity days when we would combine grapefruit juice, grape juice, and grain alcohol and dub it a "purple Jesus," a potent hooch we drank occasionally during my undergraduate days.

We later discovered that Anselmo was the shaman "go-to" when a person was in need of healing and other shamanic remedies. There was no doubt in my mind that he had helped untold numbers of people. Anselmo was not one of the workshop-circuit shamans who were only interested in power and money. Outside of the highlands, few know about this "bat shaman" of Chamula. Zinacantec literally means "land of bats."

On the way to his home, I observed numerous four-armed decorated crosses that symbolized the four-fold rain god, Chac, not the Christian cross. Crosses with designs of flowers, trees, and branches symbolized the Maya Tree of Life—the sacred Ceiba tree.

After arriving at his home, which reflected his altruistic spirit—very simple and comfortable—Anselmo indicated to us to wait in a room connected to his house that seemed to be his ceremonial room while he took the chicken into the house. A chicken dinner would definitely be served later on that night.

As much as this adventure may seem like a cool thing, there is always a little trepidation involved. Shamans like Anselmo carry great spirit-power. Healing or harming is the same power; it is only the intention of the shaman that is different. Run across the wrong shaman and you may regret it.

Anselmo began the ceremony at dusk. Certain things may not be put into print but I will give an overview. Basically, it involved Anselmo praying, lighting candles and pouring himself and each of us a shot of posh known as *agua ardiente*, or fire water. Posh connects the material world with the spiritual world and cures both physical and spiritual ailments – medicine for the soul.

I soon understood that "a shot of posh may be a blessing on a cold winter's night, but by the time the cup bearer[161] brings the ninth round, the gift has become a burden. The participants in a curing ceremony consume posh for the same reason they burn candles – it is a gift for the saints and Ancestors. Posh is considered a powerful healing substance and also a cause of sickness, for the hangovers are unbearable. Everyone who drinks offers the spirit of all that is joyous and terrible in life."[162]

For double nine rounds we each drank a shot of posh, sometimes more, while Anselmo lit candles and prayed. He would do a candle for each of us by dripping the wax of the lit candle onto the floor and then seating the candle into the soft but hardening wax. After so much posh, you would think that we would have been drunk, but the opposite was true. My senses were heightened and so was my perception of space and time. After the completion of the ceremony and before we departed, Anselmo looked at me with the sternness of a master and said, "Stop seeking, stop reading so many books (how did he know that?). You have the power, go help others."

Commentary

In our materialistic world it seems that nothing sacred is off limits. Not only have sacred sites around the world been commercialized and overrun by gaggles of tourists and New Agers, but now pox has joined the ranks of corruption, falling to materialistic greed. Since 2012, pox has been distributed outside of Chiapas.

According to Nicholas Mancall-Bitel, "Meet Pox: Whiskey, Rum and Mezcal's Mind-Altering Love Child, "for hundreds of years, Chiapas natives were the only ones to distill pox, as the Mexican government looked the other way on the unregulated, supposedly mind-altering beverage. But in 2012, the state granted certification for the spirit, allowing distillers to sell it throughout Mexico."[163]

All things said, there is one small blessing. At least the pox distilled for the public is not exactly identical to the traditional magical "medicine." This is a small victory.

A NIGHT WITH PEANUT IN TULÚM:
THE GHOSTS OF TULÚM

. . . .

PEANUT WAS A NICKNAME OF AN ELDERLY WOMAN WHO HAD adventured with us on a few journeys. She and her partner were with us in Japan in 1987 when I had the descending spirit exorcism and she deeply believed that her cancer had been cured on Kōyasan. I had a fondness within my heart for Peanut and for Tulúm – City of the Dawn.

Located on the coast of the Yucatan, cliff-side Tulúm overlooks the emerald tinged sea. I had felt a connection with this sacred place of the Descending God and the Kukulkán Group two months before my experience on Kōyasan. Kukulkán is the Mayan name for Quetzalcóatl – the Feathered Serpent.

Ever since Sher and I had first set foot on this sacred land overlooking the Caribbean in 1987, we had returned many times, primarily leading groups of adventurers to sense and experience the power and myth of this revered site and other Maya ruins.

Working with an indigenous archeologist and healer, I had learned of a secret and hidden way into Tulúm by the sea-born cliffs. On the Caribbean side there was a path that led up the cliff to the backside of Tulúm. If we wanted to do spiritual work and ceremony after Tulúm was closed to the public, this path was the only way to enter the ruins, as the front entrance was protected by two guards.

Location of the Hidden Path

We began walking up the path late in the afternoon. Even though it was daylight, it was still a difficult climb. Once we reached the top of the cliff and were safely by the pyramid, El Castillo, I realized that it would not be safe for Peanut to descend back down the path in the dark, even with my help. I put this thought aside and planned to deal with it after I finished teaching and conducting ceremony.

When sacred sites are open to the public with hordes of tourist milling about snapping picture after picture—and when the stone ruins are roped off preventing access like in present-day Tulúm—it's very difficult to practice or conduct spiritual work and ceremony. On the other hand, being in a sacred site at dusk and during the night, feeling, sensing and smelling the sacredness and power it contains and the memories held by the stones of the ruins, is awe-inspiring. The dark triggers our minds to places of power or dread, but only by scraping away the veneer of civilization's accepted norms are we able to reach to the core of our essence.

As dusk turned into night, I completed our spiritual work. There are two transitional times between day and night and night and day – dusk and dawn. At these powerful times, the blending of light and dark and dark and light are most evident as a reflection of radical nonduality. These are times when a person's dualistic consciousness has a better chance of experiencing the Otherworld.

Our group was milling about waiting for me to lead them back down the path and to our parked cars. I turned to my friend—who was assisting me because Sher was unable to join me on this journey—and asked him to lead the group back to the cars and to meet us out in front of the ruins. Peanut and I were going to go out the front entrance. Dumbfounded, he asked how we were going to get past the guards. I assured him we would be out front. He just needed to make sure he picked us up as soon as possible.

Walking with Peanut towards the entrance, my thoughts flew back to the time when Sher and I had first set foot in this blessed land and discovered our love for Tulúm. A feeling of freedom is hardwired into my soul. With Tulúm situated on cliffs facing the vast expense of the Caribbean, with the wind in my face, it allowed my core essence to feel like an eagle that could soar over the cliffs and out to sea. Prophetic this was, as fifteen years later we would be living in a home surrounded by soaring eagles, on a cliff overlooking a fjord on the west coast of the U.S.

As we moved closer to either freedom or imprisonment, I could feel and sense the ancestors of Tulúm. And it's always best to have the ancestors on your side, I thought, as I silently acknowledged and blessed them. We were in the middle of the moon cycle which made the landscape slightly visible but not full-moon bright. Perfect I thought, we'll just be nightwalkers – the Ghosts of Tulúm.

I had an idea on the length of time it would take our people to walk back to the cars and drive to the entrance of Tulúm. Timing was essential. I would need to get the guards to leave at the proper time. And then we would need to exit before they overcame their fear and returned to their posts. Peanut was curious as to how we were going to get past the guards. We were trespassing and we didn't need to land in a Mexican jail. Little did Peanut know that this was not the first time I'd had an encounter with the *Policía Federal Preventiva* – better known as the "Federales."[164]

The majority of people's minds are weak,[165] dualistic weakness based on fear, doubt, assumptions, beliefs, spiritual and religious brainwashing, and so forth. And there is the lack of undivided mental concentration, a "chattering" mind on a storm-tossed sea. These mind hindrances are what the Esoteric Buddhists refer to as "having false views." In other words, weak minds are like mirrors covered in dust that obscures clarity and the true nature and reality of things. The things that disturb the tranquility of the mind, such as fear and doubt, are the dust or the smoke that blurs the clarity of our mirror minds.

Utilizing this knowledge as well as my knowledge of how to influence the imagery within a person's mind,[166] and projecting the power of my voice, I began an Otherworldly wail that, when combined with the images within their weak minds, would basically "scare the shit" out of the guards.

The proof was in the pudding, as it is said. True to form they took off running. I knew my influence would wear off in a few minutes, so Peanut and I needed to leave promptly. As we were walking away from Tulúm towards the cars that waited for us in the shadows, Peanut turned to me and said (paraphrased), "You are something else. What did you do?"

Commentary

There is a great sadness in my heart, not only for Tulúm but for so many other sacred sites around the world. Due to greed-filled efforts to attracting more hordes of tourist to Tulúm, where the secret path was located, wooden steps were built down to the beach below El Castillo. This allows tourist easy access to the beach where they can swim and sunbathe after snapping their multitude of pictures. What a dishonoring to the land and the ancestors of Tulúm.

Presently, there's even a tulum.com! Tulúm has turned into the third most-visited site in all of Mexico. Chichen Itza is second and Teotihuacán is first among the most-visited sacred sites. Teotihuacán's status as first is not due to foreign tourism but to the sweeping numbers of Mexicans who visit. I've experienced all three and the only one where it is still possible to do spiritual work is Teotihuacán.

Greed trumps the magic of tapping into the power and sacredness of Tulúm and other sites I've experienced, such as Machu Picchu. And for generations to come, stories like this one, tales that happened before greed took over and polluted the sacred sites, will be the only way to portray the wonder, magic, and power of ancient ruins.

One final point: not only have the New Agers overrun sacred sites around the world, but there are numerous fake "Toltec-Mesoamerican" gurus offering false knowledge to a susceptible public.[167]

THE JAGUARS ARE COMING

· ·

One of the attributes for which shamans are widely known is "shapeshifting," such as becoming a werewolf or were-jaguar. Within Mesoamerican culture, this age-old shamanic belief can be traced as far back as the Olmecs, the earliest known major civilization in Mexico. It was "believed that the jaguar 'dominated' the art of the Olmecs and that 'this jaguar fixation must have had a religious motivation.' However, it is not the jaguar himself who dominates Olmec art but rather the composite being who has come to be known as the were-jaguar, a creature combining human and jaguar traits."[168]

For many of us, we have been entertained for decades with movies and televised images of shapeshifting, most often a change from man to wolf – the werewolf. Who can forget the original "Wolf Man" where we experienced for the first time Larry Talbot (Lon Chaney) changing into a werewolf after being bitten by one. And before Larry transforms under the light of the full moon, we hear the chilling words spoken by the gypsy, Maleva: "Whoever is bitten by a werewolf and lives becomes a werewolf himself." His transformation is less frightening and closer to reality than later movies depicting werewolves. Talbot's face and hands gets hairier and more beastly but still they are very human-like.

Fast forward to 1981, when the movie, "An American Werewolf in London" is released. Forty years after the original Wolf Man the producers present us with a more elaborate scene of transformation from man to wolf. The face extends out into the snarling snout of a wolf, hands and fingers elongate into sharp reddish claws (even a jaguar would be envious of such talons), and the back seems to split apart from within and extend into more of a hunch-back. Very entertaining, but very far from the truth.

Ironically, the original transformation of Larry Talbot from man to wolf was closer to the truth of shapeshifting as already stated: "combining human and animal traits." The reason why Talbot's visible shapeshifting is closer to reality may be explained by the Desana[169] Indians. According to them, the shaman shapeshifter does not turn into a real jaguar, but adopts "the 'essence' or 'state of mind,' which enforces the individual to act like a jaguar."[170] And how do I know that the Desana are correct and that Talbot's shape-changing is closer to reality than the others? Read on.

The Night of The Jaguar

Yucatan, Mexico

Come awaken your spirit adventurer consciousness during our seven-day, "Night of the Jaguar" experience in the Yucatan sacred sites of Tulúm and the Laguna Chunyaxché. Step into your personal power as a warrior and healer and explore the timeless techniques of eastern and western shamans. Transcend your separateness of mind, body and spirit and enter the awesome power of the one. . . .

The power of the one will be further experienced during our full-moon ceremony inside the cave of the "night spirit" near Tulúm. This will be the moment when the stalking jaguar leaps out of the darkness and shares the Earth beside us.

I didn't have the slightest idea how true and prophetic these words from our journey brochure would turn out to be. During August 1989, a friend, Sher and I were leading a shamanic group to various coastal and inland Maya sacred sites such as Tulúm and Coba. We were also meeting up once again with Antonio, Maya *hméen* or *h'men* (healer), who was also an archeologist who had mastered the techniques of calling in and working with the *balam* (jaguar) and *u'Pi xan akob* (night spirit) energies. Early the morning of the full moon, our Maya friend wanted to take us to an archeological site that had not been extensively unearthed, as we were bringing the group there to experience *The Night of the Jaguar*. This site was Muyil, also known as *Chunyaxché*,

Muyil, one of the oldest of Maya archeological sites, is located on the mainland side of a lagoon in the Sian Kaán ("where the sky is born") Biosphere. It is home to over 350 types of birds, as well as pumas, jaguars, and ocelots.

After we arrived, it was without our students, we were checking out the site before we brought them back later that evening. As we stepped out of our car, it was evident that no one else was around. One of the joys of the late 80s to early 90s was being the only humans at sacred sites, which is hard to experience in today's world of over-crowded, roped-off, and guarded ruins crammed with flocks of chattering tourists.

When we began walking through the jungle foliage to one of the ruins, I could feel and sense Sher going into one of her trance states to access the Otherworld. With her being a true empath, when this happens I usually freak out, concerned for her well-being. She has told me to not to be concerned and let her go through the experience without interference, but sometimes I do interfere, as you will see later.

As we got closer to the site, Sher began to tremble and panic was in her voice. "Don't you hear them?" she asked. "They're coming, I can feel them."

"Who?" I asked.

"Jaguars."

Her eyes had that strange otherworldly look to them and she kept continuously and rapidly tapping the center of her chest. "Are you O.K.?" I asked.

"They're coming," was all she replied and kept repeating. She related to me later that see could see Mayan villagers. Concerned that the jaguars were going to attack them, her heart began racing.

Sher's Account of the Walk In

When we were walking on the earth packed path through the jungle, I began to hear branches breaking and being moved coming towards our direction. I sensed and knew it was jaguars While walking I could see to my left a clearing with native Mayans in a domestic setting, cooking and preparing food around a low fire with cooking pots. There were adults and children more like a singular family than community. I passed several more and didn't think it unusual as I was unknowingly going into that state of mind of believing what I am witnessing is actually happening. When I had the sensing of the jaguars coming closer my concern shifted to the safety of the villagers and I began to feel afraid for them. It's one thing to be armed and hunting them or being attacked in your home space unexpectedly and unprepared.

My heart and breath began racing and I spontaneously began to tap my chest (basically the thymus area which I later learned is a natural way to calm the nervous system down). I began to hear the jaguars getting closer which caused me to walk faster and tap even more rapidly. I was close to what would be a panic attack. It was that tangibly real for me. I was unable to call out to Jim or our friend who were unaware of what I was experiencing.

The Temple Ruins

By this time, we had reached the site and I could see that my friend, who was a doctor, and Antonio were also getting concerned, not about jaguars, though they inhabited the Biosphere, but about Sher's state of mind. Reaching the temple ruins, Antonio said that he would work on Sher on one of the lower levels of the ruins. While she and he climbed up the ruins, we waited on the jungle floor. As I watched her ascend the steps, I felt conflicted. I considered going with her and Antonio but then thought better of it. "No," I thought, "let her go through this."

I watched as Sher knelt on the stone surface with Antonio standing behind her. Preparing for the healing, Antonio brought out from his fabric bag an overly large quartz crystal[171] and began working on her head. In the next instant, the crystal slipped out of his hand unintentionally and fell squarely on Sher's forehead – the location of her frontal lobe and third eye. Luckily, she had taken off her glasses for the healing. Without her glasses she can't see very far or clear.

With the impact of the crystal, Sher already kneeling fell forward onto her hands. I was very concerned as it was a strong hit to her head. Sher lowered her head and began slowly turning it right and left several times, and she then crawled backwards like a feline behind the remains of the wall which was in back of them. Although I wanted to race up the side of the ruins, my friend said, "Don't…" I waited to see what would happen. I could see Sher still on all fours, peering around the corner of the wall, just as a cat/jaguar would. By now Antonio was by her side, working on her to get her back. Not willing to wait any longer, by the time I reached her, she was better and had come back, but I knew not totally.[172] On the way back to the car, Sher's moon-time unexpectedly arrived. It was a few weeks early.

Later at the completion of our "site visit," Sher shared with me what her experience had been like for her:

> "When we reached the site, I was still in a state of concern about the jaguars and the villagers. Jim, our friend, and Antonio were aware that I was not in my normal state of mind. So I was led up to the lower level of the ruins by Antonio. The others remained on the jungle floor but we were still in sight of each other. Antonio reached into a bag he had with him and pulled out a very large quartz crystal. He instructed me to kneel down and as I gazed up at him he began to bring the crystal to my third eye. Within seconds he inadvertently dropped it and I was immediately in yet another realm. All of my senses were heightened; I could see clearly every detail of the jungle and Jim's face (which would not have been possible normally) but it was my hearing that was most evident to me. I heard the jaguars growling and roaring, heard their paws on the jungle floor, there were more of them spread out over the jungle and they were communicating with each other. I could smell everything in a deeper more succinct way, from the rotting vegetation, green foliage, moist earth, and the musky scent of animals. My instinct was to protect myself so I began moving backwards to be hidden behind a wall formed by the crumbling architecture. I viscerally felt that

I no longer had feet and hands of a human but padded soft 'paws' which protected my human hands from cuts from the broken stones and rubble I was leaning on. Looking outward, my vision was different as it was more like looking through tunnel vision lenses with great detail and less peripheral sight. I don't know how long I was in that state, listening to the howls and screams of the jaguars while seeing distinctive details of everything my gaze fell upon.

At some point, Antonio was working on me with that infamous crystal and chanting words over me, when Jim and the doctor got to me. I was back to being more of myself, no longer having the animal attributes. We descended the ruins and began walking back to the car using a different pathway back that did not go through the jungle. It was more open with visible sky and low grasses and some flowering plants. I remember thinking it was more like the more familiar fields I've walked through my whole life. I could feel my mind coming back to its normal state and I also felt the <u>undeniable</u> feeling of my internal blood of life flowing downwards through my body. My moon-time was not due for over two weeks but I had seemly been prematurely fast forwarded to it."[173]

Renewal of Vows Captain Lafitte's

Duty Calls

I was concerned about revisiting Muyil after Sher's shapeshifting experience within the jungle ruins. As we were once again staying at Shangri La – Captain Lafitte's, instead of returning to Muyil, I would have preferred to simply sit in the sand with Sher, watching the gentle wave action of the Caribbean Sea and gazing at the bluish-green sky above while drinking a Corona. But alas, this wasn't in the cards: duty called.

We hadn't told our students what happened to Sher as it was not necessary for them to know. On the way to the site and before it was dark we stopped at a little known sacred cave, a passage down into the Earth that contained a subterranean pool of water. This sacred virgin water, *zuhuy ha*, contained shamanic powers of transformation. Shamans have used these waters of prophecy and transformation for centuries to guide their people, and for ritual purity.

Crawling into the Earth was a unique experience. Only a few could go in at a time. Antonio went in first, next Sher, then me. Sitting next to a virgin pool (no sunlight has permeated these waters) took me back to a surreal existence of the ones before us who had used these sacred waters for healing and ceremony. As the three of us purified ourselves and then drank of these sacred waters, I realized that they were also utilized for transformation. But what type of transformation, I wondered? I contemplated the mythical knowledge that the Jaguar-god lives in caves, especially caves with pitch-black pools of water in the lower reaches – entrances to the realm of death and spiritual transformation. It made sense that I was torn between returning and not returning to Muyil. I wondered how Sher would react, being in the jungle again and revisiting the same ruined temple.

The Full Moon[174]

As we arrived at the site, the moonlit night reminded me of the myth of the werewolf. "Hopefully," I thought, "Sher doesn't revisit her feline experience." With the moonlight washing the jungle in an initial welcoming, it then shifted into a more threatening way the deeper we got in the jungle, and I realized, I was anxious. This was a feeling foreign to me. And why wouldn't I be so? This highlights why shamans-healers do not heal their own – it is difficult to stay neutral and unattached. I have a unique ability to be totally unattached in a state of immovable heart/mind (detached heart/mind, no chatter or mind-speak) in my work with others, but not my family. My love for Sher is not only this lifetime, but a soul-love of a previous life together. Of course, I was concerned, but then I let it go and trusted Sher and her powerful gifts. She has pierced the veil between realities and witnessed the otherworldly realms but she had never shapeshifted before this afternoon.

Bathed in the moonlight, the walk to the site was uneventful, even with the mystical-otherworldly atmosphere of our surroundings. With cascading light and shadows scattered throughout the jungle, I wondered how the night might play out. Previously, Antonio had told us he was going to take the group underneath one of the ruined pyramids to a hidden underground chamber. Even without Sher's strange and unique experience, I would have been worried that people might freak out in an underground, enclosed chamber.

Additionally, Ceiba trees, known as the "tree of life," were located through-out the site and were believed to be the connection to the underworld for the Maya. And we were going underground. Also, supposedly, *alux* (spirits) are thought to watch the trails.[175] According to myth, *alux* are the spirits of the Maya ancestors, or the spirits of the land itself. And we must not forget that the jaguar is linked with the full moon. A perfect storm seemed to be brewing, worthy of a horror movie, as myth could become reality.

Muyil is one of the earliest and longest-inhabited ancient Maya sites on the eastern coast of the Yucatan Peninsula. Artifacts found there date back from as early as 350 B.C.E. Since our time there in the early 90s, archeologists have discovered numerous subterranean chambers throughout Muyil.

And true to form, we were going into one of those unknown subterra-nean chambers. When we conduct this type of experiential foray we always ask the participants not to talk but to stay silent and attempt to keep their heart and mind strong and balanced. Arriving at the ruins, I could tell that people were anxious.

With the moon casting shadowed light, mystically revealing to us the entrance into the "underworld," we realized that the opening was a small space that required crawling, almost wiggling, through to reach the secret chamber. Antonio went first, and then my friend. Sher and I were going in last. Besides my concern about Sher's shapeshifting, one of our students was a large woman and I worried about her being able to fit through the opening. We didn't need a person to get stuck entering under the pyramid or be left outside alone when we were all together inside. Even though there were no guards, I didn't think the local Federales would take kindly to us doing what we were doing. And maybe they would think we were attempting to steal archeological treasures. We wouldn't be accused of grave robbing – or would we?

The moon goddess Ixchel, Lady of the Sacred Light, must have been blessing us, as our student made it thorough without a problem. Once settled within the pyramid's claustrophobic underground chamber, a very cave-like feeling, I could barely make out Sher sitting next to me. The darkness was all-pervasive save for the dim light of Antonio's candle. And at that moment, I remembered that caves, the underworld, and jaguars all intertwine. Jaguars were associated with night, tropical rainforest, caves, water and the interior of the Earth. It seemed that we had all five. We had drunk of sacred waters from the interior of the Earth, and now it was night. We had walked through the rainforest, and then entered through a passageway into a cave-like subterranean chamber. Once again, myth becoming reality.

Minutes passed. I couldn't see, but felt and sensed the change in Sher, she was beginning to transform. I waited until I could take it no longer. Foregoing Sher's instructions not to interfere, I reached out my hand to ground her with my energy. Wrong. Faster than any martial grandmaster could move, a clawed hand swept my hand away and I could hear the low, growling song of a feline. And I could feel the scratches she left behind.

Time slowed down but my interference must have worked as I sensed a lessening of her feline energy. As far as I knew, no one else knew what was happening to Sher and what had just happened to me. By the time we were ready to leave the chamber, Sher seemed to be herself once again. Antonio went out first, using his flashlight to guide the way. Sher and I are always the last to leave so that we can do our prayers of thanking and blessing the powers of this world and the Otherworld. So using my flashlight, I could determine if I was correct. And I was, the scratches were deep, very claw like, as she whispered to me, "why did you stop me; it was so incredible! I could see so clearly in the dark and hear everything in the jungle.... After hearing this, my last thought as I crawled out was, "Is this the end, or the beginning, of her shapeshifting?"

Sher's Account Returning to the Ruins

I will admit I had some trepidation returning to the ruins with our students later that afternoon, especially knowing that we would be at the same site well after dark. But as committed spiritual teachers we have an obligation to our students and the work we do to be present and allow others their own experiences and opportunities at the sacred sites we invite them to. If I felt I would be a distraction or was unable to be there with everyone, I would not have gone back to the ruins. We also had not shared with them about my earlier experience there. Up until we entered the subterranean chamber I felt like myself and I also knew that those personal kinds of experiences can occur without any further repercussions or behavior changes on my part. I could possibly re-walk that jungle path and not have anything out of the ordinary happen. But, once inside the cave like area dimly lit by the candle, my earlier experience of shapeshifting began again with my hearing the jaguars running and crying in the jungle.

Since it was evening by now I thought there was a possibility that there really were present day cats out there, in spite of being told the very sad fact that much of the jaguar population had been decimated by being killed, hunted out, or driven from their native territory by humans. It would be rare to see one in their natural habitat. So when I heard the jaguars, it was not long after that I realized I was once again able to hear, see, and smell beyond any human capacities. I felt my body begin to withdraw into a more slumped posture, my breathing sped up and then I felt my hands change into the curled semi-fist of a heavy paw again. A low growl was building in my chest and throat, somewhat like a purring in a domestic cat but a more forceful chuffing throat sound. This second time I wasn't quite as taken off guard. I was more aware and curious what I could do in this alternative state. I liked it more than feared it. Nobody knew what was happening unless they heard that sound I was making. Plus I could see all of them but they couldn't see me. I remember really wanting to run out of the chamber and go run through the jungle with all the others. As I was contemplating that, I was suddenly pulled out of this revelry by a hand on my leg. It was Jim, who sensed something was going on, and wanted to ground me. It was sheerly a reaction, not a conscious thought on my part, that I struck out with my "paw" and ripped his arm with my claws. I broke skin and left deep scratches. He realized I was not just "me" again and jostled me to bring me back into myself. I felt a sense of disappointment and anger that he broke that rare human experience of shapeshifting that I was having. I recollected looking around at all the people that were surrounding me that I had no ill intent towards humans to hurt them. Only Jim who interrupted my experience, and I only gave him a quick swipe!

After we had returned to our home, I tried to reenact the speed of that paw swipe and it was virtually impossible to replicate.

Within a few years of that initial shapeshifting, I had one other, publicly witnessed by our students. It occurred in daylight during one of our trainings—a Death Spiral experience. Again, for me, it was totally spontaneous. And for many months after, I would go out to the ocean in an isolated area and cry the sounds of the jaguar as best I could as a human….

PART IV

. . . .

The Second of Four Major Otherworldly Experiences over a Span of Ten Years

While some managed to maintain an uneasy alliance with the religious authorities of their day, most mystics were vilified and horribly persecuted for claiming direct personal knowledge of a God whom the religious establishment wished to make accessible only via their hierarchy of priests and theologians. Yet the natural experience of spiritual awakening that lies at the heart of mysticism is the birthplace of all religions, and they find their common ground in this common source. Mystical experiences inspired the founders and reformers of religion as well as its greatest heretics – indeed, they have often been the same people. The history of mysticism is the history of their revelations.[176]

PARADISE: VISION AND A VOICE
FROM HEAVEN

. . . .

Ho'opuka e-ka-la ma ka hikina.
Make a hole in sunlight and find the light behind the light.
Like the sunrise come and dawn on me.

OUR COLLECTIVE LOSS OF THE GOLDEN AGE IS NOT STRICTLY
philosophical musing but is based on the sad truth of the systematic replacement of egalitarianism with social, economic, political and religious elitist
paradigms and domination structures of institutional hierarchy.

The good news is that Lost Eden is foretold to return not only metaphorically but in reality, as it lurks right below the surface of our dualistic consciousness. In preparation for Eden's return, you may ask yourself, what was earthly
paradise like? How did it look? How did it smell and feel? I can give you a clue
because Sher and I experienced it for the first time in the summer of 1988.
Even though it is hidden from our mundane senses, it is still right below the
surface of our normal reality. I could sense it. But most importantly, I could
feel it.

After I faced death on the Royal Inka Trail into Machu Picchu and an
initiation in a sacred lagoon located on the Markawasi Plateau in the Andes,
Sher and I journeyed across the seas and discovered paradise – an island called
Kauai. As I said above, we were never banished from the garden. The garden
is still here but lost to most people's consciousness.

Departing from the furthest state on the mainland, Maine, our arrival on Kauai was like a dream come true. As we stepped off the plane in Lihue, our senses were overwhelmed with the fragrant beauty of the island, as if our souls were being bathed in rainbows. Of course, as magical as it was, the materialistic spirit was still present. But below the surface on the edge of our consciousness, and interspersed with the mundane, was the loving essence of the Hawaiian Islands – the *aloha* spirit.

Alo means "in the presence of" or "to be with" and *ha* is "the breath of life." To the Hawaiians breath symbolizes life as well as the essence of life – the divine. *Aloha* is used not only on meeting or greeting a person but also on departing. It is the honoring of the presence of the divine in each person.

Aloha spirit is the spirit of oneness and the love that is the breath of the soul. It is a loving state of mind where hate has no resting place. To the Hawaiians, aloha represents love. All of life is founded on this love, the love of the sea, the love of the sky and the love of the āina (land), and all its inhabitants – especially *aloha 'āina* (love of the land), which is a powerful core value for the native Hawaiians.

Ha is the secret key within aloha. It is the breath that we all share. It is the life-force and consciousness that connects us all. It carries our words, words that may create or destroy throughout the world. To the wise ones of old, words were no less powerful than deeds.

Breath is life, a life that is pure. But the loving breath that enters us may leave our bodies tainted and shallow with various materialistic thoughts that decay and separate people from the essence of the land and sea. And this was the case on Kauai in 1988. Even though paradise hovered just below the surface, it was still overshadowed by the materialistic spirit of capitalism.

Over the years as we returned over and over again, not only to Kauai but to the other Hawaiian Islands, we felt and saw the widening grip of progress and development as paradise slowly slid away. But to Sher and me, those islands will always be paradise.

As we drove from the south side of the island to the North Shore, we were bedazzled by the sheer beauty and awesomeness of the land, the ocean and the sky. We had chosen Kauai as our first island to visit not only due to the majesty of the Napli Coast, known to the islanders as Bali Hai, but also because of long held desire to study the lore of the *kahuna* – the magician shamans of these Hawaiian Islands. This was a desire that had its origins in my childhood.

Even though I had experienced a descending spirit exorcism on the sacred mountain Kōyasan and had faced death, survived, and been initiated in a sacred lagoon high up in the Andes, I was still seeking knowledge and power.

The Hawaiian Holy Grail

Another form of the Holy Grail is the Hawaiian "bowl of light." It is a landmark; a symbol of the way back home – back to our oneness of being. According to native Hawaiians, "each child born has at birth, a Bowl of perfect Light. If he tends his Light it will grow in strength and he can do all things – swim with the shark, fly with the birds, know and understand all things. If, however, he becomes envious or jealous he drops a stone into his Bowl of Light and some of the Light goes out. Light and the stone cannot hold the same space. If he continues to put stones in the Bowl of Light, the Light will go out and he will become a stone. A stone does not grow,[177] nor does it move. If at any time he tires of being a stone, all he needs to do is turn the bowl upside down and the stones will fall away and the Light will grow once more."[178]

We believe in the Hawaiian *aloha* spirit that lives within the *ʻāina* (the land and its spirit), the people, the sky and the sea. This is a state of mind of love and harmony, the same state of mind of Divine Humanity. For reasons unknown, when I was nine or ten, I bought a *kiʻi*[179] necklace[180] while on a family vacation to Florida. We had not been studying Hawaiian culture in school. In fact, I didn't even know that it was Hawaiian. But I was drawn to it and wanted to wear it.

Sher, Hauola Stone, Lahaina, Maui, 1989. Hauola Stone is a large stone in the shape of a low-backed chair believed to have healing powers as it sits in Lahaina harbor where both fresh and salt water mix, such waters are known for their healing power.

Little did I realize or suspect that more than thirty years later, I would be walking through the Lahaina Mall on Maui and meet a native Hawaiian carver named Jonathan. Through our discussions, Jonathan came to know me and understand that I was not your typical *haole* (refers to a Caucasian, '*ole* = lack; *hā* = breath). Of course, the discussion focused on the spiritual aspects of his people, ancestors, and his wooden carvings.

I had come to the mall to find a proper carving of the gods of the Hawaiians other than the ones that a tourist can buy in many of the stores that sell souvenirs. I asked Jonathan if I could commission him to do a carving for me. Jonathan could sense my *mana* (spirit or sacred power) and *aloha* spirit within my heart and agreed to carve a special *ki'i* for me. This was not a lightly made agreement. The carving I asked him to do was the *ki'i* (sacred carving) of the *akua Kū*.[181]

Akua (god/goddess/supernatural spirit) are the impersonal deities of the Hawaiian people. They may also be a Hawaiian's *aumākua*, or guardian spirit. The *akua* exhibit not only divine traits and supernatural qualities, but much like Greek mythology, the Hawaiians' gods and goddesses express human frailties. The four major akua are *Kāne, Lono, Kū* and *Kanaloa*. The *akua* can also take different material forms such as an owl, shark, stone, a fireball, or even an old woman, which is the form sometimes taken by *Pele*, the volcano goddess. This ability is referred to as *kino lau* or changed forms. As one of the four major gods, *Kū* is most recognizable as the war god. *Kū* energy is extremely strong and is not to be fooled with or taken lightly.

My meeting with Jonathan was prophetic, predating the happenings on the Big Island in the fall of 1993. Keep in mind that to the Polynesians who pre-dated the Hawaiian culture, *Kū* was recognized as the morning star. A year after I met Jonathan, we returned to Maui to do more spiritual work. He was glad to see me but apologized that he hadn't begun my carving because he had a lot of requests for his beautiful wooden bowls. I told him it wasn't a problem and to take his time, even though I was anxious to have the *Kū* carving finished. And why not? It was being carved by a native Hawaiian whose bowls were sought after and who carried the old ways and had great *mana*. I said that we would be going to Mexico the following year but would return in two years.

Our trips have always been tough to explain. When acquaintances would ask how our vacation was after we returned from Hawaii, Mexico or some other exotic place, their impression might be of luaus, sipping piña coladas, or drinking Coronas on a beach. Even though I did drink Coronas, in reality, our far travels were more like scripts from Indiana Jones movies featuring crawling into underground chambers of hidden Maya Temples in the Yucatan jungle or standing pre-dawn in the Hawaiian surf learning a chant to welcome the sun. And then, as if in a dream, suddenly having to leave the surf when the *kupuna* (elder) who was teaching us saw bubbles that indicated a shark. Of course, it was no coincidence that there was a shark nearby. Our daughter Jess was with us learning the chant as well. You may have guessed it. Her 'aumākua is shark.

Two years later when we returned to Maui the carving was still not done. Trusting Jonathan, I assured him that it was not a problem, but after three years I was getting concerned. I need not have worried. Jonathan contacted me and said that *Kū* was finally completed.

When we went to Jonathan's home to pick up *Kū*, he told us the reason why it had taken him so long. The energy is so strong that he had to be in the proper frame of mind, with proper prayers to carve. It was so demanding that he vowed never to carve another *Kū*. Feeling bad that it had taken him so long, he charged us very little and included one of his beautiful wooden bowls, a Hawaiian Grail, which we still cherish to this day, along with, of course, *Kū*.

In respect to *Kū*, Jonathan's carving was beautiful and striking with flaring nostrils, I wrapped him in a proper blanket and carried him aboard our flight back to the mainland. With the carving cradled in my arms, one woman approached us to look at our baby. She was shocked to say the least. Once again I smiled to myself, knowing that in many ways we were strangers in a strange land.

Island of Hawaii (Big Island) October 1993: An Otherworldly Mystical Experience

I am the Morning Star. Like many of the prophets of the past, I experienced the divine call as something heard and as something seen – in the form of a vision and a voice. I do not come from an established priesthood or hierarchy but I, as well as my wife, have had passed to us the lineages and traditions of various indigenous shamanic, spiritual and religious practices from around the world.

An island of fire and ice, where land and sea meet in one of the world's most epic scenes of creation and destruction, home to two of the world's greatest mountains and one of the world's most active volcanoes, this is the Big Island of Hawaii. And this was where my vision occurred in October of 1993.

My wife, Sherry, myself, and a native Hawaiian healer friend were leading a group of our students to various sacred sites to experience the spiritual knowledge of the Hawaiians and the magic and power of the land and the sea. This was not the first time or the first group that we had brought to the Big Island. But this time we wanted to honor the land and the Hawaiian ancestors by conducting a very sacred ceremony called a burning or feeding the spirits. Mom and Vince Stogan, Coast Salish British Columbia elders and shamans, passed on to us the power and authority to conduct this ceremonial work after an intense apprenticeship.

A burning is a timeless ceremony that actually involves cooking food and then burning the food so that the substance and energy of it is taken into the Otherworld. This type of ceremony honoring the gods, goddesses, and ancestors with a burnt offering is age-old in form and can be traced as far back as the ancient Egyptians. In fact, our friend told us that a burning was part of the Hawaiian spiritual tradition of centuries past, but was a lost ceremonial art.

In October of 1993, I had arrived early on the Big Island, two days ahead of my son, Jamie, and five days ahead of Sherry, our daughter Jessie, and our students. We had first been drawn to this island of fire and water the previous year, after having spent much time on the rainbow isle (Maui) and the valley isle (Kauai). Each island of Hawaii is different, energetically and emotionally. Some say that each isle is linked to a *chakra* – a name used for an energy vortex in the body.

Once again, I felt that I had returned home. These islands have always felt as if they were a part of my essence: fire, water and wind, all elements that make my heart smile. It is a land that I love; a paradise permeated with beauty, mystery and power.

As I breathed deeply of the salt air, I was ecstatic that I had returned to the islands of Hawaii and especially to the Big Island, the isle of the volcano goddess, Madame or *Tutu Pele*. I've always felt a close connection with *Pele*, her power and energy. It is the power of destruction, but yet again, the power of creation – of new growth. It is the power that each of us has within us but usually deny. Hers is the anger that may destroy. On the other hand, it is the anger that may right the wrongs of the world; an anger that is needed more than ever before in today's unjust world.

Shortly after I arrived, I'd conducted what these islanders call *ho'okupu*. This is a ritual of gifting and honoring. I included prayers honoring the land, the people, the *'aumākua* and the *akua*. I asked for permission to do my spirit work, and for guidance and protection for myself, my family, the seekers and my friend. My gifting was a flower. *Ho'okupu* means "to cause growth" as well as "ceremonial gift-giving." The gift can be a flower (something organic) or as simple as a prayer with the intent of giving something unconditionally back to the land and to the unseen and seen sacred ones.

Arriving early meant that I would be able to spend some time with my friend, Kimo,[182] who was also the keeper of the sacred healing pools. We had experienced many adventures together the preceding year. Kimo and my wife and I had taken a group of seekers to witness the volcano goddess giving birth (erupting) the previous November. It was a moment that words could never really describe. To be able to witness the power of the creation of new earth as it merged with the sea is a memory that will stay with us and impact us for the totality of our existence.

I had met Kimo for the first time in August of that year, and it was an experience all its own.

Kimo – The Big Island, Late August 1992

As this was our first time on the Big Island, Sher and I were amazed at the fields of hardened lava by the Kona airport so visually and energetically different from Oahu, Kauai and Maui. We were staying at a funky place over-looking the ocean that was simple but awesome in that it was one with nature. The first morning, we were awakened by the crowing of roosters welcoming the dawn of a new day, a day in paradise. A paradise stuffed full of sensory delights: the sparkling ocean in the distance; the lush green ferns; tropical flowers; sun; a warm breeze; and the never-ending sound of birds. All this and more fed our spirit and soul.

The proprietor knew Kimo, a native Hawaiian and healer, and had put us in touch with him. He'd had agreed to guide us around the island. The next morning, he would pick us up at dawn and we would visit *Tutu Pele*.

The best way to describe Kimo is laid back – a walking personification of the commonly used expression, "hang loose" or "*shaka*." Kimo is relaxed most of the time. True to form, he drives slowly, which angers other drivers to the point that when they can pass, they flip him the finger, but Kimo just returns a hand gesture that means hang loose. On our drive to Volcanoes National Park, he explained the concept of hang loose.

"We Hawaiians use our hands a lot to express ourselves. Hang loose means more than just relax or love. It also means our connection between heaven and Earth, the connection of male and female, the aspect of unconditional love for all."

By midmorning, we approached the entrance to the national park. Kimo explained that it's always a struggle for native Hawaiians to enter without paying the entrance fee.

"This is our church, all of this area, and *Pele* is one of our goddesses. You don't pay to go to church to say your prayers to leave an offering. But the government *haoles*,[183] and even some of my people that work for the government, have a hard time seeing this reality. Most of the time they make it very difficult and hassle us."

With his passion building, Kimo continues. "But brah, no one stops me from my birthright and my spiritual and family practice."

"We understand," I said. "People are stupid and ignorant concerning natural law,[184] which sometimes trumps human laws. You have the natural-law right to practice your religion without obeying the human made law of a fee to enter what in reality is your church."

As we slowdown the Hawaiian manning the booth recognizes Kimo and waves us on. "Brah, it's not always this easy. I'm happy, no hassles. Welcome to *Tutu Pele's* home. First though, before I show you around, we need to do *ho'okupu.*"

Big Island Group Journey, November 1992

Our quest to witness the fiery lava entering the ocean, as a gift to our journey participants, was not an easy one. The day we were scheduled to go to witness the eruption a tropical storm had swept over the Big Island with torrential rains that caused certain roads leading to Volcanoes National Park to flood.

Kimo decided the best strategy was to leave at 2 a.m., which would get us to the spot where the lava was flowing into the ocean before dawn.

"It's an awesome sight to see the flow in the dark," he said. "It allows us to experience what my ancestors felt living on these islands." He paused before saying, "The only problem is, the roads may still be flooded!"

"That's a chance we'll have to take," I replied before leaving to break the news to our group.

A little after 2 a.m. and it was still raining, but not as hard. Kimo, Sherry and I were in the lead car with Kimo driving and our van of students following. The road was narrow, twisting and rain slick. Darkness surrounded our small caravan of adventurers as we traveled through a landscape that could be from another dimension and time.

As we approached a bridge, Kimo smiled and said, "We made it over the one bridge I was worried about. No problem now. We have about another thirty minutes and we'll make it before first light."

The next thirty minutes could have been thirty seconds or thirty hours. Time seemed to have no meaning. As we crossed a rise in the road I saw a faint glow of red in the distance. Was it the dawn or the volcano?

"Jim and Sherry, you're going to see a wondrous sight in a few minutes that few people alive today have seen!"

Kimo was right. In the next few minutes we crossed another rise in the road and there in front of us was *Tutu Pele* in all her glory creating earth with fire while surrendering to the power of Grandmother Ocean: the blending of fire and water.

The sky had a reddish glow, a glow that would welcome the dawn. The scene was hard to describe in words: the colors of red, orange, and yellow all surrounded by the blue-blacks of the ending night. We were witnessing an ultimate act of creation and the primal power of the elements. As we parked our caravan by the barriers that mark the limit of vehicle access to the lava flow, the quiet was broken only by the occasional gust of wind. The quiet paid tribute to the sacredness of the moment and the sacredness of the new-born earth! I felt enigmatic, as if I'd been thrust into the womb of creation. With a vortex of emotions—love, fear, and others indescribable—all surging through me, I approached the actual lava, still hot, still in its infancy. Sherry, standing beside me, reverently bent down to touch the cooling lava. Moved to tears, she looked up at me and said, "This is baby earth."

The blue-blacks of early morning had given way to first light. In the dawn of a new day a circle of blue sky appeared over us while all else was still enveloped in a swirling dark mass of storm clouds.

Where we were standing, the sky had opened up in a circle honoring us with the blueness of heaven. At that same moment, twin rainbows appeared acclaiming our connection to heaven and Earth and acknowledging the love and power of our journey.

Big Island, October 1993

I was brought back into the present moment by Kimo's arrival at the Kona Airport with his typical greeting, "Eh, howzit, brah?"

Before my son arrived, my friend and I traded stories and teachings while spending the majority of our time at the place known as the City of Refuge. Its formal name is *Pu'uhonua o Hōnaunau*. At the City of Refuge, a person would be given a second-chance at life. This place of forgiveness is located on the ocean and contains the healing pools that are part of my friend's spiritual medicine. The power of the ocean and its salt water are a continuous source of healing medicine for these islanders.

The day my son was scheduled to arrive in the early evening at the Kona Airport, after leaving Kimo at the City of Refuge, I drove into *Kailua-Kona* to purchase a lei, the traditional flower greeting honoring the *Aloha* spirit and a person's arrival on the islands.

Sher, Sea Turtle, Kailua-Kona

As I waited, enjoying the open-to-nature quality of the airport, I remembered that in the near future the Iron-Man Triathlon would be held nearby. My mind was triggered by the numerous athletic men and women departing Jamie's flight.

"*Aloha*," I said as I placed the lei around Jamie's neck and hugged him. "How was your flight?"

"Long, but interesting; everyone I talked to assumed I was coming for the Iron Man," replied Jamie. "If they only knew."

Before we went to my friend's home to spend the night, we drove into *Kailua-Kona* to get something to eat. Let me explain about my friend's old Hawaiian-style home. His place was not a single building but several small ones, with a separate structure for cooking and meals, and separate buildings for his mother-in-law, for him and his wife, and so forth. When we arrived it was late at night, so no one was around. We found one small structure that must have been an exercise/storage shelter, given the free weights and the blue mats on the floor. We just looked at each other with that expression of "what the fuck" as I said in a soft voice, "welcome to Hawaii."

The little sleep we got ended with our startling wake-up call – a crowing rooster. This was shortly followed by an angry curse-filled voice. I looked out of our respite for the night to find an elderly woman spraying a rooster with a garden hose, telling him to get away from the hens. Jamie just looked at me and said, "Dad, are you kidding me?"

Fishing Village

After meeting Kimo's mother-in-law ("the rooster cleanser"), the three of us began an adventure before the arrival of the rest of our group. Our first destination was a white sand beach. Then we were to head to an ancient, no longer populated fishing village.

Stress is a silent killer in our society. People do not know how to relax. So my friend was going to show us a method of stress reduction, an old-time healing method using the heat of the sand as well as energy and body work.

When we arrived at the beach, the white sand had been bathed in the sun's fiery embrace for hours. It was one of those beautiful days that draw people to these islands, a splendor that lovingly vibrates to the depths of one's soul.

And then I made a mistake. I took off my flip-flops. This made walking barefoot across the sand comparable to walking on hot coals. Trying to look unfazed and macho, my first few steps were tolerable, but then my walk turned into a hopping chaotic dance of survival, a sight that brought mild laughter from a few locals. Grateful that our destination was in the shade, I increased my hopping stride towards the beckoning oasis of coolness. Thankful for the cool sand, I was happy that I survived my walk through the caldron of heat without making too much of a fool out of myself.

Settled in the shade, we spent time looking, listening and mimicking my friend's actions and knowledge. This is one of the key philosophies of the *kahuna*. *Nānā ka maka, ho'olohe, pa'a ka waha, ho'opili*: observe, listen, keep mouth shut, and mimic, mimic, mimic. After a few hours, including time in the surf, we headed for the fishing village.

Calling it a fishing village does not really reveal its true identity. Yes, the village sustained itself through fishing, but its primary purpose was as a gathering place for practitioners, students and teachers of the healing arts. It dated back some 600 years to when magic was a way of life. The village was deserted, with only the sound of the wind and the surf to break the silence. I could smell the ancientness of this sacred space and sense the energy that vibrated around me as ever-present *Kāne*, the sun, warmed us with its hot embrace. *Kāne*, the procreator, the provider of sunlight, fresh water, and the life substances in nature, was one of the four major deities of the islands. The others were: *Lono, Kū*, and *Kanaloa*.

As we walked the pathways that crisscrossed the ancient village, I could feel the power, the great *mana*,[185] of the site. Soon we arrived at a ledge that overlooked the ocean, which the Hawaiians refer to as grandmother.

"Here, brah, good spot to meditate, to pray," Kimo said as we took a seat on the rocky ledge.

Time passed; images came and went in my mind as the veil between the worlds became thinner and thinner. After a period of time, I was back in the present hearing the surf and feeling the hot breath of *Kāne*,[186] on the side of my face. As my eyes opened slowly, adjusting themselves to the light and to this reality, a sense of peace and happiness settled on me as if a mantle of *lehua*[187] blossoms were a part of my soul.

A few minutes passed in silence as the wind gently rocked us. "Pretty awesome, eh?" said Kimo, who was sitting on my right a few feet away.

"It sure is," replied Jamie, who was sitting on my left. "I could live here with no problem."

A few minutes passed in silence until I turned to Kimo and said, "There is something I need to ask you."

"*Kay den,* brah."

"There is a ceremony that I would like to perform for these islands and your ancestors. It's called a burning. It's an honoring and blessing to the land, the sea and your people. It's also called feeding the spirits – the ancestors,[188] the ones that have passed-over, the unknown, forgotten ones."

"You do this for my people?"

"Of course. I'd be privileged to," I replied. "However, there is one condition."

"A condition?"

"Yes, once the day of the burning is determined, it cannot be changed, no matter what happens—earthquakes, eruptions—the burning must be done."

"No problem, Jim."

"Good. Then Saturday, we'll do the burning."

As I explained the burning in detail, a bat flew towards us, circled around us and disappeared. This was in bright sunshine, at a time of day when bats usually do not appear. Our Hawaiian friend was amazed and excited by the appearance of the bat and said, "Brah, this is a great sign. Nothing will stand in our way. We will be able to flow around any obstacles, physical or otherwise just like a bat does!" Time would reveal that this was just the beginning of the magic destined to happen.

The Flying Meatloaf

After this special appearance by the bat, we bid farewell to the village and drove to our last stop of the day. We were headed to the windswept northern tip of the island. Our destination was one of the oldest and most sacred *heiaus, Mo'okini Heiau,* one of the first sacrificial temples, *luakini heiau,* of these isles. Even though it had been built as a temple honoring *Io,* the creator god of these islands, it had been changed to one that worshipped *Kunuiakea,* Great-Ku-of-the-Heavenly-Expanse – the war god. Human sacrifice had been practiced there.

Because the temple was only a short distance from fishing village, it wasn't long before we turned *makai* direction (towards the ocean) onto a one-lane, pot-hole-filled dirt road headed towards Upolu Airport. Basically, the road ended at the so-called airport. "Where are the planes," I thought. I marveled at the expansive beauty of the never-ending ocean merging into the heavens above. We turned left on a dirt path parallel to the Ocean on our right. The *heiau* was isolated and difficult to reach.

As we parked our car by the ocean cliffs, I could sense an ominous and eerie atmosphere. Have you ever been somewhere that was stark, primitive, ancient, and scary? Well, we were in that place as we walked up the hill towards the ruined temple. Even though it was not yet dusk, a dark and foreboding feeling enveloped us as we neared the ruins.

"I wanted to bring you here last year, Jim. Your wife saw a dead *pueo*, our native Hawaiian owl, lying on the side of the road in the Puna district of this island. You and Sherry had me turn my car around to get it."

"*Pueo* are special to me," I replied.

"I know, brah.[189] The *pueo* is also special *'aumakua* to the *kahuna* that cares for this *heiau*. You may be connected to this temple. But we need to be careful."

"*Mo'okini Heiau* is a temple where people were sacrificed to the old gods. It is one of the most significant historic sites in all Hawaii . . . and one of the most sacred. *Mo'okini* helped the *kahuna* (priests) and *ali'i* (chiefs) communicate with their *'aumakua* (deified ancestors) and their *akua* (gods) . . . and consolidate power. In older times, entrance was *kapu* . . . forbidden to ordinary people . . . to living people that is.

"*Luakini heiau* were dedicated to the god *Ku* for political advantages and warfare. Offerings were presented at the *luakini* to prevent hungry spirits from becoming vampire-like, or leaving. The human sacrifices were often criminals, *kapu*-breakers, enemies or slaves – with a preference for healthy young men.

"According to a *Mo'okini* family chant, this *heiau* was built under the direction of *Kuamo'o Mo'okini* around 480 A.D. and was dedicated to the god *Ku*. This *heiau* was rededicated by *Pa'ao*, a *kahuna*-chief from Samoa, whose arrival (or invasion) of Hawaii in about 1,000 A.D. commenced the *kapu* system used by Hawaiian chiefs until 1819. (In 1819 the old Hawaiian ways were abandoned following the disruption and disease precipitated by Captain Cook's 'discovery' of Hawaii.)"[190]

The temple had long been deserted, but that didn't mean that it was uninhabited. "The old stones bear silent testimony to ancient power. Traditions say that the stones for the *heiau* were carried from Pololu Valley, about fourteen miles (twenty-two kilometers) away, by a living chain of men in only one night."[191] Stones hold memories and destructive spirits may still linger in the inner recesses of such temple ruins. Caution, respect and common sense are important when approaching a *heiau*. And the proper prayers and offerings are not only necessary, but essential. Stones are never to be taken from a temple, not only out of respect, but because they may carry memories or vibrations that could adversely affect a human's heart and mind.

Since it was late afternoon we needed to be extra cautious, as that's the time the spirits begin to awaken. As we approached the *heiau*, I knew that my friend was doing prayers. No words were spoken as the three of us entered the ruins. Time suspended. I had an uneasy feeling about this sacred area that had witnessed the sacrifice of humans to feed the war god, the same feeling I've had a few times before. Once during the summer of 1981, I had a similar feeling in Glastonbury, England, when Sherry and I had an encounter with a ghost called the spirit monk.

After spending time in prayer we left the inner ruins of the *heiau*. As soon as we had left my uneasy feeling returned. I felt that we were being watched by unseen eyes. On the way back to our vehicle, I kept looking over my shoulder, expecting to see something or someone at any time.

Once back in the car, I said, "Definitely not a place to be after dark."

"No brah, you wouldn't want to be here at dark. Some of my people won't even whistle at night because it can call the spirits."

"Dad, that was intense," Jamie said.

"Brah! Did you see my 'ōkala-chicken-skin?"[192]

"Mine too," I said. But I had a feeling this was not the end of it.

"Getting late," Kimo said. "We've got to get to the other side of the island."

"Is there any place close by to get something to eat," I asked. "We haven't had anything to eat since early morning."

"There aren't many places to eat at this end of the island, but there's a small town called Hawi not far from here. We can try there," Kimo replied.

Indeed, it was a very small village. After driving up and down the street twice, we finally found a place where a traveler might find some food and drink, limited though it was. We each settled on really the only choice, a piece of meatloaf squeezed between two slabs of bread. The whole time we waited for our sandwiches, I still had an unsettling feeling that we were not alone.

I sat in the back seat of my friend's car and Jamie sat in the front with the sandwiches. As Kimo pulled out of the parking space, Jamie started to pass my meatloaf sandwich back, but instead, it flew out of his hand and landed on the seat next to me.

"Eh, brah, you see that?" Kimo shouted as he slammed the vehicle to a stop. "Something not right. That thing flew through the air."

"Dad, it just jumped out of my hand. I'm sorry."

"No need to be sorry. It wasn't your fault."

As I picked up the meatloaf and put it back between the slabs of bread I wondered about what had just happened. Was it an illusion that it had flown out of Jamie's hand? Or were we not alone? Something didn't feel right. We had just left one of the most notorious sacrificial *heiaus* that was home to a large slab of lava rock called "the *holehole* stone, where the baked bodies of sacrificed victims were laid and the flesh was stripped from their bones."[193] A human sacrifice to feed the spirits was a corruption of the original form of the ceremony that my wife and I were going to conduct in a few days at *Pu'uhonua o Honaunau*.

I thought about the implications if we were being followed by a spirit. I knew the sacred words and hand movements of power. An esoteric priest had taught me these things, a secret *mudra*, a magical finger intertwining, and a *mantra* or spirit shout that would dispel unwanted spirits. But I also believe there is great truth in the philosophy of discretion being the better part of valor.

We took off, once again headed for my friend's house outside of Hilo on the east side of the island. I had just finished eating half of my meatloaf bread, when my friend slowed the vehicle, pulled off the road and said, "I want to show you both a beautiful view of the sea and of *Waipi'o* Valley – a very sacred valley to my people. This is a good lookout place."

I could see this was indeed an awesome place to stop and feel the spirit and love of *'āina* – nature. Kimo and Jamie jumped out and walked towards the edge of the cliff. I got out, still clutching my meatloaf bread, and followed. They both turned in my direction, as if to say something to me, when all of a sudden the meatloaf and the bread flew out of my hand and landed on the ground as if it had been snatched from me.

"Ho, brah!"

"Dad, this is too weird."

My friend, looking a little pale said, "Man, leave it on the ground. I had a feeling that an *'uhane*[194] followed us from the *heiau*. Time to go."

As I looked at the meatloaf lying on the ground I hoped leaving it would satisfy the spirit and I wouldn't have to deal with it. Then, as I got back into the car I realized that once a date is set for the burning, the spirits begin gathering. This is the reason why a burning cannot be postponed. If the feeding is not done, the spirits will get very, shall we say, unruly. I guess this one was really hungry and knew I had the power to feed it.

Pu'uhonua o Honaunau

As compared to the previous ones, an uneventful day passed before we returned to the west side and *Kailua-Kona*, where my friend was determined to ask his cousin at *Pu'uhonua o Honaunau*, the City of Refuge, about conducting the burning. The City of Refuge is walled but the land outside of the walls is still considered part of the Refuge, and sacred. It was there, by the ocean, that I planned to conduct the ceremony, not within the confines of the walls.

Pu'uhonua o Honaunau, a place of sanctuary, peace and beauty, was situated on the volcanic coast south of *Kailua-Kona*. This sanctuary was originally a sacred place that provided people with a second chance – a true place of forgiveness. It was here that people who broke a *kapu* or sacred law, would flee for refuge. If they could reach the sanctuary, their life would be spared and all forgiven. This was and still is sacred ground where life can begin anew; a perfect place to honor and feed the ancestors and the spirits.

I was no stranger to this most sacred of sites. The city, the lands, and the ocean surrounding them spoke to me of a time lost in memory. Standing on the volcanic shore with the beauty of the ocean before me, I tapped into the awesome power of the elements in their virgin nature, a feeling that words cannot properly portray; only through the actual experience can you ever hope to pierce the veil that encompasses the mysteries of heaven and Earth. In other words, this sacred piece of paradise was a perfect place for the burning.

I was sitting outside the City of Refuge under a palm tree playing my *'ohe hano ihu*—my bamboo nose flute—waiting for my friend to return from asking the park ranger's permission. *'Ohe* is the name for bamboo, *hano* refers to the sound that indicates life, and *ihu*, of course, means nose. But most importantly, nose represents the source from which the breath of life comes. The flute was never played by mouth, as the mouth was impure and defiled by speech, which could give life or give death. Furthermore, the nose flute symbolized life as bamboo. *'Ohe* was the *kinolau* (other life form) of *Lono*, the *akua* who symbolizes life, harvest, fertility, and peace.

This land and the City of Refuge were protected by the mainland authorities and were designated as an historical park by the National Park Service. After I finished playing my flute, my mind traveled back to August of the preceding year when just Sherry and I were here to study and explore, and once again in the fall when we had brought a group to experience the lore and magic of the Big Island. In August, we had found the dead *pueo* and I had learned how to make and play the nose flute from a native Hawaiian named Kia. He had taught me in the old way. Before I could begin the making/teaching process, I had to agree to three things:

- I had to be able to make music on it before I left with it; if not he would burn the bamboo flute.

- I had to never put it away and play it regularly.

- Last, I had to share the music with others.

His departing words were, "*A hui hou,*" until we meet again. And then I remembered Auntie Margaret, who reminded me of my grandmother. Auntie Margaret Machado was the only authentic Hawaiian *kupuna* licensed by the state of Hawaii to train therapists in *Lomilomi.* She was one of the few people who got away with calling me Jimmy. I chuckled to myself as I recalled her strong hands as she poked my jaw at the hinge point.

"That hurt," I said, wincing in pain.

"Of course, Jimmy," she replied. "You're holding your stress there."

As soon as I finished these thoughts, I saw Kimo coming back. I stood to find out the ranger's answer.

"No can do, brah. You were right. My cousin said that all fires must be contained, and also you need to apply for a permit."

"Did you tell him that it's a religious ceremony and that it requires an open fire?"

"Yeah, brah, but it make no difference. We have to follow the rules of the National Park Service."

He went on to tell me that the rules applied not only within the city walls but outside the walls as well. After considering the circumstances we were facing, I knew what we had to do. In my estimation, what I call natural law supersedes human rules and regulations. Taking a lesson from the bat we had seen, I decided we would perform the ceremony further down the beach, but still on the sacred land of the City of Refuge.

Feeding the Spirits

A burning is always scheduled at dusk and requires a great deal of preparation. The correct food and drink, according to tradition, must be bought and cooked properly. It's important to feed the correct food to the spirits. There are certain foods that are *kapu,* or in mainland language, taboo.

For this burning, Sherry cooked and prepared the food for the various spirit groups that we were to feed, such as the ancestors and the forgotten ones. The foods presented needed to be appropriate for the culture, so Sher prepared island foods, including taro, sweet potato, *ulu* (breadfruit), and a white and red fish.

In addition to the food and plates, a "table" for the plates had to be built in a proper manner, my responsibility while Sherry was cooking. This most ancient of ceremonies allowed no deviations. Burnings are very stressful and are not something we look forward to conducting. But we still do it, without payment, of course, for the greater well-being of the Earth and humanity.

With the gentle ocean behind me and the winds quietly caressing my soul, I began to build the offering table. During this primary stage of the ceremony I could feel the spirits gathering. This is one of the reasons that once a date is set, under no circumstances may a burning be cancelled or postponed. I wondered if one of the spirits gathering was our meatloaf-loving one?

Just before I opened the ceremony, a light rain began to fall. Kimo came over and said, "Jim, this is what we Hawaiians call a 'blessing rain.'" I smiled and nodded.

After this acknowledgement by the heavens, time became meaningless as I prepared to open the gateway to the Otherworld. Becoming one with all things of heaven and Earth, I began the ceremony by calling in the ancestral spirits.

It would be improper to put into print the details of the burning. Needless to say, it was a very moving experience because it honored the ones who have died or passed-over. It's important for not only the known ones to be fed, but the forgotten ones with no names must be given food as well.

As I completed and closed the ceremony, a park ranger appeared and looked none too happy. With the sound of the ocean waves behind us, our friend walked over to him while Sherry and I, our children, and students waited. I could sense the energy ebbing and flowing between the two until they hugged and parted. The ranger was extremely angry that we had gone ahead and conducted the ceremony against the regulations of the park, but after Kimo explained the spiritual importance of honoring the land and the Hawaiian ancestors, the ranger had a change of heart. In fact, he even attempted to have the regulation amended so that ceremonies such as ours could be held in the future.

I silently chuckled at the angry park ranger confronting our friend. It was déjà vu all over again. Last year, we had driven through the gates of Hawaii Volcanoes National Park without paying because our friend felt that the park was his church and we were going to offer *ho-okupu* to the volcano and fire goddess Madame *Pele*. After completing our gifting, honoring *Pele* and "steaming," we headed home, but not before we were confronted by a park ranger. As we sped out the gates of the park, a vehicle with its lights flashing came screaming up behind us just outside the entrance.

With his anger brewing like the volcano we had just left, Kimo threw his car into park and jumped out. Let's just say tempers were flaring, and between the shouting and getting in each other's faces, I thought I was going to have to break up a fight until suddenly tempers cooled and they began to listen to each other's point of view. And then, instead of fists flying, they hugged each other. When Kimo got back in the car, he said, "Brah, you won't believe it. We discovered we're cousins!"

Now, you may have noticed I mentioned "steaming" above and you're probably wondering about it. One of the traditional practices on the Big Island is to purify oneself with Madame *Pele's* breath by standing right next to one of her steam vents. Let's just say, it's more intense than a sauna or steam room.

The coincidences of our life have been amazing, but then again, there are no coincidences. Standing by one of the volcanic vents in our underwear with clouds of steam enveloping us and sometimes obscuring our view while listening to the deep breathing of Madame *Pele*, our meditative state was interrupted by the invasion of a different sound: the mundane noise of a tour bus pulling up. As I glanced through the steam, the doors opened and out streamed not just any group of tourists, but a bus load of Japanese. It is interesting that they were Japanese, as our Japanese connection extended as far back as 1981, with the Medieval Banquet and the Japanese camera crew and their star reporter.

The Japanese visitors were obviously amused by the strange-acting, nearly naked *gaijin*. All you could hear was the click after click of their cameras and a few giggles. I always wondered if any of the Japanese had a thought, "Hey, didn't we see him and her on TV years ago?"

Vision and Voice from Heaven

Had not the Buddha himself reached awakening alone, without a master,
"when he saw the morning star"?[195]

After we had completed the burning and scattered the ashes of the fire around the base of one of the palm trees, we all returned to where we were staying to shower and share a meal together as an *ohana*. This concept is very important to these islanders, as it is to us. It stands for unity, love and always loyalty. The *ohana* refers to an extended family ideal, which includes not only the immediate family of mother, father, children and grandparents but also all things of the land, the sea and the sky. The *ohana* also includes the ancestor spirits – the *'aumākua*.

We retired early to our beds, anticipating our journey the next day. We were going back to the white sand beach and the fishing village that Jamie and I had visited only days earlier.

Burnings are stressful for Sherry and me, so the thought of a restful night's sleep before the next day's events was manna from heaven. And it was restful until the pre-dawn hours:

> Am I asleep or awake? I sit up in bed. Am I sitting or still lying? Is this a dream or am I awake? The night sky before me, that star, why is it shining brighter than any other? A Heavenly Voice: This Star is you; you are this Star! The great purification is of the people! All are One.
>
> Am I asleep? I lie back down . . .

As I woke on Sunday morning, I was in awe of my pre-dawn experience. I wasn't sure if I'd dreamed it or if I'd been awake. The star was shining ever so brightly in the east. But what star was it? Who am I? What did it mean?

I shared my experience with Sherry. We only had a short time before we needed to gather our group together and depart for the white sand beach. She suggested that I share the vision, as she called it, with our Hawaiian friend. I agreed that I needed to ask him his opinion.

Morning Star

Morning Star, there at the place where the sun comes up, you, who have the wisdom which we seek, help us in cleansing ourselves and all the people, that our generations to come will have light as they walk the sacred path. You lead the dawn as it walks forth, and the day which follows with its light, which is knowledge. This you do for us and for all the people of the world, that they may see clearly in walking the holy path, that they may know all that is holy, and that they may increase in a sacred manner.

– Lakota holy man and visionary Black Elk

We arrived at the white sand beach on one of those most beautiful late mornings on the islands. The sky was a brilliant blue touched throughout with white fluffy clouds. Kimo and I were both standing in the surf facing the ocean. There's one hard and fast rule on these islands: never turn your back to the ocean as it is disrespectful and dangerous.

A short distance away our students were relaxing and swimming. We had a few minutes to talk before we needed to continue on to the fishing village. Before I could say anything, he began talking about the burning. It was a powerful and moving experience for him. One of his ancestors had come to him in spirit form, dressed in full warrior regalia.

Kimo stared out to sea for a moment before he continued. "My ancestor brought me a message, but it's for you. My ancestor said that you are a *kahuna po'o*.[196] You are a prophet,[197] bringing back the lost knowledge[198] and sacred teachings that have been misunderstood, forgotten and corrupted. You have a message, path and way to share with this world, but do not identify it as being from these islands or other lands. This only separates people and does not unite them. Don't get discouraged with the resistance you will face; it's your destiny."

Although I was amazed, in my heart I'd always known the truth of what he said. Sometimes it can be difficult to determine if it's your own truth from your heart speaking, or your unhealthy ego. To have it verified by another, as well as by the spirit world, was important to me.

I then proceeded to tell him about my vision and the voice. After I finished explaining, he paused to think. "In the east, brighter than the other stars," he said. "Must have been the morning star."

Even though my friend had potentially identified the star as Venus, I still needed to research and discover further proof that it was the morning star. I decided to consult my astrological birth chart. Astrology predates astronomy and may be traced back to at least 2300 B.C.E. in Mesopotamia and Chaldea and was considered a sacred science.

The validity of astrology[199] may be verified by the philosophy of macrocosm and microcosm. This is the premise that all occurrences in the microcosm (humanity/Earth) are influenced by the macrocosm (the heavens). This philosophy is Greek in origin, possibly dating back to the fifth century B.C.E. Later on, an axiom developed: "As below, so above; as above, so below." Taken from *The Emerald Tablet of Hermes Trismegistus*, this axiom, "underpinned the work of the great minds of the past, such as Plato, Aristotle, Pythagoras, and Ptolemy."[200] This proposes that we are a reflection of the heavens. Thus, the way the planets and stars are arranged in heaven when we are born is an imprint and reflection of who we are – a guide to our soul.

An astrologer who had read my chart many years before said that it was one of the most unusual ones she'd ever seen in all the years that she'd been doing charts. She said it was like a mirror image of a perfect chart and that I had the energy of a visionary and a "pioneer of consciousness." I would have a knowing of my past lives, she added, and most possibly other people's past lives.

Another unusual aspect of my chart was called a "bundle," a rare grouping of planets clustered together,[201] which means there are no afflicted aspects between the planets but an abundance of helpful ones. The astrologer went on to tell me that there was a cluster of planets in the first and twelfth houses all in the balance sign of Libra, symbolically the Phoenix. Both of these houses represent the inner and outer self. Furthermore, early Christians considered Libra an emblem of Archangel Mikael,[202] who wields the sword of Truth. Libra's spiritual quest is the reconciliation of opposites, which occurs in the heart, not the mind. Libra is ruled by Venus, so a number of planets in Libra, especially in the first and twelfth houses, would be evidence of the identity of the star.[203] Both Venus and Jupiter are conjunct in the first house and are considered morning stars.

Kimo's spirit ancestor had called me a prophet. Accordingly, "it is note-worthy that among Asiatic peoples the planet Venus excites unique reverence as the shaman's source of prophetic inspiration, even being credited with orig-inating the power to shamanize."[204]

One final point: my Uranus (Planet of Rebellion) is in Gemini in the ninth house conjunct my North Node. It is the highest (or most elevated) planet in my horoscope.[205] Uranus is the archetype for equal human rights, freedom, and independence, while the ninth house is the house of luck, long distance travel, foreigners, higher education, law,[206] philosophy, religion, adventure, and wide-open spaces. It is important to note that the ninth house is the field of religion and mystical or prophetic experiences. Uranus, with androgynous energy, brings with it a new way of looking at things. It rules Aquarius and the eleventh house and is the access point to our soul and the antithesis of the lie.

Uranus, the planet of my message, is sextile Mercury in the eleventh house, trine Venus and Jupiter in the first house. Venus connected to Uranus signifies a universal brotherhood/sisterhood aspect fostering a knowing that all humans are the same. And according to the Astrology King website, "Jupiter trine Uranus in the natal chart makes you a creative genius. You are always looking ahead, experimenting, questioning, seeking new and exciting adventures. Travelling and exploring different cultures would give you the kind of experience you crave."[207]

I Am the Morning Star

. . . as revealed by my vision and the mandala of my soul. Further research also revealed the reasons for my knowledge of the ideal egalitarian society[208] and a few of my past incarnations. In my natal chart the planet Neptune, associated with past lives and spiritual enlightenment, is strongly positioned in the twelfth house with conjunctions to the Moon, Mars and my Ascendant. Neptune's paradigm is the universal sea of oneness, the unity of all existence. However, the majority of people do not live in this reality. Thus, the need for awakening.

Moreover, Neptune's paradigm is the quest for redemption and for the lost Eden or the egalitarian Golden Age, which the Mesoamericans knew as the Sixth Sun. "Neptune is the archetype of the ideal, the ineffable, transcendent, imaginal, and timeless. One of its images is the ocean of consciousness upon which the boundaries between oneself and other, oneself and the divine, are dissolved so that what is separate merges into a greater whole. Universal love and compassion come from this boundless oceanic yearning of fusion with all life. Neptune represents the longing for the ideal world, the paradisiacal garden where there is no separation from the divine source. It is in this vein that we can understand Neptune's connection to the themes of redemption and purification."[209]

Going one step further, I discovered that Neptune has both Saturn (form, time, far-seeing and structure) and Pluto (power, transformation, regeneration and rebirth) sextile. In fact, "Neptune-Pluto appears to express itself primarily on the religious level."[210] My Saturn in Leo (proud and creative) sextile to Neptune in Libra (harmony, unity, the ideal and beauty) is a soul gift, which gives me the ability to give form to the formless—vision (inspiration) into manifestation (perspiration).

The formless is not solely limited to the ideal of a non-dogmatic religious egalitarian philosophy but, and in some ways much more important, the ideal egalitarian society. To take one step further, Venus is sextile Mercury which gives me a type of perception that synthesizes and synergizes data along with the process of analyzing it; the artist and the scientist are one.[211]

Furthermore, the relationship and interplay of Saturn and Pluto in the tenth house with Neptune in the twelfth, and the addition of Uranus (the Awakener) in the ninth conjunct my North Node—known as the dragon's head—gives me another great gift of soul: knowledge of past lives.

After my vision in 1993, little did I expect that three of my past incarnations, past lives, would be physically verified: the first in 1995, the second in 1997, and the third in 2006.

Postscript

Even deeper magic and destiny was at work surrounding my vision and voice from heaven. The original journey that we'd planned and scheduled was to Japan not Hawaii, a two-week specially designed program to the Land of the Rising Sun combining the martial arts with the spiritual arts. We were working with my teacher, an incredible martial arts grandmaster in Japan and our planning was flowing very nicely. By midsummer, ten of our apprentices had already paid for the October journey. I had already completed the travel arrangements: airline tickets had been purchased and rooming deposits paid.

And then, in the middle of August, an unexpected event occurred. Out of the clear blue, I received a fax from sensei in Japan, brief and to the point. "Cannot do seminar," it said, no explanation given.

Perplexed and angry at this turn of events involving a person both Sher and I respected, I contemplated a solution to our conundrum. Canceling the journey was not an option. However, traveling to Japan would not work either. Even though I had previously adventured to Japan on five different occasions, and even though my son and I could teach the martial part of the journey and Sher and I the spiritual side, it still didn't feel right. Then again, where to go?

And then it came to me – Hawaii! We had just conducted a journey in 1992 to the Big Island with our Hawaiian healer friend. Our ten students had not been on that journey, so no one would be repeating an adventure. And who wouldn't be excited to experience the beauty and the *Aloha* spirit of the islands?

Springing into action, and with the help of others, I was able to transfer all of our deposits to Hawaii. I contacted each apprentice concerning the change to Hawaii from Japan, and even though a few were martial arts students, all agreed to travel to Hawaii. And, as it is said, "The rest is history."

Katun 4 Ahau

Decades later, in early 2018, I uncovered knowledge which I had over-looked, even when writing *The Return of the Feathered Serpent – Shining Light of First Knowledge* (Author House, 2006). This knowledge floored me and I wondered how and why I had missed it. It concerned the Maya calendar *katun* prophecies, specifically *Katun 4 Ahau*. The Maya calendar consists of the long count, a span of 5,125 years, and the short count, which is approximately twenty years (19.7) – called a *katun*.

Katun 4 Ahau began April 6, 1993 and ended December 21, 2012. Additionally, in the early morning of April 6, Venus rose from the under-world as the morning star. "How often should we expect a Venus rising to coincide with a *katun* beginning? A *katun* equals 7200 days. The Venus cycle has 583.92 days. The relationship of these two periods is such that three *katuns* equal thirty-seven Venus cycles. For both to meet on an *Ahau* day is rare: the beginning of every fifteenth *katun* coincides with a Venus morning star rising on an *Ahau* day. Fifteen katuns is almost 300 years. Actually, this is just the pure mathematics of it. Due to variations in the Venus cycle, the combination of factors which come together on April 6th, 1993 was undeniably unique."[212]

To reiterate, April 6, 1993, was designated a *katun* beginning and a Venus rising as well as a full moon! What then is the meaning and significance of this *katun* cycle that began six months before my vision as the morning star? What predictions did the Maya make for this *katun* cycle? There were two primary ones. The first: *This is the katun of remembering knowledge and recording it.* This reflects what I was told by my friend's ancestor: "You are a prophet bring-ing back the lost knowledge and sacred teachings."

The second: *Kukulkán shall come.* "This refers to the arrival of the Toltec leader known as Topiltzin-Quetzalcóatl. (Kukulkán was the Maya name for Quetzalcóatl.) This leader attempted to make reforms to violence-filled reli-gious practices of the day that included child sacrifice. He commanded that instead of human sacrifices his followers should only sacrifice butterflies."[213] According to Philip Coppens, "In the *Chilam Balam* of *Chumayel*, it says that in *Katun 4 Ahau* (the *katun* running from April 1993 to December 2012) the feathered serpent god, Kukulkan, will return. This god originated with the Toltecs as Quetzalcóatl, and the original religion surrounding this god involved a serpent-like energy rising up the spine. "[214] Within two years of the start of the *katun*—in 1995—I would be identified as Quetzalcóatl by the "Spirit Man of Teotihuacán."

"It should also be remembered that two cycles came to an end on December 21, 2012. Not only does the smaller *Katun 4 Ahau* end, but also the thirteenth *baktun* of the larger 5,126-year 'Great Cycle' which began on August 29, 3114 B.C.[215] Does this fact amplify the events associated with the smaller *katun* cycle?"[216]

One last point. According to the *Utne Reader*, 1993 was a "year like no other. Astrologers say the world may never be the same after 1993. Almost unanimously, astrologers [saw] 1993 as a watershed year for humankind. . . . Causing this big stir [was] the 1993 triple conjunction of Uranus and Neptune. In a rare celestial occurrence, these two planets align[ed] in the sky three times [that] year."[217] The last time this occurred was 1821.

Do not ask why, but only experience from the depths of your soul
the mystery, and you will know; but will you ever know?
Raven, creator to some, evil to others,
earthbound, injured wing, can't you fly?
Why, if divine, where comes the suffering?

Do you remember flying high, voice of power – black, or was it white?
Why maimed, earthbound, separate from heaven?
"Black to some is life, while white is death.
Experience the mystery for yourself," Raven shouts.
"Why do you refuse to see the mystery within me?
Always looking, judging, separating, but never seeing
the light of the mystery.

You do not know me; I am Raven,
the majestic one that suffers and weeps
for the ones I have left behind.
What is life to one as me?
Surprise will be my answer to you.
I am not what I appear;
I am you, and you are me.
We are one." – JC[218]

Spirit Dancing, Burnings, and Bathings

How is it that we came to the knowledge and the practice of bathing and burning – "feeding the spirits?" How did I find my modern-day John the Baptist – the Dipper? In 1990 Sherry and I sponsored a conference in Maine on Native American spirituality and shamanism. We were encouraged to invite as presenters two native elders, a husband and wife. Vince and Mom Stogan came from Vancouver, British Columbia. As soon as Sherry and I met them at the Portland airport, we were struck by their unassuming authenticity. It was as though we were meeting our long lost grandparents. Mom and Vince Stogan were the revered spiritual healers of the Coast Salish – Musqueam Indian Band. Vince was the fifth generation in his family to carry on the medicine of the smokehouse tradition of initiation and spirit dancing. An insight into Mom and Vince's Salish tradition and culture is the term *skalalitude*. This is being in harmony with nature – a harmonious state of heart and mind where all things are in balance.

During the conference we were unaware that Mom Stogan was watching Sherry do her spirit work and Vince was watching me. After the conference, back at our home, Vince and Mom asked to speak to both of us in private. They told us that they saw themselves in us and asked if we would like to learn their medicine ways. Of course, we were privileged and honored to be asked and willingly accepted.

Mom, Vince, Sher, and of course, the Lobster

Our apprenticeship with Mom and Vince was of the "old school," where you learned by listening, watching and doing and not writing anything down. Many of our experiences and learnings, we cannot share in print. This is typical of oral and initiatory traditions, such as the Mystery Schools of Egypt and Greece where initiates were told to be silent about the mysteries seen and experienced. However, we can tell you some things about burnings, bathings, healings, and our experiences.

The Northwest Coast First People have three primary ceremonial practices: winter spirit dancing, bathing, and burnings or "feeding the spirits." They also practice the traditional methods of shamanic healing. Bathing is their primary purification rite. Sher and I, and sometimes our daughter Jess, would travel to Vancouver and stay with Mom and Vince. Many of the stories and teachings that we heard were learned around their kitchen table. These informal sessions would sometimes last late into the night with Vince smoking Camel cigarette after Camel cigarette and drinking glass after glass of Pepsi. Many teachings were stories of Vince's experiences, and it is not our place to tell his tales.

Questing for a Spirit Song

Living with Vince and Mom, we experienced firsthand the lives and living conditions of the Coast Salish. We would go grocery shopping for them. Sher would cook and clean their house and I would help Vince on various projects, such as mending his fishing nets. As an endearment, Vince would call Sher, "baby." They were like a grandmother and grandfather to us. Living with them was like being their grandchildren, and their children were our brothers and sisters.

Many times we would not get to bed until two o'clock in the morning and have to get back up at three o'clock to go bathing. The bathing spot was about an hour's drive north of Vancouver. Bathing as a symbolic death and then rebirth from the great mother, Mother Earth, replicates our human birthing experience as we leave the waters of the Earth Mother and transition from the dark to the light on a physical as well as a metaphoric and spiritual level.

Timing is always touchy as you must enter the waters in the dark but leave the stream or river at first light, about an hour before sunrise.

A spiritual process known as questing for a song is connected with bathing. This spirit song is not handed down person to person but comes to you during bathing and is a reflection of your spiritual power. Belief holds that the songs are in the air surrounding the streams and a song will only come to a person who is spiritually ready to receive it. The quest occurs for four consecutive mornings and involves other things that I cannot reveal.

Walking up a mountain trail surrounded by towering old-growth cedar trees in the dark—darkness as dense as the bottom of a cave—is disconcerting enough. To hear the subtle roar of the stream only adds to the otherworldliness of the moment. Include a bit of fear and your sense of time dissolves into timelessness. I've always had perfectly strong eyesight and have been a swimming/lifesaving coach and instructor, so entering a mountain stream in the dark and submerging at least four times was not too scary or difficult for me. But for Sherry the opposite was true. She has worn glasses the majority of her life and almost drowned as a child. For her to enter the mountain stream in the dark and without her glasses was an act of will, courage, and trust.

Vince put us both through the quest and at the end of the four days both Sherry and I had our songs. Please do not think that doing the four days will always result in a song. In fact, just the opposite is true. Over the years, I assisted Vince when other non-natives came to seek a song. Not one received a song during the time I assisted Vince. Only when the mind is a river of silence will one be able to sing.

Even for natives, "not every spirit-quest was successful – some people searched all their lives without receiving any supernatural gift."[219] The Salish believe that the songs of dead shamans are in the air, but you must quest for them. After Vince "cooked" my song, he turned to me and said, "Your song is my uncle's spirit song. You carry his song." Vince didn't call himself a shaman, but if you needed a label, he preferred to be called an Indian doctor – a medicine man. However, he did refer to his uncle, who lived during the early part of the twentieth century, as a shaman. In fact, a "strong shaman" was his term as in "strong heart, strong mind, and strong hands for healing." Vince told my wife and me about his uncle's prophecies:

My uncle predicted all the events that would happen, and they all have been or come true – bombs, World War II, TV, cars, styles, etc. If things don't calm down over in the Middle East, it will be another war that will be big, World War III, and a part of the Earth will change. Uncle said it would be like a little boy picking on another little boy. Then, one of their big brothers will join in, and then another member, until the whole family is fighting, and it will spread to everybody joining in and choosing sides.

Concerning the spirit song, when I paint my face (a form of masking) and sing my song, magic happens. "Through the mask and song, the shaman is transformed into something other, and with the vision of an animal, ancestor, or god symbolically acquired through this transformation, he is able to see into the mysteries of the spiritual realm."[220]

Additionally, the excellent book *Masks of the Spirit* shares the following concerning myth, mask, and song:

Masks, then, are the visual equivalent of the song or chant of the shaman, and both mask and song are symbolic of the sacred discourse of myth created by the mind. All three— masks, song, and myth—are products of culture operating at its most profound level in a search for order in the invisible or spiritual world. Eliade's[221] contention that the mask makes it possible for the shaman to transcend this life by enabling him "to become what he displays," and to exist as "the mythical ancestor portrayed by his mask" suggests precisely the necessary immersion in the sacred order of the world of the spirit. Through the mask and the song, the shaman is transformed into something other, and with the vision of an animal, ancestor, or god symbolically acquired through this transformation, he is able to see into the mysteries of the spiritual realm. "He in a manner reestablishes the situation that existed *in illo tempore*, in mythical times, when the divorce between man and the animal world had not yet occurred," when the primordial order had not yet been hidden from man's view. Now outside of space and time, "he mystically unites himself with a sacred order of being, beyond the dimension of this or that person in this or that particular body." He is, in effect, reborn with the divine ability to see, behind the mask that both covers and reveals the essence of the cosmos, the divine order that alone can resolve the seeming chaos of the world of man. Thus, the mask is surely a clear reflection of and the perfect metaphor for this shamanic world view, and Mesoamerican spirituality reveals its great debt to shamanism in its pervasive symbolic and ritual use of the mask.[222]

One final point: once I achieved the power of song an interesting effect occurred. At various times, connected with different circumstances, an intrinsic song fitting the moment erupts from the power of my heart and soul. It is not my primary song but a different one, such as when I kept a person from dying. (Please see my tale in the section below titled, "Question: Native. Answer: No.")

Commentary

We do not charge a fee or request a certain payment amount for our spiritual work of healing, bathings, and burnings. Only our expenses if travel is involved. Donations are acceptable.

WINTER SPIRIT DANCING IN BIG FOOT COUNTRY

. . . .

THE FIRST TIME WE SET FOOT IN A CANADIAN FIRST PEOPLE'S longhouse was in Big Foot Country. The longhouse is called a smokehouse— most appropriate considering that the spirit dances are held at night; and the only warmth and light is provided by a large, open fire in the middle of the longhouse. The open fire provided the physical comforts of heat and light, and the interior becomes smoky. And we must not lose sight of the important point that fire is the metaphysical symbol of spirit.

Normally, only natives, not Caucasians, are allowed to view the Winter Spirit Dancing within the smokehouse. Being non-natives, there was only one reason we were allowed into the longhouse unharmed: we were with Mom and Vince, who are respected and still feared by their people. No matter who we were with, it was scary, but, of course, a great honor at the same time. Due to our promise to Mom and Vince, we cannot and would not desire to describe spirit dancing within the smokehouse. But we can tell you that when the dancers feel the presence of their spirits, the drummers begin, and the vibration of the drums sends you into another reality.

Big Foot—True or False

The legend of Big Foot, Sasquatch, is true – it exists. We have never seen one, but our experiences and travels with Mom and Vince gives credence to their existence. One time, Sher and I assisted Vince with a burning in Sasquatch Country. A small "band" up-country from Vancouver had never conducted a burning and asked Vince to do one for them. It was very evident when we arrived that they had never done one as the wood available for the fire had nails in it from a torn down building. Nails in the wood for a burning would be a no-no. And Sher, fair-freckled Irish lass that she is, had to teach the native women how to prepare the food.

After the burning and during our communal meal, the subject turned to Big Foot. The oral legend goes back to their distant ancestors who made a pact with the sentient beings known as Sasquatch. As long as they were left alone, the Sasquatch would not endanger or harm the humans.

This alone might not be enough to convince a person, but the story Vince told us did convince us, and considering who he was, there was no reason for him to lie about it. He told us this story while he was teaching us the medicine of soul retrieval. True traditional shamanic soul retrieval is nowhere close to the sham-snake-oil, neo-shamanic marketed soul retrieval. Soul retrieval is serious work. The soul needs to be put back on a person sooner than later. Furthermore, and most importantly, you need to know where the soul was dropped.[223] The location is paramount. Vince explained this to us through a tale about a native teenage girl who dropped her soul.

He and Mom Stogan were called to a hospital in Big Foot Country to work on a native teenage girl. The doctors could not figure out why she was "out of her mind," or how to cure her. Because her family knew the cause of her affliction, they called the Stogan's for help.

As teenagers do, the girl and her boyfriend had been parked in a gravel pit. Love was in the air until they heard a strange sound in front of their car. The boyfriend turned on the headlights to find a Sasquatch standing in front of the car, and the fear, shock, and trauma caused the girl to have soul loss and to "lose her mind." The boy was okay, or as well as you can be after having a close encounter with a creature such as Big Foot. Since they arrived in time and knew where the girl had dropped her soul, Vince and Mom were able to put her soul back on and she recovered.

Of course, for the science-based deniers, this is no proof of the reality of a Sasquatch. The irony is that many of these deniers are Christian and their faith makes them believe in something even more hard to swallow than the existence of Big Foot – the supposed virgin birth of Jesus. To this day a virgin birth, a birth not mythological or symbolic, still defies reason, logic, and the natural laws of creation. But the lie of the female virgin birth of Jesus helped recruit new converts to the "one and only" true religion, promoting "Jesus as God."

BATHING – SEEKING POWER AND THE INITIATORY RITE OF DEATH AND REBIRTH[224]

. . . .

"Die many times before you die."[225]

RITUALISTIC IMMERSION IN RUNNING WATER (A STREAM OR river) or the ocean is one of the oldest forms of initiation and symbolic death and rebirth. It is one of the essential steps in awakening, frightening but necessary. We need to symbolically "die" to the old to be "born again" – our second birth. Furthermore, this second birth may be referred to as a "virgin birth." As we can see, it is not membership in an earthly or religious institution. It is the beginning of an awakening to the truth of the world and one's authentic self.

Few in the world still practice and teach this form of purification. Even in Jesus's time, baptism in the River Jordan was a "unique event that even Catholic editors of the Jerusalem Bible consider to be an initiation."[226] Outside of the Mandeans of the Middle East, the greatest concentration of "dawn bathers" is to be found within the indigenous communities that still practice and adhere to the old ways. But even here, there are few still alive that can "initiate" and put people into the "living waters" of the Earth.

We are blessed to be two of those who still practice and "initiate" people into bathing. This "initiation" is not one of membership, but one of death and rebirth. After I put a person into the stream, he or she is free to revisit any stream and repeat the ritualistic immersion. Going bathing will help a person release the stress and hurt that comes from living in today's chaotic and fear-filled world. And quite possibly, it may help prevent Alzheimer's Disease.[227]

After the "initiation," there are multiple reasons for a person to revisit a stream and bathe. Bathings will increase a person's spiritual power, medicine power, and his or her inner vitality. The living waters will also help release anger, guilt, resentment, fear, and uncertainty, as well as the other emotional baggage that we seem to carry and refuse to release.

Vince once told us that anger, along with fear, is our greatest enemy: "If you keep hurt feelings, or get mad at the weather, you get a heavy feeling and it ties down your spiritual work. Anger breaks up the home and can ruin your life. It ruins hope and can separate families. Father goes one way, the mother goes the other way, and the children are left in the middle! Family love is very important, as well as the love in your heart. When you get like this (holding anger/hurt feelings), go up to the mountain to a stream and leave the anger, leave the hurt feelings, up there!"

In Ancient Peru, "after confession of guilt, an Inca bathed in a neighbouring river and repeated this formula, 'O thou River, receive the sins I have this day confessed unto the Sun, carry them down to the sea, and let them never more appear.'"[228] As we can see, bathing has been used since ancient times for the passions[229] of the mind. It then makes sense that Sher and I use bathing as one part of our releasing and healing process for deep emotional and physical trauma. Usually for others, but not always.

Broken Heart

People who experience broken-heart syndrome think they may be having a heart attack. Research points to stress as a cause, such as occurs with the loss of a loved one. What makes the condition even more puzzling to physicians is that the people who get it usually have no history of heart trouble.

Due to the separation of the spiritual from the medical, causes other than the solely physical are never considered, but our past influences our present. This is one of the reasons why forgiveness, letting go, and making peace with past traumatic events is extremely important. They affect our present state of wellness. As is usually the case, the focus of the researcher is wrongly placed on the physical without considering emotional/spiritual aspects as cause agents. But this is slowly changing: "Many physiological studies are currently being done regarding the interconnection of the heart and the brain, and why certain sensations and feelings are experienced at the level of the heart. Generally, love and certain emotional states are felt at the heart level, producing different physiological reactions of the heart."[230]

If this then is the research, are there any case studies concerning these emotional states and the physiological reactions? There is; inadvertently, I conducted a case study of this broken-heart syndrome without realizing it. I caused my dear wife to experience it.

Bathing consists not only of spirit song to open the river, and prayers, but also anointing or painting a sacred symbol on the body with red ochre.[231] The power is not within the song, prayer, or paint, but within the medicine person who applies it. As standard practice, when painting the sacred symbol on the person before they entered the river, I would always keep my mind neutral, in a state of "no mind." Except once, when we took apprentices bathing during a training.

Sher was holding onto various emotions like grief connected with the death of her sister, Beverly, and our daughter's still-born child. When she came to me to be painted, as I began, I silently said these words, "Whatever Sher is holding in her heart, let her release it . . . release . . . release . . . " Sher and I were the last ones to bathe. As I waited on the bank of the river for her to finish, I could hear her soulful cry in the swirling waters. I saw her tears as she finished and left the river. During this time, all the apprentices were under their blankets seeking vision or knowledge until I bathed and sang my song to close the river.

As we were leaving the bathing spot, after completion and closing of the river, I asked Sher how she was doing. "Okay," she replied, but this was not really true, as within a few minutes she collapsed to the ground. Two of our students helped her up and back to our cars. Since our house was only about fifteen minutes away, even though I was very worried I decided to take Sher home before calling 911.

Once home and lying down, she expressed that she had felt like she was having a heart attack but was beginning to feel better. I could see and feel that she was getting better and just needed to rest. While the apprentices were providing help and support, I realized what had happened.

Keep in mind that when I sing my song and invoke prayers to open the river, it also opens access to the Otherworld that blends with our world. My thoughts while anointing/painting her allowed her to release but the sudden release brought on the symptoms of a heart attack. A great case study, as thankfully my wife was none the worst for it, and it had the added benefit of releasing her emotional grief. And for me the learning: keep my mind neutral while painting.

Mind and Spirit Power

As I stated above, repetitive bathing will increase one's vitality (mind power) and medicine power. Accordingly, "He Who Dwells Above will never allow a man's vitality or thought to travel to their homes until he has undergone a prolonged purification, and prayed and fast unceasingly. Only one who has undergone this strenuous training, and suffered innumerable hardships, has ever become a real medicine man with power to cure human ailments."[232]

In this context, Old Pierre,[233] a Coast Salish medicine man said, "Nowadays I hear many of my friends say, 'I am a medicine man; my power is latent in this knife.' But they do not speak the truth. They are not medicine men; they have no medicine power, but only the shadow of such power. Not one of them was willing to undergo the penance that alone gives admission to the really sacred realm farther away than the realm of the ordinary guardian spirits, where dwell the spirits that give medicine power."[234]

It is interesting to note that the problem today with people calling themselves shamans who have never undergone the penance of hard, intense spirit training and who only have been trained in a workshop or seminar is the same problem that Old Pierre faced in the early 1900s.

Our message of Divine Humanity states that our world and the Otherworld blend together. In other words, spirit and matter interpenetrate each other – radical nonduality. On the other hand, dualistic paradigms view the Otherworld as being behind a veil or metaphorically separated by a body of water, such as a river. I've even used these concepts in my writings in an attempt to explain the unexplainable. But what if the exact opposite is true, and there is no separation between us and the Otherworld, no separation between spirit and matter? The Norse were closer to this truth, sometimes viewing the entrance to the Otherworld as within a holy hill or mountain; at other times, the entrance was to be found within a graveyard.

Or consider these two Icelandic folktales: "[T]he otherworld in *Grelent* and *Tidorel* seems to be in, or near, water and the characters even have to go into the water to penetrate into the other world."[235] This is exactly the case during bathing, when a person enters a river, enabling them to access the Otherworld. However, entering into a river does not unto itself provide access to the Otherworld. It is one of my spirit songs which "opens" the river and provides the access.

Winter Training

"Verily, verily, I say unto thee, except a man be born of water and of the Spirit, he cannot enter into the kingdom of God."[236]

Bathing as spirit training is not easy, especially when you consider that the training period is during the winter. Winters in Maine can be extremely brutal, cold and snowy. Many times, I had to break through the ice to bathe. One time I even wondered if I would even make it back to my car alive as I trudged through the thigh-high snow with no feeling in my legs. But the experience is awesome, even if, after countless bathing, there is still a little trepidation and fear. Only one time did I decide not to bathe after arriving at my bathing spot. I drove through the darkness to a river in New Hampshire, quite a distance from our home in Maine. As I began walking through the knee-high snow to the river, I reached a point where each time I lifted my leg to walk, my slip-on shoes came off. I thought it best to not continue further, as the river was still ten yards away. And yes, slip-on shoes. When your bathing in subzero temperatures, little clothing and easy removal is essential, especially after you exit the river with no feeling in your legs while trying to put your clothes and shoes back on. Best is easy off and easy on!

In the predawn time, the darkness is always thickest. The air brings a pleasant freshness awaiting the return of light. Imagine standing nude before first light on the edge of a flowing river while listening to the sounds of the rushing, roaring waters as if they are the sounds of a thundering heavenly chariot. This is the coldest time of the night, at first light right before dawn. It is the liminal time between dark and light. A magical moment reflecting our mortality and, most importantly, our immortality.

And further imagine your bare feet on the sacred ground of the Earth (sometimes snow-covered), your naked body feeling the winds of the Earth while your uncovered head and eyes observe the dimming night sky, one embedded with hundreds of sparkling jewels. And then you voice prayers before entering the water alone and submerging yourself. When I enter the river, with my first step, there is an explosion of my senses and dualistic reality dissolves into an oneness of truth. With my first squatting submersion, I die once again, only to be reborn as I explode straight up out of the water, into the air. A primal scream escapes my lips as the icy fire of spirit exploded through me in a wild, ecstatic rush—blood to fire, body to ice. And for a split second, my mind shifts into the realization that I must do this three more times.

After the fourth submersion, as I shoot up straight out of the waters, my spirit song erupts from the inner core of my soul. How long I remain in the freezing waters is always a mystery. The siren's song is always to stay in the power, the indestructible, to stay in the true oneness of life where human worries and fears do not exist, only you and the mystery of God – the realm of the Earth and the kingdom of heaven.

Burning Water

The awakening quest in life is to wash by fire and burn by water. This is a metaphor, and a reality, of the joining or blending of the two opposite elements of purification symbolizing a state of radical nonduality. Symbolically, this merging of fire and water represents spirit permeating matter. And, "there is proof that the dynamics of the union of two opposites is at the basis of all creation, spiritual as well as material."[237]

To awaken the spark within our bodies—which are composed of approximately seventy percent water—requires a prolong period of sacrifice. This is the sacrifice of our self to our self to release the fire within where it merges with our watery body, an interpenetration of spirit and matter: a baptism of fire. One example of a sacrifice of self-to-self is bathing. Bathing over many years will help to awaken our inner fire or spark. Considering my connection with Quetzalcóatl, and since bathing is one of my personal spiritual practices as well as one of my medicine powers, it's interesting to note that one of Quetzalcóatl's mountain ascetic training practices was bathing. "One text tells that in the year Two Reed, Ce Acatl Quetzalcóatl built a special temple facing the cardinal directions and fasted, did penance, and bathed in icy cold waters."[238]

And then there is this. The Hebrew word *shamayim* is usually translated as "heaven" in the Bible. But literally it is *Shin – Mem – Yod – Mem*, which means "fiery waters." According to great Medieval Jewish interpreter Rashi, "There is this concept that the Hebrew word *shamayim* is a word combination: fire in waters, or fire and waters or fiery waters."[239] Could the ancient Jewish concept of heaven on Earth be a veiled reference and hidden teaching of the awakening to Oneness, the interpenetration or blending of fire and water?

One final point: the cosmology creation myth of the ancient Norse portrayed the two realms of Ice and Fire blending together, resulting in water melting from the ice that was blended with fire. Once again, we have the concept of *burning water*.

Harmonia

Symbolically, Fire represents the Absolute/Heaven while Water corresponds to the Relative/Earth. Metaphorically, the blending of the opposites of Fire and Water results in harmony and a Oneness of Self. In Greek mythology, this concept corresponds to "Harmonia, which is usually translated as 'harmony,' but means any union in which the parts form a seamless whole while retaining their distinct identities. Harmonia is the daughter of sea-born Aphrodite and fiery Ares, whom Empedocles identified with Love and Strife, the two primary cosmic forces, which bring about all change in the universe. Pythagoras likewise said that cosmic Harmonia is born of the union of Love and Strife. She reconciles all oppositions."[240]

Life-Force

There is a power, a force that is the single, dynamic, sacred power or energy that is the unifying totality of all things – a universal life-force. This sacred power to the Nahua, the peoples of the Valley of Mexico at the time of the Spanish conquest, was called *teotl*, "a single, dynamic, vivifying, eternally self-generating and self-regenerating sacred power, energy or force."[241] It "permeates, encompasses, and shapes the cosmos as part of its endless process of self-generation and regeneration."[242]

This power or force on a personal level is the inner heat generated by the shaman, released in some cases by bathing. Interestingly enough, the feeling is one of icy fire. The first time I experienced it was during one of my daily runs. As it coursed through my body, I thought I was having a heart attack. This was the power reflecting the merging of the fire of my spirit with the watery essence of my body.

A balance between spirit and matter is the key to life, a life lived in love and power. "The body 'buds and flowers' only when the spirit has been through the fire of sacrifice; in the same way the Earth gives fruit only when it is penetrated by solar heat, transmuted by rain. That is to say, the creative element is not either heat or water alone, but a balance between the two."[243]

BATHING TALES

. . . .

Cold . . . Darkness . . . Death . . . but no . . . Light . . . Rebirth

Is that an Elf I See?

LAUGHTER IS MEDICINE FOR THE SOUL. IT DOESN'T SOLELY come from our mouth and throat but may be a silent vibration within our heart-filled body. I've experienced this many times while thinking about one special morning bathing. More than twenty-five years have passed since relating this tale, but each time I look back, I silently chuckle at the memory of the day the "cows stopped giving milk."

With its many natural waterways, Maine would seem like an ideal place to bathe. However, it was difficult to find a bathing spot with no homes nearby and within a suitable driving distance from our house. Over the years, I used various spots, but the one that was nearly perfect only lasted two winter bathing seasons. There was home nearby, but it was on the other side of the river and across a road. The brutal Maine winters meant closed and possibly shuttered windows. With the roar of the river, the distance of the house from the bathing spot and windows being closed, I assumed that no one would be able to hear my opening and closing song or hear my spirit song.

During the first winter at this new bathing spot, I only bathed a few times a month. But the next winter, I increased to once a week, usually on a Friday morning after fasting for approximately forty-eight hours. It had been an extremely hard winter with lots of snow and below-zero temperatures. In fact, it was during this winter that I feared I wouldn't make it back to my car alive.

The snow was up to my waist and the temperature hovered around zero. At times, I had to break through the ice to bathe. This was a fast moving river and for it to ice up meant that it was cold.

One of my bathings was near the end of March. Technically it was spring, but there was still snow on the ground. The river had iced-up. Only one opening was big enough for my four submersions. Before I sang my song and voiced my prayers to open the river, I realized I could be pulled under the ice during one of my submersions, especially the second one as I would be facing downstream. This was not an easy flowing stream but a river with a strong current. Even though it was one of my most dangerous bathings, it also turned out to be one of my most powerful, verified by the intensity of my spirit song after the fourth submersion.

After I had climbed out of the ice-cold river, I struggled to get dressed. Dressing is always problematic after bathing. Years ago, I learned very quickly that the fewer clothes you wear the easier it is, and most importantly, the faster you can get dressed after crawling out of the river. When you have no feeling in your body from the waist down and with arms and hands numb pulling on pants, such as jeans, is too difficult and time consuming. With the wet and cold, I soon discovered that the best bathing pants were a gift from my sister-in-law—a thin pair of Calvin Kline lounge pants—and a sweat shirt. I wore no underwear and stuck with thin socks and slip-off footwear.

After I dressed, and with the feeling in my lower body gradually returning, I began my final prayers and closing song. The star-studded night of my arrival had slid into the blossoming first light of dawn. As I looked across the river, I saw a small figure. A spirit elf I thought. I let that thought go as I closed my eyes to do prayers and a closing song.

When I had finished, I opened my eyes and glanced across the river again. The elf had disappeared. I wondered if it was a spirit or an actual person. But, I thought, so what? I decided not to meditate that morning, so I gathered up my blanket and towel and made my way back to my car. I must paint a picture of myself so that you may have an idea of what I looked like.

Under one arm, I had my spirit blanket and towel, and in my hand a flashlight. In my other hand I had my spirit bag containing paint for my face and the sacred red dirt or ochre that is used in bathing. The palms of my hands were red from the ochre and my face had a strange coloration from the remains of my sacred paint. I wore an awesome, wool-trimmed knee length, sleeve-free coat that was a gift from a student and looks like it belongs on the tundra of Mongolia. My hair was sticking up every which way, and my amber eyes still carried the power of the river and the spirit world. In other words, I was scary looking.

As I closed the trunk of my car, I looked up, and there in front of me walking down the road was "the elf." Definitely, he was a human being and not a spirit. I thought, "Well, I must look like quite a sight." In the next moment I noticed something very strange. Even though there were snow banks at the edge of the road, he was walking as close as he could to the other side. With no cars at this time of the morning, the logical route to walk would be down the center of the road.

He seemed to be in a trance as he walked by me without acknowledging my presence while staring straight ahead. He stopped at least twenty feet from me, then resumed walking straight ahead until he was horizontal with me. He faced the river and had not turned his head or body to look at me. He just stood still until he finally spoke in a slightly quivering voice.

"You know you scare people," he said, still not looking at me.

When I heard this, I scanned his body for a gun. This was Maine, a hunting state where the Second Amendment and gun ownership is taken seriously. At this distance a gun would be trouble unless he was a poor shoot. Luckily, he was not, as they say, "packing."

After a long pause, he continued. "Everyone is afraid of you and they talk about you constantly. In the morning over coffee you are always brought up. They feel you are some type of spirit."

With this statement, I chuckled to myself. I'd thought he was a spirit, but he and everyone else pegged me as the spirit. Again, a long pause before he continued speaking. But I could tell his initial fear had diminished because he was beginning to understand that I was a human being, just like him.

"Even farmers in the valley say that they hear you and it's disturbing their cows; they've stop giving milk!"

"Uh-oh," I thought. Not good for me; here comes the pitch forks and torches. In times past, narrow minded, arrogant and fearful Christians have burned witches at the stake. And during the Albigensian Crusade, whole cities were burned by the Pope's army: every man, woman, child, and even babies, were killed as heretics. What would this same type of people do if they thought I was an agent of the devil? But then he spoke again.

"Yah, but I think they are exaggerating," he said. And I breathed a sigh of relief. "Their farms are miles away in the valley. Your voice is loud, but not that loud."

His energy changed as he continued, "We heard you a few times last winter, but then nothing. But this winter it's been constant. My wife and I have not been able to sleep. Even with our windows closed tight, it's like you are right next to our bed. My wife is scared and very upset. This morning was the final straw; she insisted I get out of my warm bed and find out what you are. No person can go into that river during the winter. Even during the summer, it's too cold for most. What type of person are you?"

"I am sorry," I replied. "I did not know that I was disturbing people."

"Well, you are." Finally, he turned his head and looked at me. But when he got a good look—now it was full light out—he quickly turned his head back again.

In a respectful voice I said I wouldn't be back. Before I could continue, he hurried away from me while shouting back over his shoulder, "Good or I'll get my gun."

Didn't You Hear the Frogs?

After my experience with the "spirit elf" and his commandment of "return and die," I needed to find another suitable bathing spot. I found a temporary one, not ideal but suitable, as a friend had asked me to take him and his brother bathing. My friend was an organizational development manager and had used Sherry and me for a few team-building experiences out in nature, most typically in the mountains.

My friend thought that his brother would benefit from bathing and that it might spur him to change certain destructive behaviors. In addition, his brother and sister-in-law had spent thousands and thousands of dollars attempting to have a child. My friend thought that bathing might help his brother release some of his anger, resentment and guilt over this issue.

The bathing river was the total opposite of the "elf" river. It was slow moving and flowed under the bridge of a little used road. I explained the procedures and details the day before bathing given that silence is important on the drive to the river. No mind chatter or talking, just focused intent. Bathing can be a little disconcerting. You sacrifice sleep, drive possibly an hour or more in silence, and then exit your car knowing that even though it is cold and dark you are going to strip naked and dip yourself in the waters of a possibly swift flowing river not just once but at least four times. One of bathing's tricky issues involves timing. It is a death and rebirth ritual through which you are symbolically reborn. This means that, metaphorically, your final dip and rise straight up from the dark, watery womb of the Earth Mother occurs at first light. Only experience can teach you the timing on this. A perfect bathing would involve entering the river womb of the Mother in darkness and exiting the river in lightness (first light). When I am alone timing is not a problem, but when I put others into the river it may become an issue. If the light is approaching, I face the spiritual struggle of keeping my human mind from chattering, "Come on, hurry up," because of the people still in the water, and of not letting such chatter interfere with my divine, focused intent.

Even though it was spring, it was spring in Maine – cold with some snow still on the ground. However, this river was not mountain fed so it was not as cold as some I'd encountered. Since the river ran under a bridge the walk to get there was only down the sloping shoulder of the road, plus few more yards to the bathing spot. As I did my prayers and "opened" the river with a song, the brothers undressed. Before they went in, I was to anoint each of their chests with a sacred symbol using my red paint.

Once a person is painted they enter the river facing east, do prayers then dip down under the water and come straight up. They then turn to the south, repeat the process, and then again facing the west. North is the final direction, where a spirit song may be revealed. After this final dip, the person leaves the river, sits under a blanket and meditates, remaining open to whatever images, messages or insights that may come from spirit.

I put my friend's brother in first and watched with slight amusement his interpretation of my instructions. As I said before, this river was not mountain fed and was not that cold. In fact, it turned out to be the warmest water I'd ever bathed in. I didn't need to go into the river to realize this fact. The brother broadcasted it loud and clear with his body image. It was as if I was watching someone at the beach floating in the water, with his arms spread wide and shoulders back like he was relaxing in a comfortable chair. No dipping, just relaxing. I couldn't wait for him to finish the four dips, which at this rate would take us to high noon, so I painted my friend and put him into the river at the same time.

Being an only child, the sibling relationships are foreign to me. With more quiet amusement, I watched as my friend positioned himself downstream, in front of his brother. So far so good as I waited for his first dip. And I waited and waited while he turned his head around to check on his brother not once but a multitude of times before, at last, the first dip. I guess this spurred his brother to replicate his elder sibling. He took his first plunge beneath the waters.

I do not go in and bathe until everyone is out of the river and I know they are safe and under their blankets. Thankfully, the next three directions and dips of the boys didn't take as long as the first ones. I was able to enter, bathe, sing my song and exit the river with the rising of first light. If I am alone, I will sit under a blanket, but if I am bathing others, I do not. I "closed" the river with prayers, a special song and a gifting, then sat next to the water marveling at the sights, smells and sounds of the birth of a new day. After a little while, I called the brothers out from under their blankets and waited while they got dressed. Then we returned to the car.

Once inside the car I let them know that it was okay to talk now and that they could ask any question or make any comments. Before I could even take a breath, the younger brother, who was in the back seat, exclaimed, "I have never heard so many frogs make so much noise in my whole life. I couldn't concentrate. They were everywhere, even hopping on my blanket."

My friend and I just looked at each other with surprise etched on our faces. He stared at us with a questioning look. After a few seconds, I said, "But, there were no frogs!"

Lost Opportunity

Life is ever mysterious and presents us with many challenges. But it also may present us with opportunities and gifts if we have the eyes to see and the ears to hear. Sadly, many people only have the sight and sound of an unhealthy ego-based materialism with a "chattering" mind. Gifts from spirit may go unrecognized and unrealized.

I explained to the younger brother the symbolic significance of the frogs that came to him in spirit form. Symbolically, the frog represents fertility. The frog-headed deity of eternity (the timelessness of now or the present moment) of the ancient Egyptians, *Hehu*, represents the transformation and evolution of Earth/Matter, Water and Fire – the elements connected with the base of the spine and below the navel, the stomach at the navel, and the chest at the heart.

But that brief explanation was as far as it went. He never asked for me and Sher's help with he and his wife's inability to have a child. I still feel sad about this. In the years to come, three of our students who felt they would never have a child, and one who was told it was medically impossible, birthed three new human beings on this Earth through the counseling and healing work of Sher and her support of their efforts to release their past.

This true story is also a teaching story in three ways. First, if Divine Humanity was a dogmatic religion or philosophy, the way the brothers bathed would be unacceptable and deemed ineffective because they did not follow the rules.

Second, the transformational power of bathing occurs through the principle of interpenetration of spirit and matter. Even awakened, a person may be stupid and enlightened at the same time as the Absolute and Relative interpenetrate. The river is spirit/matter. When I do my opening song and prayers, the river takes on the primary attribute of the spirit or divine realm while still being water. It's also important to keep in mind that water has always been considered the portal to the Otherworld.

From a scientific point of view, the best way I can explain this transformational power of bathing is through the work of Masaru Emoto. "From Mr. Emoto's work we are provided with factual evidence, that human vibrational energy, thoughts, words, ideas and music, affect the molecular structure of water, the very same water that comprises over seventy percent of a mature human body and covers the same amount of our planet. Water is the very source of all life on this planet, the quality and integrity are vitally important to all forms of life."[244]

Mr. Emoto's research gives us scientific proof and a glimpse into the validity of spiritual mysteries and practices that indigenous people have known for millennia without having the need for such proof. When I open a river with my song, prayers and thoughts, the molecular structure of the water actually changes and becomes blessed or divine water. When I close the river it goes back to its previous self. However, there is a lingering effect as the river is not quite what it was before.

If we go one step further, we may realize that the pollution affecting the Earth and all of its creatures is not just human-made physical pollution. A large share of the biosphere destruction is being caused not solely by human actions, but by our words and thoughts as well.

Third, many of us have been told that we have to believe in something to see or hear it. I know this is not true. Besides this bathing story, there was the time in the mountains in the 1990s when we were doing our version of corporate team building, which we called community building because team indicates hierarchy while community infers more equality. Our camp site was one which we had used numerous times for our own shamanic apprenticeship. In other words, the land and the spirits knew us.

To put the scene in the proper context, these were employees of a large corporation. And this was not a voluntary training but a mandatory one. None of them believed at all in any form of spirituality or shamanic practice and many were none too comfortable in nature. We were located next to a river and a waterfall in an isolated area. Being on a mountain next to a waterfall and stream provided Sher and I with an invisible assistant – an overabundance of negative ions. These ions are beneficial to our wellbeing and provide a relaxing effect on the body.

If a body is relaxed the mind will be more open to new experiences and beliefs. Our choice of location was one of the reasons we achieved great success in community building in a very short period of time. The training was experiential, but not in a manner that threatened anyone's belief systems. We didn't bathe them, but we did teach them a simple chant and put them under the waterfall. We did a fire without any shamanic overtones where they released some issue in their life and brought some personal quality to the group that would make their work together more harmonious and effective. During these activities, Sher drummed. Interestingly, drumming is usually acceptable to most people.

After the fire, everyone turned in except for my friend—their organizational development manager—Sher and me. As we sat around the fire going over the day's activities, one by one, people came out of their tents and back to the fire. I could see fear etched on their faces. Something was wrong. Finally, someone said, "Who's drumming and chanting?"

I looked at Sher with a smile, and Sher looked at me and then she said, "Don't be afraid. It's only the spirits. They are always happy when we bring groups here."

Why Did You Awaken Me?

The dragon (together with the unicorn) is like a secret theme through time, surfacing like a chimera, touching the lives of the great, then disappearing.[245]

After we relocated from the East Coast to the West Coast's Olympic Peninsula,[246] we needed to discover a new bathing spot. We bought a home, which we christened the *Moorish Castle*. Our home overlooked the only fjord on the West Coast came with a great joy – a view of the white-mountain, Mount Rainier.

The first time we'd set foot in the Pacific Northwest on a journey to live and study with Mom and Vince Stogan, we fell in love with this special place. A familiar refrain reminds us that there's love in the air. And where there is love, there is magic. This is no truer that in the Pacific Northwest. The legacy of spirit, community, love, power and giving (Potlatch) is embedded within the mountains and the sea of this most pristine, primal corner of the world. The love of the land and the sea is woven throughout the myths and the legends of the First Nations People that lived and communed through and with this most sacred part of paradise. Their songs are still alive today, held within the essence of the bubbling of a stream, in the whisper of the wind, or in the cry of an eagle. One may hear and know if one listens with the heart.

And then there is the Olympic Peninsula, a rain-glistening, golden-lit landscape, reminiscent of the mythical land of Lothlórien from J.R.R. Tolkien's Middle-earth trilogy, the Lord of the Rings. It is a special place where magic lives and elves and dragons may very well dwell. As you will discover.

Even thou we lived in the shadow of the Olympic mountains with eagles flying overhead and mountain lions nearby, finding the proper river or stream in which to bathe was not easy. Nor was the right place a short distance from our home. Once again a road trip was needed to discover the proper site. One of our apprentices who lived not far from us suggested a place that might work – Rocky Brook Falls.

The falls turned out to be the perfect bathing spot. Not only did the spot have a small parking area for a few cars, but the path in was only about a five-minute walk. And it was isolated, with no homes nearby. The falls were massive with water cascading down the rocky slope with extreme power and persistence to end in a perfect bathing pool to the right of the falls. The water flowed from the pool into Rocky Brook (actually a river not a brook). The next steps? Open the falls and the river and bathe.

Opening of a Virgin Bathing Spot

In the dark of a moonless night a few weeks after our first visit to Rocky Brook, I was driving the mountainous and tree-lined twisting roads to the falls. After forty minutes, give-or-take, I arrived at the small parking area across the road from the path. The first time walking to a new bathing spot in the dark is always a bit disconcerting. Walking the path in the light of day is different from walking the same path in the dark. Most people use their eyes to identify threats. They seldom use their other senses.

As I applied my face-paint, it was appropriately dark and windy outside the car. I was excited to experience the virgin living waters of this magical place. But then again, after all the years of solo bathing, being alone in this new place was chilling and unsettling. Anyone who would say otherwise is a liar and fool.

Walking to the waterfall in the deep and chilly dark, I couldn't see much in the dim light of my flashlight. But I could strongly feel the primordial primitiveness of the land. The base of the waterfall and the bathing pool were hidden from view by gigantic boulders that had to be traversed to get to the waters. I viewed this as a type of gate, separating the profane from the sacred. Just before I approached this symbolic barrier, I could hear the roar of the falls as if a pride of lions were waiting for me on the other side of the boulders. Once over the rocks of varied sizes, I arrived at the base of the falls. Immediately, with the cold spray from the cascading waters anointing me with its sacredness, I was thrust into a timelessness of force and power.

With a feeling I was not alone, and with the roar of the falls in front of me, I sang my "opening" spirit song, vibrating the land and the waters of this primal place. And then I knelt to pray and offered some of my sacred red paint to the waters of the fall.

The river was now open with access to the Otherworld as I stripped down to "drown" myself not once but four times in the mythical pool. There are few words to describe the bathing experience. All such experiences are powerful, but this sacred place was power incarnate. After my "closing" song, prayers, and gifting, and now in the light of the approaching sunrise, I took in the beauty of this magical place. What an awesome site! I looked forward to bringing our apprentices here for their first West-Coast bathing. And for myself, to bathe once again was to hear the siren's song, to experience the energy of the icy-fire, the burning water, coursing through my body and soul: sacred power,[247] the primal force of creation.[248]

It Simply isn't a Tale to be Told if There not be Dragons

There are dragons of sun and ice, dragons of the moon and the earth,
dragons of salty waters, dragons of thunder;
There is the spangled dragon of the stars at large.
And far at the centre, with one unblinking eye, the dragon of
the Morning Star.[249]

Weeks later we arrived at the Rocky Brook parking area with our apprentices. Once again it was dark, but no wind, only silence. As I applied my face-paint, the apprentices knew to wait in their cars. They also knew that on the drive and once there, no talking, no chatter. The silence within the cars reflected the silence outside. Fear is an insidious "passion" that disturbs the tranquility of the mind. Bathing helps people face their fears of the unknown, the dark, and the cold. And let's not forget submerging in cold, dark, living (flowing) waters.

As Sher and I exited the car, everyone else got out with their bathing blankets under their arms and flashlights in their hands. Once across the road I stopped at the beginning of the path to offer prayers to the spirits of the land. I asked permission to enter the sacred space, conduct bathing, and I asked for the safety and wellbeing of each of us.

During group bathings, I lead the group in while Sher is the last in line. After bathing we reverse the order. Sher leads and I bring up the rear, the last to leave. With my first step on the path, I could feel a difference. Something had changed from the last time I was there. I sensed that we were not alone. In the deep dark of the forested path there seemed to be a presence up ahead. Was it of this world or the otherworld? At this point, I felt uncomfortable as we continued up the path to the waterfall until, in the words of an apprentice who was walking right behind me:

When I go bathing my senses are usually heightened,
mingled with trepidation, knowing that I will immerse
myself in cold, dark, unknown waters before first light.

But on this particular occasion I received a jolt of fear like nothing I've ever experienced, before we even reached the river.

As I walked right behind my spiritual teacher, Dr. Husfelt, headed into the forest, the crown of my head suddenly began to tingle, and the hair rose on the back of my neck. I sensed something powerful, yet invisible, coming down the pathway to meet us. The energy of this spiritual being/entity felt immense, primal, ancient and otherworldly. I could not imagine taking another step towards this looming presence (without grabbing onto the back of my teacher). At that moment he ordered, "Lights off." Into the silent darkness he commenced to sing a spirit song, a vibration unique to his strong mind and powerful spirit. Immediately the energy began to dissipate, and with it my terror. I found I could take the next step when he said, "Lights on," and we continued along the pathway of the primordial forest, headed to the dragon's pool.

It seems that I had awoken the guardian of the waterfall when I opened the bathing spot. After this occurrence, every time we bathed I felt comfort in the knowledge and the knowing that we were accepted, watched, and protected.

BURNINGS – FEEDING THE ANCESTORS

. . . .

A BURNING, FEEDING THE ANCESTORS, IS A TIMELESS AND MOST important ceremony that actually involves cooking food and then burning the food so that the substance and energy of it is taken into the Otherworld. This type of ceremony honoring the gods, goddess, and ancestors by a burnt offering is ancient in form and can be traced as far back as the Egyptians. "The funeral custom is almost universal for the mortuary meal to be made to feed the spirits of the departed, and communion with the ancestral spirits was an object of the totemic eucharist. The sacrifices offered to the dead, the burial rites and funerary ceremonies, generally imply the existence of a living consciousness to which the piteous appeal was made."[250]

A ceremonial burnt offering is also recorded in the *Pentateuch*, the Old Testament, in the story of Abraham and his son Isaac. Abraham is supposed to take his son into the mountains and offer him as a burnt offering to God. At the last moment, God sends an angel to stop him from sacrificing his son, and provides a ram for Abraham to sacrifice in his son's stead. This story does point out a sad fact of history. At certain times and in certain cultures, humans have become the sacrificial food of the gods through the corruption of this most sacred ceremony to honor God and all the unseen reflections of God. (Slightly off the subject, cannibalism, the eating of human flesh, is a deplorable corruption of the spirit and soul.)

Of course, the corruption of this ceremonial practice extends not only to the cultures in the past that have used slaughtered humans as "food" for the gods, but is present today in the Catholic Church rite of communion where the spiritually blind participants eat a wafer symbolic of the body of Jesus and drink wine representing his blood – a corruption, but very effective brain-washing.

Many times, it is the returning cultural hero who brings a new message and method of feeding the Otherworld. Such a person was Quetzalcóatl who brought wisdom as well as peace, knowledge and equality to the people. In his wake, he substituted a burning, or a gifting to the spirit-world of quail, rabbits, snakes and butterflies, for the priestly controlled brutal feeding of the gods the blood sacrifice of human beings.

Conducting a burning is very stressful to say the least. Since this knowledge was and still is orally transmitted, we can only reveal a few things. Before we open the ceremony by calling in the spirits, I paint myself and my wife with red paint, symbolic of blood. Three plates of food are always required: for the ancient ones; the spirits of the land; and most importantly, the forgotten ones.

In preparation for the burning, you prepare a full meal (favorite food) for each spirit to be honored, either as an individual person that has passed over or as a group. The group may comprise the ancestors, the area and the land. Each meal is referred to as a plate, and is put on paper plates. While Sher cooks the food, I prepare the "table" that the food will be put on to be burnt.

Burnings may be performed for openings and closings including but not limited to weddings, funerals, cleansings of homes and land (the exorcising of spirits that are causing problems), memorials and the beginning of spiritual seasons such as the opening of the smokehouses, also known as longhouses, in the Pacific Northwest for the winter dance season.

BURNING TALES

· ·

The Toast that Didn't Burn

BURNINGS ARE THE SOURCE OF MANY TALES THAT FLY IN THE face of accepted scientific fact. One such example comes from our own experience. We were conducting a memorial burning for my father who had passed over the year before. The plate of food for my father would include foods that he liked and would have eaten while he was alive. After calling in the spirits, the plates of food were then put on the "table" as an offering. As Sherry handed me my father's plate, I saw that it contained a piece of wheat bread, something that my father did not like and would not eat. The brief thought that flowed through my mind was: Wheat bread, Dad hates this.

Once I finished laying the rest of the plates, cups, and other things on the table, I lit the fire. Time passed as we each conversed silently with our loved ones who had passed over. During this time, we each observed the impossible.

The wheat bread did not burn while everything else around it, all the other food, burned to ashes. The wheat bread was untouched.

After I closed the ceremony, I turned to Sherry and said, "How come wheat bread? You know my father hated it."

"I know," she replied, "but your mother said she hasn't had white bread in the house since your father died." Sherry paused and smiled. "She said that it was the only bread she had and he would have to eat it!"

Ice Cream

Let me tell you of our friend Dr. Walter Houston Clark, who passed over in December of 1994 while in his nineties. His memory always brought a smile to our faces in more ways than one. One time he was reading to our daughter who was on his lap and he fell asleep and our daughter felt that he had died and didn't know what to do until he suddenly began reading again.

My story takes place in January 1995, when we conducted a burning for the beginning of our year-long apprentice program. Once the date is set for a burning, it cannot be changed under any circumstances, even intense snow storms. The Friday of the burning dawned gray and overcast with snow forecast to fall at any time. We couldn't conduct the burning sooner in hopes of beating the snow as burnings have to be held late in the afternoon after a certain time when it is felt the spirits have woken from their rest.

The location for the burning was on an apprentice's property located on the shores of a lake. The logistics are never simple. Food needs to be cooked and brought to the site while an open fire is built. Open being the key word. Have you ever attempted to light a fire in the open while it is raining or heavily snowing? And then keep it burning?

On top of the snow, Sher was on her moon-time – bleeding. To many shamanic cultures this is a time of great power for women, but the belief is that the spirits are uncomfortable with the menstrual blood. Thus some cultures will prohibit women from participating in any religious ceremonies while bleeding. On the contrary, Vince and Mom Stogan had taught us the proper procedures (painting with red ochre) for a bleeding woman, which would allow her to participate or conduct the ceremony.

If there had been a camera crew filming the burning, this is what it would have recorded: A dozen bundled people with heavy snow falling down on them, already standing in knee-deep snow as the wind whipped off the frozen lake at their backs, decreasing the all-ready brutally cold temperature. In front of them are layers upon layers of wood and paper open to the falling snow. And next to the wood and paper, a table holding plates of food and blankets for the burning.

In the next scene, a few yards away from the burning area, Sher had her back to the lake and students with me in front of her, I painted her body with sacred red paint in an ancient design that would allow her to conduct the ceremony with me.

After I painted Sher, we proceeded to call in the spirits and begin the ceremony. Even with the heavy snow falling, all the wood and food burnt up. During the ceremony, ice cream came into my consciousness, possibly a request of one of the spirits. It is usually Sher who hears and sees the spirits so I needed to ask her if I was correct or if it was just a random thought. If I was correct, then we needed to provide ice cream for the next burning. If a spirit requests something then it is our responsibility to provide it the next time.

After the burning was completed, I turned to Sher and said, "I think one of the spirits wants ice cream." She laughed as tears rolled down her cheek. "That was Dr. Clark. He loved ice cream. During the whole ceremony he was sitting up in the tree to our right having a good time watching us."

To this day, we greatly miss Dr. Clark. And we are grateful to him for many things, especially one. Pure and simple, it was due to Sher working with Dr. Clark, and us not moving to Maryland, that we ended up in the Yucatan in August of 1987. And as it is said, "the rest is history." Our journey to the Yucatan led us to many great adventures and eventually to Mom and Vince Stogan.

No Tea for You. So Cold!

Friends who were establishing a New Age center on Martha's Vineyard asked us to do a burning for their opening weekend. Never having been on Martha's Vineyard, we were looking forward to seeing our friends again and experiencing the island.

Depending on the time of year, burnings are conducted late afternoon to early evening. While Sher was inside our friend's home preparing the food and liquid such as hot tea, I prepared the table to be burned with layers and layers of wood and paper. The food would be put on the table and then burnt, transmuting it into sustenance for the Otherworld. Besides the food, we would burn at least one cotton blanket for spirits still on Earth who possibly drowned or died in the cold.

Once everything was completed and the food and other items were brought out to the burning site, no words were spoken. After I applied my face-paint, I painted Sher with red paint and then called in the spirits to open the ceremonial feeding of the Otherworld. Before I began, I took a quick look at the other table holding the food, tea, water, and blankets which Sher was to present one at a time to me to be put on the burning table before we lit the fire. I realized there were no cups of tea. Letting this thought go, I proceeded to call in the spirits. Once the spirits had gathered we could begin the feeding.

Burnings are powerful and can be dangerous. You never turn your back to the fire as the spirits are feeding. One may reach out and touch you, which would result in Sher and I having to do a spirit extraction on you after the ceremony.

One most important point: Sher and I are equally important and necessary to the ceremony. The spirits expect food and drink and our attention. I can't go into more detail regarding the actual process with the plates, cups and blankets. The knowledge must be given orally along with the medicine power to conduct such ceremonies.[251]

Usually in a burning, once we have called in the spirits, Sher passes me the food to place on the food table. Works well, except this time. After a few plates of food had been placed, as I turned to get the next plate from Sher, she hesitated and then collapsed to the ground.

After Sher collapsed I attempted to ground her because I knew whatever spirits she saw or heard in the Otherworld were affecting her. As they say, the ceremony must go on. It became a struggle of plates, ground and hold Sher, cup of water, ground and hold Sher, until finally, I was able to ground her enough that she came back and was able to continue.

Finally finished with the food and other things, it was time to burn the blanket. And boy, did it go up quickly as the flames rose high into the air. My thought was, "One or more of the spirits was very, very cold."

Thankful that the burning was complete, and concerned about Sher because I knew she was an empath, I turned to her and asked how she was feeling.

"So cold, so wet," she replied with a grieved look within her eyes. "A family, they drowned." I took her in my arms and held her with a love that transcends time.

Before our group—the witnesses of the burning—had its sharing/discussion and communal meal, Sher told me what had happened.

"At first I thought, why are those people coming from the woods and walking towards the fire. You're not supposed to be in front of the fire where the spirits are feeding. And then I realized, they were spirits, a family, two adults and a child. The sorrow was so overwhelming I couldn't stand. They were so cold and we only had one blanket. They asked for more blankets. We need to burn more than one next burning."

During the sharing, after Sher explained what had happened and what she saw, the person who requested the burning told the group that recently a boat had sunk and the family on board had drowned! And the spirits had walked out of the woods from the direction of that tragic accident!

From the Viewpoint of an Apprentice

Back in the early to mid-1990s Jim and Sherry Husfelt co-led an old-time burning ceremony on Martha's Vineyard that I was fortunate enough to attend. Although the day was sunny and calm, I felt a sense of pressure during the preparations for the burning. Horses in the adjacent field also seemed agitated and began to whinny, nicker and skitter. Dr. JC Husfelt explained that the horses could pick up on the energy of the gathering of spirits. The air felt electric and wild. The wind stirred. Emotion welled up inside of me as Sherry Husfelt sang her spirit song for the opening of the ceremony, which pierced the veil between the worlds. Within a short period of time, her eyes glittered and focused on something that I could not see. Her knees buckled, and she was wracked with grief.

JC, while conducting the ceremony, stepped closer to assist her, to prevent her from collapsing. He had a tough job to do, to keep her upright while tending to the ceremony. The wind swelled and swished the trees. Sherry's empathic nature, tears and trembling body communicated to all witnesses the anguish of those who had passed over. JC laid his powerful healing hands upon her shoulders and neck numerous times to help keep her functional and on her feet. The hot and hungry fire surged and billowed, devouring the spirit food with its orange flames. Once the spirits were fed, the fire died down and so did the wind. The horses fell silent and a peaceful hush settled over the land. The ceremony complete, the Husfelt's shared their stories, insights and experiences of this unusually intense burning.

One last comment on the missing tea. I wasn't in the kitchen, but outside helping with the fire. Thus the vivid remembrance of the horses.

What I recall is that there were three signs around the tea making. First, there was the unexpected commotion of the pitcher shattering when the boiling water was poured over the tea bags, and onto Sherry's hands, which miraculously did not get burned. Then there was the last-minute re-brewing of a new batch of tea, which mysteriously never made it out to the table. It was too late in the proceedings of the burning to go retrieve it, once the discovery was made that it was missing.

Afterwards, during the sharing and discussion of the ceremony, Peanut[252] explained that during the embargo on tea during the era of the Boston Tea Party, boxes of tea had been smuggled into Martha's Vineyard to hide on the island!

SPIRIT EXORCISM – CASTING AWAY
UNWANTED INTRUSIONS

. . . .

VINCE AND MOM STOGAN TAUGHT US THIS METHOD OF
shamanic extraction of unwanted spirit energies based on knowledge handed
down for hundreds and hundreds of years. This knowledge is only orally
taught. It cannot be learned in any neo-shamanic workshop.

It is also important to know that there are no bad or evil spirits from which
we need to protect ourselves. Protection is physical and/or mental separation,
which only influences and promotes the continuance of a dualistic consciousness. Energy is energy; however, there are unseen energetic forms that may
attach themselves to our bodies, which may cause physical symptoms and
problems that traditional medicine would not able to diagnose or heal. These
vibrational energies are, in most cases, not compatible or in harmony with our
vibrational bodies and minds. As an example, this is the reason why it is best
not to remove lava from the Big Island of Hawaii. The lava is not cursed by the
Goddess *Pele*, but the vibrational energy of the lava may not be compatible
with your energetic vibration and may present to you as headaches, stomach
problems, and so forth.

Extracting the energetic form is only the first part of the process. The
second phase, and almost as important as the first, is the command not to
return. This is as true today as in the past. According to Morton Smith, "almost
as important as the command to leave the patients was the command not to

return, which we find Jesus and other magicians adding to their exorcisms."[253] This fact as truth you will discover in the tales that follow.

The Cursed Sword

If we were writing this book a decade ago, this section would not be as necessary as it is today. I still would have shared cautionary thoughts about purchasing or accepting older esoteric items, but it's more important in today's world of eBay and other online auction sites. No travel to foreign lands – it's all done from the comfort of your home. There is a problem, however, which you will discover or maybe already have experienced.

The majority of my sacred objects have stories connected with them and were found during my various adventures over the past thirty-plus years. Not only do they carry the power of the lands they were wedded to, but they also hold my memories of time, place, and adventure. I know the circumstances surrounding them. They are not an unknown, purchased off the Internet. For many armchair adventurers, the memories are only of the winning bid.

Sacred items may retain the energetic memories of their previous use. This also extends to martial items, such as swords. Many factors, including how they have been used, will determine their effect on the present owner. This effect may be neutral, positive, or negative.

These effects may also stem from a spirit that has attached itself to the item. Casting out serpents is not metaphor but literal. It is a form of healing where an energetic serpent is taken off a person and cast away. This is one of the oldest and more advanced forms of shamanic/spiritual healing. It is the hands-on healing of extracting old energies, which are usually in the form of a serpent, but not always. This energy may wrap itself around a person's limb during a time of intense trauma. Most often this is not a physical trauma, but one of an emotional, mental, and/or spiritual nature. It may lie dormant for years until something triggers its activation.

In the same manner, a person may trigger an item's spiritual stowaway. One story portrays this vividly. Sherry and I had flown to New York to conduct an apprentice training and were staying at an apprentice's house on Long

Island. Like myself, the apprentice was a martial artist. He was also an avid buyer of items on eBay. Even though it was late at night when we finally arrived at his house and we were tired, having traveled all day, he still wanted to show me something as soon as we walked into his house. What he showed me was a *nodachi*, a horse sword, used by Japanese cavalry or foot soldiers. This sword is nearly a five-feet-long, a two-handed sword that was basically used to take down a horse and its rider or soldiers on the ground. The apprentice handed me the sword, and within seconds, I handed it back to him.

I'm not a night dreamer. Yes, I dream, and I have had some powerful dreams, but primarily I'm a daytime dreamer. The next morning, I was in that twilight stage between sleeping and waking. In that gray area of existence, the dream/waking state, the image I had was of a centipede on my back, choking me. And then I woke up, gasping for air, my heart pounding as if I had sprinted the first mile of my typical four-mile runs. Perspiration formed on my forehead. Even though I was slightly shaken in both body and mind, I shrugged it off as my being overly tired from traveling and didn't think much more about it until I took a shower.

Initially, a spirit intrusion will affect our bodies at their weakest points. I know my body, and its weakest point is my lower back. One time, when I was studying the martial arts in Japan, I unconsciously disrespected a former grandmaster of the arts by calling him by just his last name. This is a grave offense to any Japanese, but it was especially disrespectful to my former grandmaster. I didn't do it intentionally; it was just a slip of the tongue. When his hand touched my hand, it was stone cold and an image popped into my mind of writhing maggots. I didn't even realize the disrespect until, as we were walking away, my son said, "Dad, you just called him by his last name. His whole energy changed at that moment. He was none too happy."

Within the hour, I began to feel a little dizzy and sick. I wondered, "Did he put something on me? No," I thought, "he wouldn't have done that for a simple slip of the tongue." Of course, he didn't know it was unintentional. Sherry and I had been taught the knowledge of extracting unwanted spirit entities as well as putting them on others, and the cold hand and wriggling maggots had all the hallmarks of this practice.

Later that night, at martial arts training with my current grandmaster, all doubt left my mind because my lower back went out for no reason at all. It was not until the next day, when the grandmaster conducted *kuji kiri* (esoteric spirit power) over me that my back got better.

Ten years after that experience, it was déjà vu all over again. As I was taking my shower, I bent over and felt the first pangs of pain. Straightening, I quickly exited the shower, threw on some clothes, and went downstairs to find my wife.

"Sherry," I said. "Something's on my back. Would you please take it off?"

Without hesitation, she asked, "Where can I do it?"

"Out front, next to the driveway is a tree stump. I can sit on it, and you can work on my back," I replied.

Discreetly, we excused ourselves and went outside. Once Sherry began working on me, I could feel her pulling it off. Depending on the spirit entity, this healing can become almost like an epic battle, with the healer having one foot in the Otherworld and one foot in our material world. And so it seemed that Sherry was engaged in one of these struggles. There are two important parts to this form of healing. The first part is, of course, taking the entity off the person. The second part is equally important: casting it away so that it stays in the Otherworld and doesn't return to the person.

I had not told Sherry about my waking experience, of a centipede choking me. She had no idea what was on me. However, I now knew that it had attached itself to me when I had held the horse sword. This was also why I had only handled it for a short time. Brief or not, it was still time enough for it to have taken up residence on my body. It felt my martial spirit and attached to me, not to my student.

Finally, I could feel that it was off me as Sherry cast it away. After a few minutes she said, "Wow. It didn't want to be taken off of you. And this was a first."

"What do you mean?" I asked.

"I've never come across this type of spirit. It began at the base of your spine and was all the way up to your neck. It was a giant centipede!"

Interesting postscript: There was a special group of mounted samurai messengers called *Mukade* – centipede. These mounted warriors were supposedly known as "one worth a thousand," and their weapon of choice was the *nodachi*. The feudal Japanese did not think of the centipede as having positive qualities, but it was considered good luck in battle and was the battle banner of the famous general Takada Shingen. The folklore about the centipede is that they will bite you in the behind!

Spirit Serpent

Mexico is a land full of mystery and enchantment, but sad to say, also sustains a socio-economic system of poverty. The gulf between the haves and the have-nots is a great one. Accordingly, when you travel away from the tourist areas and the major cities, you will discover a land full of proud people, which in their own way are living out a legacy of the white invaders and the narrow-minded dogmatic Christian zealots who destroyed their culture and lifeblood many centuries before. To these people and this land of the feathered serpent, this place of magic, Sherry and I came once again. Many times we had journeyed to these jungles and to the highlands of this enigmatic nation, experiencing the wonder and hidden gifts of the people and the land. And again, we were bringing a group to learn, heal and awaken to their own love and power.

Some of the people on this trip had been with us the previous year in Hawaii, where I experienced my vision, and had now come to experience the primal energy and the surreal beauty of the Yucatán. Mexico and Hawaii are two of our favorite pilgrimage destinations. The transformational energy of each is distinct, and thus, both lands provide a different gateway and access point to the healing of one's soul.

Over the previous year (1993) I'd researched the symbolic and mythological knowledge of the Morning Star. Having spent many years of spiritual seeking within the mystical traditions of Mexico, I was familiar with the mythology of Quetzalcóatl as the Morning Star but never really paid much attention to it until that year, when Venus and its aspect as the Morning Star became a constant in my consciousness. Thus, I awoke to the fact that many of the sites around the world that we'd visited were connected with Venus. However, there was one important historical site linked with the religion of Quetzalcóatl that I hadn't yet visited: Teotihuacán. In my heart I felt that sooner rather than later I needed to visit this "City of the Gods." But for this trip, the beaches and the jungles of the Yucatán were our focus.

Since the late 1980s, we've been bringing groups to a wonderful, and most importantly, isolated resort about forty-five minutes south of Cancun. Over the years I've observed the changes in this part of Mexico. When I first came here there were few tourists and very little resort development. Of course that has changed, but still, there is never an absence of enchantment. Magic lingers in the air, a pristine aura suspended over these spirit filled lands. Jaguars, and their spiritual essence, move just beyond our consciousness, always dwelling in a space between fear and fascination. "Whilst Quetzalcóatl is often referred to as the feathered or plumed serpent (i.e. a composite bird-snake), a closer examination reveals that it may in fact be a mixture of three separate animals – with a jaguar's face and fangs, a serpent's body, and a bird's feathers."[254]

Yucatán with its jungles is a land of death, and all the fears connected with it. But it is also a realm of rebirth and all the joys that are connected with that.

Our group was to get an opportunity to experience this first hand, not just with the mind, but also with the body.

There are many ways to experience the process of death and rebirth. One of the oldest forms of this transcendent wisdom is submersion, either in water or through burial in the earth. Each form has a similar but different focus and purpose. Both allow us to come face to face with our greatest enemies: fear and death. One day on the 1994 trip, the sky had turned to dusk and our dear students had been fasting since breakfast. Since we didn't want to seed their minds with worry and dread, we hadn't told them what experience we would be conducting. They trusted Sherry and me, but they also knew that every activity was optional.

Burial

Standing in the near darkness on an isolated stretch of beach, the lush jungle to our backs and the bluish-green, clear waters to our front, we explained the spiritual exercise:

- Each person had a partner who was going to witness the experience as well as act in the role of a guardian angel. As I handed each person a straw and a small cloth to cover their eyes, I sensed their level of fear and observed their eyes, the windows to the soul. I took note of the ones that I would need to keep more of an eye on. For some, this was one of the worst things that I could ask them to do – be buried alive!

- One of the partners would dig their own grave, keeping in mind the impermanence of the body while letting go of a quality of self that no longer served them. As they let go of this quality they would also need to replace it with a positive one, such as increased patience. Meanwhile their partner—their guardian angel—would silently witness this courageous act of digging one's own tomb of spirit.

225

- When they were ready, they would lay in the "arms of the mothering Earth" while their guardian angel covered them completely with sand except for the straw they would breathe through. Now, if you've ever tried to breathe through a straw, you know the limitation. This added the additional fear of not getting enough air. And of course, the more tense that you are, the more difficult it is to breathe.

- Some of the graves were deep enough that when covered, a person would need assistance to get out. So there was, if you will, an angel line. The person buried would keep one hand out of the grave and their angel would hold their hand. When they completed the exercise to the best of their ability, they would squeeze their angel's hand and the angel would dig them out. There was no time limit or required depth of the grave. It was up to the individual. Over the years, I have seen many shallow graves and a few very deep ones. And the time spent spanned from a few seconds to upwards of a half an hour. We never judge the people we work with, how they accomplish the exercises or whether they choose to even participate in a certain one. They know best. We are only teachers and guides that offer support and encouragement.

As the exercise began, all were in silence with one partner digging and the other witnessing. As I walked up and down the beach offering encouragement through my smile, I never took my focus or awareness off the one student who was the most terrified. She had been in our program a few years, and in that time, had healed many of her past's woundings, but I knew this activity was bringing an old, deep wounding to the surface, one from the core of her soul.

The grave was dug. She slowly crawled in and began to lie back, but suddenly, she bolted back up into a sitting position, fear and terror etched on her face. With a deep breath and a courageous spirit, she tried again and again, until finally, she stayed down. As her guardian angel began to cover her, I stood right by her side. I could rely on Sherry to watch the rest of our group. I was needed here.

She was only under a few seconds, which probably felt like an eternity to her. As she kicked her way out of the sand, I saw an old, an ancient serpent wrapped around her right leg! This was a spirit serpent, an old energy that had probably been attached to her leg for years. Her right leg had caused her pain and problems for years. No physician or alternative health practitioner had been able to diagnosis the cause of her limping and painful leg, nor had anyone been able to heal it.

I positioned myself at the bottom of her leg and begin an extraction healing, a shamanic practice that has been utilized for thousands of years. As I prayed and began the extraction, I knew that no one else but Sherry saw the serpent. The sweat built as I worked on this serpent energy, which did not want to be released. This type of extraction can be dangerous to me; if doubt or fear had entered my mind, the serpent could have attached to me. I needed to be one with the heavens and the Earth, virgin in spirit, fully focused in the moment and with total confidence. The struggle reflected the cosmic dance and blending of dark and light, and then my voice erupted into my spirit song. I know that I am never alone, my heavenly "buddies" are always available and my earthly other half, Sherry is always there. With the power of the heavens, the Earth, and my song, I extracted the serpent with my hands and cast it away!

Serpents in the Night

In the aftermath of this type of spirit healing, the person who has been healed needs to rest and be quiet. Without any explanation, Sherry and the woman's partner helped her back to their cabana to sleep. No food was needed, just pure water. It was not necessary to explain the details of what happened. It's always best to keep in mind that the greatest spiritual lessons are not found in books, but are learned by listening, observing, doing spirit work, having spirit work done on you, and then asking questions.

The next morning at breakfast, both the woman and her roommate came over to thank us. As they approached the table, I noticed how strong and confident she seemed. In fact, she walked with more confidence than I had ever seen her walk with before. We asked her how she was feeling and if she had slept okay. At that moment, a strange look crossed both their faces. "I'm feeling much better, just a little weak," she replied. "But neither of us could sleep. We both swear there was a gigantic snake in our room, and many smaller ones. We heard them moving in the dark and sensed them. But each time we turned on the light, we searched the complete cabana and there were no snakes!"

Pesky Snakes

The following is an account of an exorcism of a spirit in the form of a serpent I performed on one of our apprentices in 1997. These are her own words, written the morning after the visitation.

"From the start it was a strange injury. I do several sports: karate, where I was a purple belt; and tennis, which I play competitively at the club level. And so I always have plenty of opportunities to get injured. But I didn't get injured while I did a sport. I didn't even get injured within several days of doing one of my sports. I just woke up one morning and my heel hurt. Within two days my leg started to hurt, and within hours after that, I couldn't put any weight onto my leg at all. I had ruptured my calf muscle. Recovery involved about six weeks in an air cast and physical therapy that included everything from swimming to special stretches.

"After about three months, I returned slowly to my sports. After about nine months, I was back fully to my sports. There was, however, a nagging tightness and sometimes aching in my leg that never seemed to fully leave me. After a strenuous workout, it would even develop spasms, and these came at times when I had the full range of motion and didn't seem to be hindered sports-wise other than the discomfort, so I knew something else was going on. I spoke to JC and asked if he would do a healing on my leg.

"Early one August morning, after a very powerful baptism ceremony, JC performed the healing. I don't know what energy he tapped into. I did feel tingling up and down my spine. It was excruciatingly painful when he put his hands on my leg and pulled off whatever it was he was pulling off. That night when everyone had gone to bed at my house, I went into my meditation room to do some chanting and ceremony. My chanting kept getting interrupted because I felt like snakes were crawling over my body. I knew from the rational world that there were no snakes in my room or in my house. But they felt so real that I couldn't concentrate. Finally, after several fruitless attempts, I decided to call it a night. As I was closing up my altar, I suddenly heard a very distinctive hissing sound coming from the corner of the room. I couldn't see anything, but the noise had a distinctly otherworldly feel to it. It made the hair on the back of my head stand on end, and my blood instantly ran cold in my veins. It had the effect that a good horror film will have on someone – paralyzing. I ran out of the room, closed the door, and called JC even though it was near midnight. Normally, JC and his wife have an answering machine on so they don't have to answer the phone at night. But on this night, JC had fallen asleep downstairs by the phone. He'd gotten up and was standing by the phone when it rang at midnight. I remember sobbing to him that something was hissing at me. I was terrified. JC said that he had taken a serpent off of my leg that morning and had cast it away, but sometimes this serpent energy will follow the person and stalk him or her. He taught me a secret *mudra* (a hand position), a *mantra* (a vocalization or prayer), and a movement to chase it away.

"When I touched the doorknob of the room, I immediately felt the same cold horror. My hair stood up, and my blood felt chilled again. I walked carefully into the room with my arms crossed in front of me and my hands tightly holding onto the *mudra*. In the corner where the energy was most intense, I performed the combined movement and *mantra* twice.

"Immediately, my blood warmed up and the fear dissipated. And since this time, my leg has been wonderful. Other than occasional bouts of stiffness, I am able to move much more energetically, and I can feel the energy flow has returned to its normal levels. I am very grateful."

Mason Jars

In some healing situations, mason jars are an essential tool for the shaman. I know. Mason jars? Of course, there are different healing methods and tools depending on the indigenous culture. But in Vince's medicine tradition, under certain circumstances a mason jar may be needed.

In the early 1990s, Vince received a request for healing on the Lummi Reservation located across the Canadian border in Washington state. We just happened to be staying with Vince and Mom when Vince received the request. It is important to mention at this point a primary responsibility of an Indian doctor or shaman in Vince's tradition. He had taught us that every request for healing or ceremony had to be accepted. There were no exceptions. Even if a person had committed the vilest act against you or your family, their request would have to be honored. The only wiggle room on ceremonies such as a burning is timing. It is the responsibility of the shaman to determine the proper day to conduct the burning.

This request for healing involved a different form of extraction healing. This type of healing could be referred to as a form of countering "love magic." In this case, it involved a romantic love triangle. As I mentioned in the story of "The Cursed Sword" above, a person of power may put their spirit power on another person, though not for their benefit.

Timing was perfect, with us being in Vancouver. We were able to learn how to accomplish this type of extraction healing work. Learning the "old ways" does not involve workshops or seminars. It's similar to being an intern or resident in a hospital setting. You learn by doing and assisting an Indian doctor like Vince.

Lummi

We arrived at a woman's home on the Lummi Reservation late in the afternoon. Vince introduced us to the woman and told her that we were going to assist him in the healing. The backstory concerned the woman's husband and his girlfriend. The girlfriend had paid a local medicine man to put something on the wife that would cause the husband to leave his wife for his girlfriend. Surprisingly, these types of things still happen today and are not just stories from the distant past.

We can't go into the details of the extraction except that when Vince had removed what was basically the energetic essence, the spirit power, of the medicine man, it was not "thrown away" as spirit entities such as serpents are, but was put into a container – a mason jar.

As Vince held the extraction in his cupped hands, I held the jar and Sher the lid so that when Vince placed it in the jar the lid could be put on immediately to trap the essence in the mason jar. In this way, the person who'd put that on the wife would need to go to Vince to apologize and vow not to do that type of work again. If the person did not do this, the person would slowly sicken, have problems breathing and, well, you can imagine the rest.

On the lighter side, when Sher helped Mom Stogan in the kitchen and was asked to get an "empty mason jar," she was always a little apprehensive about which one to pick!

Commentary

Many people emphasize learning the technique for such healing work. However, the key to success is not just technique, but the strength of the shaman's mind and heart. In other words, it is not solely the technique that works but the internal power of the healer, which is revealed by the "gateway" to the soul – the eyes.

HEALING – HARMING: IDENTICAL

. . . .

THE ABOVE TITLE MAY SEEM STRANGE AT FIRST AND THE WORDS seemingly at odds with each other, but this is not the case. There is no such thing as Black Magic or White Magic – only Magic. The intention determines whether the results are beneficial or harmful. According to James Maffie's *Aztec Philosophy*, "Creative energy and destructive energy are not two different kinds of energy but two aspects of one and the same teotlizing[255] energy."[256]

In other words, healing or harming is dependent on the will and intention of the Indian doctor, shaman or mystic. The difference between healing and harming has nothing to do with technique, only the shaman's intent. And the effectiveness of either healing or harming is directly proportional to the strength of the Indian doctor's heart and mind. This reality further verifies radical nonduality, which is based on nondifferentiating knowledge where there is no distinction between dualistic terms. It is not healing and harming, two terms, but healing/harming as one term. They are one and the same.

One example of this concept is portrayed by cutting (harming) the energy of a person and then making them whole again (healing). As preparation for our apprentice program, we would offer a workshop called "Awakening." What follows is a participant's own words:

> I started the martial arts in the year of 1972. As a martial
> artist, I have always heard the stories about masters who
> could perform incredible feats of what many may call magic.

232

In 1988, I met a Japanese grandmaster. I was fortunate enough to be accepted to training with him.

On a return trip from Japan, I stopped over in Los Angles where I met James Husfelt, Jr. We both trained under the same Japanese grandmaster and we both ended up in Los Angles for a seminar being conducted by this grandmaster.

One thing led to another and I was introduced to James' father, JC Husfelt. This was in 1991. Through the next four years, James and I became close friends and I talked with his Dad occasionally. In 1995, we attended another seminar with the same grandmaster. This time I sat directly across from JC and was able to listen to him talk about his philosophy of Divine Humanity, which heightened my curiosity. JC explained to me that he and his wife did a weekend workshop which they had aptly named The "Awakening" Weekend. After thinking about it, I called and registered to attend the following weekend. This was in June of 1996.

I managed to enlist two other friends to attend with me because frankly, I was a bit apprehensive. James explained to me that his Dad was a little different than most teachers and the weekend would be grueling, fun, and possibly a little scary. I figured, how bad could it be? I didn't think he would kill me, but I thought it was best to have friends along just in case.

We arrived on Friday evening and settled in for the weekend's teachings. On Sunday, the last day of the workshop, JC explained that everyone is capable of some type of energy work; some more than others. My interest level rose immediately. I'd been earnestly searching for something like this since I'd begun my martial arts journey.

JC asked if anyone would like to volunteer for an impromptu demonstration. Being the person I am—I have to see it to believe it—my hand shot up. I still remember him smiling and saying, "I am not surprised."

He taught me a way to breathe and relax and then went on to explain what he was going to do, which was to cut my energy. I have to say right then and there I said to myself, b—s—, never going to happen. I planned to resist in any way I could.

First, JC moved about ten feet away from me. In the next moment, he was holding a silver shining sword and it was cutting me from hip to hip. My upper body fell forward as if I had been cut across the waist. The next thing I knew, I couldn't move my arms or my legs, and although I seemed to be able to breathe okay, everything was getting somewhat cloudy and fuzzy.

I am not sure about the next part. One of the participants said that JC came next to me and did some motions with his hands. It was then that my vision cleared as JC asked me to move my arms and legs, which I was now able to do. I looked over at one of my friends and asked, "What the heck just happened?" He said at the same time, "Are you OK?"

To say I was stunned and awed would be an understatement. Never in my life, had I experienced anything close to that. I had heard tales about masters being able to cut energy, flow energy, or whatever you want to call it, but no one ever showed it.

When I sat back down, again I asked my friends what happened. They told me they saw what appeared to be a sword cut through me. I looked at JC and he showed me he was holding a small twig about five inches long. I immediately signed on and became a direct personal student of him and his wife. Many years later my teacher explained to me that he had a knowing that a demonstration of power would be the only way I would become a student.

Despite what I did with this student, I seldom demonstrate this act of power. The most interesting comments from those few people in the past whose energy I have cut were never so much about the cutting or harming but more about the healing, the making them whole again.

Cutting Attachments

One of the most important spiritual practices is forgiveness.[257] Forgiveness is the light that pierces the darkness and dispels the mists of hatred, anger, guilt, and resentment to name a few of the negative emotions. Forgiveness is of the heart and mind. It is the cornerstone of love and all spiritual practice and the key that unlocks the doorways to peace – peace within and peace on Earth.

Forgiveness, on the other hand, is often misunderstood and misrepresented. It is important to understand that forgiveness from the Great Mystery is automatic; we do not need an intermediary such as a priest between us and the Great Mystery. But what is not automatic is our own earthly forgiveness of others, and of ourselves.

Forgiveness is simply the letting go of our emotional and mental enemies. Four of the greatest enemies that attach to our mind are fear, anger, resentment and guilt. Pure and simple, these emotions are the chains that bind us and prevent us from being happy. The more we hold on to these emotions, the stronger the chains become, but freedom is always within reach. Freedom is within our mind and heart; freedom is forgiveness. It frees us from the bondage of these emotions and allows us the courage to be fearless. Forgiveness does not condone the wrongdoing of others nor is it about forgetting; it does, however, release us from the emotional prison of the past. To the degree that we release our past through forgiveness, we will experience the same amount of happiness and freedom in our present life.

However, there is one aspect of forgiveness that is seldom discussed, possibly due to lack of knowledge and training. We may have forgiven others and cut our emotional ties or attachment to them, but that does not guarantee that they are not emotionally attached to us. Under this circumstance, "cutting" may be needed.

We are all connected in a symbolic web of life. If we have never met, a person, the thread connecting them to us is very, shall we say, thin. It makes sense, then, that the threads between family members are much stronger and thicker and transmit greater energetic vibration. In a nut shell, this explains sympathetic magic or imitation magic which involves using an effigy such as a voodoo doll.

These threads may be cut away from an individual leaving only a thinner thread with no adverse emotional connection. The question often asked: "Will this cut the person totally out of my life?" The answer is no, just the dysfunctional connection between both of you. However, without an emotional connection, the person may disappear out of your life. (Cutting the attachment of an abusive person is much more effective than an restraining order!)

This spirit power of "cutting" cannot be taught in a seminar or training. This is one of the reasons why it is not widespread. Furthermore, the effectiveness of the "cutting" is directly proportional to the power of the shaman.

This form of healing may be done at any time and in any place even though many times it is done during a Peruvian Fire Ceremony. The cutting is usually performed with a sword, but not always. As with any spiritual work, the medicine man or shaman needs to be asked for healing or for a certain ceremony. Most importantly, there is no fee for healing work or ceremony. "Cutting" is one of the medicine powers that I possess.

The following is an account of an apprentice I cut during a fire ceremony:

Ponderings of the Fire Ceremony and Cutting

Been sitting and thinking about how to try to put a lot of this into understandable words. Tough.

During the actual cutting it was almost as if I wasn't there. Time seemed to suspend, stop if you will. I had no inkling of how long or short a time I was there.

It seemed as if a tornado of power was swirling around me, but not really touching, or so I thought. It was almost dreamlike. Making my way back to the guardian position was vague. That's when I kind of knew that stuff was going on around me. Perception seemed to return for me.

When we finally finished—it seemed to go on all night— my legs just said, time to go down. I had to put my forehead against the ground to get a semblance of being in the present time period. Grounded so to speak.

That night was rough. Up and not feeling well, in and out of the toilet. That lasted for almost a week. My insides were really messed up. Very weird.

Then today I decided to get out and run. Running for the last two years has been difficult. I could never seem to get the proper breathing and pacing. Today was way different. I felt lighter and running was incredibly easy. Pacing, breathing all seemed to work. I got through the two miles much more easily than I have been able to do for a long time. I found that very strange.

To say that I am completely back is not entirely correct. But I do feel I am very much better than I have been. Lighter, more open, maybe a little less sad.

So we'll see what the tomorrows bring.

Weeks later:

As to the cutting, nothing new. Still feel lighter and the relationships that I was looking to detach from are detached, which is a good thing. No sadness or remorse, which I am happy about.

The Sword

The sword has its own intrinsic power and is also an extension of my power. The sword I usually use for a cutting is the *Espada de San Pablo* (Sword of Saint Paul). In Belize, I purchased and used a Belizean machete to perform cutting on the edge of the New River Lagoon while staying at the Lamanai Outpost Lodge. But there may be times when a sword is not available. What happens then?

Depending on the power of the shaman, a sword may not be necessary. Not having a sword available, I may cut energy using my fingers in positioned in the sword *mudra*. Basically, *mudras* are various ways to use our hands. They include the intertwining of our fingers. The most commonly recognized religious *mudras* would be the Christian hands pressed together in prayer or the Islamic uplifted palms of the hands in reverence to Allah. Another *mudra* has probably escaped most people's conscious awareness. In many paintings of Jesus, he is shown with his right hand held up in what looks to be the Japanese Esoteric Buddhism *ken-in*, or the sword *mudra*. In other paintings, his hand posture is similar to the esoteric *mudra* called *Tōmyōo-no-in*. Appropriately, this is the *mudra* of light.[258] This seems to indicate either that the artists were practitioners of an esoteric form of Buddhism or Jesus was an esoteric teacher who had studied with the "Buddhists missionaries who had overrun Egypt, Greece, and even Judea,"[259] during this time period.

On the Sands of Kauai:
An Apprentice Story

Years ago, after a long distance move, I gradually let go of many friendships. They naturally dissolved and faded away, except for one that I chose to end through a letter, which caused my friend deep emotional pain and anger towards me. I felt remorse, apologized and hoped for forgiveness. I also knew that I needed to forgive myself, along with forgiving my friend's anger and hurt. Although I made a conscious effort to do this, over the next few years I noticed that my general ease at making new acquaintances never developed or deepened into lasting friendships. I was mystified, because authenticity and trust in relationships had always come easily to me. Could that relationship I had ended be affecting my new friendships somehow? I knew that I had let it go, but my spiritual teacher Dr. JC Husfelt told me that though one person may let go, the other person may still hold on and remain emotionally attached, which can indeed impact other relationships.

During a spiritual journey to the Hawaiian island of Kauai, Dr. Husfelt asked if anyone wanted a cutting of an attachment. I knew in my heart that I needed this and said, "Yes please!" He said that he did not even need to know who or what the incident was. We stood by the great Pacific Ocean with sand underfoot, wind blowing and sun blazing as Dr. Husfelt used his spiritual power to cut the attachments of my friend's connection to me. He did the cutting with his hand in the *mudra* position of a sword, even thumping my heart to break the cords. I actually cried with relief from the physical, tangible release. I felt profoundly liberated. He later told me that the filaments or threads were thick. It was a profound healing that brought freedom and forgiveness on a spiritual level.

The gift of the cutting of attachment had immediate results and authentic friendships flowed right back into my life. I continue to have those wonderful relationships to this day. I am deeply grateful for this cutting, as it has allowed my life to bloom with relationships once again. I am forever grateful for my teachers who carry the wisdom, knowledge and power of the old ways and practices to those fortunate enough to stand before them.

THE READING OF MY PALM

. . . .

IN 1964, AS A FRESHMAN IN COLLEGE, I BEGAN TO STUDY *JUDO*, a Japanese martial art. I was more interested in seeking and learning the mind power of the legendary martial wizards than in learning physical fighting ability. I could street fight, but I yearned for spirit and mind power. From that point forward, my martial and spiritual seeking took me far afield, to various isolated and remote places on this Earth. Finally, my quest for knowledge and power led me to study with two different Japanese Grandmasters. One of these was Shoto Tanemura *Sensei* – a *soke* or family head of many ancient martial *ryūha* (schools) as well as the esoteric science of *kuji kiri* ("nine symbolic cuts"). He was also a master of palm reading, taught to him by his grandmother.

Sensei (teacher) called me the "puma that smiles" and had a vision that the name for my *dojo* was Hakusan (sacred white mountain). As it turned out, it was perfect.

Mount Hakusan

Hakusan is one of Japan's three most famous mountains, famous because they are the three most significant and holiest Buddhist mountains in Japan. The other two are Fujisan and Tateyama. Hakusan is one of Japan's most important and ancient sites of religious mountain worship. From ancient times, this mountain has been the object of religious worship based on a spiritual philosophy that emphasizes oneness with nature and the spiritual rebirth possible for all human beings because of this harmonious blending of humanity and nature. This is the enduring message that grew from the mythological beginnings of the spirituality of Mount Hakusan.

Most importantly, the common people regarded the mountain as special and sacred. Being snow-capped even during the summer, the local people depended on it to provide water year round for their rice fields. It was the home of the dragon goddess, *Kukurihime no Kami*, and sacred to the ascetic *Shugendo* mountain wizards. The name *Kukurihime* suggests the deity possesses the power to bind or join together (to create harmony). Besides *Kukurihime no Kami*, the two creator gods in Japanese mythology *Izanagi no Kami* and *Izanami no Kami* are the primary deities of Mount Hakusan, along with the Buddhist bodhisattva, the eleven-faced Kannon, the personification of watchful listening.

Jamie and Me on the Holy Mountain, Hakusan, Japan

Based on my far traveling consciousness, my sense of authenticity,[260] and as a seeker of knowledge, I needed to experience firsthand with all my senses the holy mountain, Hakusan, a stratovolcano overlooking the Japan Sea. Accordingly, during the spring of 2005, my son, one of our students, and I traveled to the namesake of our *dojo*, the mystical white mountain that straddles Ishikawa and Gifu prefectures. Awesome it was, and mythical, as our student tested for his black belt, which consisted of *randori* (fighting) my son for over an hour. As I witnessed the test, the past became the present as crows gathered to sit and watch the struggle of our student to endure the pain in an attempt to best my son. That didn't happen, but the test was not about winning. It was about the steeliness of our student's spirit, the ability to endure and not quit. He endured, cried tears; it was a humbling experience for him. I awarded him a black belt. Anyone can fight; just pick up a baseball bat and start swinging. What is most important for a martial artist is the power of their mind and spirit, as well as humbleness and an enduring heart.

And the crows! We were beside a cedar tree where crows would come and sit on a branch, and then fly off, except for one. This one stayed and watched. Mythically, being on a mountain sacred to the ascetic wizards, these crows may have been *tengu*, slayers of vanity and pride. *Karasu* or "crow" *tengu* (nature spirits) are mythical bird-like beings who are the guardians of mountainous regions and highly skilled in the martial arts. And then there is Taicho Daishi (the great teacher), founder of Hakusan Shugendo Monastery, who later became a *tengu* of Mount Hakusan. Supposedly, practitioners of the austerities who loved Hakusan would appear as *tengu* after they died to protect the mountain and repay an obligation. Was the crow that stayed a *tengu*? Possibly. What do you think?

Vanity and Pride

The most plausible answer to the *tengu* question is that yes, it was a *tengu*. My student always had a fascination with the *tengu*. And here he was fighting for a black belt on a mountain sacred to them. But that alone would not let me believe that *tengu* were present at the testing. What happened later that evening pointed to their presence.

I have a knowing that in the ebb and flow of life a person may be tested by the Otherworld. And then there is this: *tengu* were known for their mastery of the martial arts and being renowned swordsmen. Would my student face another test?

Back at our hotel we met up with the other martial artists on our journey for a celebratory meal, and of course, *sake* and beer. The alcohol was flowing freely and so was my student's mouth. Basically, he told the others that testing was not difficult, and that he had held his own. Not only a lie but the height of vanity and pride – a long way from humble. My son and I just looked at each other with an expression that said, "What the fuck?"

After all of us had returned to our rooms for the night, my son and I knocked on our student's door. As we walked into his room I said, "Please give me back your black belt."

I must say at this point that I have had a connection with the *tengu*. One experience revealed itself while in Kyoto in 1987. Seeking esoteric items, I had wandered through a large seasonal market within the environs of a castle. I was drawn to a small vendor in a secluded corner of the market. There were scrolls for sale that drew me like a bee to honey. The last scroll in the lot was one of *Akiba Daigongen*, a deity who resembles a raven-like *tengu* and who rides on a white fox done in the imagery of *Fudō Myō-ō*.

When we were dating, Sher's nickname for me was "fox." And this deity was in charge of fire prevention. It had only been six months before, while on Kōyasan, that I had made the decision not to move back to my hometown and take over my father's business. The name of the business was, "Fire Prevention Co."

To take back my student's black belt was not an act most *sensei* (teachers) would do for fear the student would quit and they would lose revenue. But in my case, I may have been subconsciously doing the bidding of the *tengu*.

On our flight back to the States, I returned his black belt. He had shown the measure of his heart and mind as he had not complained or attempted to give excuses for his words and behavior. He realized why I took his belt. The lesson had been learned, and to this day, he is my senior black belt.

President?

During the 1990s, after attending one of Tanemura Sensei's seminars, my son, his girlfriend and I invited the *sensei* to lunch. Initially, our conversation focused on martial training, but it didn't take long for the talk to morph into a discussion of various spiritual aspects of life and training. While waiting for our food to be delivered, *sensei* asked if we would like our palms read.

Knowing his martial and spiritual mastership, I readily agreed. He gently turned over my right hand and glanced at my palm. A sudden intake of breath indicted that he had seen something. I was concerned until I heard him say softly, "President." Then he glanced at my face and back to my palm. Reflecting on this, there is an interesting connection with his initial assessment and his mumbling of president. The president of the United States as I write, Donald Trump, was born in June 1946 – a Gemini. President George W. Bush born in July 1946 – a Cancer. President Bill Clinton born in August 1946 – a Leo, and I was born later in August 1946 – a Virgo. We can add Dennis Kucinich to this list, who was a candidate for the Democratic nomination for president in 2004 and 2008. He is our Libra, born October 8, 1946.

Without any further explanation as to why he had said, "President," *sensei* went on to tell me that I would have a long life as long as I reduced the frequency of my practice of cold-water submersion bathings. I needed to keep warm and not keep exposing myself to such extreme cold. He then read my son's palm until our food arrived, which stopped any further discussions about palm reading.

The next morning we picked *sensei* up at his hotel and took him to the airport. While we waited for his plane to depart, *sensei* pulled me aside and said he wanted to tell me something. "Jim," he said, "your palm; it is not destined that you will become president, which at first is what I thought I saw in the lines of your palm, but something greater. Your destiny is to bring a spiritual savior system to humanity, just like Jesus."

Before *sensei* told me this, and even before the descending spirit exorcism, I had known within my heart my destiny and its connection to one or more of my past lives. I am ever amazed at life and the mysteries of creation. It's simply astounding that my soul's destiny is encoded and etched on the lines of my palm. Most important, this fact lends further credence to my theory that our soul settles over our DNA as "golden dew."

PART V

The Third of Four Major Otherworldly Experiences over a Span of Ten Years

But I am the Morning and the Evening Star, and lord of the day and the night.
By the power that is put in my left hand, and the power that I grasp in my
right, I am lord of the two ways.

The Lord of the Morning Star
Stood between the day and the night:
As a bird that lifts its wings and stands
With the bright wing on the right
And the wing of the dark on the left,
The Dawn Star stood into sight.

Lo! I am always here!
Far in the hollow of space
I brush the wing of the day
And put light on your face.
The other wing brushes the dark.
But I, I am always in place.

Yea, I am always here. I am Lord
In every way. And the lords among men

See me through the flashing of wings.
They see me and lose me again.
But lo! I am always here
Within them.

The multitudes see me not.
They see only the waving of wings,
The coming and going of things.
The cold and the hot.

But ye that perceive me between
The tremors of night and the day,
I make you the Lords of the
Way Unseen.

The path between gulfs of the dark and the steeps of the light,
The path like a snake that is gone, like the length of a fuse to ignite
The substance of shadow, that bursts and explodes into sight.

I am here undeparting. I sit tight
Between wings of the endless flight,
At the depths of the peace and the fight.

Deep in the moistures of peace,
And far down the muzzle of the fight
You shall find me, who am neither increase
Nor destruction, different quite.

I am far beyond
The horizons of love and strife.
Like a star, like a pond
That washes the lords of life.[261]

SPIRIT MAN OF TEOTIHUACÁN

· ·

When
In all places,
His belly is upon the ground,
His spine upon the sky,
And the core of his being
Lies equally between the two worlds
Of North and South,
Day and Night,
Heaven and Earth,
Woman and Man,
When at once he shines
As the Morning and the Evening Star,
Look upon your Heart
And you will see him,
Quetzalcóatl.

Do not shudder or turn away,
For it is the time of Becoming.
Open yourself.
Give yourself.
Let him wave within you
To feel the split
That no longer exists.
Your two halves are One.[262]

249

Teotihuacán, City of Water – City of Fire, known as, "The place where one becomes a god – a place of deification," is the birthplace of the Fifth Sun and the home of the prophet Quetzalcóatl and his religion. In recognition of this, Teotihuacán's Temple of the Sun was built over a sacred cave symbolizing birth and was shaped like a four-leafed clover. If we explore Teotihuacán's title as the place where humans become deified, we may clearly recognize that Quetzalcóatl's religion was based on overcoming our consciousness of dualism by awakening to unity (oneness)—the merging of fire and water, spirit and matter—and giving wings to the serpent. This is the same message that we bring today.

"Where Men Become Gods" (in Nahuatl)

According to legend, Teotihuacán is where wisdom flourished, and the arts and sacred science originated two thousand years ago. The city was a ceremonial and spiritual/religious center and all of its people were extremely religious. As a religious symbol and image of the cosmos, Teotihuacán's primary ceremonies were timed with the appearance of Venus as the morning and evening star. Teotihuacán's primary temples symbolized the Sun, Moon and Venus (Quetzalcóatl, as the Morning Star). The Mesoamericans called Venus the Dawn Star in its morning star phase and equated it with their god Quetzalcóatl, the Feathered Serpent.

Teotihuacán had soil rich in volcanic preserves and, being at the basin of the Cerro Gordo, streams flowed throughout the territory. Today the ruins of this theocratic city lie in a semiarid valley on a plateau thirty miles north of Mexico City. The enormous four-step pyramid—the Pyramid of the Sun— dominates this magical place two-thousand meters above sea level. This pyramid was situated so that the sun set exactly in front of it on the day of the summer solstice. The cave that was discovered under the Pyramid of the Sun was "artificially reshaped and decorated into the form of a four-petalled flower. In some of the later paintings and pictorial narratives the Mesoamerican cosmos is symbolized by a four-petalled flower representing the division of space into four cardinal regions around a center. It is possible that the cave was Teotihuacán's earliest *imago mundi*, or sacred image of the cosmos."[263] Furthermore, "the great stairway of the Pyramid of the Sun faces a westerly point on the horizon where the *Pleiades*, called *Tianquitzli*, meaning 'market-place' (or *miec* meaning 'heap') by later Nahuatl peoples, sat directly in front of it."[264]

Possibly symbolizing the four-directional cave, Teotihuacán is situated with a north to south main ceremonial pathway (avenue), and in the center of the city at a right angle to the ceremonial pathway lays the east-west avenue, which then divides the city into four sections. The ceremonial pathway, beginning in the southern part of the city and extending northward, ends at the Pyramid of the Moon. It is called the Avenue of the Dead. Spiritually, it is referred to as the Belly of the Serpent – a Two-headed Serpent. Along its entire length it is lined with palaces, pyramids and temples. It is interesting to note that the Belly of the Serpent is oriented fifteen to twenty-five degrees east of true north.

Jamie and me standing on the Pyramid of the Moon with the Pyramid of the Sun in the background

At the south end of the avenue sitting in the east is the compound that contains the Citadel and the Temple of Quetzalcóatl. In the center of the compound is a small step pyramid with a flat platform on top. In the Mesoamerican journey of awakening, this is called the Island of Hell (first *chakra* issues[265]) and is surrounded by the Ocean of Fear. The initiate or student has to be willing and have the courage to leave their known Island of Hell and enter the Ocean of Fear, which is an unknown. This begins their journey up the Belly of the Serpent. Their first destination is the Island of Temptation – the Earth. We are still tempted to return to our Island of Hell because it is known, safe and secure; even if it causes us and others great pain and suffering. It is a known existence, for example an abusive marriage.

If we stay disciplined, determined and maintain a heroic will, we will continue and persevere to our next destination, the Place of Water. We continue up the Belly of the Serpent arriving at the Place of Air and the Place of Fire. Next we move to the Place of Sacrifice and the Temple of the Jaguar; finally the Temple of the Moon, and if worthy, completion on the Temple of the Sun. The thousands of casual tourists that tread this path may know little of these ancient and ageless ceremonial acts of death and rebirth.

Another interesting fact about this mysterious place: according to American engineer Hugh Harleston, Teotihuacán is a perfect model of our solar system. The buildings correspond proportionally to the position and size of the planets.[266]

Quetzalcóatl

Quetzalcóatl, Feathered Serpent and priest – King of Teotihuacán, may be legendary, but he is not a myth. The name refers to an actual person who was a prophet, teacher and messenger to the people. According to David Carrasco in his book *Quetzalcóatl and the Irony of Empire*, "Quetzalcóatl was the first shaman-priest, a symbol of sacred authority, and a justification for leaders to pull and hold populations together."[267]

To the Mayans, he was Kukulkán, the double-headed serpent. According to Frank Waters in his *Mexico Mystique*:

> Quetzalcóatl was a uniting symbol achieving union of oppo-
> sites: heaven and Earth, morning and evening star, matter
> and spirit. . . . [T]he transcendental meaning of this great
> myth is clear. It is an expression of the universal doctrine of
> sin and redemption, of death and resurrection, the trans-
> figuration of man into god. . . . [T]his myth, in the broad-
> est possible terms, enunciates the principle of all Creation:
> the incarnation of divine light, purity, and spirituality into
> gross matter; and then the agonizing redemption of matter
> by spirituality – the immortal theme of all world religions.[268]

Quetzalcóatl's connection with Teotihuacán would seem to be obvious according to Laurette Séjourné: "It should now be evident that the religion of Quetzalcóatl . . . was a highly inspired system of intuitive thought yielding insights about life, death, and rebirth that provided the basis for a culture—Teotihuacán—that ranks with those of ancient Egypt, and more recently Tibet, in the splendor and integrity of its spiritual purpose."[269]

It was in Teotihuacán where Quetzalcóatl was deemed a god-man – a divine human. He "taught that human greatness grows out of the awareness of a spiritual order; his image must therefore be the symbol of this truth."[270] Most vividly, this symbol is the feathered or plumed serpent. "The serpent plumes must be speaking to us of the spirit which makes it possible for man—even while his body, like the reptile's, is dragged in the dust—to know the superhuman joy of creation. They are thus, as it were, a song to the most exalted inner freedom. This hypothesis is confirmed by the Nahuatl symbolism where the serpent represents matter—being always associated with terrestrial gods—and the bird heaven. The plumed serpent is thus the sign of the revelation of the heavenly origin of man."[271] Furthermore, the cultural hero Ce Ácatl Topiltzin Quetzalcóatl, who taught the goal of inner perfection, represented the union of heaven and Earth evidenced by the volume of plumed serpent and plumed jaguar imagery everywhere throughout Teotihuacán.

"Myths embody the universal quest for meaning in life, and the desire to know the transcendent spiritual world. Quetzalcóatl, as the legendary Topiltzin, tried to overcome the duality of spirit and matter, and reconciled them in a holistic vision as embodied in the Plumed Serpent. Topiltzin becomes the Redeemer of humankind through his reconciliation of opposites."[272]

Heroic Return of the Plumed Serpent

"The return of Quetzalcóatl or the return of his knowledge (also the knowledge of the Indigenous [sic] people of the Americas) appeared in many prophecies between the people of Mesoamerica. Including our Yucatec Maya ancient texts. Ce Ácatl Topiltzin Quetzalcóatl teachings (These teachings are fully taken from traditional Toltec texts): And here is the mature man: a firm heart like a stone, a wise face. He owns his face and his heart. Skillful and understanding, good composer of texts, is a Toltec of black and red ink, an expert. God is in his heart and divinizes things with his heart; dialogs with his own heart. Note: The term Toltec is used here as someone who fallows [sic] the toltecayotl which means 'The art of living' among the people of Mesoamerica. Quetzalcóatl was known by the Maya as Kukulkán."[273]

The true essence of every religious system lies in the revelation of an individual soul closely bound to the soul of the cosmos: it has to do, in other words, with making man divine.[274]

I first far traveled to Teotihuacán in 1995. It is hard to describe in words; it needs to be experienced. For myself, I have meditated at the Temple of Quetzalcóatl. I've journeyed the Avenue of the Dead as a pilgrim and experienced its initiatory affect. I have sat on the crest of the Sun Pyramid and experienced its power. Bees, our family *nagual*, have visited me on the top of the Pyramid of the Moon. And I have experienced the magical other-worldly power of Teotihuacán. But the most mystical event happened here at midnight in 1995 on a lonely dusty street, when I encountered the Spirit Man of Teotihuacán.

Spirit Man

For me the serpent of middle-earth sleeps in my loins and my belly, the bird of the outer air perches on my brow and sweeps her bill across my breast. But I, I am lord of two ways. I am master of up and down. I am as a man who is a new man, with new limbs and life, and the light of the Morning Star in his eyes. And I, I am on the threshold. I am stepping across the border. I am Quetzalcóatl, lord of both ways, star between day and the dark.[275]

In late May of 1995, I once again found myself in Mexico, not in the jungles of the Yucatan or the mountainous highlands of Chiapas, but a short way outside of Mexico City. After I had determined that the star of my vision was Venus, the Morning Star, I had a feeling within my heart that I needed to visit Teotihuacán.

Words can only portray a small portion of the magical feeling one has when they first set their eyes on the ruins of Teotihuacán. The twin pyramids of the Sun and the Moon—awe inspiring to say the least—crown the ruined city in its majesty. This mysterious archeological site is surrounded by a tall, barbed-wire fence, and the fantasy of my mind makes me wonder if it's to keep people out or to keep people in! At night the pyramids are lit with an unearthly glow, suggesting a possible landing point for extra-terrestrials. Not far from the entrance to this "City of Gods" lies the hotel where I stayed, Villas Arqueologicas Teotihuacán.

Many people have a problem falling asleep at night, which for various reasons is very often connected with the stress and the worry in their life. Falling asleep is usually not a problem for me. But this night, I was excited and my "land of dreams" was far away. I focused on letting the chatter in my mind disappear. And then in a semi-awake state, a voice within my mind said, "Go for run!" And repeated a second time, "Go for run."

I've been a runner and a martial artist for thirty years and in that time I have always preferred late afternoon for my runs, never late at night. And after all those years of training and running, and of course the injuries (not to mention being in my late 40s), when the sun sets my body determines it's time to rest, not run. I looked at the clock. It was close to midnight. I was in

Mexico in an area that I'd never seen before. Did I want to be a white man running down a dark, moonless Mexican road at midnight? If you can imagine, this could possibly be the opening scene for a Quentin Tarantino movie. Hey, but the voice said, "Go for run," and I couldn't sleep. Being who I am, I also thought that maybe I could find a way in through the fence and explore the ruins at night. I've done this before at other sacred sites such as Machu Picchu in Peru and Tulúm in the Yucatan.

As I walked outside the hotel, the quiet and the aromatic scents triggered memories of times long lost to my genetic being and soul. In the years of my travels, many of the ancient sites where I have journeyed have resonated deep within my soul's memory. As I walked through the darkness, feeling without seeing, the soul memories of Teotihuacán began to vibrate within the core of my being.

I came to the deserted road surrounding the fenced ruins. The air was still, with an unsettling quiet, as if I had been thrust into an early Clint Eastwood, "man with no name" movie. Very little light was cast by the few overworked street lamps. As I began my run, off to the left in the distance, the illuminated Pyramid of the Sun glowed as a welcoming beacon to all who dared travel these lands by night. Little time was needed for me to determine that it would not be a good idea to try and get through the fence. I figured I would just enjoy the run and wait for the morning.

Over the years I've been involved in some frightful situations. Little did I know that this run was going to be very unique. People run for a variety of reasons: for exercise, as an escape from the stresses of their life and for competition, either against themselves or others. In my case, I run to keep my weight under control and to connect with the heavens. Various ideas, insights and knowledge come to me while I'm putting in the sweat-riddled miles. Tonight was no different; as I explored with my mind the symbology of Teotihuacán, I rounded a corner and out of the darkness came a pack of wild dogs, snarling and snapping.[276] I had a choice to be made very quickly – keep running towards them and engage them in battle, and perhaps get bit or scratched and risk an infection or worse, or slowly back away, turn and retrace my steps. The last thing I needed that night was to kill someone's pet and possibly end up in a Mexican jail. I'd come close to it before. What would you do?

Of course, I slowly backed up and turned to run. Suddenly, out of the darkness and seemingly out of the void, a figure came running towards me. I wondered if it was the owner of the dogs. But the dogs had come from the other direction. In no more time than it took for this thought to enter my mind and then disappear, there was a young, but ageless, man standing in front of me. As I looked back on this experience later the next day, I realized that the dogs had suddenly disappeared.

This young man seemed to be agitated, or maybe scared. He spoke a language (not Spanish) that I hadn't heard before, except for a short phrase in English. Pointing at me he said, "Quetzalcóatl – the Sixth Sun." Then other words that I couldn't understand, then he said, again and again, pointing at me: "Quetzalcóatl – the Sixth Sun!"

Time seemed to have stood still as he was now pointing to my feet. Did he want my running shoes? But his shoes looked brand new! More strange words, and then once again he repeated, "Quetzalcóatl – the Sixth Sun" while pointing at my shoes. I'd just run into a pack of vicious dogs that seemed to have disappeared. Now, this strange person was calling me "Quetzalcóatl – the Sixth Sun".

Next he removed his non-descript baseball cap, which also appeared brand new, and offered it to me. In my many travels I have learned that in many cultures it is impolite and dis-respectful to refuse a gift. I took the cap even though I didn't want it. Then deciding that this interchange was not getting us anywhere, I handed back the cap. Next, a strange thing happened. As I placed the cap in his hands I looked closely into his eyes. The eyes are windows into the soul, to the depths of creation; I felt rather than saw an endless, timeless space reflected in his eyes. This feeling is very difficult to put into words – it was sadness but not sadness, it was compassion but not compassion, it was reality but not reality, it was the meeting point of chaos and order and order and chaos! As he accepted the hat back, I had this overwhelming urge to hug him. There were no words exchanged as I broke the hug, which didn't feel real. Realizing this would be a good time to leave, I smiled slightly, bowed, turned and started running back the way I came. After a few steps, I looked back. He was not there. He had disappeared.

Well, so much for an uneventful run! After what happened, the mere act of running seemed boring. A few more minutes passed and then the sound – a rifle shot in the distance and the undeniable ricochet near me!

In times of danger our mind and our body can respond to the threat in a variety of ways; fear may freeze us or courage may move us and sometimes we just react without any conscious though at all. It wasn't fear or courage, just reaction, as my legs moved the fastest that they'd moved in many years. But at that moment, my mind, being the wondrous thing that it is, remembered a scene from a movie called *The In-Laws* starring Peter Falk. As the characters are running and being shot at (I believe on an airstrip in Central America), Peter Falk yells, "Serpentine!" Guess what? That's what I did. I zigzagged. Another shot, no ricochet and finally safety, not in the light but in the dark!

Commentary

Over the years since 1995, I've wondered about the mysterious man's emphasis on my shoes while saying: "Quetzalcóatl – the Sixth Sun," and the exchange of the hat. Both gestures remained an enigma to me until several years later when it struck me out of the clear blue. All shoes have one thing in common – soles (soul). And as for the hat, that covers the head – a symbol of mind. He was saying that I had the mind and soul of Quetzalcóatl – the Morning Star! Additionally, did the dogs have any significance or was it just a coincidence?

In Nahual mythology, dogs were associated with *Xolotl*, this psychopomp, sorcerer and dog-faced god is twin to Quetzalcóatl. *Xolotl* is identified with Venus as the evening star, and as Quetzalcóatl's *nagual*. It's important to note here the symbolic spiritual meaning and differences between the evening star and the morning star, even though both are the planet Venus. Mythically, *Xolotl* is the evening star while Quetzalcóatl is the morning star.

What happens when the evening star in the western sky disappears from the nightly heavens? For eight days it goes through a period of inferior conjunction when it is invisible to us until it raises and becomes visible again as the Herald of the Dawn, the Morning Star.

In other words, the evening star symbolizes our incarnated soul; it is the descending spirit of the fragment of divine light, a small piece of the "Sun behind the sun." The morning star in the eastern sky is the star of hope and reflects our earth journey back to our true divine nature, a transformational journey through the "underworld" seeking awakening and the liberation of the enlightening energy within our heart as we become a Quetzalcóatl – a Divine Human.

Even though the star of my vision was the morning star, when I was born Venus was in its evening star phase – twin symbology. The evening star of my birth reflects my past life, revealed by the visitation, while the morning star is the energetic symbology of my present incarnation.

One final point: it is important to note that the creation of the Fifth Sun took place at Teotihuacán.[277] And the Sixth Sun? Read on.

Plumed Jaguars and Water

At the base and to the west of the Pyramid of the Moon sits the Palace of the Butterfly. To the west of that, you find the Palace of the Jaguars, *Palacio de los Jaguares*. Within this sacred space honoring the jaguar, we discover a unique representation of jaguars with feathered heads blowing conch shells held in their forepaws. These are big felines that fly.

> The familiar signs are there: the jaguar's plumed head-dress stretches back behind his ears; vacant-eyed star/Venus-glyphs with downturned mouths and two-pronged tongues keep watch above him. Elongated raindrops hang from the conch shell, itself a plumed sea symbol. The green-feathered jaguar frescoes and murals discovered at the foot of the Pyramid of the Sun and elsewhere on the site are "linked with the symbol of heaven, the quetzal or the eagle . . . representing the union of two opposites, heaven and Earth." Indeed, the red-and-orange-tinted Teotihuacan jaguars, agape jaws baring curved, tusk-like teeth, spew forth with abandon

puffy clouds, watery streams bordered with flowers, and wind-borne rain.[278]

In 1988, at Machu Picchu, Don Eduardo Calderon identified me as the "big cat that flies" – a feathered/plumed jaguar. Seven years later, at midnight outside the fence of Teotihuacán, I was identified as Quetzalcóatl.

One of the keys to fathoming Teotihuacán is to understand the meaning of the multiple representations of plumed jaguars, plumed serpents, and throughout the sacred site, the emphasis on symbols of water:

> The Quetzalcóatl temple facade is "a tribute to things that flow: the water in rivers, the course of a road, the sinuous winding of a serpent, blood through the veins, the ruffling of feathers on a banner in a breeze . . . presenting the visual statement of the sacred value of the nearby river."
>
> In an agricultural society what could be more important than water, the source of all life, venerated in the body of Plumed Serpent? Even in today's Mexico, in the Huastec region, a heavy shower is described as a quetzalcóatl.[279]

In addition to my birth Maya day-sign, "storm," and just as jaguars are comfortable in rivers and streams, my connection to water ranges from my past multiple aquatic certificates and trainings to being one of the few Caucasians who has the power and authority to "bathe" others. It does seem as if Teotihuacán is a familiar residence within my soul.

THE CONSCIOUSNESS OF TREES

. . . .

With the death of the last tree, comes death to the last human.[280]

The winds speak to all whose minds are still and uncluttered . . .

with Oneness being the sacred beauty of words unspoken
– JC, 1989

WHAT IS YOUR FUNDAMENTAL WORLDVIEW? IS IT DUALISTIC, non-dualistic, or radical nondualistic? If we view the fundamental essence of the world dualistically, spirit and matter are separate. This mindset breeds inequality, with the view that humans are superior to all other things. In other words, trees, rocks, animals, and so forth are not conscious as they are nonhuman and, according to the Bible, inferior to humans. Needlessly killing animals is acceptable as they are nothing more than "dumb animals." We can see where this leads us in the environmental habitat destruction caused by the dualistic consciousness within patriarchal dualistic institutional and capitalistic paradigms.

On the contrary, if we awaken to a consciousness of radical nonduality, all things of heaven and Earth are equal, conscious, and aware with the divine spark or fire of creation within each. And all things are connected as one in a "web" of love, i.e., oneness. Furthermore, as humans, when our hearts awaken with this radical consciousness our decisions in life are no longer solely based on our dualistic mind. A dualistic mind is ever seeking security and power of self with little thought to the heart essence of compassion and empathy. With a consciousness of radical nonduality, and the thoughts that flow from it, our decisions take into account the messages from our heart. The following is excerpted from my book, *Do You Like Jesus – Not the Church?*

Wondrous and magical is the heart physically and spiritually. It is the center of our consciousness of oneness, while the brain is the center of our dualistic consciousness. Amazingly, the heart possesses its own nervous system. And the heart thinks! It is an intelligence system. In fact, the brain receives more orders from the heart than the heart receives from the brain.

Furthermore, our indigenous ancestors "understood the heart's ability to intelligently perceive and decipher the world around them, and acknowledged the limitations and reductionist nature of living in a manner in which one relies primarily on the mind.

"They went beyond the thoughts in their heads, using the heart as an organ of perception to connect with the energy fields of other organisms—not just other humans, but the Earth as well—in order to fully immerse themselves in the deeper meanings embodying their thoughts."[281]

Moreover, new research has discovered that the heart has a sense of smell. Even more amazing is the hormone it secretes – oxytocin.[282] This is the bonding or love hormone that brings things together. In this bonding we experience feelings of compassion, harmony, love, and peace. In other words, the heart is the key to our awakening of radical nondualistic consciousness.

dod yn ôl at fy nghoed
Welsh phrase meaning "to return to a balanced state of mind" – translates
literally as "to return to my trees."

The standing sentinels of our world whose roots bury deep within the body of the Great Mother and whose bare or green-covered branches reach towards the sky provide life and beauty for all. The grandeur Sher and I have experienced on forested mountain tops and in verdant valleys has brought us joy and peace of mind and memories that are priceless.

On a forested slope north of Vancouver, B.C., after bathing and being under the blanket, we were welcomed back to this reality with a vision and the sensory impact of a cedar-filled paradise. This experience has been repeated over and over again on forested slopes around the world.

Trees, like all other things, are conscious and aware. In fact, they communicate with each other and will listen to our words and thoughts. "Two decades ago, while researching her doctoral thesis, ecologist Suzanne Simard discovered that trees communicate their needs and send each other nutrients via a network of latticed fungi buried in the soil – in other words, she found they "talk" to each other. Since then, Simard, now at the University of British Columbia, has pioneered further research into how trees converse, including how these fungal filigrees help trees send warning signals about environmental change, search for kin, and transfer their nutrients to neighboring plants before they die."[283]

It seems that few humans understand the impact of the gifts that trees provide to the Earth and humanity. Following a reflection on trees and forests, Artur Lundkvist, one of Swedish literature's greatest tree worshippers, wrote:

In every human there is a tree, and in every tree there is a human. I feel this, the tree wanders inside a human being, and the human being is caught in the tree.... I serenade the forests, the forest sea is the second sea on Earth, the sea in which man wanders. The forests work in silence, fulfilling nature's mighty work; working with the winds, cleaning the

air, mitigating the climate, forming soil, preserving all our
essentials without wearing them out.[284]

*We must protect the forests for our children, grandchildren, and children yet to
be born. We must protect the forests for those who can't speak for themselves,
such as the birds, animals, fish, and trees.*

– Qwatsinas, Nuxalk Nation

Tree Whisperer

One of my favorite memories as a young child is of cutting down a
Christmas tree. This was in the fifties in rural Maryland. My vision of wonder
was centered on forging through the snow on a cold afternoon, through a
magical forest of silence, with three of my great-uncles. I spent many of my
days visiting with my grandmother and her brothers and sisters on their
small farm.

Sherry and I and our two children continued this ancestral tree-cutting
tradition for many wintry seasons. Once during a snowstorm, I had to carry
our young daughter through knee-high snow, and the tree we selected turned
out to be not so perfect when the snow melted off. There were few branches.

Having family together to choose the perfect tree for honoring and celebration is wondrous and the memories last for life. The selection of which
tree to cut was not fully a democratic process. Sherry made the final decision. My wife is a true empath. This soul ability also takes the form of "tree
speak." We would pick out a tree and Sherry would talk to it to see if it wanted
to go home with us. Usually, Sherry would address the tree, except for one
time during Christmas of 2014. I had spotted a tree that looked perfect for
us. Meanwhile, Sherry was talking to another person while I was roaming
around. As she walked toward me and the tree, the tree spoke to her: "Hey,
come here." Needless to say, she was a little taken aback. Usually she initiates
the dialogue. As she put her hand on the tree, it said, "I want to go home with
you. I want to go where there are hidden ones, but don't let that cat run up me."

Our magical tree stayed alive within our home for just shy of three months; one day it was still viable, and the next day, the branches were stiff as a board.[285]

Karma

Any harming, abusing, or cutting down of trees has a direct detrimental impact and effect on both me and my wife, but more so on Sher's spirit. My dear wife is a true empath and tree whisperer.

Yes, we have cut down a tree for Christmas following our ancestral tradition; but the tradition also involves asking the trees permission to take its life, an honoring and blessing of its life and beauty, and a gifting back to the earth.

Trees speak to Sher. In Maine, our home was surrounded by trees. Having the ocean at the end of the street meant that we would, over the years, be hit with storm-driven high winds, especially during Nor'easters. Since we regularly talked to our trees and blessed them, during the twenty-four years we lived in our home, our trees always stood tall, providing protection that no insurance could ever buy.

One of our trees did cause destruction, however, not to us but to our neighbor. One of our trees sat at the corner of our property. A few of its massive branches hung over our neighbor's fenced yard. It was also right by the corner of our teaching space and my office, which we called the sanctuary. One morning I heard voices by the corner of our sanctuary. Rushing outside, with the fury of a storm, I realized what was happening. There were three men by the tree with ropes and chainsaws. One was already up the tree. In short order, with my "angry face on," I let them know in simple terms to get off our property. I met little resistance as they said they had been hired by our neighbors to cut the branches hanging over their fence and yard. They said the neighbors were worried that one of the branches might damage their roof or fence. Without further ado, they left.

Within a month or so, a late afternoon wind-driven storm was upon us. The wind howled through the night with rain pelting a chorus of purity on our land and home. The next morning as I walked to the sanctuary, I began laughing. A middle section of their fence—not near the sanctuary—had been destroyed by a large branch, and yes, it came from our sanctuary tree. Maybe in your minds this doesn't sound too mystical, but here's the thing: the branch broke off over the sanctuary. Logic and gravity would deem it to fall on, and possibly putting a hole in, the sanctuary's roof. Instead, it flew at an impossible angle at least twenty-four feet to fall on the fence.

All we can say is that trees know your thoughts, words, and actions. Respect and care for them and they will care and respect you. Do unto them with love not greed.

IS THAT A NAKED MAN I SEE?

· ·

I CARRY THE LINEAGE AND MEDICINE OF BATHING AS A QUEST motif. I have received a vision and my spirit song. I do not carry the medicine of the pipe or the stone-people's lodge commonly referred to as a sweat lodge. Both of these practices are connected with the Native American form of the vision quest or as it is known, "going up the mountain."

I didn't go up the mountain, but instead went to the seashore for a modi-fied quest. This was a choice I made after having a disturbing night dream. I am not what you would call a night dreamer. In other words, I access knowl-edge during the day, a daydreamer if you will, but not during sleep.

Even though I usually do not view many of my night-time dreams as being prophetic, this dream prompted me to do an isolated-style quest, normally something I would not do as it is not part of the spiritual lineages that I carry. In addition, the thought of staying isolated in one place is antithesis to my spirit as it's difficult for me to be contained with no movement. Even so (was I crazy?), I still decided to do this form of questing.

As this experience would teach me, many times we don't need to take our spiritual or mundane life too seriously. Sometimes the best medicine is to laugh at ourselves and the situations that we put ourselves in.

The Highest Form of Bliss is Living
with a Certain Degree of Folly.[286]

It was the summer of 1995 on the coast of Maine. After researching, evidently not too well, a location for my quest, I enlisted Sherry and Jessie to take me to a state park. My preparation was simply packing my essential gear: a sword, water, blanket and a few of my medicine bundles.

As I was putting my backpack with the sword strapped to it into the car, my daughter Jessie said, "Dad what are you doing with a sword?"

"Practice," I replied.

"I thought you were going on a vision quest."

Closing the trunk of the car I said, "Well, not really. I'm just doing my own thing. I'm not seeking a vision or really anything like that but it's a long story."

Sherry heard this as she approached the car. "Jess, he's crazy. He doesn't like to sit alone and do nothing. He hasn't even told me why he's doing this."

"He has a sword," Jess said.

Sherry turned to me and said, "A sword? Are you out of your mind? I've never heard of someone going on a quest with a sword."

"It's not a quest," I replied.

"Well, whatever you're calling it, why a sword?"

"Practice," I said.

"Practice," she replied. "You have been practicing since college, for thirty years." She paused and added, "I know why. Boredom."

I just smiled as we all got in the car.

The ride to the park was uneventful except for a few light-hearted comments about the forthcoming myth of the crazy gray-haired swordsman of the sea. It was early afternoon when we arrived at the park. The sun was shining in a crystal-clear sky and since it was still early in the season, there were few people in the park or on the beach.

I was unloading my gear from the car as Sherry said, "You're sure you want to do this?"

As I turned, smiled and then kissed my wife and daughter, I said, "Well, no I don't want to do this, but I need to."

After they took a few pictures of me with my gear sitting on a picnic table, plus another hug and kiss, I waved goodbye as they drove off. I went back to the table and sat down once again.

"This is going to be tough and challenging," I thought. I could feel my perspective of time slowing down as if all of a sudden I was cast into a silent film. Having not worn a watch for many years, I was not imprisoned by the umbilical cord of linear time. However, the down side of this is that I have a keen sense of passing time and realized that being without books was going to be torturous for me. But I did have my sword.

Knowing that I couldn't stay on the picnic bench all night, I decided to explore the beach and set up camp at its very end, far away from visitors or park rangers. This was a park that did not allow you to camp or stay overnight. But at the far end, out of sight, no one would discover me. At least that's what I thought.

Do You Want to be My Friend?

The beach was relatively deserted. The few people I did pass smiled, but with that forced smile of not knowing what to make of you. To reach the end of the beach was a long walk, which I thought was a good thing. Finally, I came to the very south end of the park and beach and saw a perfect spot to make camp. Some large driftwood had been deposited further back from the shore and would make a perfect little enclosure where I could spend my time. I tried not to think of it as spending time in jail, but as an opportunity to be in nature.

"Who am I kidding," I thought to myself. "I spend a lot of time in nature but not this way, just sitting. I'm in a 'prison of my own making'!"

To pass the time, I decided to build up the sides of my shelter with other pieces of drift wood, which probably took up the better part of only thirty minutes. "Now," I thought. "What do I do? Ah, I'll practice sword cuts."

After thirty-plus years in the martial arts, I was not a novice with the sword. So accordingly, after only a few minutes had passed, I got bored again. And boredom leads to, yes, a nap. I laid down in my make-shift cave and attempted to sleep. I estimated that it was now probably late afternoon.

I never take naps, even after getting up at three in the morning to go bathing. I don't lay down to take a nap even when I get home from dipping in the stream. In short order, I discovered that napping was not the answer. I couldn't sleep. Awake and lying on the sand on my back, I suddenly got the feeling that I wasn't alone.

As I sat up and looked to my left where there were a few other pieces of large driftwood, a head peeked up and looked my way. "Oh man," I thought. "What is another person doing all the way out here?"

With that thought having just left my mind, the head rose further up and I saw it was attached to a male body – that was nude! Now the head was smiling at me. "I can't believe this," I thought. "On an isolated beach in Maine and I'm possibly getting hit on."

He was definitely not sunbathing, as the sun was low on the horizon. His next actions revealed that he seemed to be interested in getting to know me. He marched back and forth in front of my driftwood cave with all of his male glory waving and hopping in the wind.

And then, he stops in front of me, smiles over his shoulder and begins doing jumping jacks. First, he had his back to me, but then he turned and continued his wide, legs-spread jumping. After a few minutes of this showcase of his manly equipment, he fell into a full split and started doing some modified extreme yoga movements. I had to give it to him, he was in good shape!

Finally he tired and realized that I didn't want to be his "friend" in that way and proceeded to go back to his lair and get dressed. During all of this, not a word had been spoken. "Well," I thought, "a good story for the family and the apprentices."

The episode of the naked man had taken up some time and it had broken my boredom. I laid back down and kept smiling to myself thinking about the tale I could tell. And then I got the not-alone feeling again. As I sat up, I saw a park ranger approaching. Evidently, it was later than I had thought and I was not as isolated as I had hoped.

I have a habit of upsetting park rangers. I remembered how upset a park ranger was on the Big Island in 1993 after we had gone ahead against park rules and had conducted a burning to feed the Hawaiian ancestors. This Maine ranger looked none too happy, either.

"You can't camp here," she said. "And gay sex is not allowed."

I wanted to reply, "So other sex is okay?" But thought better of it. Then I did a strange thing. I pretended I was deaf and couldn't speak. I pointed to my mouth and ears and spread my arms wide indicting I didn't understand, but she wasn't buying it. Then I went to plan B. I began speaking a nonsensical language that I made up on the spot.

Plan B didn't work either. "Are you going to explain to me why you are here?" she said. "You need to leave. Or do I need to call for backup?"

As has been said before, the "caper was up." So I said, "No, I'll leave."

"Yes you will, and I will follow you out," she replied.

I almost felt like a kid caught stealing candy. Her intense stare didn't help. And then she spied the sword.

Taking a few steps back, she said, "What are you doing with that sword?"

Having taught self-defense to officers at the Maine State Police Academy and having worked with the police in the Greater Portland area, I was known by many officers throughout the state. It never occurred to me that I would be questioned as to why I, of all people, would have a sword. But she didn't know me. And in her mind, especially given my behavior over the previous few minutes, she might have been thinking that I was mentally unstable.

"I teach an old style of the martial arts that includes sword work," I replied, trying not to be threatening.

"Well those are illegal, also," she said as she glared at me.

I didn't want to contradict her and tell her that wasn't true. I thought it was best to keep my mouth shut and follow her, but she indicated that I was to walk ahead of her and she would follow.

I tried to initiate some conversation as we walked back to the entrance of the park, but she wanted nothing to do with speaking to me. I could hear her talking on her radio but couldn't make out the words.

As we approached the parking lot, I realized the gist of her radio conversation. An overly large park ranger was waiting by the open door of his vehicle. And as we got closer I could see he didn't look too friendly. Well, I guess it's not every day they have a crazed, sword-wielding, homeless and possibly gay man on their beach. I had to smile to myself as Sherry and Jess were right about the myth about the crazy gray-haired swordsman of the sea but with the addendum of homeless and gay.

As we approached the ranger and his vehicle, my sullen escort said, "He will follow you out to the road. And don't come back."

Well, I thought, "I won't." The good news was that I hadn't been bored, although there would be no quest that day. I needed to find a phone and call home. In that moment, I felt like ET, the Extraterrestrial, in more ways than one.

Eagles we see

What is this?

A sun angel, no two

So close I know you

Wounded I am, so green and red

Flower of my heart

Your nectar heals

MYTH OF THE HUMMINGBIRD CLAN[287]

. . . .

THE PLACE WAS SACRED. YOU COULD FEEL THE SACREDNESS when you crossed over the bed of rocks that were the floor of the Stream that guarded the Place. You put on the sacredness like a shawl over your shoulders and you knew that you were crossing a line and that things would never be the same. At least that's how it feels now looking back on that hot July day when we, a group of Searchers, and our teachers crossed the Stream.

Trees like giants dwarfed us from above and as we got closer, we could hear the sound of Water falling over the ancient rocks. We had no doubt that there was much wisdom to be learned from this Place.

But this, like many sacred places, had been dishonored and we, the Searchers, were witness to the dishonoring. We came seeking and looking for gifts, but our first task was not to receive, but to give and to make right the Place which had been so dishonored. We worked for several hours cleaning and nurturing the Place before we could begin our work of personal healing and learning.

As we worked, the Watchers were about – Rabbit and Fox and Owl and Bear and Squirrel and Deer and Hawk and Salmon and Bee and Duck and Great Blue Heron, and many others who hid in the trees and the hollows and the waters and watched. They were afraid at first, thinking that we brought more destruction to their home, but watched with love as we did for the Place what they could not do. There was another Watcher among them, tiny Hummingbird who had followed the warm ocean breezes from Mexico and had come home to this Northern Place for the summer. She had been coming to this Place for many years and had grown sadder every year as she watched the Place being destroyed by people. So it was with joy and gratitude that she watched us honor the Place which had been so dishonored.

We stayed at the Place for six days. Six days when time stood still and the world outside waited while we did our work. We prayed and fasted and for four mornings, we rose at First Light and offered ourselves to the Stream and the Four Winds in a sacred way. We came together as a community to do this work, but then came the time when we were to do our work alone, so we took our blankets and our sacred objects and went deeper into the woods of this Place. And through this all, the Watchers were about and made themselves known from time to time.

One of the Watchers, Hummingbird, watched from her nest high in the pine trees as each of us settled into our own little nests in the forest. She saw that many of us had feelings of loneliness and sadness and terror and many other feelings as we sat alone in the woods. She knew her own loneliness here in her Northern Home and she had not forgotten that we had blessed her Home, so she blessed us. She flew from one to the other of us, bringing with her a tiny golden thread which she had carried with her from Mexico. The thread was the thread of family and was a gift unlike no other. This she carried to each of us that she could find, binding us together forever. There were two among us that she could not find, and for this, she shed a tear of sadness into the Waterfall. The next day, she sent two leeches to kiss the feet of those she had missed, telling them that they too were of this family.

Yes, the Place was sacred, as was the gift that we took back to others of our family who could not be with us on our six-day quest. When we crossed the Stream to go back into the world we had left behind, nothing would ever be the same, for we were forever, the Hummingbird Clan.

THE RIVER RISES AND THE HUMMINGBIRD CLAN IS BORN

. . . .

According to Mesoamerican mythology, Quetzalcóatl is equated with the Hummingbird, symbol of creation and resurrection.

In the medicine traditions of the Andes, the hummingbird is a compelling archetype. It is small but powerful. It feeds off the living plant without taking the life of the plant and converts that nectar into the energy to fly great distances – to be a bridge between two cultures, two worlds. The hummingbird is featured in Andean mythology, representing the invitation from Spirit to source ourselves from direct knowledge – to gain our spiritual insights directly from Spirit, not from an intermediary.[288]

DURING THE SUMMER OF 1995, A FEW MONTHS AFTER MY SPIRIT Man experience and the encounter with the naked man in the Maine state park, Sherry and I conducted a special six-day spiritual/shamanic training by a river in Maine. We needed to be by a river as our apprentices were on a quest for a spirit song. This required bathing four mornings in a row.

We arrived at our camping and teaching spot right before noon, not a public campground, but an isolated spot next to the river. Mostly unknown except to the locals, one of our friends was familiar with the spot and thought it would be perfect for our work. Unspoiled and isolated, were his words. But instead of discovering a pure natural paradise, we found the area littered with garbage, the result of uncaring human actions. Evidently, the site had been used by the locals as a camping and party spot.

276

We cleaned for many hours before we set up camp. We stuffed dozens and dozens of large bags full of trash—enough to fill a small truck—that had accumulated over many years of misuse. When we arrived, Sher and I had both noticed a lack of birds and an energetic sadness to the land. But we both knew that nature and the Earth respond to the thoughts, words and actions of humans. Of course, the land was sad, as it had been desecrated and taken advantage of by humans for the sole purpose of their so-called pleasure. However, we also knew that for the next six days, we would care for and respect the land, the animals, the birds and the river, and that the land would respond and return to a more pristine state of being.

During the opening ceremony, a bee stung Sher on her third eye. Appropriate, as it seemed this would be a magical training. We had never been to this river before, so after prayers asking permission to do our spirit work, the first thing we did was explore the river and the surrounding area. We decided to take the apprentices along with us. It was now late afternoon and hot. We let everyone swim and relax before the intense spirit work began. In addition, I searched for an appropriate spot to conduct waterfall ascetic training – basically standing or sitting meditation under a waterfall.

I've been a water baby my whole life, so swimming with the apprentices was not totally unconditional. I looked forward to discovering the ideal water-fall. About a kilometer upstream I found it. While the apprentices swam, I decided to float over the falls and drop into the waters below. I'll admit that my unhealthy ego was involved. As a former lifeguard, I know better. It is a no-no to jump or fall into unknown waters because you don't know what is below the surface.

As soon as I hit the water, I knew my fate. Fortunately, I didn't break any bones when I landed on the rocks hidden beneath the surface. But I did put a deep and long gash in my left buttock. And how did I know the cut was deep? By the bloody waters surrounding me.

Sher immediately knew that something was wrong. I shouted to her, "I'm okay, but I did cut my hip. And it's bleeding pretty well." I could sense her alarm, but she knew that with my strong focus and intent I handled emergencies well. "Do you need help?" she shouted back.

"No, but get everyone back to camp. I'm going to stay in the river and slowly make my way downstream back there, too," I answered.

If you've ever been in Maine during the summer, you know that the rivers are still cold. So I determined that my best strategy was to keep my injury in the cold waters and slowly make my way downstream using my arms, not my hips or legs. One of our apprentices was a nurse and we had a first aid kit. By the time I reached camp, everyone else would be there, so when I got out of the river she would be able to assess the damage and patch me up.

By more or less floating downstream and not stressing my body by walking or swimming, I kept my blood pressure lower and didn't stress my leg or hip muscles. At the same time the cold water inhibited the bleeding while I used my mind to help heal my body and reduce the blood flow to the gash in my hip.

It all worked. I finally reached the shore of the camp and slowly limped out of the river. The nurse took over and surveyed the damage. I could tell she was concerned. Being a good and proper nurse, she wanted to get me to a hospital as quickly as possible to get stitches because the wound was deep and wide.

"Do you have any butterflies," I asked? I figured she knew I wasn't talking about the beautiful, winged ones.

"Yes, but I feel we need to get you to a hospital."

"I'm okay, I'll be fine," I said. "I know you can do it. Just use the butterflies to close the cut – patch me up and I'll be brand-new."

Spirit Song, the River Rises and Hummingbirds

It seemed the magic had already begun. My hip stopped bleeding and I continued teaching along with Sherry. Sleeping on the ground, however, was a little problematic. I didn't want to sleep on the side of my injured hip.

One solution came with bathing. Having to open the river with a song right before first light, I didn't have the chance to sleep very long, or worry about putting undo pressure on my gash.

This was the first of four dawn bathings. Conveniently, the spot in the river where the apprentices would submerge was right by our camp. The waters were low and slow running but still deep enough for bathing. I thought back to the many times Sher and I had gone bathing with Vince Stogan at a spot a few hours' drive north of Vancouver, B.C. We would leave three hours before dawn and then have to hike up the mountain to a frigid stream accessible only by climbing down a steep bank. How easy for the apprentices to roll out of bed to bathe. But soon they would be sacrificing in other ways.

Bathing has very strict rules. One is that a woman who is on her "moon-time"—menstruating—cannot bathe. The women who were menstruating would still participate but in a different, separate, powerful ceremony conducted by Sher further downstream. As you may have guessed, it was important to have them be downstream from the bathing spot. It was not that the women were being ostracized. Instead, they were being honored for the sacred and powerful time of their bleeding.

For the rest of the day we taught our apprentices and conducted various experiential exercises culminating in a very special fire ceremony at night. After bathing the next morning, we put each of the apprentices out on a quest for vision and power. Each would be alone and fasting for the next two days except when they would bath at pre-dawn. This was their sacrifice: fasting and solitude without the various mundane distractions of life.

A person's spirit song is a reflection and vibration of their inner spiritual power. To receive a song is not easy, but once you have your song, it is your "open sesame" for the spirit world. You may have more than one song and there are even secret teachings to separate songs if they start to combine. These are just a few of the many teachings that Vince and Mom Stogan passed on to me and Sher.

As part of the opening ceremony of our six-day training, both Sher and I sang our spirit songs. While I was clowning around, gashing my hip and sacrificing blood to the river, Sher was doing a heavy-duty healing on one of the apprentices. Sher sings her song as part of her healings. She may repeat it many times.

After bathing the second morning, we put the apprentices out on their quest. This left Sher and I time alone to do our own spirit work, and gave us time to relax and put our heads together regarding ways to help each of the apprentices heal their pasts and grow in their spiritual power. Little did we realize that sooner rather than later, magic would happen as the spirit of the land and river awakened.

After brutal winters, Maine summers were usually jewels to be savored. The only drawback was the tourist traffic. But the summer weather, the mountains, rivers, forests, and the sea—and we can't forget the lobsters—are the reasons Mainers suffer through the winters. And this summer was one of those gems, with daily sun and very little rain.

In late afternoon on the third crystal clear day, I was away from camp interacting with nature, doing my thing, when all of a sudden I heard Sher singing her song. I was taken back because you usually don't have your song just come out for no apparent reason. I was mystified because Sher was alone. The mystery only deepened as I kept hearing her song over and over again, to the point I couldn't concentrate anymore and decided to return to camp and see what was happening.

As I entered camp, I saw her sitting silently on the rocks by the edge of the river. As I approached her, she just turned and smiled.

"What are you doing?" I asked.

"Listening to my song," she replied while motioning for me to sit down next to her. "The river has been singing my song."

"I thought it was you, and wondered why you were singing so much."

"It's the river. The river is singing my song over and over again."

I sat in awe next to my beautiful wife watching the rippling waters pass in front of us while listening to the soul of the river mimicking and honoring my wife's spirit song, a song of joy and life. Just as I noticed that the waters of the river seemed to be higher and faster moving than before, a hummingbird appeared in front of us with that familiar sound that I liken to a light saber. It stayed suspended in the air, looking at us. Minutes pasted before it took off, only to return in a short time to repeat the same action.

"Sher, this is strange. Not as strange as the river, but still quite unusual," I said.

The next moment in the blue draped sky above us, two eagles circled overhead as the hummingbird made a third appearance.[289] We just looked at each other and sat in silence until dusk.

The Rising of the Waters

Bathing is not the most popular activity that we put our apprentices through. In fact, it is probably the most dreaded. You must sacrifice sleep and enter fast moving waters, living waters, to submerge yourself not once but at least four times, in the dark, in a simulation of drowning. But if one can let go of the fear, the dread, the cold and losing sleep, it is the most wondrous rejuvenation of one's body and soul – a rebirth out of the materialistic sluggishness of life. And with first light, nature's symphony awakens and serenades you with the beauty and the promise of golden memories of life's purpose and your connection to all things – no worries, no stress, just being as the Creator intended.

I opened the river for the last time, once again with a spirit song. I prayed and anointed each apprentice with the blood of Mother Earth before they entered and submerged into the roaring, life-giving—as well as life-taking—waters. I always wait until everyone has dunked and are under their spirit blanket before I bathe. As I entered the waters my last thought was: "I'm glad no one was swept away by this potent current."

After being out questing with no food for two days, the apprentices were eagerly preparing breakfast as Sher and I spent time witnessing the miracle before us. The river was still singing Sher's song but the waters had risen at least threefold from the time we'd arrived. There was no earthly explanation. No rain or storms or opening of dams. Salmon swam and jumped up-stream in waters that were now so alive, active and happy.

As a final activity before the closing and breaking of camp, we held a sharing circle to hear and witness everyone's experience of their quest, bathing, and training. To begin, we gave an overview of our observations and comments about the six days. Everyone was shocked when they found out that it wasn't Sherry singing her song, but the river. The rising of the river's waters added to their amazement – a physical demonstration of the land and river responding to the power of spirit and love.

During the first apprentice's sharing of her experience, she mentioned a strange visitation. "I was under my blanket trying to escape from the mosquitoes when I heard this sound. I lifted the blanket off of my head and there in front of me was a hummingbird." Before she could continue another apprentice said, "I had a hummingbird come to me more than once!" And then another, "Me, also." Each of our long-term apprentices were visited by a hummingbird. And so the Hummingbird Clan of our Apprentice Program was born.

I should note that a few months earlier I'd had my Spirit Man experience at Teotihuacán where there are numerous images of hummingbirds, for instance a wall painting of a hummingbird feeding a jaguar. As a redeemer, Quetzalcóatl brought a message of resurrection. Consequently, Quetzalcóatl was equated with the hummingbird, a symbol of creation and resurrection among Mesoamericans. Furthermore, according to the Maya, hummingbirds are an avian aspect of the sun. "With their iridescent feathers, these small birds look like glints of sunlight as they dart back and forth."[290] This is one of the reasons hummingbirds are sometimes referred to as "sun angels." Two years after our hummingbird encounters, heavenly angels would appear to Sherry and me and twelve of our apprentices. Magic is real and miracles do happen.

RHONDA THE HONDA

. . . .

To Dad

Eagle feathers glowing in the moonlight.
Sky of brilliance Night rhythms heard in the distance.
A man full of pride and wisdom.
Gray owl full of wonder.
Faces blank fill my sight, but owl man glows in the passage above.
Stars of light Moon Fawn standing in the corner, circled and
embraced by Corn Spirit.
Animal Boy watches with his heart and soul.
We gather around gray owl to celebrate the new moon.
Boldness fills the picture.
All of our hearts come together to form our circle of love.
Love, Jess (6-21-92)

IN EARLY AUGUST 1995, AFTER OUR SIX-DAY TRAINING, SHER AND
I and our daughter Jess began a cross-country journey to Seattle from our
home in Cape Elizabeth, Maine. We were considering relocating to Seattle
where we would be closer to Mom and Vince Stogan. Before we decided to
pack up our roots in Maine and move coast to coast, we wanted to experience
the greater Seattle area. Instead of driving our car cross-country, we bought
an older used car. We found the perfect one – Rhonda the Honda.

Rhonda was awesome. She got us to the West Coast and back to our
home the following April. But this story is not about our journey out or what

happened while we were there, but the journey back to Maine, just me and my daughter. In fact, I would encourage every father and daughter, every parent and child, to drive cross-country together – a great experience and a memory to last many lifetimes.

We decided that Sher would fly back to Maine while Jess and I drove Rhonda home. When we had arrived in September, we rented an apartment in Redmond, WA, the home of Microsoft. After the disruption of my beach quest,[291] I decided that I needed to quest by bathing four mornings in a row. Searching off I-90, I discovered a perfect river: swift-flowing, isolated and a little scary in the dark. The river had easy access via a trail that led to an often visited waterfall. Of course, people didn't walk to the waterfall in the dark so I wouldn't have to worry about visitors, at least not human ones. At certain times on this trail just before first light, I had smelled wild animals like coyotes or possibly a bear. This was a little disconcerting. My focus was on bathing, not the residents of the land. After my final dunk, I didn't want to turn towards the bank and see a bear waiting for me. Fortunately, this never happened.

In January 1996, we decided to experience island living, so we relocated to Vashon Island, outside of Seattle. And then reality set in. To be subject to a ferry schedule for civilized shopping (book stores) and eating out (ethnic restaurants such as Mexican and Japanese), we discovered that this type of small island living was not for us – Vashon was a far cry from Maui. For numerous reasons, including that we missed our home, our son Jamie, and Shadow, our hybrid wolf, we decided to return to Maine at the beginning of April.

Because I was staying on Vashon, I hadn't returned to my bathing spot since late fall. In all likelihood, I wouldn't be bathing there again, at least within the foreseeable future. This meant that I needed to bathe one last time and, so to speak, "close" the river. True to nature as a champion procrastinator, I waited until the last moment. I caught the first ferry, around 4 a.m., the morning we were leaving to travel cross-country. A little frustrating to say the least, given that within hours we would be driving past the I-90 turnoff for the bathing spot as we headed towards Idaho and Montana.

Once I got off the car ferry in Southworth, I needed the traffic to cooperate if I was to arrive right before first light. As if time had been suspended, I got there in time to bathe and close the river. With no time to meditate after bathing, I hurried back down the trail and back to Vashon to finish loading Rhonda and pick up Jess. Like a scene out of a manic, comical movie, we headed to the ferry repeating a journey I had just made. It was comical as Rhonda was packed to the gills.

After we exited the ferry, it soon became obvious that we were so over-packed I couldn't see to change lanes. Jess had to lean out of the passenger side window and yell to let me know when we could get over. With traffic zooming past us on I-405, outside of Bellevue and Redmond, I realized, as did Jess, that we couldn't drive cross-country like that. The solution was less stuff. We couldn't and didn't want to throw things out on the side of the road, so we stopped in Redmond at the postal service. Three large boxes later—all headed to the East Coast—we continued driving. I realized we would never reach Montana that day, and we'd be lucky if we made it to Spokane. And I was correct. Montana was not in the cards. We pulled into Spokane early in the evening.

Jess and I were looking forward to Montana, a state we hadn't traveled through. We left our humble lodgings early in the morning. The scenery through Idaho was awe-inspiring. As we entered Montana on I-90, nature still took our breath away, but it was an isolated area. We were on a section of I-90 that cuts through the Lolo National Forest on its way to Missoula. With nature's beauty surrounding us, I thought, "Rhonda, please don't let us down now."

As we exited the forest that straddled both sides of I-90, I could sense and feel a change in Rhonda's motion. I sensed that we were not far from Missoula, but a breakdown would put us in a difficult position. As I silently urged Rhonda to keep going, Jess looked at me and said, "Dad somethings not right."

"Don't worry," I replied.

A few more miles and I thought, "It feels as if the front wheel is going to come off."

More minutes passed, and then, as we came up and over a hill, we saw at the base of the hill a garage and restaurant. Both Jess and I cheered. And

Rhonda had not let us down but her front passenger-side wheel was about ready to fall off.

Life happens. Attempting to keep life from happening is foolish and pointless. Most important is how we react. As our Zen priest said in the Yucatan, "Don't complain, don't explain and, most importantly, laugh." Rhonda's wheel could have come off in the isolated wilds of Montana and possibly caused us to crash. Instead, the wheel stayed on until, safe and sound, we reached "civilization" and a garage. We can be thankful we were in the right place at the right time.

The Badlands and Fire Works

After two very restful and peaceful but unexpected nights in Missoula, we were back on the road. And Rhonda was her old self again. We spent the next night in Sheridan, Wyoming, in what I can only describe as a creepy room. Jess even wanted me to push my bed in front of the door to keep anyone from entering. Not a Marriott by any means; not even a Motel 6.

The next morning we continued our eastward journey. Leaving Wyoming, we entered South Dakota. In South Dakota, I-90 just happens to skirt the edge of the desolate land known as the Badlands, the only place Jess had told me she would like to visit on our journey home. For myself, I had no interest or desire to stop and pay a visit.

As we approached Wall, South Dakota, signs began appearing for the Badlands. Jess seemed to be asleep as her eyes were closed. I thought, "Great! We'll just go past the exit and by the time Jess wakes up we'll be too far away to backtrack."

I zoomed past the turnoff thinking, "Awesome, no Badlands today." With that thought still vibrating within my mind. Jess opened her eyes and said, "Dad, the Badlands. You passed the turnoff. I really want to see them."

"Okay," I replied, with no idea how she'd known we'd passed the exit. "I'll turnaround." Attempting one last time to get her to change her mind, I continued, "Are you sure you want to see it?"

"Yes," was her short and to the point answer.

I must say, I'm glad we did stop and see the Badlands. They were amazing in their stark beauty. After that, the rest of our journey was uneventful except for the fireworks.

We were outside of Gary, Indiana, when we passed a sign for fireworks. Since Maine allows only the weenie ones, we decided to find the place. We pulled off the main road onto a secondary one and came upon a country store. And this wooden two-story general store could have been right out of a Quentin Tarantino movie. I parked in front. Even though there was no indication that they sold fireworks, I thought we could ask if they knew where we could buy some. Before we got out of Ronda, Jess and I looked at each other with a mind-meld of, "Do we really want to go in?" But then we did.

The wooden boards creaked as we walked inside. The clerk (I believe) behind the counter looked at us with a facial expression that said, "Why are you bothering me? What do you want?" His mannerisms reminded me of the bartender played by Cheech Marin in the movie *Desperado*.

"Hi," I said. "We're looking for some fireworks."

"What type?"

This question had not been spoken by the clerk, but came from a voice behind us. Both Jess and I turned. The questioner was a large man who just happened to be wearing a badge – a Sheriff's badge.

"I'm not sure," I replied, cautious because I didn't know the local laws concerning fireworks.

"Follow me," was his simple reply.

We followed him outside and around the side of the store to a set of wooden stairs at the back of the building. I looked at Jess and she looked at me. Did we dare follow him up?

We did. I went first in case it was some type of trap. I'm not paranoid, but the past few minutes had been strange, to have the Sheriff right there and then have him lead us to a stash of fireworks.

By the time we had reached the top of the stairs, the Sheriff had opened the door to the attic, which housed, with no exaggeration, thousands of fireworks. There were all kinds, and more than a town would need for a community Fourth of July celebration.

I looked at Jess and she looked at me and we both smiled as we stepped over the threshold.

We'd been gone from our home for nine months, I can tell you the adage, "there's no place like home," is so very true. This is one of the reasons why the homeless situation in this country is so morally and spiritually repugnant, considering the amount of wealth held by a small percentage of people.

Commentary

My journey coast to coast, west to east with my daughter, just the two of us with no distractions—and of course at that time no iPads, no smartphones, no selfies—just memories, was more valuable than all the excessive wealth in the world. In a most vivid and cosmic term, life is short. We do not know what tomorrow will bring, or for that fact, the next moment. Our lives can change in a heartbeat. Don't spend your life accumulating and consuming material items. Spend quality time with loved ones, family and friends. Spread peace and love with a smile. And most definitely, take a road trip and far travel with your son or daughter. Just you and your child – no distractions!

THE CHATTERING RETREATERS

. . . .

May the stars carry your sadness away. May the flowers fill your heart with beauty. May hope forever wipe away your tears, and, above all, may silence make you strong.

– Chief Dan George

IN 1996, FOR MY FIFTIETH BIRTHDAY, SHER AND I CONDUCTED A spiritual journey to Maui. I wanted to welcome the dawn and the sun on Haleakala on the fiftieth anniversary of my birth. To witness the rising sun on Haleakala, "house of the rising sun," is an awesome spiritual experience, but it does involve a sacrifice – a sacrifice of sleep. As a group, we needed to leave while it was still a few hours before dawn so we could reach the summit in time to witness its unknown number of "sun births." For me, it was the mere fiftieth year of "sun births" for my soul.

Bee Clan, Maui, August 29, 1996

For the majority of tourists, a visit to *"Ala Hea Ka La,"*—Haleakala's ancient name meaning "Path to Call the Sun,"—is nothing more than an unhealthy-ego-producing entertainment with the added opportunity of cycling down from the summit. I would suspect very few tourists view it as a religious experience or even understand the significance and mythology of this volcanic mountain. To the ancient Hawaiians this mountain was *wahi pana* (legendary place, sacred place) and *wau akua* (place where the gods live). According to myth, on this sacred place the demi-god *Maui* lassoed the sun so that his mother, *Hina* the moon goddess, could dry her *tapa* cloth. The thought of this transported me back to Machu Picchu and meditating on Intihuatana, "the hitching post of the sun," and my visionary experience of a time before the Inkas.

I wanted to celebrate my birth and share this experience with my family and our students in this sacred and legendary place. We arrived at the summit with plenty of time to spare. Even though we were on Maui, we were not at sea level but at 10,000 feet, which meant it was cold. The parking lots were almost full by the time we reached the top, with large numbers of people milling around.

Silence is golden as the saying goes. And then there is Spartan philosophy, which valued silence over empty words. Unfortunately enough, for most people silence is an unknown quality and in fact something to be shunned. The more external chatter and internal mind talk, the less opportunity to come face to face with our true authentic selves with all our imperfections and woundings that may be unveiled.

The divine and mundane interpenetrate. What this means is that the quieter the mind and tongue, the more we can hear nature and nature's divine voice. If we desire to speak to trees, we must first listen to them. One of the key teachings of the Northwest Coast First People, as well as other indigenous cultures, is the refrain to listen, look and learn.

It has been said about God, whom "no words can tell, no tongue can speak, whom silence only can declare," that this Great Mystery may only be "served through silence alone." This knowledge seems to be absent from the public, including many spiritual seekers. However, many cannot be faulted for their tongue wagging and mind chaos. They are still living in a reality of dualism and have not been taught the axiom of the interpenetration of spirit and matter. Thus, they do not live according to that axiom and only seek spiritual growth and enlightenment through classes and workshops and not through hearing the first bird sound of the morning.

The key is to see where our heart and mind are in the present moment. Even the mundane moment, which may often be more important and affecting than when we are in a formal spiritual/religious/shamanic workshop or spiritual/religious setting. As a child forced many times to going to church, I could never understand the smiles and behaviors of people at church compared to their mean-spirited actions and faces outside of church.

Pointedly, this cultural pattern of dualistic belief and action was very much in evidence on the summit of Haleakala. As we stood in awe and anticipation of sunrise, it became evident to me that visually we would not experience it due to the early morning weather conditions. When others began to realize this fact, their tongue wagging with empty words increased in intensity. One group behind us was by far the worst of all within ear shot. It wasn't so much what they were saying, but the arrogance and superior tone of their voices. I felt they were some type of spiritual group.

To check out my theory, I sent one of our students to talk to a couple of them who had wandered away a few yards from the main group. My student returned shaking his head and asking how I knew. It seems that not only were they a spiritual group but they had just come off a thirty-day silent retreat! "Maybe I need to tell them to get a refund of monies spent," I said.

Because moments in time like this one are not a structured spiritual time, they can be a glimpse into people's true spiritual makeup. You see, it's easy to be spiritual in a spiritual setting or religious in church and easy to be martial in a *dojo*, but the proof of a person's power is being spiritual and martial outside of those settings – in other words, with every breath, in every moment. It is right action: a divine heart and mind contained within our holy temple of body and what we do today and every new day about self and other. No one in today's world needs their consciousness raised. What we need is for each person to be aware of what they do to themselves and to others (others being not only human but all things of the Earth). If a person suffers dysfunctional actions and thoughts, the person needs to transform them and stop repeating them.

Ask yourself today and every day: are my actions of body and mind helping the greater wellbeing of self and of others? Am I a better person today? Or, am I the same person? Have I repeated dysfunctional patterns? And one last question, am I happy and fulfilled? If not, do something about it. Or not.

RENNES-LE-CHÂTEAU

. . . .

Our tale is dedicated to our friend Elizabeth Van Buren who passed-over on
September 6, 2011. May you be enjoying your time with the
Archangel Mikael.
Do not stay long, the earth needs you back.
Know that you are missed. – JC and Sher

The owl is the secret symbol for the guardian of the invisible world.
To those who have understood that Love is the
key, the White Owl will appear, and will lead them
into another time. One cycle ends, but another
commences – and a seed group will go forward into
the Age of Aquarius, the Age of the Holy Spirit.[292]

HOW DID WE DISCOVER RENNES-LE-CHÂTEAU BEFORE THE
publication of *The Da Vinci Code*? Was it from a dream? On the contrary, the
knowledge came from a book and a soul need. During the spring of 1998,
while conducting a spiritual journey to various sacred sites in England and
Wales, I stumbled upon Elizabeth Van Buren's book *Refuge of the Apocalypse*.
I was awestruck with the book and determined that Sherry and I needed
to visit Elizabeth and the focus of her book, the Rennes-le-Château area of
Southern France.

Sadly, it was a bitter sweet discovery, as the previous evening we had a call
from our daughter in Maine that our beloved wolf hybrid, Shadow, had died.

After we experienced much grief, we took solace in our new interest. I had already read parts of *Holy Blood, Holy Grail*, the original bestselling book about Rennes and the bloodline of Jesus and Mary, and had planned on visiting this area, but Elizabeth's book spurred us into action. Within six months, we arrived in the Languedoc-Roussillon region of France.

After flying into Montpellier, we drove to the medieval city of Carcassonne to spend the night. We arrived at our hotel late in the afternoon. Since it was situated right outside the medieval city, I decided to explore Carcassonne while Sherry stayed in the room, resting. I have a vivid imagination and am a romantic at heart. As I entered over the drawbridge and through the castle gates, I was transported back to the time of the Knights Templar and the troubadours. I wandered the streets like a kid in a fantasy world, then heard music and singing coming my way. The full moon had just risen over the city, providing some natural light.

I decided to wait on the battlements to discover what merriment was approaching. As I closed my eyes, I could sense the shades of the defenders of these stone walls. I wondered how much laughter these stones had seen and how many tears had been shed over the centuries. In the next moment, I was drawn out of my reverie by five medieval-clothed figures who were now personally serenading me. And they say magic doesn't happen!

Elizabeth Van Buren

Over the next few days we were able to track down Elizabeth and became fast friends with her. An eccentric and rebel much like us, she graciously shared her knowledge and experience of the mysteries surrounding Rennes-le-Château and its sacred landscape. Her home was on the outskirts of Limoux where once, dressed as the Archangel Mikael, she stopped traffic in the middle of the city as a form of protest. She never revealed to us the reason for her protest.

What intrigued me about Elizabeth and her book were her discussions of the relationships that Rennes-le-Château has with alchemy, the Holy Grail, the Archangel Mikael, and Venus. But there was still something more about

Elizabeth's book, and it had to do with the theories surrounding Jesus and Mary Magdalene.

The theory of the marriage between Jesus and Mary was initially made popular by the book *Holy Blood, Holy Grail*. However, Elizabeth's book speaks more to the esoteric aspects of Rennes-le-Château and the hidden teachings of Jesus and Mary rather than simply to the bloodline that flows from them. One of the keys to understanding this region is symbology. Scattered throughout the landscape and churches are symbols not found (or rarely found) in any other Christian churches, such as pentagrams and the Jewish six-pointed star.

One of our first stops with Elizabeth was the church at Esperanza dedicated to Saint Michel. There are two extremely important images here. One is a statue of the archangel Mikael with his or her spear tip inside the mouth of a dragon. This is the true esoteric meaning of transmuting the base, dualistic energy within us, symbolically represented by a serpent or dragon, into the nondualistic energy of creation. Throughout history the church has led us to believe that it is the devil being slain, not a dragon or serpent being transmuted.

The second image is of a large painting hanging over the main altar. Again it is of the archangel, this time posed with a sword, standing on what appears to be the devil. But closer scrutiny reveals that the figure has the head and body of an old man. This is Father Time, or Saturn, conveying the teaching that we must learn to "press down" linear time so our lives are not controlled by the fear of aging and death. Neither of these are dogmatic teachings of Christianity. In fact, they counter the dualistic-fear-induced propaganda of the church.

Our next stop was the hilltop site of Rennes-le-Château and its small church, which overlooks the valleys of the Aude and Sals known as *La Val-Dieu* (the Valley of the Gods), where abundant crops and rich soil bask under the golden sun. The star of Venus travels over this valley for eight years to form the five-pointed star defined in the heavens. Inside the church, her reflection is painted on the ceiling. The twins are depicted at the altar and the Star of David is mysteriously engraved on an outside headstone. Out of Egypt and the holy lands came the mystery-school teachings.

Sher, Tour Magdala, Rennes-le-Chateau

Since the release of *The Da Vinci Code* in May of 2002, more people are aware of the various mysteries that shroud Rennes-le-Château like a dreary mist in a good, old-fashioned Dracula movie. The main mystery has to do with treasure. What is the true treasure here? Is it that of the heretic Cathars, decimated by the church through the Albigensian Crusades? Is it

297

Solomon's treasure, discovered beneath Jerusalem by the Knights Templar and subsequently brought to and hidden in the mountains surrounding Rennes-le-Château? Or is it Jesus and Mary Magdalene's gravesite? Of course, any physical evidence that Jesus survived the cross and died at a later time would destroy the church and would have to have been well hidden.

On the other hand, if the priceless treasure is the hidden knowledge of Jesus's true message and teachings, would it be possible to prove this by using common sense, logical thinking, and intuition? The clues could possibly be found within a parchment, and most certainly in the many symbolic images scattered throughout the region. This knowledge of Jesus's true teachings and beliefs would be easier to discover than the physical evidence proving his survival of crucifixion.

The decade-ago controversy surrounding *The Da Vinci Code* and a possible bloodline would pale in comparison to revealed truth about Jesus and his message. Yes, he was married to his special Mary of Bethany, but the "greatest lie ever told" is not about his marital status. The fact is, his being married or not does not really collapse the foundation of Christianity. The truth about him and his message does.

One important point remains to be made. There is one painting of Jesus with his students that really stands out and reveals truth. Out of the dozen or so students, only three are male, and the rest are female. The truth is, when Jesus taught, there were many times more female students than males.[293] Of course, Christianity wants us to believe that there were only male disciples to justify their patriarchal rule. I pose a question: why do men fear women's power and equality?

A Two-thousand-year-old Anointment in a Sacred Stone Chair in Southern France

I know the power of anointment. During the fall of 2008, we returned to France, leading a spiritual group to the Rennes-le-Château area. We had last brought a group of our students there in 1999.

Flying into Toulouse, our destination was the Languedoc region, where many spiritual and esoteric traditions flourished, such as the keepers of the

Holy Grail, medieval alchemists, the Knights Templars, the Black Madonna and the Gnostic Cathars. Plus, the area was the wellspring of the romantic age of chivalry, the troubadour tradition and the courts of love.

As we entered the town of Alet-les-Bain, we crossed the singing, babbling river (oh the stories it could tell!) and passed two stone pillars before we glided under the heavenly carpet of a massive, ancient tree's canopy. The shelter of its branches and leaves whispered and quieted our thoughts. We had arrived at our lodging, the *Bishop's Palace*.

Night had fallen and the air was thick. This was our place of refuge. Under that ancient tree, hundreds of years old, we enjoyed our first meal of French cuisine: green salads, breads, cheeses, trout and local red and white wines.

Legendary home to Nostradamus, "*Alet*" means chosen place, and has a long history of being home to seekers of wisdom through the Mystery Schools, the Druids, and the Knights Templar. The next day after a wonderful breakfast buffet, we explored La Val-Dieu – Valley of the Gods. Our focus was a small town known for its healing baths and its natural hot spring: Rennes-les-Bains. Hidden in a cleft in the Corbière mountains, Rennes-les-Bains is thought to be the place where Mary Magdalene and Jesus first came to live when they escaped from the Holy Land. Here we explored the sacred land, its timeless and ancient healing waters, and the sacred streams nearby, Sals and La Blanque.

After experiencing the healing waters of Rennes-les-Bains, we traveled to the small village of Sougraigne, the source of the spring that gives birth to the river Sals. What makes this unique and extraordinary is that the spring is salt water – a salt spring. Yes, the river Sals, the red stream, is salt water, not fresh water. The fact that it is naturally salty is extremely unusual for an inland river. It flows downstream until it meets the fresh waters of the stream La Blanque, the white stream, at a place called Benitier, which means a basin to hold holy water.

This is a sacred place, the confluence of salt and fresh water, red and white, masculine and feminine energies. With the fresh and salt waters blending together in such an alchemical merging, it is symbolic of the primordial waters of creation.

After leaving Sougraigne, we followed the Sals downstream. Our first stop was at the *Fontaine des Amours* – the Fountain of Love. It's important to note that the waters of the Sals are cold, rising from deep underground. It's believed that Mary Magdalene bathed apprentices at this spot. Sher and I both recognized this as an excellent place to bathe, to put seekers into the living waters of the Sals. There was a perfect place to stand on the rocks beside a deep pool of swirling cold water. Dipper John[294] believed that the colder the water was, the better the purification. Adding to the sacredness of this place of love was a smaller heart-shaped pool. A heart often represents Mary Magdalene, as well as representing love.

Our next and final stop before the sacred site known as the devil's chair," was Benitier, the confluence of salt and fresh water, red and white, masculine and feminine energies. Here we conducted a ceremonial purification symbolizing the blending of spirit (Sals, the red stream) and matter (La Blanque, the white stream) – Oneness.

After this purification, we ascended a steep, little-used trail to the "devil's chair." Named by the Catholic Church, it is a stone chair on the side of a mountain that looks toward the rising sun in the east. A five-thousand-year-old pre-Christian site, this pagan stone throne commands an imposing place on the mountainside. Due to its location, a church could not be built over it. Whenever this was the case, the church would demonize the spot in various ways, one being to identify it as a site sacred to Satan. In opposition to the Christians, I renamed the stone seat the Morning Star Seat.

Mary Magdalene is often compared with the eternal Goddess Isis. Appropriately, this stone seat was also known as the "Seat of Isis." There is an old legend that states, "The Spirit of Nodens—God of the Great Deep—flashed forth as lightning from the depths and formed a throne in celestial realms—a seat of stone—whereon the Goddess was established. She ruled from the throne of stone which Nodens had fashioned, and about her the Temple of Nu-Isis grew into being. This also was of stone, hollowed out, and of the lightning. And this Seat of Stone whirled forth in the heavens—the vehicle of Noden's fire—veiled from mortal eyes by a vitreous curtain of deep unyielding ocean."[295] It has been proposed "that the name Isis literally means a stone seat."[296] Isis is also identifiable as Venus. Even though I renamed the seat the Morning Star Seat, it would be just as appropriate for it to be called the Magdalene Seat.

The seat has a power that is hard to describe. Right next to it is a spring in a circular shape that is further proof of the power of this site. At this spot, three dragon lines or ley lines merge together creating an electromagnetic energy vortex in the middle of the stone seat where time and space may be suspended. Seated on the stone chair, Sherry performed an ancient anointing ceremony on me, witnessed by three of our apprentices.[297] As I watched her, her face physically changed. She was not herself but I knew her. And the anointment she did on my head with the sacred oil was known to my soul. She had anointed me like this before. Further details are not necessary to share, but the stone seat was honored in a manner that possibly had not been done for thousands of years. (Please see endnote 160.)

QUESTION: NATIVE. ANSWER: NO.

. . . .

SEPTEMBER 2000, AND WE WERE RETURNING FROM A SPIRITUAL
journey to Hawaii. We stopped over in Seattle to spend a few days with one
of our apprentices and her family. After a few enjoyable days on the Olympic
Peninsula, we were headed back to Seattle's SeaTac Airport. We were on a four-
lane highway outside of Tacoma that was divided by a grassy median strip.
Our apprentice Jane was driving with my wife in the passenger seat, and I was
in the back attempting to nap. With eyes closed all I heard was, "Oh no." With
that, my eyes flew open. I saw a car settle on its wheels on the median. "Stop,"
I yelled. I jumped out and hobbled[298] across the highway to the car. Later, I
was told that I did some type of arm motion as I went across the highway that
seemed to slow down time. They also related that the car had rolled side over
side numerous times before it came to rest upright on its wheels. Jane said she
saw the driver's head violently whipping around.

As I approached the vehicle, I saw two Native American men unconscious. Once by the car, I knew the passenger was injured but not dying. The
driver was another story. He was dying; his soul was leaving him. When I
had broken the sensory separation between this world and the Otherworld,
I was aware of both. This was like the feeling and knowing I had during the
descending spirit exorcism.

In an attempt to keep him from dying, I put my hands on him and a spirit
song sprang from my lips. This was not my usual song; this one I had never
sung before. When you are in this timeless space, you still have a conscious
awareness. It is not a trance state but one of full awareness, total focus, and

302

intent with a minimum of mind talk. Time had no meaning as my awareness shifted to the other side of the car where a woman, definitely Native American, was walking back and forth while looking at me. It is difficult to put into words: her intense focus was on me, not the two in the car. I thought, "She must be pissed that a white guy is healing with a Northwest Coast spirit song." Then I refocused on the driver. Again, time was lost to me until the driver opened his eyes turned, looked at me, and said, "Native."

I replied, "No." He closed his eyes, and I knew then that his soul was back and he was not dying. With that, I left, as I heard the sounds of an ambulance coming. In that moment, I had a fleeting thought, "Where was the native woman?" She had disappeared.

In hindsight, I realize that no other cars had stopped to help. This in itself was very unusual, as accidents seem to draw humans like bees to honey.

The odd thing is that at the time, I never gave the native woman's disappearance any further consideration. It was only years later, out of the clear blue, that the thought came into my mind: "She was a spirit psychopomp to assist the native man passing over. And however the sisters[299] weave the threads, I had prevented it." With this awareness, I asked both my wife and Jane about the woman. They never saw her.

So, is the guide who helps us pass over a female? Does she appear as one of our own race? If we use common sense, a woman births us and delivers us into our earthly existence. Why would a female not assist us in departing?

Within a short time after the accident an event occurred that shows there are no coincidences and that sometimes there is great meaning in a seemingly random event.[300] One of the reasons we had stopped in Seattle was not only to spend time with our apprentice and her family, but because we were considering a move to Washington state. As we approached the Tacoma Dome on I-5, traveling at least sixty-five miles per hour, a hawk swooped down in front of our car, disappeared for a fraction of a second and then came back up carrying a wriggling serpent in its claws – a seemingly impossible feat as we didn't collide with the hawk. It was divine timing. And a hawk with a serpent in its claws – a feathered serpent! Why, of course. The heavens and Earth had spoken![301]

AND THEN IT RAINED

· ·

On that day, a cloud arises,
On that day, a mountain rises,
On that day, a strong man seizes the land,
On that day, things fall to ruin. . . .
– Chilam Balam

AS DARKNESS TURNS TO LIGHT, THE SUN ONCE AGAIN RETURNS to the central lands of the Americas. The crystal blue tapestry of sky is studded throughout with billowy white clouds, the discarded pillows of the gods and goddesses. But at another time, an age that the indigenous people wished had never happened, there appeared white clouds low on the horizon as well. But these were not white clouds. They were the sails of invaders.

In the dawn light, these clouds never rose higher into the sky, but only came ever-closer to shore. That morning, as the winds blew in off of the sea, what thoughts, feelings and wishes were in the hearts of these people? These lands were home to an advanced civilization that lived in harmony with nature. Perfect they were not. But the slavers who approached were even further from perfection. In their lust for power and gold, they transformed this land forever, and not for the better.

Hernando Cortéz and his Spanish conquistadors, who set foot on the sands of the Americas that sad morning, were slavers, though not in the usual sense. Bolstered by their sense of righteousness and doing the work of God— the work of the Catholic Church—they brought with them a slavery of the heart and mind. With fire, brimstone and smiles, the spirit was ripped from

REV. DR. JC HUSFELT AND REV. SHERRY HUSFELT

the deepest, inner core of these native people, resulting in a life of economic inequality and fear-based religious practices. Through their greed and materialism, these conquerors left a legacy of death and destruction, which is most evident today in the on-going devastation of the rainforests and the ecological biosphere.[302]

Belize is often referred to as the
"Heart of the Maya" due to its high concentration of Maya sites.

AT THE END OF JULY 2004, I FLEW INTO BELIZE. THE AIRPORT reminded me of Cancun circa 1987. It was a breath of fresh air compared to many other tourist destination airports. Belize is a land of jaguars, iguanas, parrots, butterflies, hummingbirds, an abundance of medicinal plants and the endangered *Morelet's* crocodile, also known as a water dragon. This is a sacred land of mountains and jungles, waterfalls, caves and lagoons, and literally thousands of Maya sites, with more being discovered every year. It is the Caribbean at its best. No wonder the buccaneers of the past fell in love with it, English being the official language.

I've been blessed to have journeyed to many distant lands before the advent of eco-tourism and New Agers. When there is an increase in tourism, restrictions are put in place on sacred sites and the ability to conduct spiritual practice is limited. The silence of the land disappears. I felt that Belize had not been discovered and was still a virgin land.

I also chose Belize for another reason. As the Morning Star, this was a most auspicious time to visit Belize. We had just entered an eight-year period beginning with the passage, or transit, of Venus, across the sun on June 8, when Venus goes from the evening star to the morning star. Venus was now the morning star, the last Venus cycle of the Fifth Sun that was birthed by Venus on August 29, 3113 B.C.E.[303] The cycle ended on the winter solstice, December 21, 2012 C.E. According to prophecies, 2012 forward is a difficult time of labor foreshadowing Earth changes that usher in the birth of the enlightened age of the Sixth Sun. During this transition time, the Maya World Tree, *Ceiba*, will shake but not fall. The shaking symbolizes earthquakes, and changes in the Earth, and societal transformations.

306

Vampire Bats, Crocodiles and Howler Monkeys

My first night I stayed at the distant Lamanai Outpost Lodge named for the nearby Maya ruins. *Lamanai* comes from the Yucatec Maya word *Lam'an'ain*, which means, "submerged crocodile," and the Outpost was located on the New River Lagoon. A natural name, as the New River Lagoon is full of crocodiles.

Because access to the lodge and the ruins was by boat up the New River from Orange Walk town, the lodge provided transfer from and to Belize International Airport, a combination road and river trip.

The wild and isolated New River is the main waterway and access route to the Outpost and the Maya ruins. Stepping aboard the small boat, I felt totally alive. The sights, the sounds, the smells, the feelings – my heart was happy. Many people vacation in the safety of known, civilized places, never traveling off the beaten path. But it is only in the uncivilized lands, surrounded by nature, that we can feel the essence of life – that we can discover and know the meaning and purpose of life and, most importantly, "who we are."

Our jungle boat sped past lush vegetation that grew right to the edge of the sun-drenched waters as we headed south to the New River Lagoon. The moment made me feel as if I had been thrust into an Indian Jones movie. I marveled at my surroundings. I didn't spy any jaguars hidden in the thick tangle of riverside jungle, only iguanas and egrets, but also no crocodiles. Within an hour and a half, we reached the dock of the Outpost, and came upon what could be a scene out of any jungle-themed movie.

As I walked from the dock to the lodge, I could feel the power of the land and the lagoon. It was like I had been transported to a different world. A dangerous one, as the power and beauty of the land hid the danger concealed within the jungle. Two dangers were the Fer de Lance and the Maya Coral Snake. These are just two of the nine deadly serpents in Belize. Of the nine, the coral snake's neurotoxic venom is the most dangerous. Fortunately, the coral snake is not aggressive. If you watch where you step, there should be no problem. However, I was ready if I did come across a colorful serpent. A local had taught me the rhyme to determine the deadly coral from a harmless king snake: Red Touch Yellow – Kills a Fellow; Red Touch Black – Friend of Jack.

I soon realized that the Outpost's reputation as one of Belize's finest jungle lodges seemed to be true. The open-air reception desk was an invitation to settle in and become one with my surroundings. This was surely not your typical sterile hotel setting for puppet corporate executives, but one better fitted for a person with an adventurous spirit. This sense of adventure was only heightened by the jungle surrounding the lodge and the Maya ruins. The jungle was comprised of giant Guanacaste, Ceiba and Breadnut trees, as well as Allspice, Strangler Figs and Belize's national flower, the Black Orchid.

Since it was late afternoon, I decided to rest, to get a decent night's sleep before visiting the Maya temples on the morn. Over a cold Belizean beer, *Belikin*, I relaxed, reflecting on my journey so far while immersing my soul in the sounds and smells of this small sliver of paradise. After a few moments, I struck up a conversion with another lodger, a British woman traveling alone who was the executive secretary to the head of a worldwide management consulting company. After a few minutes of the usual polite chit chat, she poured out her true feelings to me. I was a stranger, but a safe one, reflecting a feeling within her heart that I would listen to her unconditionally while making no judgments or assumptions about her. She opened her heart to me: "I know everything about my boss, his financial affairs, even his dosage of blood pressure medication, but do you suppose that he knows anything about me? No. He's rude to me. Even one time he told me that I wasn't being paid to think." How sad, but on the other hand, how angering that one human being, so giving and loyal, would be treated as such by another human being.

After she left, I had a second *Belikin* before I retired to my room with the promise of a peaceful and sound night's sleep. Hopefully, now that it was dark, I wouldn't have an encounter with Lamanai's Great False Vampire Bat (vampyrum spectrum).

Thankfully, No bats swooped down as I approached my lodging for the night. I was staying in a Lagoon View Cabaña, a fully screened, thatch-roof cabin, built with hardwood and mahogany. It was well ventilated and fitted with a high-output ceiling fan. The jungle came right up to my cabin, giving me the feeling of the presence of hidden denizens and shrouding what little light was cast by the cloud-covered moon. It was a little scary, but then again exciting.

My sleep was deep and sound until I heard a cry. If I had been dreaming the cry would have been disturbing enough, but it wasn't a dream. My eyes shot open as the howl echoed through the darkness-encased jungle. It sounded as if it came from right under my window. Then silence, an eerie feeling of anticipation. My primitive brain woke up, generating that instinct we all have of "fight or flee," our beast within. Could it have been a jaguar seeking prey? I grabbed my flashlight and cautiously looked out the window. I scanned the nearby jungle foliage. I wasn't about to open the door and explore outside. The third option, neither fight nor flight, washed away my primitive feelings – stay inside!

Once again the howl shattered the silence of the night; the sound didn't seem to come from the ground, but from the branches of the trees. As I raised my light towards the source of the howl, I was greeted with nothing but jungle foliage. Silence once again reigned as I headed back to bed wondering what had just happened. Sleep came fast, with no dreams of jaguars, friendly or otherwise.

As first light broke through the dark of the night, the willowy mist swirled and rose off the jungle-edged lagoon and through the jungle canopy beginning a new day of adventure. Mystified about the howl, I headed to breakfast, taking in the scents and beautiful essence of a new Belizean day before I headed out to the temples of Lamanai. Curiosity got the best of me. I asked one of the staff if there were jaguars prowling around. He shook his head no, then he smiled and said, "The howl you heard last night was our local residents, black howler monkeys."

After breakfast, on my walk to the temples I did indeed spot the howlers hanging out in the trees. It's amazing what our minds will conjure up in the dark of night.

In a short time, I arrived at the sacred site of Lamanai, a place that enlivens your imagination while thrusting you back into an era of Maya glory. The awesomeness of the site belies the fact that there are still hundreds of unexcavated ruins lying hidden within the nearby jungle. Three of the most impressive excavated temples are the Jaguar Temple, the Mask Temple, and the High Temple.

Before entering, I prayed and asked permission to enter the sacred site. I poured a little Belizean rum on the ground as a gifting to the hidden ones and the ancestors. I explored the various temple areas, such as the Rain God Temple and the magnificent High Temple, which rises an imperious thirty-three meters above the jungle canopy to provide an excellent view over the river. And I must say the view from the top was awesome. Next, I visited the Mask Temple and then the ball court, where back in the day, the winners of the game supposedly were sacrificial food for the gods—but why would you sacrifice your best athletes/warriors?

Jaguar Temple Lamanai

Out of the entire sacred site, I spent most of my time at the Jaguar Temple as the big cat and I have a very special relationship. The temple is named for the shaman's *nagual* due to the two jaguar masks on its base. The masks "are made from carved stone rather than molded stucco plaster. The builders cleverly chose to create a stylized image that could be created quite simplistically by arranging bricks, saving the effort of carving out the jaguar's various features and then slotting them together. The design was also a very elegant solution, because the spaces that were created to define the eyes, nostrils, cheeks and ears, made perfect niches for leaving offerings to the Jaguar God."[304]

Knowing what it is to have jaguar as a *nagual*, I opened myself to the Otherworld as I sat next to the jaguar masks. Images came and went as I felt the past and present power of place merge together. How long I was in this state I do not know. But awakening back to this world, my senses and my visual acuity were heightened, as they always are after such a journey. Leaving the site, I did a final blessing and "thank you," and headed back to the lodge.

The next day dawned beautiful with no rain in sight. In fact, I was told that even though it was the rainy season little rain had fallen throughout Belize. I wondered if anyone had attempted to pray or sing for rain. After breakfast, I was heading back to the airport to pick up a rental car. There wasn't enough time to return to the High Temple to pray and sing. I thought I would do that at my next sacred stop, Xunantunich: Lords of War and Fertility, with the emphasis on fertility.

My next lodging destination was The Lodge at Chaa Creek outside of rustic San Ignacio, the cultural-economic hub of Cayo District. After an interesting drive through the Belizean countryside, I arrived at Chaa Cheek. It soon became apparent to me that the Lamanai Outpost was heads and tails better than Chaa Creek. In fact, right then and there, I decided that our group would not stay at Chaa Cheek during our October journey.

Xunantunich

Evam maya e ma ho! (All hail the harmony of mind and nature!)

One of the reasons I had chosen Chaa Creek was its proximity to the sacred site Xunantunich, the largest ceremonial center in the Belize River

Valley. The ancient name of this place was *Katyaatz Witz*, meaning Clay Mountain. *Witz* meaning sacred mountain.

In Maya, *Xunantunich* means "Maiden of the Rock" or "Stone Woman," and is derived from a local legend referring to the ghost of a woman claimed by several people to inhabit the site. Beginning in 1892, this ghostly maiden was seen dressed completely in white with red glowing eyes. The tale reminded me of Sher and I awakening to the glowing red eyes of a long-dead monk, frightening experience we'd had back in 1981.

Xunantunich consists of six major plazas surrounded by more than twenty-five temples and palaces. The most prominent structure located at the south end of the site is the pyramid *El -Castillo* (The Castle), which towers 130 feet above the plaza. It consists of two temples. The lower temple is famous for its large stucco frieze, a mask possibly representing the sun god. Next to this mask, there is a moon sign with sigils representing Venus.

Xunantunich lay across the green crystalline waters of the Mopan River. The only means to cross the river was by a quaint hand-cranked ferry. As I drove onto the ferry, which has space for only one car, I once again felt thrust back in time. In short order, we reached the other side, which seemed to be only fifty feet or so across the river.

The guide books and the archeologists will tell you that the temples of Xunantunich, although at a major ceremonial site, were not as important as Caracol or Tikal. On the contrary, as soon as I approached the entrance, I felt the power of Xunantunich. After prayers and gifting, I asked permission of the ancestors and hidden ones to enter the sacred site. Since it was morning with few people around, I was able to explore and feel the essence of the land and the memories encoded within the stones of the temples without the constant chatter of tourists. Stones are memory keepers and will reveal their knowledge when your mind is silent and your heart is pure.

I explored the various temples as if I had been thrust back in time to the heyday of this Maya city.

El Castillo Xunantunich

When I felt the time was right, I sat on the steps of *El Castillo* and prayed and sang for rain. As I was singing with my eyes closed, I sensed someone walking down the pyramid steps and passing near me. As I finished my song and blessing, I opened my eyes and saw the back of a tattooed guy and, I would suppose, his girlfriend walking away from the pyramid. I wondered what they must have been thinking about me.

Intuitively, I knew it was time to depart. As I left the sacredness, I gave blessings and thanks and said, "I'll be back." Before I left, I stopped in the small gift shop by the parking lot, where I struck up a conversation with the Belizean native in charge of the shop. I mentioned that Xunantunich has great power, probably more than most people realize. He smiled and agreed. He said that very few ever recognize the scope of the power, and that one of his friends had used a "forked stick" (used for dowsing) to find energy lines (ley lines) within the ruins. His friend had discovered that major energy lines (also known as dragon lines) within the Earth meet here at this site. This meant that Xunantunich was an electromagnetic energy vortex, formed where ley lines connect. The result is an increase in the electromagnetic energy produced and released. This energy amplifies, heightens, and magnifies our physical, mental, emotional, and spiritual essence as it acts through prayer and song.

As I was walking to my car after thanking my new friend, I gazed at the sky, still blue and cloudless. Instead of returning to the lodge, I decided to venture into San Ignacio because it was Saturday, the best market day. The farmers market is the place to be if you want to experience Belize's multiple cultures and see for yourself why the country is known as a "melting pot of cultures." The market is a feast of colors and scents for the eyes and senses, with mangoes, starfruit, oranges, guavas, papayas, big bananas, green bananas, clothes, carvings, flowers, handmade soaps, and a multitude of spices. Combined with the visual overload, there is the smell of local street food. But most unique is the sounds of conversation. It's hard to determine in what country you stand as you hear a melodic mix of Maya, Creole, English and Spanish, while Mennonite farmers can be heard conversing in German.

As I wandered through the market, I found some great honey to purchase, and then I felt it coming. I looked off into the distance. Dark clouds were forming! Loving rain and storms as I do, I wanted to reach my room before the storm hit, kick back, sip a *Belikin* and enjoy the show. But as sometimes happens in life, I didn't make it in time. I got soaked. Actually, drenched is a better word; it was definitely a downpour. The storm and rains came two hours after I left Xunantunich. Outside my room I poured some *Belikin* on the ground while blessing and thanking the sky and spirits for watering a thirsty Earth and for responding to my prayers and song.

Tikal

Even though we were not taking our group to Guatemala in October, I decided to go because I had never been there myself. And let us not forget, it is the location of world famous Tikal. Since the border with Guatemala was not far from Chaa Creek, I decided to visit the sacred site. It lies relatively close to the border in the El Petén District of Guatemala.

Crossing the border was not a problem; I didn't even get searched. But as soon as I entered Guatemala, I felt, sensed and could visually notice how different it was from Belize. The feeling was difficult to put into words. The best way to say it might be that it was dark and depressing. The energy of the land changed as soon as I passed over the border.

Tikal ("City of Echoes") was at one time the sprawling capital of one of the greatest empires of the ancient Maya. Supposedly, its peak population was 90,000 and the city flourished during the Maya Classic period of 200 to 900 C.E. However, the birth of Tikal happened around 600 B.C.E.

The dark and depressed feeling that I had when I crossed the border was still there when I reached Tikal. Stones hold memories, so I wondered, "What memories were the stones of Tikal holding?" Exploring this "City of Echoes," I didn't feel the power I had experienced at Xunantunich. Maybe it had been there at one time, but I could only think, "What happened to the power of this site and the land?"

Temple 1, Temple of the Jaguar, Tikal

As I explored, I struck up a conversation with a local who just happened to be a Maya healer. I expressed my feelings and he agreed. He explained what led to the downfall and abandonment of Tikal. The seeds of the collapse were rooted in a problem that we face today in the 21st century – deforestation.

Tikal's downfall was the clearcutting of the forests that had once surrounded it. The purpose of the destruction of trees was not limited to providing agricultural land; the primary reason was to provide fuel to feed the limestone ovens of Tikal. The limestone was utilized in pathways and the outer coverings of the temples. As Tikal was a theocracy, the priestly class demanded beautiful temples to honor their deities – trees to placate religion. This was vividly portrayed in Mel Gibson's movie *Apocalypto*.

In today's world, the elites and their "temples" of capitalism are no different. They encourage the removal of what happens to be the lungs of our planet: the Amazonian rainforest. This time around, due to the destruction of the rainforest, forests and woodlands, as well as other vile desecrations of resources and species, we are on the verge of a macro-collapse of the whole civilized world instead of the micro-destruction illustrated by Tikal's downfall.

And there is something more to consider when discussing clearcutting – the ability of the soil to store carbon. The large swathes of land deforested by the Maya affected the soil's ability to store carbon instead of releasing it into the air. For a moment, please consider the ramifications of this clearcutting. The final nail in the coffin for the Maya was drought, a worldwide condition facing humanity today.

Return Flight Home

Leaving Chaa Creek, I drove to the Caribbean coast to relax and write for a few days before I returned to Seattle. I was sad to leave but missed my wife and adult children. The flight back was difficult. The Dallas/Fort Worth airport was closed due to storm cells moving through the area. As a result, we circled Dallas for about two hours until fuel was low and then we were diverted to Houston to refuel.

As we were sitting on the ground in Houston, I realized it would be a nightmare for Sher and Jess to drive into Seattle at midnight with me being still in Dallas. A person in the row in front of me had a cell phone and I asked him if I could use it and pay him for the use. He replied, "Don't worry." I called Sher and got her voice mail and explained my situation. Luckily, she got the message before going to the airport. And most thankfully, she booked me on a flight out the next morning. I was probably one of hundreds who had missed their connections and Sher got me the final seat and final flight out of Dallas to SeaTac. Everything worked out perfectly due to the kindness of the guy with his cell phone.

But my tale doesn't end there. We had flown out of Belize at 3:45 p.m., or 4:45 p.m. Dallas time; it was 1:00 a.m. when we finely cleared customs in Dallas. Since no flights had landed in or left Dallas since the late afternoon, the airport was a zoo. As I was walking through the crowds of people trying to find a comfortable place to rest for the remainder of the night, I saw the cell phone guy walking towards me with his girlfriend. They said they were headed back to San Francisco. I thanked him again. Then with a strange look in his eyes, he said "Didn't we see you sitting on the pyramid steps at Xunantunich?" It was the couple who had walked by me as I finished my prayers and song for rain! If you didn't realize it – life is magical.

THE BIG CAT THAT FLIES

. . . .

"The jaguar was to the Mexicans first of all the strong, the brave beast, the companion of the eagle; quauhtli-océlotl 'eagle and jaguar' is the conventional designation for the brave warriors."[305]

I FELL IN LOVE WITH BELIZE, ESPECIALLY LAMANAI AND Xunantunich and their ruins, ever seeking the power of the memories held within the stones while climbing their pyramids' narrow and steep stone steps. Not once did I have a problem climbing the steps of the pyramids.

Having awoken to a consciousness of radical nonduality resulting from my descending spirit exorcism in 1987, I walk through life in a blending of the Otherworld and this world. The Otherworld is always there on the edge of my consciousness that can be accessed at any time in any place. But I am human, so most of the time my consciousness is focused on this world. And then sometimes I find myself more in the Otherworld and not this world, which may result in surprising happenings.

I had only been back from Belize for a few weeks. On one misty Sunday morning at our home on the Olympic Peninsula, I planned to do some writing. It had rained during the night and the early hours revealed a hazy, fog-coated fjord. I thought, what an awesome morning to write as I do my best writing in the morning. But first I thought I would help our daughter, Jess.

Jess was watching our neighbors' dog, Autumn, while the neighbors were away. Early each morning, she would feed her and let her out. Instead of waking her, I decided to do it myself.

Life is awesome, tragic and mysterious. Our actions and decisions in the moment point us in a direction. A different action or non-action could have portended a different future and none of us are islands unto ourselves, as all things are connected and interconnected in a web of consciousness and oneness. Each moment is precious as in the next moment our lives may change drastically.

Walking to our neighbors' home in flip-flops (at the time my favorite footwear), my mind and body were in the moment, enjoying the tactile sensations of a stereotypical Northwest Coast early morning. Watching one of our local eagles soar overhead, life was wonderful.

I climbed the steep stairs to the second-floor landing, with my mind basically silent. The stairs were wet, as was the decking. When I opened the door Autumn greeted me enthusiastically, jumping and licking, and then bounded down the steps past two large boulders in a rock garden at the bottom of the stairs. I followed. As soon as my flip-flop hit the top step, I slipped and fell towards the boulders at the bottom of the steps, with the potential for death or great injury.

Our minds are amazing. As I was falling, my consciousness realized death waited for me below. Being a martial artist, I know how to shoulder roll. While falling face-forward in mid-air, I did a 108-degree turn and threw myself out (flew) onto the lawn to shoulder roll out of the fall. It was if a gentle hand had me in its palm and took me out of death's grip. All these thoughts went through my mind faster than can be measured.

My life didn't pass before my eyes, but my perception was that I was stationary, and the ground was coming towards me. Visually, it was really cool. And then, thump, no shoulder roll, despite my intention.

Lying there I knew I'd broken some ribs. My concern was an internal puncture of my lung or another organ. It was not lost on me that I was going to be fifty-eight in a few days and my father had passed-over at fifty-eight! His father had died in his forties. And a few weeks ago, I had been climbing very steep pyramid steps in Belize and Guatemala without difficulty.

No one was around to find me. I could lie there and possibly fulfill my patriarchal lineage's destiny to die young. Or I could get up, walk home and get help. No self-fulfilling destiny for me. My will was to live not pass-over.

With only one flip-flop, I crashed through our front door yelling: call 911! And yes, I did break ribs – all the ribs on my left side. Looking back on my fall, it is verifiable, evident, and blessed that I am the Big Cat That Flies.

TEARS OF THE SOUL – ASKING FORGIVENESS

. . . .

The King with half the East at heel is marched from lands of morning;
Their fighters drink the rivers up, their shafts benight the air.
And he that stands will die for nought, and home there's no returning.
The Spartans on the sea-wet rock sat down and combed their hair.

— A.E. Housman, from "The Oracles"

IN 2004, I HAD A KNOWING THAT I NEEDED TO BE AT Thermopylae on my sixtieth birthday, coming in 2006. Accordingly, in late August of that year, twenty-one of our students and their families, plus my wife and I and our two adult children journeyed to Greece. Our warrior pilgrimage took us from the sacred sites of Athens onward to Eleusis, location of the Sanctuary of Demeter and its ancient Mystery School and finally to the oracle sites of mountainous Delphi—the beating heart of Greece—and the Temple of Apollo and Athena.

Sher Temple of Athena August 2006

Since I was a teenager, I've had a knowing, but I still doubted a few of my past incarnations. The proof of one was revealed in 1997 at the Visitation, the fourth of my major Otherworldly experiences, which in turn verified the others. A past life of mine had occurred in Sparta, or Sparti as it is known today, and this past lifetime ended at the Hot Gates of Thermopylae.

As I mentioned before, when I was sixteen, a visual tale triggered a soul memory. The visual tale was *The 300 Spartans*. The ancient Spartans were the saviors of Western civilization as a result of their heroic action and sacrifice at the Pass of Thermopylae, also known as the Hot Gates.

As soon as I returned home from seeing the movie, I ran into my room, grabbed two encyclopedias and began doing bicep curls. Since I was one of the first corporate fitness and wellness consultants in the country in the mid-70s, you might find it odd that I didn't have any weights to lift as a teenager.

Let's just say that my parents probably thought I was an alien baby switched at birth (there is my O-negative blood type). You could say my worldview and theirs were 180 degrees apart. As a young kid, I wanted to be an architect. I would spend hours designing and drawing home plans. Almost visionary in scope, one of my favorite designs I did as a kid looks just like our present home, curves and all.

But my parents were not in support of this profession. One of their closest friends was an architect and influenced them by saying that it was a tough field with not much future. So, I went to college not knowing what the hell I was going to do with my life, one of the reasons I was willing to go to Vietnam. The other reason? My warrior soul.

I find irony in all of this. In one manner, I did become an architect, but not a designer and builder of structures and homes. I became something totally Otherworldly, a spiritual architect, a designer and builder of awakening souls.

Thermopylae, August 29, 2006

The Hot Gates of Thermopylae – Late August 480 B.C.E.

"Our army is great," the Persian says, "and because
of the number of our arrows you will not see the sky!"
Then a Spartan answers: "In the shade, therefore, we will fight!"
And Leonidas, king of the Spartans, shouts: "Fight with spirit
Spartans; perhaps we will dine today among the ghosts!"

– Cicero

Thermopylae is a place in Greece where a narrow coastal passage existed in antiquity. It derives its name from its hot Sulphur springs. The Hot Gates is "the place of hot springs" and in Greek mythology it is the place where Herakles had jumped into the river in an attempt to wash off the Hydra poison infused in the cloak that he could not take off. The river was said to have turned hot and stayed that way ever since.

In the spring of 480 B.C.E., King Xerxes of Persia set forth to achieve what his father (King Darius) had failed to achieve ten years previously in 490 B.C.E.—the conquest of the Greek city-states with the final goal being the whole of Europe. At that time, the Athenians valiantly crushed King Darius' empire-building desires on the plains of Marathon. The extremely religious Spartans missed the triumphant victory by arriving late to the battlefield due to their honor-bound observance of the feast of Apollo.

But there is doubt about this being the reason for their lateness: was it a religious observance that kept them arriving late to assist the Athenians or some other reason—remember the Spartans and Athenians were not, what you would call, on friendly terms (as a consequence of Athens involvement in the Ionian Revolt – 499 B.C.E. – 493 B.C.E.).

Since the Persian defeat at Marathon, Darius' son, King Xerxes, had been amassing an army of over 200,000 men as well as a massive fleet rumored to be close to 1,300 vessels. This time King Xerxes was not going to repeat his father's failure by invading from the sea, but was going to attack Greece by land.

Once again the Persians were invading Greece and history seemed to be repeating itself—the Spartans, once more, were involved in a religious observation. This meant that, as before, the best warriors in Greece would arrive late. This time there was a difference: King Leonidas. His personal bodyguard of 300 was not honor-bound by the religious laws of Sparta. These laws kept the rest of the Spartan army from marching to battle, but not the King and his personal bodyguard. This is usually the commonly accepted historical account. But is it true?

Suicide Mission?

(When I discovered, *Beyond the Gates of Fire*, it answered questions I have had my whole life and provided clarity to my Spartan past-life—its truth spoke to my heart.)

By all commonly accepted accounts, the Greeks sent to Thermopylae would have been on a suicide mission. Within my heart, this never seemed to make sense. There was always something, in the corner of my mind and heart, mostly my heart, that did not make sense.

First, there was the Congress of Corinth, where strategic planners were discussing how to stop the Persian invasion. It seems that Thermopylae was only the "most favored" initial place of defense against the Persians hordes. This "suggests that the delegates at Corinth were not unanimous in their decision to send troops to defend the pass."[306]

Furthermore, "it has been suggested that many representatives on the council from the Peloponnesian states (including the Spartans) may have been more in favour of the establishment of a defensive line at the Isthmus in order to protect the Peloponnese directly."[307]

What then was the reasoning for the selection of the narrow pass of Thermopylae? According to Herodotus,[308] the "decision was made to hold the pass in order to prevent the Persians from advancing further into Greece while Greek ships kept the Persian fleet in check at Artemisium. Diodorus[309] elaborates on the nature of the land campaign by stating that the purpose of the defence was to forestall the Persians and prevent them from moving further into Greece."

And then we have the religious festival of *Carneia* held in honor of Apollo Carneus, supposedly the reason why Leonidas could only call-up his Royal Bodyguard. "However, it appears that the reports of these religious restrictions are a later insertion into the text to seemly justify why the Greeks mounted what appeared to be, with hindsight, an inadequate defence at Thermopylae. These reports are most likely part of the legend which grew almost instantaneously around reports of the defeat and turned it into myth:"[310]

The Carneia was based on the rising of the full moon which, in mid-480 BC, happened on July 21 and August 19. Similarly, the Olympic festival for 480 BC concluded around July 21. This would initially suggest that the advance troops for the Thermopylae holding action, and the ships for the Artemisium blockade, were assembled and dispatched shortly after either of these dates. When the time required to assemble these contingents and move them into position is considered, this would place the date of the actual battles themselves to sometime in either late July at the earliest or in late August of 480 BC depending upon which Carneia festival the calculation is based upon. Importantly, Herodotus states that the subsequent naval engagement at Salamis occurred on the day after the celebration of the Elusian Mysteries which occurred on the twentieth day of Boedromion. This would place the battle of Salamis in mid-late September in 480 BC. Additionally, Herodotus records that a solar eclipse occurred not long after the battle of Salamis. This eclipse can be dated to the 2 October 480 BC. This further evidence for the battle of Salamis taking place in late September 480 BC, in turn, places the battle of Thermopylae in late August – after the Spartan Carneia festival and more than a month after the end of the Olympic festival in July.[311]

Keep in mind that "the most important priests in Sparta were the kings. They were regarded as descendants of Herakles and therefore of divine ancestry. Sparta had an interest and awareness of oracles and portents. Officials dealt with oracles from Delphi and state ministers kept records of signs from the gods. If a Spartan king had a reasonable religious excuse, he could be forgiven for not winning a battle or even for not fighting one in the first place. The gods were to be obeyed unquestioningly. They stood at the very top of the chain of command which all Spartans were taught to respect completely."[312] Since Thermopylae occurred at the end of August, Carneia would not have had any influence on the timing or deployment of hoplites to defend the pass.

The next question we must ask is why only 300 men? "Clearly the Spartans had to send troops as they were in overall command of the campaign and had to set an example. The reasoning behind the dispatch of 300 Spartans to Thermopylae appears to be that a unit of 300 was the standard contingent of Spartan hoplites sent on any 'special operation'; and may constitute something of an elite unit within the Spartan army."[313] And having living sons would indicate an older hoplite; a more experienced veteran. Even, "Leonidas himself appears to have been about 60 years of age at the time of the battle of Thermopylae."[314]

And one final question; what was the objection of an holding action at the pass of Thermopylae? Keep in mind that food can be a weapon as well as weather, water, and disease. Xerxes possibly had a land army of around 400,000. A gigantic feat to feed, water, and keep well such a large number of troops.

Did this fact influence the Greeks strategic policy? It did; "the Greeks regarded the actions at Thermopylae and Artemisium neither as an attempt to win a decisive victory or as a feint designed to give time to muster forces for Salamis.[315] Instead, they conceived of the operation as a forward line of defence, which could be reinforced as needed by reserves in the rear, and the aim of these tactics was to hold up Xerxes' advance until weather and lack of supplies forced him to abandon his campaign for that year, and perhaps indefinitely."[316]

The Final Day – Day Three

"The result of day three of the engagement at Thermopylae is well known, even if the events and motives behind many of the decisions made on the day are not. Once the Persians had found a way around the Greek position, the defence of the Thermopylae pass was on a much more precarious footing. Regardless of why some of the Greek forces did not stay in the pass, and regardless of the tactics employed by those that remained, the outcome of the fighting on day three appears to have been anything but a foregone conclusion...

"The fact that the remaining Greeks were able to inflict substantial casualties among the Persians on this final day, even after many of their weapons had been broken and the position had been overrun by Persian troops coming over the Anopea path and attacking from the rear, attests to the capability of the Greek hoplite over a more lightly armoured opponent in hand-to-hand combat... It seems to be clear from the available evidence that the action at Thermopylae in 480 BC: was never seen as, nor intended to be, a 'suicide mission' but was part of a 'grand plan' for the defence of Greece which followed a sound strategic logic which utilized terrain, numbers, a strong comprehension of the required logistics, coordinated actions by both land and sea forces, and the superior fighting ability of the Greek hoplite."[317]

The Day of Tears

Oh foreigner, give a message to the Lacedaemonians
that here lie we, their words obeying.

—Simonides of Keos

I awoke the morning of my sixtieth birthday with a knowing within my heart that it would be a bittersweet day. Almost to keep the day from happening, I lingered in bed, which I never do, reflecting on a most telling experience that happened a day after our group had arrived in Delphi. I had wandered into a souvenir shop that seemed to be closed. There were no lights on but the front door was standing half-open. I'm the spiritual item shopper in the family, so lights or no lights, I was drawn inside like a moth to a candle flame. Before I could begin browsing through the various statues and other items, I noticed a Greek man hurrying across the street towards the shop. As he briskly entered, he turned on the lights while apologizing in English.

And then he turned and looked at me and said, "Greek."

I replied, "No American."

The man's name was Constantinos, the owner of the store. He smiled and said, "No, you are Greek."

One of our fellow journeyers, an apprentice, smiled in return and said, "Why, of course."

As he walked towards me, Constantinos continued, "You are Greek. I sense it and can see it on you."

"Yes a long time ago," I replied.

And then out of the blue, he said, "You know that Leonidas was sixty[318] or so when he died at Thermopylae."

I just nodded my head.

Constantinos' ancestors have lived in Delphi for an unknown time and he carries secret teachings and knowledge of Delphi. We became immediate friends (he would refer to me and call me Socrates). When he discovered I was in Delphi to celebrate my sixtieth birthday, he arranged for our group to formally meet with the mayor at city hall as well as arranging the perfect restaurant for my birthday celebration.

The last time I walked onto this battlefield, I did not leave. Today, I walked onto the battlefield and I will walk off.[319]

The drive from Delphi to Thermopylae takes a little over one hour. In one sense, it seemed a short time but then again, it felt like an eternity. As our bus pulled into the parking lot across the road from the site of the last stand, I could feel the tightness beginning in my chest and gut. Despite being raised in a society where men were not supposed to show emotions or cry, I was not inhibited in that way. But for some reason, as I stepped off the bus and crossed the road to the site, I kept my tears bound within me even though they struggled to escape.

Before setting foot on the battleground, I removed my shoes and walked barefoot across the sacred and hallowed ground of Thermopylae. My family knew to leave me alone with my thoughts and memories. The sparsely treed ground was hard and scorching as if that time almost 2,500 years ago was imbedded forever in the cracked Earth beneath my feet.

Walking as if in a trance, I could smell why this sacred ground was known as the Hot Gates. In front of me were the purified waters of the flowing, volcanic sulphurous springs. As an act of purification, remembrance, and personal penance, I dipped my feet into their indescribably hot waters. I endured the pain that I felt I needed to feel as a tear slowly slid down my cheek. The searing waters and the rocky ground mirrored to me their witness and my soul's knowing of that heroic battle.

In this lifetime, I would discover that it wasn't a defeat but a victory, or rather a victory in defeat—a glorious defeat. This didn't matter to me on that day because I carried a self-wounding of the soul, one that I needed to heal. And I knew in my heart that it was not a so-called suicide mission as indicated by historians. Our group kept a very respectful distance and finally wandered back to where the bus was parked.

Alone now, without the group nearby, I slowly walked to the mound where the last of the 300, and the other Greek warriors had lost their lives. If it hadn't been for the Visitation in 1997, I would have thought, "Am I totally crazy? Who am I to think I had been . . . ?" But in my heart I knew, just as I knew my other past lives, revealed by the physical proof of the Spirit Man and the Visitation.

Not deterred by the sounds of the modern highway that now separates the battlefield from the monument of Leonidas, I kneeled on the sacred mound. At that moment, my tears exploded out of the depths of my heart, watering this hallowed space of sacrifice and pain. I spoke my words of forgiveness—asking forgiveness for an action not taken—a feeling of guilt that has been part of my soul for 2,500 years. I was in a state of timelessness, and the words I spoke through the torrent of tears and spittle echoed through the millennium as I asked to be forgiven, especially by my peers, the veterans known as the 300, and the other Greek warriors.

Heroes become legendary thanks to a storyteller's musings or a historical writer's pen while the true heroic emotions are buried beneath layers of bravado and myth. Truth is sometimes manipulated and hidden. Why was the decision made to stay and not fall back? Was it made too late… a miscalculation of the amount of time left to escape to fight another day?

Whatever the reason; it does not decrease the sacrifice, loyalty, courage, honor, vigilance, and perseverance and the fortitude, struggle, bravery, and heroic action of each and every Greek at the pass—known today as the Gates of Fire.

Commentary

City Hall 60th Birthday Celebration, Jess, Me, Sher, and Jamie

It's hard to put into words my state of being, heart and mind, after leaving Thermopylae. It was if I was still in a trance; one foot here, one foot there. That night, during my 60th celebration, the honors and words I received touched my heart with their caring and love. But, it was like I was outside myself, seeing the present through a mist as if I was still in the past. It is hard to explain. It was a bittersweet celebration.

RETURN: 2010 LACEDAEMON—A BITTER/ SWEET JOURNEY

. . . .

The most ancient and fertile homes of philosophy among the Greeks are Crete and Sparta. They (the Spartans) conceal their wisdom and pretend to be blockheads, so that they may seem to be superior only because of their prowess in battle, rather than by virtue of their wisdom.

~ Socrates

THE MOMENT WAS FROZEN IN TIME AS MY HAND OBEYED THE prayers in my mind. I tossed three coins in the air so they could catch the glint of Apollo's sun before they descended into the watery realm of Poseidon.

Yards out, I could see black heads bobbing in the waves. In another time they would have been Apollo's dolphins answering my ceremonial gifting. Minutes passed as I prepared to submerge myself in the sparkling crystal-clear sea. As I stood unclothed, an honoring to the Olympians of my human vulnerability, power and strength, I wondered what my actions must have seemed like to the swimming Greeks.

Photo by Ian Owens

Today, the Greek Orthodox Church has a strangle hold on Greece and my actions would speak of pagan worship of the old Olympic gods and goddesses. In the realm of materialism, statues of the Olympians are okay to sell to the tourists, but such things as offerings, prayers, invoking Apollo (god of the shamans), and three coins to the Olympians would smack of idol worship and unchristian behavior. Heaven forbid: what next?

Would this lead to philosophical discourse on street corners questioning current dogmatic beliefs? Or worse, to divination, a well-known practice of ancient Lacedaemon, better known as Sparta? My honoring and prayers were not playful actions, but part of a philosophical/spiritual/religious practice that I have conducted for more than thirty years whenever I far traveled to foreign countries seeking the mysteries of heaven and Earth and indigenous spiritual knowledge. This ritualistic ceremony is a blessing for the journey. It is asking permission to do spiritual work. My actions, words and thoughts were addressed to energetic forces that I know are still alive and conscious and will respond to heartfelt intent.

I do not have faith, I do not believe. I have a knowing of this truth. The three coins symbolized me and the two martial and spiritual students who were traveling with me. We had spent the first night in Corinth and were now headed to Sparti (Sparta) with a stopover at Nemea, the location of Herakles first Labor.

In 2006, I needed to be in Thermopylae not Sparta. Now in the fall of 2010, I needed to journey to Sparta. My two students, who had been with me in 2006, asked if we were going back to Thermopylae. An emphatic "No" was my response. I completed what I needed to do in 2006 and I will never return to the Hot Gates.

Sparti

Arriving in Sparti is visually unexciting. There are no signs acknowledging this land, this city, as the homeland of the great warrior philosophers except for an awesome statue of King Leonidas by the stadium. With this being said, the most important aspect that is missing is any sense of the warrior spirit that was and still is Sparta's historical birthright. Not that I would want to see workers of the Municipality of Sparta walking around dressed as ancient Spartan knights, but I would love to see a shift in the consciousness. This would be a shift from the purely mundane and materialistic to a sense of spirit, honor and pride in their warrior-philosopher ancestral heritage and to the restoration of equality, given that the ancient Spartans referred to themselves as "Equals." And we must not forget one of the most important ingredients, the equality of men and women.

If you've ever been to Sparti, you may question this statement about spirit, honor and pride. When historical ruins are left to linger as an afterthought, or an absence of thought, of the glory days gone by, this act alone paints a vivid picture of an absolute rejection of one's ancestral heritage. This is the case here.

Photo by Ian Owens

We arrived in Sparti late in the afternoon and checked into the Menelaion Hotel, named after the site of the Sanctuary of Menelaus and Helen, the deified heroes of Sparta. The next day, a Sunday, was to be a martial and spiritual training day. I wanted to first meditate and train at the Sanctuary of Artemis Orthia. We would then finish the day with a session at the hilltop site of the step-pyramid structure and hero shrine of the Menelaion in honor of Menelaus, Helen (of Troy) and the *Dioscuri*—the twin heroic brothers of Helen—Castor and Polydeuces. Castor, the mortal one of the twins, was a martial artist and a teacher of swordsmanship to Herakles. Both were Spartan heroes, Polydeuces being an unbeatable boxer, while Castor was the fearless warrior. How appropriate for us to train on the sacred ground of the *Dioscuri* and to honor them and Herakles with prayers, meditation and martial activity.

This myth of the *Dioscuri* led the ancient Spartans to have two kings. The *Dioscuri* were Spartan's patrons and protectors. Additionally, the Spartan kings were the priests of the *Dioscuri*. After breakfast we headed to the Sanctuary of Artemis Orthia (the Upright). I chose this as our first training and meditation site as it was the most sacred place and religious gathering site within ancient Sparta. Now, I have an excellent sense of direction but attempting to discover the location of this sanctuary was, to say the least, difficult. Finally, we saw a small sign pointing down a side road. What we discovered brought both anger and sadness. Artemis's sacred ground, the religious navel of Sparta, appeared extremely unkempt, desecrated by lack of attention. A locked gate and fence circled the site and prevented us from entering. I was extremely upset at this turn of events but hoped the sacred site of the *Dioscuri* would be different.

We headed out of town in search of the mythical, but real, ridge-top site of the *Dioscuri*, who symbolized the spiritual and physical in humans. We found the turnoff and proceeded up a narrow road that seemingly ended at a small chapel. But there was an even narrower road, better described as a path, that continued up the mountainside. It appeared as if it had not been used often as the foliage encroached on the road in certain places. Not to be deterred and in the spirit of Artemis, whose domain is the dangerous and exciting moments of life, we continued up the mountain in our four-door BMW, which we'd dubbed the "black chariot."

After a slightly harrowing ride up the curvy mountain trail, we finally arrived at the sacred site of the *Dioscuri*. And what a beautiful scene awaited our arrival: the Valley of Lacedaemon, the name Homer attached to it. We could see the River Eurotas running through the entire fertile and lush valley. The beauty of the valley was magnificently and magically framed by Mt. Taygetus, the mythical haunt of Artemis. The day was crystal clear and the azure sky held within it a radiant sun ruled by none other than Hades. It was boiling hot. Taking a deep breath of the energetic splendor, I could almost hear Zeus, Hera, Poseidon, Athena, Hades and the other Olympians shouting their approval. Finally, humans were going to bless and honor this sacred ground of the Age of Heroes and the *Dioscuri*, sacred stones and soil that for so long had been neglected.

My desire was to honor this holy ground, not only spiritually, but martially, in tribute and reverence to the Age of Heroes and the spirit of the Spartan warriors. Perchance this simple and heartfelt act would be the beginning of another Age of Heroes.

As I exited our chariot, a surreal sight met my eyes. An abandoned vehicle sat by the corner of the ruins farthest from where we were parked. The passenger's side door was open, and its car seat was missing. As I walked closer, I realized we were not alone. It seemed that a local had taken this opportunity on a Sunday to drive up here and work on his car. Our new friend, and soon-to-be spectator, looked up from his work and smiled. I returned the smile while thinking, "What a story he's going to be able to tell his friends over *ouzo*."

Talk about the ironies of life. There was only one Greek here on this sacred site on a Sunday. And he was working on his car no less. This was hallowed ground. This was the sacred site and birthplace of one of the most recognizable Western myths and legends, —that of the beautiful Helen and the fall of Troy, which the ancient Greeks considered one of the greatest and most important events in the Age of Heroes and, in fact, marked its end. It seems to me that the modern citizens of Sparti don't cherish their Spartan heritage. An even larger irony is that the ancient Spartans were the most spiritual, religious and philosophical of all the Greeks at that time in history. One only needs to visit the museum in town to verify this truth (more about this later).

Once my students and I had changed into our black, and let me not forget to mention heavy, training uniforms, we proceeded to climb to the highest and hottest part of the ruins—barefoot.

As we made our way across the broken stones and dirt of the once glorious, but now all but forgotten, temple and shrine, I could sense the latent power beneath my feet. With Apollo's darts beaming into my back, I stepped through the fabric of time and felt the joy and sorrow of this place. In the next moment, I was kneeling and offering prayers to the land and the ancestors.

After further prayers and meditation, we began our physical training in various areas of the ruins. The sharp stones and uneven ground provided an excellent stage for the realization of hand-to-hand martial training. The sun, energizing but not debilitating, and the awakened Earth flowed together within me and brought a heightened spirit and memory to every cell of my body and mind. My body was happy. My mind was happy. And my spirit was happy.

Next, I taught my students the strategic use of terrain through positioning, distancing, timing and most importantly feeling (intuition). This was an exercise in mind power, or what I call a strong mind, as a misstep could cause a loss of footing and stability that could propel one down on the edge of a jagged and unforgiving rock. Moreover, this exercise allowed my students to learn a lot about themselves under these non-*dojo* conditions, in other words, outside the training hall.

Physical training is important in the martial arts, but what is mostly overlooked, and what is even more important, is to know ourselves and to train our mind. The importance of strategy and knowing ourselves has its roots here in Lacedaemon. "Know thyself" is essential for all people's evolution of heart, mind, and spirit. This central Delphic maxim was attributed to Chilon, a Spartan Philosopher and one of the seven ancient sages of Greece. During our training, it was more than appropriate to honor not only the Lacedaemonian Chilon but furthermore, Athena, the goddess of the heroic, martial ideal, who personified excellence in close combat and strategy.

I completed our training session with a meditative journey of martial power and then we ended with further meditation and prayers and bid farewell to our new Sparti friend. However, our day was not yet complete as we were headed for the ruins of ancient Sparta – the Acropolis.

Once again, the lack of attention and care was maddening. Ironically, this uncaring attitude of the Sparti government and citizens was beneficial for our training. There is always a gifting in a wounding. And our gift was the freedom to explore and train with nothing restricting our ability to be one with the sacredness of the ancient site. There were no crowds, no guards or roped off areas like most other sacred sites around the world. We were not going to train there today, but I needed to get a feel for the Acropolis of Sparta and the Sanctuary of Athena *Poliouchos* (Athena Guardian of the City) before our training session the next morning.

We spent a short time walking among the ruins of the Acropolis, but there was no indication of the location of the Sanctuary of Athena (representing intelligent courage). Historically, it was located on the slope above the Acropolis. Even though the sanctuary was one of the most important cult locations in ancient Sparta, there were no ruins left or even a sign honoring and explaining the importance of Athena's cult.

As we returned to the car, I spied an awesome gifting from the Spartan ancestors. To my dismay, one of my students had seen it first on the walk into the Acropolis. Thus, it was a gifting for him and not for me. This made it even more powerful for him as my "owl eyes" didn't see it on the way in and I usually miss nothing. The gifting was a pristine luculent luminous, or translucent serpent's skin, that was ascending a rock face. It was the most perfect serpent's skin that I had ever seen. It was perfectly positioned on the stone and mirrored the ascending serpents on the insignia of the *Dioscuri*. This was a magical gift and an acknowledgement of our purpose and the training that we had just completed and would conduct the following morning.

Back at the hotel, I lectured on divination and the "god in chains." There is a commonly accepted truth that in Sparta there was a statue of Ares, the Greek War God. Ares represented violence, war-like frenzy and slaughter. This statue was wrapped in chains and supposedly symbolized that the spirit of Ares (blind violence) was never to leave the environs of the Spartan lands. This meaning was the conclusion the second century C.E. Greek travel writer, Pausanias. People take as truth Pausanias' assumption and conclusion that "in Lakonia they think the god of war will never desert them if they keep him in chains."[320] However, as a spiritual/religious philosopher and martial artist, this explanation and symbolism doesn't make sense to me. One of Ares' principle attributes was bloodlust, but this was not a feature of the Spartans. In fact, bloodlust was the antithesis of the Spartan mind and heart. So, what is the truth?

The Spartans recognized the totality of human emotion, always striving to achieve harmony within themselves and within the Spartan community. They intimately followed the maxim, "know thyself." The importance to the Spartan mind of understanding fear, of detachment and the "pressing down"[321] of fear, is revealed by the chained statue of Ares. The chains did not symbolize that the spirit of war should never exit the city of Sparta. They symbolized the detachment and pressing down of fear and the resultant bloodlust, which was not acceptable in their philosophical culture of perfected minds and hearts. Surely, the Athenians, and others would want you to think otherwise.

The Museum in Sparti

I know the ancient Spartans were first and foremost warrior philosophers. To many people they were just the opposite; unintelligent warriors bent on war. This has been a viewpoint put forth by historians and scholars who base their theories, premises and assumptions on second-hand information or knowledge. They may also base their theories on their life experiences as an observer and not as a participant in martial/spiritual studies.

Another glaring problem with discovering the truth of the past: it is written by the victors not the vanquished. Thus, the majority of the written history of the Spartans has been viewed through the prejudicial prism of the Athenians, the Spartans' archenemies. What then is the truth? Are we going to believe historians and a travel writer? Or is there some type of proof that would contradict them?

Undoubtedly, the Spartans were the most religiously pious of all the Greeks. In addition, there is my esoteric theory on the chained statue of Ares. The statue of Ares was not the only chain-wrapped statue in Sparta. A statue of Aphrodite, the wife of Ares, was similarly fettered. Why, we may ask.

In Greek mythology, there is a concept called "*harmonia*," which is usually translated as "harmony," but means any union in which the parts form a seamless whole while retaining their distinct identities. Harmonia is the daughter of sea-born Aphrodite and fiery Ares, whom Empedocles[322] identified with Love and Strife, the two primary cosmic forces, which bring about all change in the universe. Pythagoras[323] likewise said that cosmic Harmonia is born of the union of Love and Strife. She reconciles all oppositions."[324]

In other words, the chains on both statues symbolized the concept of control or pressing down the energy of both the blind violence and bloodlust of Ares and the desire of Aphrodite. This is the desire, the worldly lust (*voluptas mundi*), which may lead to illicit love, the type of love that causes dysfunctional behavior and actions. It is interesting to note that the Spartans didn't cover up their women or make them second-class citizens as cultures and societies since the time of the Spartans have done to control the worldly lust of their people.

Is there still more proof outside of my theory on the reason for the chains? What else is there to verify that the Spartans were warrior philosophers? Is there a clue within the mythology of Greece? Is there truth to be found within the mythology of the serpent?

Both the Spartans and the Athenians considered themselves of serpent origin. The Temple of Apollo at Delphi, where Chilon's maxim "know thyself" was inscribed, may have been located on the site of an ancient serpent temple.

One of Athena's symbols was the serpent. The Greek god of healing, Asklepios was also represented by an ascending serpent coiling around his staff.

Photo Ian Owens

There is the insignia of the *Dioscuri* with two ascending serpents. And we had been gifted with the ascending serpent skin by the Temple of Athena overlooking the Acropolis. The majority of spiritual and religious traditions of the past have recognized the wisdom and power of the serpent as well as its various allegories. The serpent represents immortal energy and consciousness,

343

which is connected with the ageless myths of death, rebirth and resurrection. The serpent's movements are serpentine, symbolic of the rhythm of life. And with its lidless eyes, it reminds us to be ever vigilant, aware and awake, a necessary quality of a warrior.

Additionally, the serpent was recognized as a symbol of prophecy as its venom was used for altered states of consciousness and mystical trances. I have spent my life seeking the mysteries of heaven and Earth. I have a very close relationship with the serpent; even my heliacal rising star at birth was Alphard—the heart of the Hydra—as is Sher's. This means that our life has been connected to the great serpent.

Accordingly, when I entered the museum in Sparti the next morning, I was awestruck by the abundance of ascending serpent imagery. Percentagewise, there were more than I had ever seen in any other museum around the world. I happily realized that along with the cult of the *Dioscuri*, this was the proof that I needed to support my theory that the Spartans were a culture of enlightened warrior philosophers. The imagery was not only of ascending serpents, but the serpents were drinking out of a cup.

Ascending serpents symbolize the awakening of the serpent energy within us. Philosophically, awakening our serpent power allows the energy of the Earth, the angels of the earth mother, to ascend and marry the energy of the stars, angels of the heavenly father, to join in a union of opposites. Philosophy aside, this occurs physiologically within our bodies. Once awakened, our serpent energy begins ascending our spinal column activating each *chakra* or energy center until union is completed at the pineal gland (enlightenment) within the skull, which is sometimes symbolized as a cup. At this point our serpent is no longer just of the Earth, but is now of the Earth and the heavens.

This inner fire of spiritual awakening occurs within our body and mind (heart). This divine solar force arouses the serpent energy in our first energy center or *chakra*.[325] This is the water serpent that is aroused by the fire of our spirit – a supreme interpenetration of heavenly and earthly elements: fire and water. This is a union of opposites, a baptism of fire and water that leads to healing and enlightenment and the resurrection of the androgynous lifeforce. This was the knowledge and the wisdom utilized by the ancient Spartans, an enlightened culture of warrior philosophers.

I'm amazed, but then again, I'm not surprised that no one ever connected the serpent knowledge utilized by the Spartan culture and society as a foundation of truth to their enlightened culture. Instead, people have accepted the word of a travel writer projecting his own preconceived notions about the Spartans as gospel. I understand that this may be partially because the primary focus has been on Thermopylae and not on Sparta.

Please understand that the Hot Gates are closer to my heart than anyone could ever know, but Thermopylae was just one moment in time that exemplified struggle, sacrifice, honor, courage, perseverance, loyalty, tears and freedom – the desire to be free people and to live in peace. It was a victory in defeat that presented a noble but sober image of life and death. However, the divine and human qualities embodied at Thermopylae were not birthed there; they were birthed someplace else. Quite simply, they were born out of the soil and the vibrant mountains of Lacedaemon, all framed by the wide-open skies.

But primarily, they were birthed within the heart and the mind of a people: the brothers and sisters of Sparta. The next day after training at the Acropolis, we bid farewell to Sparti and headed to Olympia, and then on to our final destination – Delphi. It had been four years since I had last seen my friend, Konstantinos, and I looked forward to spending time with him again.

As we left town, I mused on our time there. The memories, experiences and training had been awesome. We had met and talked to some of the locals and made some friends, enjoyed good food and drink. Still, even with all that we'd discovered and experienced, my time in Sparti was bittersweet. But then again; isn't that life?

Commentary

One thing about Sparti struck me as very odd. All the tables in the main plaza across from our hotel were always filled with men, just men. No woman at all. If they were trying to propagate the so-called homosexuality of the ancient Spartans, they were doing a great job of it. Even though I believe in gay rights, gay marriage, choice and equality, it was still very strange to see a crowd with no females. There was something different, an attitude; something beneath the surface.

The day we were leaving Sparti, I wandered into one of the few gift shops in town. As usual, I stuck up a light conversation with the owner and her daughter and saw an opportunity to ask a question of them.

"Ancient Spartan culture," I began, "was based on the equality of men and women. But I've noticed that the plaza is always filled with just men with no women in sight. What happened to the equality of men and women? I would have expected to see couples not just men."

The owner and her daughter looked at each other while vibrating a sadness of spirit. The owner turned to me and said one word, "Turks." She continued with a venomous tone, "The Turks invaded Greece and with the Turks came Islamic rule and faith – Sharia Law. And women became subservient to men. This is still the way it is even in today's world."

I could feel their pain and sadness as I replied, "I'm sorry to hear this… maybe I need to return and run for mayor!"

Without hesitation, they both said, "we'll vote for you….!"

THE ICELANDIC *HULDUFÓLK* (HIDDEN ONES)

· ·

AFTER MY FIRSTHAND PHYSICAL EXPERIENCE WITH OTHER-worldly energetic beings in 1997, I concluded that there would also be earthly energetic beings, commonly referred to as faeries and elves. This conclusion came from my experiences, intuitive sense, scholarly knowledge, and oral teachings from elders around the world.

Speaking of these energetic beings, in the nineties my family and I journeyed to Cornwall, England, where some of my family's items went missing and later showed up, a sign of the Cornish faeries known as piskies. Of course, it might not have been the piskies playing tricks on us but our own human forgetfulness. But the experiences didn't stop there.

The fall of 2012 found me traveling to Iceland with my son and one of our students. Even though Sher and I had visited in 2010, I felt an urge to return and further explore this mysterious island. For the first part of our journey, we explored the most magical region of Iceland, Snæfellsnes, a peninsula, and its volcano, Snæfellsjökull. Jules Verne used this volcano as the setting for his novel *A Journey to the Centre of the Earth*. This was a mystical and strange land, where the hidden ones, elves, and dwarves hide in dark crevices and caves while strange rock formations become ogres and trolls. This is the land of fire and ice. It is nature in all its glory, creative and destructive though it may be. The wind, the sea, and the hundreds of waterfalls vibrate a song of primal pureness seldom found on our beautiful but wounded Earth.

When in a mystical place, spiritual protocols are important. These are not dogma-and-doctrine-based but more rooted in common sense and respect for the spirit world. Asking the Otherworld's permission when conducting our spirit work is a protocol we follow faithfully and teach to our students. When we travel to a new place or return to one, we think it best to do prayers and an offering—which could be as simple as a piece of our hair—and to ask permission to be there and do our work. I also ask for safety for myself and others while we are on our journey. Sometimes this rite is short and simple, and at other times more extensive and intense. There is no format to follow, just your heart. As soon as I set foot in this magical land, I felt a strong connection and kinship. For this reason, early the next morning, facing the cloud-covered volcano with the icy winds crashing into me, I did an extensive and complete rite of permission. At least I thought I did.

Iceland was a virgin land in the sense that the New Agers had not discovered it and few tourists spent any time there, at least as of 2012. Not only was it an unspoiled land, but it was home to many legends and myths and one of the most famous Icelandic Viking shamans, Bárður. This legendary shaman was born in northern Norway and his grandmother was a Sami—the people of northern Scandinavia—who passed on her shamanic and magical knowledge to him. One of the sacred sites on the edge of the volcano is known as the Singing Cave. This is Bárður's cave, where he would spend time conducting his shamanic practice.

Since it was October, a time of the year with few tourists, we were just about guaranteed to be the only ones visiting the various sacred sites on the peninsula. Late in the afternoon on the second day, we spent time in the Singing Cave. As its name indicates, one of the most obvious and important practices to conduct here would be *galdr*, a Norse magical chant/song. Once again, I needed to make myself known to the spirit world and ask permission to enter the cave and do our work. Inside the cave, I conducted a blessing, an honoring and opening ceremony. Then we proceeded with other practices including an old magical chant. The sound of our voices vibrated off the cave walls, and once more, Bárður's cave was singing.

We spent another day and half on the peninsula before we returned to Reykjavik, the capital of Iceland. While in Reykjavik, we stayed at the Grand Hotel, which would be our residence for the final days of our journey. The Grand Hotel is beautiful. However, I did not choose it for its beauty but for the its honoring of Norse mythology. When you enter the hotel, you are greeted with a phenomenal piece of glass artwork portraying the creation of the world based on the *Völuspá*. The front desk is decorated with small poems from the *Poetic Edda's Hávamál*, which provides advice for living, proper conduct, and wisdom. Staying in that hotel captured the feeling and essence of the Norse who had settled there after leaving Norway.

My room was on the twelfth floor overlooking the ocean and the fog-covered Snæfellsnes. Even though the hotel's focus was on mythology, it was your typical, ordinary hotel. Or so I thought. The next day, we were leaving early to explore Thingvellir National Park, where Iceland's parliament, Althing, was founded. Heeding the advice "early to bed, early to rise," I turned in around ten o'clock. I had only been asleep a few minutes before the phone rang. A voice said, "I'm calling to make sure the four Russians we sent over arrived safely since we're overbooked here." I told them they'd reached a private room and not the front desk and promptly hung up to keep myself from totally waking up. A few more minutes passed, and the phone rang again.

This time, the voice spoke Icelandic until I explained I didn't understand. Finally, the person said in English, "This is not the front desk?" Hanging up once again and crawling back to bed, I thought, "What is going on?"

The phone rang constantly until I wised up and unplugged it at two in the morning. The next morning after breakfast, I plugged the phone back in and once again the calls came, all wanting information from the front desk. Realizing it was not a fluke, I informed the front desk about the strange occurrence. They apologized and said that they would investigate it. They said it had never happened before and was seemingly impossible.

After a full day of exploring Thingvellir, I checked in at the front desk before going back to my room. The problem had been fixed, but there was no explanation for how it had happened. There was no logical reason to explain it. Later that night, as I was pondering this mystery, it finally came to me – the hidden ones. I had forgotten to include them in my prayers. And they will let you know if they have been offended or slighted in some manner. I immediately did prayers and an offering to them. The result: the rest of our journey was uneventful.

Is this the end of my story? Not at all. It seems that one or more hidden ones decided to hop a ride on our flight home and now reside with us on another peninsula – this one in Washington state, overlooking the only fjord in the western continental United States!

Loki – A Hidden One?

Nine months later, we had a very young feral cat show up at our back door. During one of its morning feedings, he bit me, a deep puncture. It was my fault. I frightened him when I turned over his feeding dish. Common sense dictated a visit to the physician. Of course, the thought within the physician's mind was rabies. He emphasized that I needed to trap the cat to discover if it had rabies. I replied that I didn't want to, as he was living outside our home. "Well," the doctor said, "the cat may get hit by a truck and you will not know until it is too late if it was rabid, as rabies untreated will kill you."

My wife and I didn't trap the cat to discover if it was rabid, but rather due to a wicked-looking injury near his tail and his dreadful appearance. Let's just say that he was very wild. In fact, after we trapped him and took him to a vet, the rescue cat woman felt he might be better off as a mouser at one of the farms. But she did ask if we would like him back.

We decided to take him back to our home and let him loose. We hoped he would stick around, which he did. He was getting regular meals, so why wouldn't he? Add to this our home's location overlooking a fjord with eagles, coyotes, mountain lions, and bears nearby. Staying close could mean life over death.

A month passed with our feral cat still outside our home. And then came the night of July 4, and fireworks. Where my wife was sitting, she could see our barbecue outside on our back deck. Sitting on it, looking in at my wife, was the shivering, scared little cat who, by now, had put on weight. We opened the sliding glass door. With no hesitation, he ran in and became a part of our family, joining our three other cats, all three strays, including our Maine Coon, a Viking cat.

The next day, Sherry named our new cat Loki. It was as if someone had whispered his name into her ear. We wouldn't have chosen that name for him. At the time, we didn't even know his breed. Amazingly, Loki adapted to our home rapidly. In fact, after a few weeks, you wouldn't have believed he'd ever been a feral cat.

Within a short period, we knew Loki was different from your average cat, feral or otherwise. His behaviors and eyes were strange to say the least. Loki had a baby face but was large for one so young. In my research for a journey to Norway and Iceland, I stumbled across Loki's breed: *Norsk Skogkatt*, Norwegian Forest Cat. It seemed another Viking cat had found us, even though there were no known Norwegian Forest Cats in our area of the state.

The mystery and essence—yes essence—of the enigmatic Loki does not stop there. His eyes are otherworldly and of this world. Eyes are the portals to the soul, and in researching the Norwegian Forest Cat, I discovered something that shed some light on this mysterious new member of our family. With deep roots in Norse mythology, "the Norwegian Forest Cat (*Norsk Skogkatt*) is the gift of the Norse gods to the cat kingdom. Celebrated in Norse mythology and nineteenth century Nordic fables, this cat has an air of enchantment. It has awed Þórr and pulled Freya's chariot. Asbjomsen and Moe embellished their Norwegian fairy tales with descriptions of these 'huge and furry Troll cats.'"[326]

Mystery solved – Loki was a faerie cat! And it all made sense. At certain times, he was not of this world, his eyes changing into Otherworldly orbs, a trait noticed not only by us, but others as well. Could it be possible that our dear Loki has the spirit of the hidden ones within him? Maybe not. Maybe so. And then there is this: in Denmark, these cats are called *huldrekat* – hidden folk!

PART VI

· ·

The Fourth of Four Major Otherworldly Experiences over a Span of Ten Years

It is the soul of man which is capable of the knowledge of being. It carries in it a knowledge which it has not won in this life: knowledge is recollection, anamnesis. With this the knowing soul rises above existence as stretched between birth and death... Death affects only the body; the soul is immortal.[327]

Photo Jim Kalnins This was taken late afternoon not seen by us but captured by the camera.

THE VISITATION: REVEALING WHO WE WERE IN A PREVIOUS LIFETIME

August 3, 1997 – New Moon

．．．

My Jupiter in the First House is Trine Uranus in the Ninth House of Our Message. Jupiter- Uranus relationships and cycles are referred to as Quantum Shifts such as the one that occurred in 1997, the year of the Visitation. Twenty-seven Quantum Scientists and Physics have had Jupiter Uranus relationships including Einstein, Oppenheimer and Bohm.

REINCARNATION[328] IS A PHILOSOPHICAL PARADIGM THAT causes "shock and awe" in Christian and Muslim circles. It is a threat to the power of organized religion. Early on, the Church of Rome saw the danger in people's belief in reincarnation. Consequently, "those early Church Fathers who taught or believed in reincarnation were declared heretics, excommunicated, and their books were burned. Other heretics faced horrible deaths, such as being burned alive. Why? Think about it. If you believe you will reincarnate in another body, you cannot be controlled by fear of an eternity in the fires of hell.

"The church existed to hold power over the people, to tell them what to believe rather than have them think for themselves. Control by fear is not possible if an individual knows who she/he is (astrology) and that he will reincarnate again and again. There is nothing to fear when we know Truth; therefore, Truth must be hidden from the people."[329]

Let's compare my knowing of the truth of reincarnation to Christianity's dogma of a single lifetime with death resulting in the gift of heaven or the punishment of hell. This dogma subtly insinuates that we are not responsible for the future well-being of the land or the Earth and its creatures or future generations, as we will not reincarnate back on Earth at a future time. As we are observing in this twenty-first century, this belief has opened a Pandora's Box of ecological destruction.

If we look back, we discover that "by the 7th century the Church had rewritten Catholic dogma to obliterate most of the original teachings of esoteric Christian groups such as the Essenes. . . . Most importantly, they edited out all references to the universal doctrine of reincarnation, a central theme throughout Eastern religion as well as Druidic and early Christian life.

"This had a profound effect on all succeeding ages. Before, people believed that their ancestors were still alive in the Otherworld, and that like themselves, they would be reborn into the group or tribe to which they belonged. In this way, warriors felt it an honour to die in order to protect their people. But there was a deeper responsibility; if you were to be reborn, then the land must be preserved not only for your children, but for yourself when you returned. Short-term exploitation would have been inconceivable. You and your children were, in a very real sense, the land."[330]

Purification

The rabbis declare that "wherever the angel appears the shechina (the divine Presence) appears (Exodus Rabbah 32:9)."[331]

Early on Sunday afternoon, August 3, 1997, the day of the angelic visitation, we experienced an otherworldly storm. One moment, the sky was crystal clear, tinged only with a few clouds, and in the next moment, the sky darkened into an ominous, swirling, bluish-black tempest. Sound and movement paused as if a giant were holding its breath. And then the storm. All around us, torrents of rain fell as thunder boomed and lightning struck.

At the time, we didn't know what to make of such an unusual natural occurrence. Considering what happened about eight hours later, we realized it was a purification. The volume and intensity of the thunder and rain and the strength and force of the lightning that struck all around us was a purification of the Earth and its elements. A major sanctification had taken place.

At the visitation, as messengers of God and in answer to my prayer, the archangel and the two assisting angels announced—through their presence and the signs that accompanied their appearance—who we had been in previous incarnations. "In biblical accounts, angels traditionally appeared in order to make an annunciation or a revelation of transcendent import. Usually an angel's message is one of concern not only to the individual who sees the vision, but to the collective group as well. Such visionary experiences mark dramatic turning points personally and culturally." In the case of our twelve apprentices and my wife and me, the visitation was not a visionary experience, but an actual physical, sensory, extraordinary event.

The Visitation:
Revealing Who We Were In A Previous Lifetime

Starting from the east they follow the course of the sun in the name of the Holy Three. . . .As they move from left to right they sing the song of Michael the Victorious.[332]

"If you are blind and have never seen the sun rise it doesn't matter how many hypotheses you can array, you still don't know. Belief is simply the adoption of someone else's idea. Once you have seen the sun you don't believe in it, you know it."[333]

I've seen angels. This is the reason that I don't believe in angels; I **know** angels. Most importantly, I have not seen angels in my mind, in a cloud formation, or in my dreams. I've been in the presence of and witness to an archangel and the two assisting angels. My wife, Sherry, and twelve of our apprentices were witnesses to the same sacred visitation. It occurred on the night of the new moon on August 3, 1997, in the woods of Maine. And it just happens that I was born on a new moon.

Numerically, the date is a ten.[334] The number one symbolizes the Absolute, the One, the Divine, the Great Mystery, the Creator. The number ten symbolizes the reflection of the Divine or the perfection of creation. "In the number 10 creation reaches perfection and fulfillment. The masculine-positive, creative principle of God has penetrated and fertilized space, the negative, maternal aspect, and has become one with it."[335] In the Jewish tradition, the tenth letter of the alphabet is *yod*. "*Yod* is the very first flame of the divine fire, of the spirit of God."[336] In the Jewish esoteric system of *kabbala*, "the tenth *sefirah*[337] is *Malkhuth*[338] and means kingdom."[339] And in the original tarot, the tenth card is the Wheel of Fortune. This is a card of choice where we continue to maintain our dualistic consciousness or let go of it and begin the journey to awaken to a consciousness of radical non-duality where we shift our focus from materialism to one of spirit. The witnesses to the Visitation had a choice regarding the future path of their lives.

Winter 1997

I received the first indication of what was to come in the winter of 1997. At that time, even in the wildest part of my imaginative mind, I had no idea or inclination what the future might hold for our apprentices and us. In addition, this was the winter of the appearance of the comet Hale-Bopp in the Northern Hemisphere. It was only many years later that I would recognize its connection to the visitation.

It was early April, and I was conducting a weekend corporate community-building seminar in the foothills of Maine. There was still snow on the ground, but the temperature was tolerable. To say the least, our seminars were not your typical corporate fare. We would explore territory that was many times taboo within the corporate mindset. We got away with it because we got results and great feedback from the participants. One exercise that pushed the envelope of acceptability was an experience demonstrating the power of the mind over the body.

On Saturday evening I asked for volunteers, who would like to "go for it." After I explained the exercise, only a handful out of the twenty-some volunteered. In simple terms, through directed, focused attention and intention, they would comfortably spend time barefoot in the snow without the benefit of coat or hat. Even though the sun had been shining throughout the day, once the sun died, it got very cold. When I took the few outside and explained the exercise in detail, it was well below freezing.

Standing barefoot in the snow, I slightly adapted the exercise, as the comet Hale-Bopp (the twins – two tails; the Hopi Blue Star)[340] was visibly streaming through the heavens like an icy-blue angel. This was a very special occasion and an extraordinary view, to say the least. The last time Hale-Bopp had appeared was during the time Noah built the ark.[341] And it was the Archangel Michael who influenced and was the messenger angel to the prophet Noah.

Down through the ages, according to mythology, comets such as Hale-Bopp have been considered celestial messengers and harbingers of prophecy. The Hawaiian king Kamehameha, the great warrior and unifier of the Hawaiian Islands, was born during the appearance of Halley's Comet. Since Hale-Bopp was a greater comet and seldom visited the Earth, what then was the message this time around?

As the comet flew overhead, I had each person focus his or her eyes on it – a once-in-a-lifetime vision of heavenly magic. What a sight it was, a memory forever etched within our souls. At the conclusion of the exercise, everyone was simply amazed that they hadn't felt the cold. While watching the mystical sight of the comet overhead, everyone's feet stayed warm and melted the snow. Little did I realize that the magic was just beginning.

The next morning was Sunday, the conclusion of the seminar. As I ended class, a strange and inexplicable thing happened. In front of everyone in the meeting room, a white feather mysteriously fell out of the air and dropped into the palm of my hand. Since it was early spring and still cold outside, all the windows in the room had been closed and locked for months. There was no rational explanation for the feather's appearance. It just manifested out of thin air.

Over the next several months, the mystery deepened. Two more feathers inexplicably appeared. Again they manifested out of thin air and in front of our students. During one of our weekend teaching sessions, two of our apprentices had independent visions of me riding on a white horse, even though it was known that I was not a horse person due to an incident in my childhood.

During the summer in Maryland where I grew up, a carnival would set up for a few days every year in our small town. I was young, probably eight or nine years old, when my grandmother took me to the local carnival. This one summer night, they had pony rides. As I was waiting in line, I happened to move to a spot behind one of the ponies. Before I knew it, I was in intense pain and crying. The pony had kicked and hit me in the groin!

Spring 1997

The last time that we'd visited England was in 1982. After an absence of fifteen years later, for reasons known and unknown, we needed to return to the British Isles. Over the years we had focused on journeys to Japan, Hawaii, Mexico, and Peru. It seemed that I was being drawn back to England because of its connection with the Holy Grail and other legends and mysteries, such as the one surrounding Joseph of Arimathea.

On our previous visit to England, we had not ventured to Cornwall and its many mystical sites. Since we were last there, my many visionary and otherworldly experiences had led me to research the legends and lore of this part of Britain. As in times past, I stumbled on information and knowledge that tugged at the inner recesses of my heart and mind.

We were headed to the north coast of Cornwall, a dramatic and isolated land filled with strange tales of ancient kings and shipwrecks, and some of the county's most beautifully situated coastal towns and villages. From my research, I knew Tintagel and St. Nectan's Glen, a place of legends and ghosts, were two sites we needed to visit. St. Nectan's Glen is where the "River Trevillet tumbles amongst ancient woodland. The water expertly cuts its way through the layers of Devonian slate to form a series of waterfalls. The largest fall drops roughly [sixty feet] into a rock basin. Then the water pours out through a perfect window or arch of stone before falling again and continuing its journey towards the sea. This pool is known as Saint Nectan's Kieve (*Kieve* is basin in Cornish)."[342]

But there was something more. On our first visit to England, we had spent time in Glastonbury and on the Tor with its tower dedicated to the Celtic Goddess Bride and the Archangel Michael. We had also visited Avebury, a supposed serpent temple also connected with the archangel. Could it be that the archangel and his[343] connection to Cornwall were pulling me back to England? If so, it was not the only reason. There was another purpose to our return that only my wife and I knew.

I determined we would bring a group here at the end of May, but first, we needed to check out the sacred sites and lodging in Cornwall. In mid-April we arrived in England and headed for Cornwall and the small town of Tintagel, the magical birthplace of King Arthur. In addition, this was the land of Merlin and the Archangel Michael, the ancient patron saint of Cornwall and its hills and high places.

Michael, whom I call Mikaël, is known as the dragon slayer. The archangel is also known as, "the spirit of revelation, giving inspiration and visionary glimpses of divinity, the great initiator into the hidden mysteries. In the esoteric tradition, he is the one that transmutes lower, base energies into those of a more refined, spiritual type. . . . This would seem to be the real meaning behind the glyph of the slain dragon – the archangel transfixes the raw-dragon energy of the Earth with the Will (of which the sword is the traditional symbol), and transmutes it to a higher rate of vibration."[344]

Tintagel was everything we expected and more. It was situated on the cliffs overlooking the sea. I immediately felt at home, feeling the breeze and the sun shining on my face and seeing the sparkling blue ocean before me. Tintagel was more of a village than a town, with few options for lodging within the town itself, except for the Wootons Country Hotel, which we fell in love with. The inn was situated right next to the cliffs and overlooked Tintagel Island and the mythological ruins of Arthur's castle. Located below the castle ruins was an ocean cave known as Merlin's Cave, the supposed part-time sanctuary of the legendary wizard. Since we conduct many experiences at first light or after dusk, staying at the inn would allow us easier access to the cave than other lodgings outside of town.

Even if Merlin never set foot in the cave, it was still a reputed place of power. Partially, this was due to the geomancy of the area, the meeting place of land and sea. But there was more to it than just this aspect. Tintagel Island's origins were volcanic, with an ample supply of quartz crystals deep within the interior of the island. It seemed that the odds of it being a place of power and an energetic vortex were great.

From a shamanic point of view, caves are considered repositories of power and the birthplaces of legendary people. Caves, since the earliest times, have been places of enchantment, invocation, and initiation. Being in the womb of Mother Earth generates magical power as one experiences a symbolic death in the dark only to be reborn in the light as one emerges from the cave.

To enter Merlin's Cave required knowing the schedule of the ocean tides. During high tide the cave was partially underwater, which would cause an unaware person to be trapped within the cave until the tide receded. In addition, it was a tourist and New-Age site. Planning a visit to do spiritual work required the proper timing of the tides, the ocean, and the people.

We made our way down the partial stairs on the side of the cliffs in late afternoon, and reached the beach that fronted Merlin's Cave. It was a ways away over the stony landscape, but we could sense the power. As with all places of power, care and respect were essential. We needed to do the proper prayers and ask the land, the sea, and the spirits of this area permission to enter the cave. We did this, as well as a simple purification of ourselves using what was naturally available to us.

As we silently entered, I noticed Sherry looking down at the floor of the cave as she walked. There was little light within the cave, giving it a further mystical feeling. Interestingly enough, there was light at the symbolic end of the tunnel, which happened to be the opening to the sea at the other end of the cave.

Time seemed to be frozen in a vortex of sounds – the ocean and the wind and every so often a subtle thump as if a dragon's heart were beating. With a look of amazement etched on her face, Sherry asked, "Did you see what I just saw?"

"No," I wondered what she was talking about.

"After we passed the entrance, I saw purple lights arranged in a serpentine form, almost like a purple serpent moving across the floor of the cave.[345] My first thought was, oh, they have lights in the floor of the cave to help visitors see. And then I realized this wasn't Disneyland, and with that thought, they disappeared."

There is another cave opposite Merlin's Cave that we entered on a future journey. In the words of one of our fellow far travelers: "We entered the Dragon's Lair, where one of the old Earth energies, a sleeping dragon, was awakened and tamed by the Captain."[346]

The next day we awoke to an overcast sky but brightness within our souls after our experience in Merlin's Cave. We were going to explore the mystical valley that contained St. Nectan's Glen and its magical waterfall, rumored to be the place where King Arthur's twelve knights were purified and then took their vows to quest for the Holy Grail.

Twelve is a magical number, the number of constellations and months in a solar year. With the twelve knights symbolizing the twelve constellations, and with King Arthur as the sun god and Queen Guinevere as the moon goddess, we have presented to us a heavenly cosmology mythologically reflected on the Earth. Additionally, the Norse recognized twelve heavens, as related in the poem *Grímnismál* of the *Poetic Edda*.

Many myths have common threads. Arthur fought twelve battles as well as having his twelve knights. This may "recall a mystical system of initiation that was once universal. All the different cultures have memories of this, from Hercules and his twelve labors to Odysseus, Samson and the twelve-part Babylonian epic of Gilgamesh. For each, there are twelve trials of the spirit that mark the progress of the adventurer on his quest. In the Celtic world, this twelvefold system was translated into a central heroic figure surrounded by twelve followers. Charlemagne had his twelve peers, King Lot of Orkney ruled over twelve minor kings, King Conchobar of Ulster was supported by twelve of his best warriors, and King Arthur had his twelve knights."[347]

Arthur's "twelve battles have a zodiacal significance: the progress of the candidate on his pilgrimage through life reflects the passage of the Sun through the constellations on its annual cycle from birth to death, and rebirth. The actual nature of the trials or battles may vary in different cultures in accordance with the psychological makeup of their people, but they all seem to refer to the evolution of the individualized human consciousness."[348] Last but not least, we must not forget to mention the power of twelve in the Twelve Tribes of Israel.

As with Tintagel, we were not disappointed with St. Nectan's Glen. The secretive glen had an otherworldly feeling and aura to it, and its waterfall and location only added to the land's mystical power. It was a place of initiation into the mysteries of life and death. We were told that King Arthur and his knights were said to haunt this place. This valley was undoubtedly a place of legends, ghost stories and myths.

St. Nectan's Glen, April 1997

In this place, "nature has contrived to create a most unusual waterfall. The river rushes out from a dark hole and cascades for some forty feet into a rocky basin (or *kieve* in Cornish) that has been sculpted by the timeless rushing of the waters. Here it forms a foaming cauldron of boiling water, which issues out through another remarkable hole in the rock outcrop, to hiss and splash into a pool below. A vertical rock face is covered with dripping dark-green weeds, and billows of spray spread a glistening dampness over everything. It is an intensely magical place."[349]

Standing on a rocky platform to the left of the waterfall and its pool, I turned to my wife and said, "This is awesome."

"I know," she replied.

We spent time doing inner work and energetic work, becoming one with the elements of this Earth and the magic of the Otherworld. This was so powerful a place that at any time, an elf or a faerie might appear, laugh at our humanness, and then disappear. This was definitely a place of vow-making, and it was here that we decided we would conduct a vow ceremony. Our students would vow to participate in a three-year quest for the Holy Grail. This quest would emphasize not only the experiential knowledge of the Grail but also the experiential knowledge connected with the Archangel Michael and his places of power. This knowledge would include his roles as warrior, captain of the heavenly hosts, psychopomp, purveyor of divine justice, and dragon slayer (subduing not killing).

Four weeks later, after a purification and initiatory ceremony, we were standing on the same rocky platform to the left of the waterfall, listening to each of our questors dedicate himself or herself to his or her own personal quest for the Holy Grail. My heart was happy as Sherry and I listened to each one state his or her vows as we began the first of three adventures questing for knowledge and power – questing for the Holy Grail.

After their vows, we spent the next few days exploring the dragon ley line known as St Michael's line (sun), an alignment of sacred sites across southern England, as well as the partner ley line, Mary, the Magdalene's line (moon). We completed our far traveling journey in London, staying at the Sherlock Holmes Hotel, Holmes being one of my literary heroes.

Summer 1997

Our adventures in England had been extraordinary. However, something kept gnawing at the edge of my mind. I felt there was a hidden reason for our need to return to England after so long an absence. It certainly wasn't that we were bored with the other lands where we had far traveled.

During the summer we always conduct longer-term trainings out in nature. This summer we'd scheduled a four-day training, beginning on Friday, August 1, and ending on Monday, August 4. The theme of the training was initiation, fear, and death and rebirth, including the experiences of a twenty-four-hour solitary quest, a stone-built ceremonial death spiral,[350] and bathing.

Since we mostly take novices into the outdoors, I always perform prayers for safety, love, and power before the trainings. This time I did a different prayer. Based on what I knew within my heart and my vision, I prayed for a sign to be given of who I was in my last incarnation: "Let them see a sign knowing that I was [name stated]." I mentioned the name as people would recognize it today.[351] I then let go of any expectations about the prayer. Little did I expect the sign—in reality, signs—that would be given.

The Sunday of the four-day training dawned bright and very dry. Little rain had fallen that spring and summer. We had planned on constructing the death spiral early in the afternoon so we could conduct the ceremony late in the afternoon. In addition, during the evening, I wanted to work on the issue of *phobos*, the Greek word for fear and the origin for the word phobia. The exercise I had chosen was one I had conducted many times before. In my mind, it was an excellent way to help a person release a fear that had haunted him or her.

It was a very simple exercise. Our apprentices had to identify a fear and then fashion an image of their fear out of natural materials. At night they would fight their fear with a wooden sword and burn the remains in a ceremonial fire.

This was an excellent exercise of body, mind, and spirit, and besides, many of our apprentices were martial artists. The assumption was that they would take to this exercise like ducks to water. On the contrary, many were too structured in their bodily movements. This inhibited their creativity and spontaneous "immovable and no-mind" actions.[352]

However, we were concerned that we might not be able to conduct this exercise. Sherry and I faced a major hurdle in the dry condition of the land. With little and infrequent rain we basically had drought conditions that summer, which prohibit an open fire. Without the fire, the experience would not work. But the heavens provided a solution to our dilemma.

Early in the afternoon, an intense thunderstorm developed. And "intense" does not do it justice. In a scant moment, the crystal-clear sky darkened into an ominous, swirling, mass of bluish black. For a beat, all sound and movement hushed, and then came the crashing storm.

Torrents of rain fell as thunder boomed overhead and lightning struck the ground all around us. Everyone ran to huddle underneath the cooking tarp, shaking and scared by the otherworldly intensity. People were terrified at the suddenness and force of the wind and the rain, the thunder and the lightning.[353]

As the storm abated, the Earth felt different – as if it had been purified. Later I realized that the pre-Christian Hawaiians would recognize this sudden downpour as a sign of the presence of the *Akua Lono*, the white god.[354] Our apprentices milled around, slightly disoriented by the storm. The good news was that now we could have a fire. However, the storm changed the timing of building the death spiral. It would now occur later than planned.

Building the Death Spiral, August 3, 1997

For the remainder of the afternoon, we finished building the death spiral and prepared for the death-and-rebirth ceremony. When we were almost finished building the spiral—a universal symbol of the serpent—one of our apprentices took a picture of me within the center of the spiral. . Our apprentices would travel a narrow path, the way of the serpent, to reach the center of the spiral where they would experience the death of their old selves (shedding the skin and leaving the old self behind) and be reborn as their new selves.

As with all things, there is an opening, a middle, and an ending to the ceremony. I've opened many spirals, but this one was different. I had a feeling that this was not any ordinary spiral. When I was ready to open it, I let go of any attachment or anticipation, cleared my mind, and prepared to enter.

Sherry and I had chosen two apprentices as symbolic birth guardians. They would stand at the mouth of the birth canal of the spiral, which was also the entrance, and pull the new ones into existence. The others would stand on the outside of the outermost spiral, chanting a phrase linking heaven and Earth, until it was their turn to enter and face their symbolic deaths. Each one who chose to enter the spiral would stand at the entrance, praying and contemplating his or her desire to enter the spiral. If the person still chose to enter, he or she would take the first step into the vortex with the left leg as a sign of intent and focused will to let go of his or her old self.

Before anyone entered, I needed to sanctify and open the spiral by walking to its center and then repeating my steps to leave it empowered and blessed. As I stood at the entrance, I could feel that this was an extremely powerful death spiral, possibly due to the thunderstorm. As I took my first step into the spiral, my last fully conscious thought was, "My spirit song's coming."[355]

And with that, my left foot stomped the ground inside the spiral. As my right leg caught up with my left, my spirit song sprang from my lips. I began walking the spiral with serpentine movements of my body. Sherry later related to me that the response from our apprentices was immediate: fear and wonder became etched on their faces. It was so intense that a few apprentices chose not to participate, one being a person that had been raised in a strong Catholic household and had been an altar boy.

Angels

*Every blade of grass has its angel that bends over it and
whispers, "Grow, grow."*

– Talmud

After the death spiral, the apprentices fashioned images out of wood of
one of their fears. The fear was to be minor, one that they could let go of in
the night's exercise. Darkness came around nine o'clock when I lit the fire to
begin the experiential exercise. Everyone sat on the ground in a semicircle
with the fire in the center and the west direction open so that each apprentice
could approach the fire from the west. Symbolically, this is the black direction
of fear, but also the direction of rebirth.

One after another, the apprentices approached the fire and laid the
symbolic image of their fear before them. When they were ready, they fought
their fear with the wooden sword and then tossed the remains into the fire.

Whether it was tiredness or the effects of the death spiral, the apprentices
only halfheartedly fought their fear. When all were finished, I looked around
the semicircle. Each apprentice's head hung low, staring into the fire. It was
evident they knew they had listlessly and with little heart fought their fear.
A few were accomplished martial artists. How was I going to tell them that
they blew it? They had squandered an awesome opportunity to release one of
their fears. With these thoughts going through my mind, I decided to stand
and talk more philosophically about releasing fear rather than giving them a
searing commentary along the lines of, "You blew it."

I stood and began a more nurturing synopsis of the exercise. I'd only
uttered a few words before I felt my neck twitching and an icy-fire sensation
around my head. I recognized the feeling, the one I always get when there
are otherworldly energies around. But this time it was different, much more
intense and stranger. I looked behind me into the woods. Everyone else was
still seated on the ground, staring into the fire. No one else was looking up.

This was the night of the new moon, and the only light in the clearing was
cast by the small fire. The night before, while the apprentices were sitting alone

in the woods on their vision quest, I had stood in this very same spot observing the dark woods, listening and making sure that everyone was all right. When I had turned off my flashlight, I couldn't see more than a few feet in front of me. Therefore, I was stunned to see searing translucent lights illumine the forest.

"What? No." These two short thoughts coursed through my mind as I turned around to see if there was some light source coming from in front of me other than the small fire. I observed nothing that could explain what I had just seen. I turned around again in disbelief, to make sure I saw what I saw. This all took less than a minute.

"Please stand, and be quiet. We have visitors," I said as calmly as possible, all the while not knowing what I saw.

As Sherry stood next to me, looking at the lights, I leaned over and whispered into her ear, "What are they?"

Without hesitation she said, "Why, they're angels!"

And then I remembered my prayer for a sign of who I had been. It all made sense, but I never expected a sign like this. I hadn't told anyone about the content of my prayer, not even Sherry.

"A shooting star," someone said as we all looked up as it blazed across the night sky.

"A white dove," an apprentice exclaimed as it flew over our heads.

"Look at the stones of the death spiral," another said.

The stones had increased at least fivefold in size; some were now the size of boulders. But the most unusual thing was their greenish, otherworldly glow. Each was an emerald stone of celestial pulsing energy.

After this, no further words were spoken. Time seemed to be suspended as Sherry and I and our twelve apprentices witnessed in awe a massive pillar of light,[356] a living pillar of translucent-ethereal light (do endnote) a few feet off the ground, at least six feet wide and five or six times as tall. This light was in the north by the entrance to the death spiral, whitish and not of this world.

Suspended higher up were two other pillars of light, not quite as bright or as large. The legends tell that an archangel is always assisted by two helping angels. Many traditions believe that the north direction is symbolically the direction of the ancestors and heavenly, otherworldly beings, such as angels.

I don't know how long we'd been standing rapt in their presence when Sherry whispered to me, "We need to leave and go to bed now. There are only a few hours left until we have to get up and go bathing."

"You're right," I replied.

"It's only a few hours until we put you in the stream and bathe each of you," I said to the others quietly. "We all need to get some sleep, so please return to your tents; be respectful as you leave, and give prayers, blessings, and a thank-you for this experience."

Sherry and I were the last to leave and return to our shelter. She slept soundly for the few hours we had left, while I couldn't sleep. My mind was focused on the visitation, trying to figure out the identity of the archangel. The last little doubt of who I was had left my mind. I gave blessings for the answer to my prayer and for the sign of my past incarnation. Right before I was going to wake my wife to go bathing, I thought, "Will they figure it out, who I was? Will they figure out who Sherry was?"

The Picture

Summer turned into fall. I had finally solved the mystery of the identity of the archangel, one that was perfectly congruent with my past-life. The archangel was Mikaël, known to most as the Archangel Michael.[357] I had determined this through my research of the connection between myself and the archangel.

- Michael, angel of Israel and the light-bringer, was denominated by the Kabbalists and the Gnostics as "the Savior," the angel of the sun, and the angel of light.[358]

- The Archangel Michael's day is Sunday, and the astrological sign is Leo. The Visitation was on the first Sunday in August, *Lughnasadh*, Mikaël's (Celtic Lugh's) day of honoring.

- The visitation was on the night of the new moon, and I was born under a new moon, symbolic of the virgin. The full moon symbolizes the mother. Additionally, both Sherry and I were born under the sign Virgo – the virgin.[359] It is interesting to note that Sher's and my original death and rebirth ceremony of bathing, performed by Vince Stogan, wherein we emerged from waters of the Great Mother, was a "virgin birth" for both of us as explained in our section on bathing. Additionally, on the morning of my birth in late August, the sun was in Virgo in the 11th house. In the twelfth house I have the new moon at 8 degrees 51' Libra, symbolically, the new moon lies under the feet of the Virgin. Furthermore, on top of the Virgin's head, I have Mercury in Leo in the 11th house, Pluto in Leo in the tenth, and Saturn in Leo, also in the tenth house. These three stars/planets plus the nine stars of Leo symbolize a crown of twelve stars.

- Michael is the fiery manifestation in the burning bush (Exod. 2:5).[360] The angelic fire and light (spirit) interpenetrated with the bush (matter). This is the earliest known biblical reference to radical nondualistic interpenetration.

- Michael is the angel of sanctification and is recorded in the Talmud as the prince of water. My wife and I are two of the few Caucasians who carry on the sanctification practice of bathing.

- Michael is the warrior archangel, captain of the heavenly hosts, and the guardian of the mysteries. I've spent fifty years in the mystical and practical exploration of the martial arts.

- The archangel is the celestial savior and purveyor of divine justice signified by the imagery of Mikaël holding the scales of justice. Libra's symbology is the scales of justice, and I was born with seven Libra energies, all within the first and twelfth house. Furthermore, I was born in the year of the Chinese Fire Dog, which is linked with Libra and represents justice and equality.

- Michael is the guardian of labyrinths (death spirals included), and the organizer of Earth energies. The Visitation was in the North, next to the entrance into the death spiral, which faces East. According to René Guénon, "the 'gateway of the gods' is at the North and turned towards the East which is always considered as the side of light and of life."[361]

- Michael has always been connected with wind, water, and lightning—the storm (my Maya birth-day sign is storm). He oversees nature, rain, snow, thunder, lightning, wind, and clouds. He represents the ability to conquer or over-come any obstacle and the struggles of life. And according to various prophecies, great events are often heralded by unusual weather conditions. The storm before the visitation was extremely unusual. In addition, Michael is identifiable as one of the Seraphim, who are "known as the 'fiery, flying serpents of lightning' who 'roar like lions.'"[362] This is exactly how I would describe the intensity of the lightning and the sound of the storm.

- Michael is known as the angelic psychopomp, the mediator between life and death, and the archangel of the shamans.

- Michael assists the messengers—the light-bringers of the different ages of humanity—and is the messenger of the prophets. He was the messenger angel to the prophet Noah. And, "in the Book of Revelation, [Michael] is to clear the way for the second coming."[363]

- Michael is the archangel of the incarnation and the Holy Grail.

- One most important point: Michael's present day battle is against the forces of greed that are corrupting the world. Due to greed and the need for power, wars are fought, people-oppressed, populations go hungry, and the Earth is polluted. In other words, Michael is in opposition to the liar, who is the lover of self and praise, the Antichrist.

- Finally, "it is foretold in Daniel that when the world is once again in real trouble, Michael will reappear. Some religious scholars claim that this century is the one in which he will reveal himself once again."[364]

On an October afternoon of the same year, one of our apprentices contacted me. "JC, you'll never guess what I have," he said in an excited tone. "While you were finishing the late-afternoon building of the spiral, I took a picture of you in the center of it. When I got home, I just threw the camera into my truck. Last week, I finally got around to getting the pictures developed. I knew something was up when the photo shop lady said, 'One of your pictures has caused quite a stir.'

Photo Jim Kalnins taken during the completion of building the Death Spiral.

"Guess what?" he continued. "I have a daylight photograph of the archangel and the two assisting angels. They were observing us building the spiral, and no one ever suspected!"

The picture is sacred and precious. It revealed a very faint image of what looks like the shape of a sword (a sword of light) or an elongated star pointing to the heavens. This dim image is within the center of the reflected light. This is the picture above and at the beginning of this story.[365]

"Just a little note to say thank you so much for all you have done for the two of us. God has given you many gifts. But now you have Gods, Angels, and with them the chance to fly to higher places. So, fly high . . . " – M and S, two of the twelve who witnessed the Visitation

One final note. Three months before the Visitation, we far traveled to Cornwall, the sacred land of King Arthur and Michael:

Both are different versions of Sun-Gods, ruling the high places and the destiny of the land. Both are to return, victorious, at the time of the second coming. Michael, leader of the heavenly hosts, according to the apocryphal message in the Book of Enoch, 20.55: "holds the secrets of the mighty Word by which God created heaven and Earth."[366] That Word is Love.[367]

August 1998

We returned one year later to the sacred place of the Visitation. The owner of the land didn't want the Visitation publicized, afraid masses of people would want to visit the angelic site. Consequently, few people knew about this earth-shattering event that had, and still has, the potential to undermine the foundation of Christianity given the twelve who witnessed the phenomenon offered in answer to my prayer to know my past lifetime.

To honor the Visitation, a statue of Mikaël was placed in the North at the entrance to the death spiral where the largest pillar of light had appeared. In front of this statue, I would pierce the dragon with the sword of Mikaël. As noted above, the archangel is known as the dragon-slayer. Additionally as a metaphoric feathered serpent, Mikaël symbolizes the joining of the energies of the heaven and Earth. As the archangel of the sun, he uses his sword as a channel of heavenly energy, setting it into the Earth and connecting both – a blending of heaven and Earth. By piercing the serpent with his sword, he releases the Earth energies allowing both energies to flow together.

The time had come for me to pierce the dragon energy of the Earth as an honoring of the Visitation. Silence enveloped us all as nature held its breath. With our apprentices in a semicircle behind Sher and me, I lifted my large, sacred, angelic doubled-edged sword to the heavens as I prayed and entered the blended state of heaven and Earth. With full nonattached will to honor the Visitation, I drove Mikaël's sword into the dragon (Earth) with the power of my spirit. When I pierced the ground with my sword, one of our apprentices became agitated as she and others actually saw the ground undulate as if a serpent had been stabbed. The dragon had been transmuted and the Visitation honored. As we all experienced that moment of love and power, I could feel the energies pulsating through my sword. Silently, I thanked all things of Creation for the blessed experience of the Visitation, a confirmation and proof of reincarnation.

Summary

Is it so bad, then, to be misunderstood? Pythagoras was misunderstood, and Socrates, and Jesus, and Luther, and Copernicus, and Galileo, and Newton,

*and every pure and wise spirit that ever took flesh. To be great is to be
misunderstood.*

– Ralph Waldo Emerson

After twenty-two years, of the twelve students who were present at this
visitation, only one remains as our apprentice. The reason the eleven apprentices left our circle is a reflection of the downside to this experience. It was, and
still is, not understood as it was so far outside the normal dualistic consciousness of people that the truth is veiled from their minds. Even for those who
were physically there and experienced the presence of the angels with all their
senses, most still could not rationalize the event within their consciousness or
their basic beliefs, especially ingrained Catholic beliefs. The following are the
words written three months later by one Catholic of the twelve:

> I have been raised to believe in angels. When I was
> young, I was filled with the tales of Fatima and Lourdes. On
> several occasions I traveled to St. Anne de Beaupre and St.
> Joseph's Oratory to see for myself the evidence of miracles
> that had occurred there. As a child in parochial school, I was
> constantly reminded that I had the good fortune to have a
> guardian angel, and frequently prayed that I would be kept
> safe from the potential terrors of the world, both seen and
> unseen.
>
> There, in the forest, on the fringe of the field, stood
> several columns of bright light. There were rectangular in
> nature, clearly divided by space between them. One column
> appeared larger and brighter than the others. Its luminosity
> was curious to me. I stepped back and tried to find a light
> source, a reason for its existence. I knew that there was no
> source of backlight, and it was quickly apparent to me that
> the spotlight on the garage was too diffused by the trees to
> account for this effect.
>
> We decided to sit up for a while under the shelter. Pete
> was visibly moved by the experience; Jim L. was confounded,

and I wanted to go to bed. I walked out from the shelter, towards the spiral, and stopped dead in my tracks. The outer perimeter of the spiral had changed. The stones, which I had helped to place, had grown! They had taken on a soft glow; they seemed to pulse in place. The stones that I had placed, which were about hand-sized, now seemed to be boulder sized!

I have thought about this night for a long time. In fact, I think about it frequently. Did I see angels? I still don't know. Perhaps my mind, filled with expectations of what angelic visitations should be, refused to believe. I did see the lights, and I acknowledge that there is no physical reason for their existence. I did not experience any profound feelings, any state of grace that I have always assumed would accompany an angelic experience.

For the religiously indoctrinated, especially Catholics,[368] even with total sensory awareness when in the presence of the Otherworld, their expectation of an angelic visitation is not in tune with the actual reality of the Visitation. This is specifically true when a person has swallowed the doctrine of grace[369] as stated above. But what is the meaning of a "state of grace?" According to the Catholic dictionary, it is the "condition of a person who is free from mortal sin and pleasing to God. It is the state of being in God's friendship and the necessary condition of the soul at death in order to attain heaven."[370] My question is, "How would you know in the moment if there is a "state of grace?" Do you hear harps, angelic singing, does God's voice boom from heaven saying, "Hey, you are my friend and are pleasing to me." Of course, I'm being facetious, but only to an extent. We can see how deep the influence of dogmatic brainwashing extends. So sad that indoctrinated people are not able to trust their senses or common sense over deeply imbedded religious beliefs.

Furthermore, not only for the religious, but for the majority of people, it would have seemed impossibility with no precedent for such an unbelievable event. How could it be true, as there was no such physical manifestation or event ever recorded in the Hebrew Bible, the Christian Bible, or the Koran? Of course, there were accounts of angelic visitations or interactions, sometimes in visions and other times with angels appearing as men. But none had twelve witnesses, as we had, or the appearance of other physical signs: a dove, which has symbolized the Holy Spirit as well as the bird of Venus; a falling star; and ceremonial stones that increased at least fivefold in size and glowed with a greenish aura. Preceding this visitation, we also witnessed an otherworldly thunder-and-lightning storm, which purified the land – a reflection of my Maya Day sign: Storm, and that fact that and great events are often heralded by unusual weather conditions.

And very importantly, none of the accounts in the Bible were ever written down by the people who experienced them. All the accounts of angelic events in the Hebrew Tanakh were written down by priestly scribes after having been orally passed down for centuries.

The following are a few of the recorded biblical angelic events:[371]

- Abraham, when he was willing to offer his only son as a sacrifice

  (Genesis 22:11-12, 15-18).

- Jacob, after his famous dream of a stairway to heaven (Genesis 28:12;

  31:11; 32:1-2).

- Joshua, before the battle of Jericho (Joshua 5:13-15).

Furthermore, from my experience, knowledge, and knowing, I would have to state that of all the stories recorded in the holy books, the one that holds the most truth in revealing an angelic or divine encounter is that of Moses and the burning bush. As brightness is a common description of divine beings throughout the ancient world, they are often described as luminous or fiery. Two factors point to this truth.

- The image within the bush was one of fire and light. It was not in human form. The angelic fire and light (spirit) inter-penetrated with the bush (matter). This is the earliest known biblical reference to radical nondualistic interpenetration (my basic belief and the belief of Divine Humanity). For Moses this was not a dream or vision, but a physical-sensory, firsthand experience.

- I have personally experienced firsthand radical nondualistic interpenetration with my descending-spirit experience. Another revealing truth was Jesus's descending-spirit experience while bathing in the Jordan. The descent of the dove into Jesus, symbolic of the Holy Spirit, was a visual reference to radical nondualism – spirit interpenetrating matter, the body of Jesus, through his head. This was his awakening and the formal beginning of his quest to bring his message of the divine in all things to all people of the world. In reality, extraordinary spiritual and religious experiences are difficult to metaphorically "swallow" for the average person.

Truth

Truth is an interesting concept to consider. What is truth? Is there a definition of truth that provides us with more insight than, "Truth is an individual perspective?" I believe so. The Nahua (Aztecs) concept of truth provides more insight into the meaning and essence of it. Truth means "well-rootedness."

"What an entity is rooted in that makes it well-rooted is *teotl*,[372] which is ultimate reality and a continual active process. Truth is understood primarily in terms of its support of instances of knowledge, where knowledge specifically has to do with skill or performance. Aztec philosophy considers human beings, in addition to activities, objects, and statements, as truth bearers."[373]

To clarify, according to James Maffie in *Aztec Philosophy*, "Truth is a way of being and doing; a way of living, conducting one's life, and so forth."[374] He goes on to state "that which is well-rooted, well-ordered, and well-balanced more fully disclose (sic) the nature of teotl. In what sense, exactly, does it do this? I submit it does so by disclosing teotl's diachronic balancing, ordering, and unifying of complementary polarities, such as order and disorder, male and female, and fire and water."[375]

According to the Nahua, I'm a truth bearer. Difficult to be a truth bearer, in one sense, considering the consistent deceptiveness and the lies of people in power, including the U.S. President. But on the other hand, it is easy for me, as seeking and speaking truth is part of my soul. So, what truths do the Visitation reveal?

The Effect of the Visitation on Spiritual, Philosophical or Religious Knowledge

Everyone who is seriously involved in the pursuit of science becomes convinced that a spirit is manifest in the laws of the universe – a spirit vastly superior to that of men."

– Albert Einstein.

The knowledge revealed by the Visitation is very important as it reveals the truth of various spiritual/religious mysteries such as reincarnation. The visitation was a sensory, materialistic, firsthand experience witnessed by twelve apprentices and my wife and me. In other words, we experienced something that humans can only believe in, not know. The majority of humanity's spiritual, philosophical, or religious belief is based on secondhand, thirdhand, and so forth knowledge, either written or oral, which has come from others who have also based their belief on secondhand, thirdhand, and further-removed oral or written knowledge.

This miraculous happening opened the gateway to knowing certain truths concerning spiritual, philosophical, or religious beliefs. I will attempt to lay them out as best as I can. One further note: I believe that the visitation provides Occam's-razor validation for some aspects of physicist David Bohm's theories.

There was a "Quantum Shift in 1997"[376]

Knowledge: The Interconnection and Interpenetration of Consciousness throughout the Seen and Unseen Universe.

- David Bohm theorized as to the reality of the universe, which he named the implicate order – the hidden aspect of the universe. "The theory of the implicate order contains an ultra-holistic cosmic view; it connects everything with everything else. In principle, any individual element could reveal 'detailed information about every other element in the universe.' The central underlying theme of Bohm's theory is the 'unbroken wholeness of the totality of existence as an undivided flowing movement without borders.'"[377] In other words, "within the implicate order everything is connected; and, in theory, any individual element could reveal information about every other element in the universe."[378]

- Bohm named the known or visible universe or manifest world the explicate order. In the implicate order, "everything is enfolded into everything. This is in contrast to the explicate order where things are unfolded."[379]

- The Visitation provides proof of Bohm's theory, as the physical appearance of the angels as immense pillars of light was due to my prayer. For the angels to respond while in the implicate order, they would have to have received the information from me in the explicate order.[380]

- After the intense, unusual storm, they were present in the afternoon but hidden[381] while they were still in a layer of the implicate order. It was only in the evening that they became visible to us in the explicate order. In Bohm's terms, they unfolded.

Knowledge: Divine Light/Spark Within

- The three immense pillars of light reflect Michael's name. The name Michael is Hebrew for "likeness of God." His name reflects Divine Light to which our own divine spark is akin.

- Most assuredly, Mikael is our guide. He assists us in overcoming ignorance, including the ignorance of our divine origin, our root. Ignorance derives from stupidity. The trademarks of stupidity are ignorance, overall dullness of spirit, a naive incompetence, fear and arrogance. Arrogance shows up as many secondary evils, including greed, pride, vanity, lying and false pretenses, incompetence, savagery, cold hard-heartedness, and the desire to stay ignorant.[382]

Knowledge: Reincarnation

- Based on what I knew within my heart and my vision as the morning star, I prayed for a sign to indicate my identity in a past incarnation: "Let them see a sign knowing that I was [name stated]." I mentioned the name as people would recognize it today. So that there is no confusion, the name I stated in my prayer was not Quetzalcóatl, but it seems most assured that *one* of my past incarnations was the human named, Topiltzin Quetzalcóatl – the Morning Star.

And then this from Joseph Campbell:

"Just as in the legend of Christ and the Virgin to whose mystery the cathedrals arose, so also in the legends to which the temple gongs are resounding, there is signified the knowledge of a seed or part within ourselves and all things that is antecedent to time and space, part and parcel of eternity, and which, like the everlasting light that in the sun, the moon, and the morning star seems to rise and set according to laws, never dies but is ever renewed. Begotten as it were of fire and wind, born as it were of water and Earth, it is what lives in all lives, but also antecedes and survives them.

"All accounts agree, therefore, that the vanished Quetzalcóatl is to return. From the shining East he will one day arise with a feathered, fair-faced retinue, to resume his reign and the guardianship of his people. For those same irreversible laws of time that brought to pass the dissolution of his glorious palace-city Tollan must also inevitably bring about its restoration."[383]

The angels who visited, as well as other signs in response to my prayer, indicate that I was alive before in a different body, place, and time. I am no different from anyone else. If I have had a past life/lives, everyone else has had a past life/lives. This is proof—as far as we can take it, considering we are attempting to prove the unprovable mysteries of life and creation—that our lives on Earth are not a one-shot deal with heaven, hell, or oblivion all that waits for us. I make this statement from direct experience, not faith. Truth will set you free.

Our life is an ongoing death-and-rebirth evolution of our souls – our golden DNA, our divine spark, our starlight.

Knowledge of Reincarnation: Its Impact on Prejudice and the Earth

- Since most people have had numerous past lives, it is common sense that we have all been different races from different cultures. In other words, a present-day Neo-Nazi, KKK member, or even Donald Trump likely were not white in some of their other lifetimes. I am not talking about our human DNA but our soul's heavenly golden DNA of the total accumulation of past lives.[384] Even with this knowledge people will still be prejudiced, but possibly a seed will be planted that will bear fruit in the future.

- Understanding that we will all reincarnate, we need to embrace an ancient Iroquois philosophy, The Seventh Generation Principle: "In every deliberation, we must consider the impact of our decisions on the next seven generations." The core of this philosophy holds that the decisions we make today should result in a sustainable, green world seven generations (a generation equals one hundred years) into the future.

Knowledge: the Most Obvious

- Sentient beings, which humanity has named angels ("A rose by any other name would smell as sweet."[385]), physically exist even though they are usually hidden from sight while they remain in Bohm's implicate order. This leads to a conclusion that other sentient beings exist, such as faeries and, in Iceland, the hidden ones. But once again they are in the implicate order and hidden from our senses and sight.

Knowledge: Silence

- With the Visitation came silence, or what one apprentice referred to as the cone of silence. There were no summer sounds of nature, only silence. I'm still attempting to figure this one out. Possibly, silence is a key element in spiritual growth. But then again, given that I don't understanding or even know the natural laws of the Otherworld, it could have been some type of barrier, a dome possibly, that separated our sacred, divine space from mundane earthly space, considering the sense of prevailing timelessness.

Knowledge: Sacred Power of Stones

- The stones of the death spiral increased at least fivefold in size during the Visitation, some to the size of boulders. But the most unusual thing was the greenish, otherworldly glow that surrounded each. Green is the middle of the light spectrum and esoterically connected to the heart, the Heart *Chakra*'s color being green. Green is the color of truth and of Venus, the morning/evening star. Evergreen is the color assigned to ever-living and eternal truth. Biblically, green is symbolic of resurrection and immortality.[386]

The purification and silence seem to suggest that the known laws of physics were suspended as the phenomena of the Visitation revealed the Otherworld and our world visually and with all our senses as one world.

Philosophically, due to the greenish glow of the stones, the space we occupied for that moment in time could be considered the Heart of the Earth. You may come to your own conclusions on this.

- All things in the seen and unseen world are sentient (conscious). Stones are known to hold memories and prove of their sentience through their response to the presence of Otherworldly sentient beings.

- Proof of being in the presence of the heavenly or divine power of the three pillars of light is reflected in the growth of the stones into boulders from ones that you could hold in one or two hands. Indigenous cultures believe in the spiritual power of stones. The Japanese believe that sacred power is often manifested within a sealed vessel that may grow. The vessels that contain this sacred power are known as *utsubo*. The stone is an *utsubo* vessel. It contains a sacred force that may grow under the right circumstances. The Japanese national anthem contains these words addressed to the emperor: "May your reign last for thousands of years until pebbles have become moss-covered rocks." Very interesting that they refer to the rocks as moss-covered. In other words, green, just as the stones of the spiral had a greenish glow to them!

Knowledge: Change of Ages

- As with all extraordinary events like the Visitation, many times its connecting threads are not readily apparent, observed, or considered. What thread connected to the Visitation could be easily missed? Three: the prophet Noah; the comet Hale- Bopp; and the Archangel Mikaël. All three together point to one thing – a change of ages.

As I have already stated, Mikaël was the messenger angel to the prophet Noah and has assisted all the other prophets since that time. The last time Hale-Bopp visited the Earth was during the time of Noah. And we know the myths about

Noah surviving the flood. This Earth-wide deluge would have been the event that ended one age and birthed the beginning of the next age. Could this age have been our current one, the Fifth Sun? Basically, the Fifth Sun corresponds to the Western Ages of Ares and Pisces.

According to the Mesoamericans, the Fourth Sun, known as the "four-water" sun, was governed by the goddess Chalchihuitlicue, sister and wife of Tlaloc. The destruction of that age came in the form of torrential rains. In other words, a flood. The myth of an Earth-changing flood is recorded in various myths across the world, including the Pacific Northwest First People.

Dating the flood myth and the changes of ages is problematic, as any written sources originated from oral histories. Even archeological knowledge may not give us a true picture of the past. But the appearance of the comet Hale-Bopp and, due to my prayer, the appearance of Archangel Mikaël in 1997 could possibly point to a period in the transition from the Fifth Sun to the Sixth Sun. The Sixth Sun would be the Ages of Aquarius and Capricorn.

And then there was the spirit man of Teotihuacán identifying me as Quetzalcóatl – the Sixth Sun. Let's not forget that Teotihuacán was the birthplace of the Fifth Sun and the home of the prophet Quetzalcóatl. These are interesting and mythic times we live in.

A final point: the last time comet Hale-Bopp, the prophet[387] Noah, and Mikaël appeared together, there was a change of ages. This time, something more profound is happening, with their appearance connected to the precession cycle of 26,000 years. Precession is caused by the gravitational pull of the sun and the moon on the Earth. One great cycle is 26,000 years. We are not just at the change of ages, but at the end of the great cycle of ages that spanned

26,000 years. With endings there are beginnings. And the beginning of the next 26,000-year cycle has been prophesied as the Golden Age, known by many as the Age of Aquarius, and to the Mesoamericans – the Sixth Sun.

50 – 30 – 20
Love – Magic – Light

. . . .

Magic is the unveiling of the Mysteries.

THE YEAR 2017 WAS VERY SPECIAL FOR SHER AND ME. THE
month of August 2017 marked: our fiftieth wedding anniversary – Love:
thirty years since the descending spirit exorcism on Kōyasan, Japan, and
our first fire ceremony on the beaches of the Yucatan during the Harmonic
Convergence – Magic; and twenty years since the Visitation of the Archangel
Mikaël and two Assisting Angels – Light.

To celebrate and honor these events, we conducted an invitational journey
to Cornwall, England, at the end of August. Love, magic, and light not only
reflect our years together but are the three essentials of marriage.

Marriage is a partnership of love where the bonds of marriage are
strengthened by support (being there for each other), compassion, loving
kindness, and forgiveness. These are essential to life, an authentic life of love
and personal power. Magic is not only the extraordinary but ordinary acts
of being in each other's presence while gazing at the beauty and splendor of
a sunrise or a full moon in the tapestry of a starlit night tapestry. Light is the
laughter of a loved one; the eyes of a baby; the awakening of the Earth on a
new day of mystery and, possibly, toil.

On another note, another fiftieth anniversary has a significant but sad
meaning for me. Che Guevara was murdered by the CIA on October 9, 1967.
Oddly enough, our daughter was born on October 9th. According to *The*

Nation magazine, "Dead now for 50 years, Che wasn't much older than those of us who were radicalized in the 1960s, and he was formed by conditions not altogether different than those that affected us. To us, Che was a symbol of boldness, intelligence, internationalism, self-sacrifice, solidarity and, as he said, 'at the risk of appearing ridiculous,' love. Che rejected personal gain and privilege for the leaders in a struggle for a fair and just society; he lived as he asked others to live.

"It's been said that Che was a citizen of the world. Perhaps more accurately, Che was a citizen of a world that did not yet exist."[388]

St. Nectan's Kieve and Waterfall

I write this in the seventy-first year of my birth as I view Glastonbury Tor and the Tower of Mikaël and Bride. Seventeen years have passed since we last set foot in Glastonbury and in the mystical and magical land of Cornwall, the birthplace of Arthur, the once and future king. On the surface in Tintagel, Cornwall, it seemed as if nothing had changed aside from the number of Brits on holiday. But as we all know, there may be more than what meets the eye. And so it was with one of the most sacred sites in this part of Britain – St. Nectan's Kieve a few miles outside of Tintagel.

In our past journeys to Cornwall, we would always begin our quest in mystical Rocky Valley at St. Nectan's Kieve and Waterfall. The Kieve has been a place of reverence, worship and healing since pre-Christian times. People of many faiths have walked the ancient route to the waterfall to bathe in its mysterious and therapeutic atmosphere. St. Nectan's wooded glen and water-fall are magical and maintain an atmosphere of Celtic mystery and reverence. The Celts saw the natural stone *kieve* made by the waterfall as a cauldron of knowledge, healing and regeneration. In legend, the knights of King Arthur began their Grail quest from St. Nectan's Glen.

Furthermore, it "is one of the most strangely beautiful and powerful of all Cornish sites. Everyone who visits it for the first time is invariably awed into silence as they stand at the bottom of the tree-covered gorge, looking up at a stunning sight. The waters of the River Trevillet pour over a rocky cleft to tumble in a spray of silver mist into a great rock bowl, or *kieve* in Cornish, whose sides have been smoothed by the power of the water. This is dramatic enough, but then the water brims through a large hole in the rock, just wide enough for someone to climb through."[389]

Expecting to renew our marriage vows in front of the great rock chalice where we had first heard the spiritual vows of our apprentices twenty years past, the change we discovered, wrought by greed, was heartbreaking. This sacred cascading waterfall, a haven of peace, a place of tranquility, had been desecrated and destroyed. And of course, not by nature but by greed-filled humans. The waterfall was not physically destroyed but its spirit of sacredness and the freedom to visit it had been obliterated.

At the head of the waterfall on such sacred and special land now stood a blight on the spirit of the place – a commercial gift shop, café, and gallery. To reach the bottom of the waterfall where vows and prayers were once voiced, we needed to pass through the gift shop and pay our entrance fee. Money given to enter nature's church. But the desecration didn't end once we passed by the materialistic gatekeeper.

The original path to the waterfall was simple and impacted the Earth only very slightly. Now a wooden-railed sharply serpentine long walkway takes you down to the base of the waterfall. People simply talk too much, chatter that shatters the power of nature's moment. With this much easier path to the basin at the base of the waterfall and the brainwashing of marketing, the once-magical site was guaranteed to be crowded with selfie-taking, ever-talking people. We chose not to enter.

Please do not misunderstand about the rampant desecration of sacred sites. The sacred spirit power of nature and the great Mother has not left the sites no matter the actions, thoughts, and words of unevolved materialistic humans. The power is asleep, the land is asleep, Arthur is asleep, all to be awakened and to return at the proper time. All are the sleeping beauty who will be awakened by the "kiss of love." The once and future king must wake, the question needs to be asked, and the wounded wasteland needs to be healed.

Many myths and legends are teaching sagas based on real events. The mythic aspect is nothing more than the usage of imagery and wording revealing the Otherworld. We are in a transition, a change of ages; this is a mythic time. What myths and legends will be written?

The legendary birth of Arthur, the Bear King and Solar Hero, may mythically symbolized the transition from the Age of the Dragon to the Age of the Bear. According to Paul Broadhurst, "We can begin to see how the story of Arthur's birth at Tintagel is an ancestral memory of the changing ages of humanity's occupation of the planet. The legend of Uther Pendragon shape-shifting so that he conceives King Arthur on Tintagel Island, when stripped of its later accretions, is surely a reference to the gradual shifting of the Pole Star at the centre of the Round Table, which may have first been observed by astronomer priests who used the Island as a polar observatory. Around 2500 B.C.E. the apparent centre of the universe was located in Draco, the constellation of the Dragon, marked by Thuban or Alpha Draconis, its main star, which due to the cosmology of earthly precession slowly changed and transformed into the Bear. So Arthur the Bear King who rules the Round Table is born of the Pendragon – the Dragon's Head who presided over the age when these legends were first formulated. Arthurian mythology is in many ways the story of the changing ages of the evolution of the Earth, and humanity's role in it."[390]

At the present we are in the Age of the Fish (Pisces) in transition to the Age of the Water-Bearer (Aquarius), which is determined by the precession (movement) of the equinoxes and the shift of the Polar Star. Each age lasts approximately 2,150 years and a full cycle of twelve ages equates to a "great year" of approximately 26,000 years. The Age of the Fish completes a great-year cycle with the Age of Aquarius, the Water-Bearer, the foretold Golden Age beginning the next 26,000 year cycle.

The symbolism of Aquarius is important. During each age, humanity learns the lessons of each zodiacal influence. As the next stage in humanity's evolution, Aquarius is the archetype of the universal mystic, the seeker of truth, and is depicted as a water-bearing angel—an immortal messenger—pouring from an urn that is open at both ends. Its imagery signifies our human capacity to become one with the divine consciousness of the universe. It takes us beyond the egocentricity of the previous ages and transports us to a oneness of being where we may directly access heavenly knowledge. It will be an age of individualized religion, not dogmatic, organized religion, and a time to accept our divine sides as well as our human ones; a time to acknowledge our connectedness, not separateness, to all of creation. Archangel Mikaël is said to be the angel guiding this time of transformation from the Age of Pisces to the Golden Age, known to the Mesoamericans as the Sixth Sun: the Age of Aquarius.

Our lodging in Tintagel was at the Bossiney House Hotel, which we recommend if you are ever in Tintagel. We'd been drawn to Cornwall and Tintagel twenty years previous, a few months before the Visitation of the Archangel Mikaël and two assisting angels. We visited Cornwall and Tintagel in April of 1997, and returned with a group at the end of May.

After our explorations in April, we reconnected with the friends we'd meant at the Ruthin Castle Medieval Banquet in 1981. The four of us then journeyed to Majorca off the coast of Spain. I only note this as, during our stay on the island, I ran out to a high point of land where you could see an awesome panorama of the island plus the harbor. The moment I looked back towards the harbor, I knew. The view triggered a past-life soul memory: I had once sailed into this harbor.

Celebration of our 50th Wedding Anniversary

The apprentices who journeyed with us to celebrate 50 – 30 – 20 designed our renewal wedding ceremony (an awesome and perfect gift to Sher and me). The ceremonial location was awe inspiring: the Bossiney headland cliffs overlooking the sea, named Willapark. In the distance, sat Tintagel Island, the Island of the Kings. In Cornish *willapark* means "enclosure with a view." Supposedly during the Iron Age, there was a cliff castle on this land overlooking the sea, the west, and the setting sun with ramparts built across the neck of the headland to seal it from the mainland. And in the sea off the northern side of Willapark stands The Sisters, two gigantic rocks that guard this sacred land as sea-born sentinels and a portal to the Otherworld.

Photo Mark Speranza

Our renewal ceremony was held late in the afternoon near sunset. After a procession from the Bossiney House, we gathered on the edge of the cliff to the right of the Sisters. Peace and beauty enfolded us with the energy and sounds of this coastal paradise. Our eyes beheld grandeur. The roof of our cathedral was the crystal-clear sky above and the walls the four winds of the Earth. Sher and I were far from wealthy, but no amount of money could have bought a more profound, sacred, and beautiful setting. The Earth in purity, scent of eternity. There at that moment was earthly paradise – our hearts were happy and our minds at peace. It was thus that *"zum raum wird hier die zeit"* (time here turns into space)[391] words were spoken, some funny and in jest but mostly, out of love and respect. One of our apprentices who had brought his guitar from across the sea serenaded us with a beautiful song of love. Our hands were bound together as our hearts were fifty years before, rings exchanged, honey-bread-salt graced our lips, and the gift of the bees, mead, was shared.

As the sun slowly slipped into the ocean, we departed the sacred site with the memory of Love, Magic, and Light within each of our hearts. The only thing that was missing was the presence of our two children, who due to various circumstances could not journey with us to England – a sadness held within our love.

Photo Mark Speranza

Our last few days we spent outside of Glastonbury at the Crossways Hotel, another lodging we would highly recommend. Our last day with our apprentices was Sunday, August 27, on the Tor—known to some as The Michael Tor—where Sher and I had begun our journey of far traveling thirty-six years before. In 1981, it was only the sheep, Sher and I on the Tor, a magical time and place that foreshadowed our life to be.

In 2017, with the sun beating down (it was unusually hot), we were hardly alone. Dozens and dozens of people were coming and going, but it was a fitting completion for our journey of love-magic-light. We toasted the completion of the journey by Mikaël's Tower and honored the title of our memoirs with, of course, tequila and chocolate.

But for ourselves, we were not yet complete. The friends we'd met at Ruthin Castle thirty-six years before, and who went with us to Majorca, arranged to meet us in Glastonbury on my birthday. And our meeting place for lunch? The George and Pilgrims Hotel, where Sher and I had seen a ghostly monk, the full mystical circle of this world and the Otherworld. The potential for magic in life is boundless. What may the next fifty years hold for us?

Life Eternal

Once again our earthly journey,
Separating from the loving womb of mother.
We take our first breath of life, of God's breath,
And we remember
The love and purity of the heavens,
The perfection and oneness of all.
With our cry our journey of life,
Of life's joys and struggles, begins,
And remembrance slowly fades
But is never totally gone.
Throughout the joys and struggles,
The joys of family and friends,
Of pets, music, and the delights of life,
There are the struggles.
Ones that may strengthen our spirit,
The turbulence of life, the cares and sorrows
That hang heavy over our heart,
the grief and sorrow of death.
But we remember at certain times
the love and perfection,
Times when we gaze into the eyes of loved ones,
The closeness of family and friends,
The sounds of laughter, the playful glee of children, the innocence of a baby.
Freshly falling snow may bring remembrance,
As may the first blossom of spring,
A visit by hummingbird, the beauty of a butterfly,
The first star of night,
The mystery and beauty of nature.
Our remembrance is of our heart and soul,
Of the starlight eternal.
Remember, remember, remember.
Then it is time, the heavens call.

A time to return,
Return to the purity of heavenly love,
To the perfection and oneness of heaven.
In the heavens a star shines brighter.
To the ones we leave behind,
Know that you are loved,
And know you are never alone.

– JC, 2014

APPENDIX

. . . .

A Confused Mind or a Clear Mind

The Ocean Waves Beckon us to Know the Depths of the Sea

Divine Humanity is a spiritual and religious philosophy[392] based on radical nonduality—where spirit and matter mutually permeate, with no separation between the seen and unseen worlds or between mind and body—in which all things have consciousness and are connected in a web of love.[393] This philosophy is substantiated by the work of the physicist David Bohm (1917 – 1992) a colleague of Albert Einstein.

Additionally, our firsthand experiences of the Otherworld have been of the type that William James documented in *The Varieties of Religious Experience*. In this classic study, he "finds the origin of belief in an 'unseen' world in the experience of 'religious geniuses' who experience firsthand the realities of which religion speaks, and carefully distinguishes this primal experience from what he calls 'secondhand' religion, the beliefs that people acquire through tradition."[394]

Superimplicate, Implicate and Explicate Orders of the Universe

Physicist David Bohm theorized a different view of the universe than the one that is commonly accepted by science. Briefly, he theorized a model of wholeness that constituted reality, which consisted of two orders: the explicate order and the implicate order. The explicate order is the manifest realm of the physical universe in space and time. The other order, implicate, is the unmanifested, unseen (hidden) universe that has an unknown number of layers. The primary universe is not the explicate order but the implicate order. Additionally, he conceived of a 'deeper' hidden unmanifest layer of the implicate order, which he named the superimplicate order – the eternal order. Bohm also used a comparable term for the implicate order: the holomovement. This indicated the implicate order was always in dynamic flux.

From his research and from his own intuitive side, Bohm concluded that the universe, seen and unseen, is an inseparable whole that is full of energy and contains an unknowable number of universes enfolded, intertwined and interpenetrated into each other.

Like Einstein, Bohm was not a narrow-focused physicist as he extended his theories outwardly to the fields of philosophy and ontology. His ontological ideas are well summarized in the introduction to a popular paper from his own hand:

> In my work in physics, which was originally aimed at understanding relativity and the quantum theory on a deeper basis common to both, I developed the notion on the enfolded or implicate order (Bohm, 1980). The essential feature of this idea was that the whole of the universe is in some way enfolded in everything and that each thing is enfolded in the whole. From this it follows that in some ways, and to a certain degree, everything enfolds or implicates everything. The basic proposal is that this enfoldment relationship is not merely passive or superficial. Rather it is active and essential to what each is. It follows that each thing

is internally related to the whole and therefore to everything else. The external relationships are then displayed in the unfolded or explicate order in which each thing is seen as separate and extended and related only externally to other things. The explicate order, which dominates everyday experience as well as classical physics, is however secondary in the sense that ultimately it flows out of the primary reality of the implicate order.

Since the implicate order is basically dynamic in nature, I called it the holomovement. All things found in the unfolded explicate order emerge from the holomovement in which they are enfolded as potentialities, and ultimately they fall back into it. They endure only for some time, and while they last, their existence is sustained in a constant process of unfoldment and reenfoldment that gives rise to the relatively stable and independent forms in which they appear in the explicate order."[395]

Bohm and Consciousness

Today's world is still based on Descartes' philosophy of the separation of body and mind – dualism.[396] Bohm, however, felt that Descartes was off the mark and that reality was simply composed of one energy – oneness not dualism. This would then indicate that mind and matter are united as one and are not separate entities as proposed by Descartes.

Bohm felt that this separation of mind and matter, as well as humanity only recognizing the explicate order and its illusion of separateness, had resulted in people's minds fragmenting into a reality of separateness that then dictated their thoughts, actions and behaviors:

A major problem of the world today, according to Bohm, is that our minds as well as society have become overly explicate, so to speak, or fragmented, in Bohm's terms. This happens when the order of our thoughts is projected onto reality, that is, when we think that the world actually has compartments and divisions that correspond to the concepts we use to grasp it. The remedy proposed against fragmentation is, to put it simply, getting in touch with the energy of the implicate order. This will dispel confusion and fragmentation, bring about clarity and help people realize their "true potential for participating harmoniously in universal creativity[.]"[397]

The writings on Bohm go on to express:

> Recommendations as to how to get out of fragmentation and restore wholeness may be thought of as general guidelines for human action. However, Bohm is extremely reluctant about calling fragmentation "bad" and wholeness "good," since he considers precisely this kind of division of the world into opposing categories the essence of the fragmentary approach. Thinking in terms of good and evil only propagates the antagonisms and conflicts between people and within the individual.
>
> Instead, he prefers to speak of the mind as being in a state of "confusion" or "clarity," respectively, the latter describing the state associated with direct insight and "serious attention." In another analogy, he speaks of the confused mind as missing the point and being "off the mark." In a conversation he remarks: "There are not two things, good and evil, but rather there is . . . attention which keeps you on the mark, or failure of attention which makes you go off."[398]

Interestingly, Bohm's solution to fragmentation mirrors to an extent Divine Humanity's concept of Awakening, Firsthand Experience and "Second Attention." The unawakened person views the world in separate and dualistic terms (good and evil, light and dark, male and female) where the seen and materialistic world are the primary aspects of life. Consciousness is based on a separation of subject and object. Contrary to this, the awakened person views the world as One and in non-dualistic terms that interpenetrate or mutually permeate. Awakening is not immediate but gradually occurs with the realization of the Oneness of subject and object.

First Attention/Second Attention

Our basic patterns of life are based on what I call "first attention," based on our dualistic consciousness. You may have heard the expression, "energy flows where attention goes." Repetitive energy flow, a constant focus of our mind and our thoughts, will establish our reality and our beliefs about life – about the Earth, nature, others, and ourselves. It will erect core beliefs about all kinds of things including life, death and religion. From these core beliefs, our rules of life, assumptions, and our attitudes will be formed.

Each of us is more of a product of our past than we even realize. Troubling behaviors become ignored or unconscious in our stress-filled, hectic, materialistic lives. In addition, these behaviors are connected to our basic rules of life or belief system. All are a result of our "first attention." This is where our patterns of life were formed growing up.

An example would be represented by a belief resulting from our "first attention" that made our mind view the glass as half-empty. Our "second attention," where we would focus on optimism and the positive potentialities of life, would then produce a belief where we would view the glass as half-full and not half-empty.

All our reality comes from our mind. First and foremost, we need to practice forgiveness and release the past's destructive emotional baggage of resentment, anger, guilt, fear, uncertainty and doubt. Then by transforming our "first attention" to a "second attention," we change our patterns, our rules of life and our beliefs. Usually the greatest "first attention" that we accept is fear. The opposite emotion from fear is the emotion of love. Take a moment and list the "first attentions" that you feel need to be changed to a "second attention." Then compose and implement an action plan to replace your dysfunctional (and possibly destructive) "first attentions" with functional "second attentions."

Sixth Sun

In Mesoamerican belief our present age is known as the Fifth Sun. The First Sun was known as *Nahui Ocelotl*, the Sun of Jaguars; the Second as *Nahui Ehecatl*, the Sun of Wind; the Third as *Nahui Quiahuitl*, the Sun of Rain; and the Fourth as *Nahui Atl*, the Sun of Water. Each of these ages ended with the destruction or death of the current age which then allowed the rebirth of the next or "new age." The destruction of the world by water at the end of the Fourth Age corresponds with the worldwide destructive flood mythology of many cultures.

Our Fifth Sun is the Sun of Movement (*Nahui Ollin*), meaning Earth shaking or change. The glyph for movement is called *Ollin* and is positioned in the center of the Mesoamerican Calendar of the Five Ages. This is a glimpse into the ending of our Fifth Sun and the transition to the enlightened Age of the Sixth Sun.

Each Solar Age has an undertaking. When that mission is completed, we move on to the next Sun. The mission of the Fifth Sun has been to bring our entire planet together through the principles of movement and measure – think air travel and internet. The transition from the Fifth Sun to the Sixth Sun of Consciousness will be a time of Earth shaking and change from the greed and inequality of the Fifth Sun to the enlightened Age of the Sixth Sun.

Additionally, "We know that the Fifth Sun appears after four others have come and gone, and that this Fifth Sun is itself destined to be superseded by another. We cannot believe that these myths of solar cataclysms were inspired only by the eternal cosmic renewal manifest in natural cycles. Apart from the fact that Nahuatl religious phenomena, which are so highly spiritual, could never be so simply explained—in terms, that is, that have no inner meaning—there are various indications that the Fifth Sun is the creator of a great and indestructible work: that of freeing creation from duality."[399]

According to Mayan Elder Don Tomás Calvo an "image to illustrate the end of the Mesoamerican calendar is a serpent swallowing its tail. He and the other Elders believe a self-consuming snake symbolizes the upcoming era of the 'Sixth Sun,' one which brings the past to the present in order to construct a brighter future. The Elders also say they want to remind the world how important it is to live in harmony with oneself, the ancestors, the Earth, our environment, all living creatures and the greater cosmic order."[400] Please note that the serpent swallowing its tail is symbolic of Quetzalcóatl.

And I do agree with the elders. A snake eating its own tail is named an Ouroboros, a "tail biter," with the meaning of infinity or wholeness. In an eternal cycle of renewal, the tail-eating serpent symbolizes the cyclic nature of the Universe: creation out of destruction, life out of death. It is essential to recognize that the Ouroboros "was also the symbol of the early Christian religion and philosophy known as Gnosticism. In its doctrines, Jesus tells the Virgin Mary: 'The outer darkness is a great serpent, the tail of which is in its mouth, and it is outside the whole world, and surroundeth the whole world.' Gnosticism also taught that the serpent and the Christ were interchangeable figures, and that both were saviours or 'redeemers.'"[401]

The death of the Fifth Sun results in the life of the Sixth Sun – an age of wholeness or Oneness. This is Jesus' Sun and Quetzalcóatl's Sun, the Sun of Consciousness. It will be the Age of the Divine Human – *Hombre-Dios*. It will be an age of the heart, truth, freedom, and equality.

The Sixth Sun will be *Xochitl Tonatiuh*, the Sun of Flowers. Our Fifth Sun and the Sixth Sun are reflections of the last two day-signs of the Nahuatl *tonalámatl*, the Sacred Calendar. The nineteenth day-sign, "*Quiáhuitl*, rain, signifies not rain of water – but rain of fire such as destroyed the Third World, and represents the fiery torments of self-sacrificing penitents. Its deity is of course Tonatiuh, the solar god of the Fifth World. The twentieth and last day-sign is *xóchitl*, flower. The deity is Xochiquétzal, goddess of flowers. As the 'House of Flowers.'[402] the human heart, we understand that *xóchitl* here symbolizes the budding blossom of the human spirit at last freed from duality."[403]

The Sixth Sun – a time to look forward to as *xóchitl* is love and the search for union. It's happiness. It's sex. The Sun of Flowers is when humanity comes to flower.

The End and the Beginning

Humanity will no longer see through a glass darkly but face to face. No longer will man and woman be a mirror of the Truth but the Truth itself. In the church at Esperaza, France stands a statue witness to this message. In the left hand is an open book on which a child sits, caressing the statues face lovingly. In the right hand is held a bunch of lilies. The solar Forces are portrayed by the child who is the little king, the Love which is the Sulphur of the alchemists, and the pure white lilies, the Philosophical Mercury. At last the earthly twin has learned the lesson of Love and the balance is restored, the male becoming the female, the female, the male. And the open book? It is "The Book of Love."[404]

Rev. Dr. JC Husfelt and Rev. Sherry Husfelt

Sher and JC, July 2019 Apprentice Training

JC and Sherry have been referred to as "magicians who are able to take a group of people into the dimensions of their souls – fluid dancers that know where a group needs to go!"

Rev. Dr. JC Husfelt is a philosopher and mystic, teacher, martial artist and practitioner of the mystic arts, and a *tlamatini*[405]: a wise man, philosopher, sage, priest, and preserver of divine knowledge. In modern Nahuatl, he is *tlamátiquetl*: a "person of knowledge." He is the author of *I Am a Sun of God and So Are You*, *The Return of the Feathered Serpent*, *Return of a Green Philosophy*, and *Do You Like Jesus – Not the Church*? And in 2020, he plans

409

to release *The Morning Star's Guide to a New Consciousness: The Awakening of our Divinity and Humanity* and *Return of the Morning Star, Quetzalcóatl – Sixth Sun, Awakening to a New Consciousness: Becoming a Quetzalcóatl – a Feathered Serpent.*

Rev. Sherry Husfelt is a wise woman and teacher, empath, counselor, healer, and a Certified Integrative Nutrition Health Coach. The Husfelt's have undertaken a literal and metaphorical journey through the mystical and practical aspects of the mystery, myth, and spiritual lore of indigenous cultures throughout the world. They have traveled across the Americas to the icy plateaus and volcanoes of Iceland, through the windswept barrens of the British Isles and the Orkneys, and across Norway, Europe, the Mediterranean, Asia, and the Polynesian Islands.

Their teachings grew from their firsthand experience with multiple cultures, as well as their spirituality. For more information, please email the Husfelt's at bigcatthatflies@gmail.com or visit their blog: www.snowyowl-speaks.info, or any of their websites: http://divinehumanity.com; http://www.revolutioninreligion.com; http://www.spartanwarriorphilosophers.com

Please join us in Greece for our Gates of Fire II, May 3 – 18, 2020, to mark the 2,500th anniversary of Thermopylae: http://www.spartanwarriorphilosophers.com.

ENDNOTES

· ·

[1] Virgo's ancient name meant, "The Branch."

[2] According to Greek mythology, Zeus split the human body into two because he feared it was too powerful. Out of the one being came man and woman, separated by Zeus in order to prevent it from rising against the gods. Legend says these two now separate beings are destined to roam the world until they find their other half. When they find each other, they will unite and their spirits will join and become that one being separated by gods. (https://hackspirit.com/10-undeniable-signs-youve-found-soulmate-never-let-go/)

[3] Line from the 2018 movie *Aquaman,* starring Jason Momoa.

[4] Title of a 1987 film starring Robin Williams.

[5] The Norse-Germanic concept of fate and destiny is based on a triple-goddess (sisters) paradigm, the Nornir. The three sisters are Urðr, origin/fate/"that which is"; Verdandi, being/becoming; and Skuld, necessity/debt. I explain this concept fully in my book, *The Return of a Green Philosophy: The Wisdom of Óðinn, the Power of Þórr, and Freyja's Power of Nature* (Snowy Owl, 2015).

[6] As a teenager, I wanted to be an architect. I would spend time designing houses and building models. The home we live in now is eerily similar to one I designed as a kid. I was discouraged by a friend of the family from studying architecture in college or pursuing it as a career, but in one sense, I did become an architect: a

divine architect, designing the way reality is structured; a heavenly builder, an esoteric carpenter.

7 The fact that Venus was a "wandering star" soon became obvious to ancient sky watchers, who noticed its motion relative to the background stars, going from the eastern sky in the morning to the western sky in the early evening. Nicolas Camille Flammarion, a noted French astronomer in the late 19th and early 20th centuries, referred to Venus as "The Shepherd's Star." I myself like to refer to Venus as the "night light of the sky." So, it's easier to understand the origin of the terms "evening star" and "morning star" if we only consider Venus. (Joe Rao, "What Is a 'Morning Star,' and What Is an 'Evening Star'?" *Space.com*, February 6, 2016.)

8 Video introduction – Delta Airlines.

9 This is appropriate when you consider that I am the Morning Star. Venus as the morning star rises in the darkest part of the night and is seen by only a few who are awake (awakened) at a time when the majority of the world is asleep. Thus, Venus, in its morning-star cycle, is like the thief in the night as it is noticed by only a few. The name morning star in the original Hebrew and Arabic meant "that which comes in the night or one who knocks at the door."

10 This is the well of knowledge from the most ancient of civilizations which spread throughout the world and is known to us through the patinas of many different cultures and their writings.

11 As the great mythic accounts of the Grail Quest reveal, there is a great need in today's world to Far Travel and heal the "wound" of the separation, suppression, abuse, and control of the feminine.

Even though the Grail is enigmatic in its identity, it is essential to understand that the Holy Grail is not an item to possess. It is not an external "thing." It is our awakened hearts and minds, and in a grand sense, it symbolizes what has been lost – humanity's, and our own, lost values. The primary loss is that of the feminine nature and the equality of men and women, he lost Feminine Principle (terrestrial Mother Nature and celestial) of the cosmos, the seen world.

This troubled world of ours only recognizes the light as authentic, not the dark; the material, not the spiritual; the male principle, not the feminine. This then is the quest to recover the feminine and nature—to heal the "wound."

12 As an irony, we don't have to far travel outside of America to discover poverty, social injustice, and inequality. These things are rampant throughout the United States.

13 http://www.imdb.com/title/tt0318462/plotsummary

14 The martlet is the heraldic form of the swallow or martin and is frequently depicted with a very short beak, long wings, and no legs or feet. The martlet is a symbol of swiftness in travel, or on the battlefield. Represented with feathers where there should be feet and so unable to land, the martlet is a mythical bird representing the ceaseless pursuit of learning.

In ancient Egypt, the swallow was associated with stars and the souls of the dead. In paintings from that time, the bird often appears perched on the prow of a boat, announcing the approaching dawn. In Egyptian love poetry, the swallow brings tidings of new love. In ancient Rome, as well as China and Japan, swallows nesting on a house are symbols of good luck. Swallows are associated with prophecy and are messengers, arriving from afar. They are also harbingers of spring. Because of this, the bird is associated with the resurrection in a Christian context.

15 Chris Irvine, "Tourists plunge 100 feet to their death while taking selfie on wall above popular Portuguese beach," Fox News, June 13, 2018:

A British woman and Australian man have died after falling 100 feet off a beach wall in Portugal while taking a selfie.

The man, who was in his 40s, and the woman in her 30s were apparently taking a picture on top of a wall that overlooks Pescadores Beach in Ericeira when they plunged to their deaths between 1 a.m. and 6 a.m.

Their bodies were found by a beach cleaner on Tuesday morning and a cell phone was found at the top of the wall.

"Everything seems to indicate that the fall happened when they were probably trying to take a selfie," said Rui Pereira da Terra, a captain of the local naval authority.

"It seems they dropped their mobile phone and fell down while leaning over to retrieve it."

16 Justin Wise, "These aren't our kids," *Fox & Friends,* June 22, 2018.

17 Angelina Chapin, "In Their Own Words, Migrant Children Describe Horrific Conditions At Border Patrol Facilities - Kids told lawyers they're sick, cold, wake up hungry in the middle of the night, sleep on cement floors, and take care of babies separated from their families," 06/28/2019, https://www.huffpost.com/entry/migrant-children-describe-detention_n_5d1646ffe4b-03d61163af666

18 Anthony Bourdain, *"No Reservations: Around the World on an Empty Stomach*

19 The unknown separates and causes fear. Thus the reason to far travel is to change the unknown of other lands, cultures, and people into the known, an antidote to xenophobia.

20 A liquid tobacco mixture that acts as a catalyst for vision. When taken through the nose, it touches olfactory papillae that go directly to the brain.

21 She believed that her cancer had been cured on Kōyasan in 1987 ("The Tale of the Descending Spirit Exorcism"). Also please see my tale: "A Night with Peanut in Tulúm."

22 Old Norse poem *Hávamál—The Sayings of the High One—Óðinn.*

23 https://www.themathesontrust.org/library/oldmeadow-rene-guenon

24 Miguel León-Portilla, *Aztec Thought and Culture* (University of Oklahoma Press, 1990) 27.

25 http://www.primordialtraditions.net.

26 G. Philippe Menos and Karen A. Jones Menos, "Revelation and Inspiration: Paranormal Phenomena in Light of the Kundalini Paradigm," Presented at the 14th Annual Conference of the Academy of Religion and Psychical Research, Rosemont College, Rosemont, Pa., May 21–23, 1989, 3.

27 Ibid., 3-4.

28 Ibid., 5.

29 Jürg Glauser and Susanne Kramarz-Bein (Hrsg.), *Rittersagas: Übersetzung, Überlieferung, Transmission* (Strengleikar in Iceland, 2014) 119–131, 127 (https://www.academia.edu/10666162/Strengleikar_in_Iceland._2014._Rittersagas_%C3%9Cbersetzung_%C3%9Cberlieferung_Transmission_pp._119_131).

30 What is the definition of sacrifice self to self? Is it the same as self-sacrifice? Not quite. Sacrifice self to self is slightly different. Self-sacrifice means some type of personal sacrifice for the benefit of others. This could take the form of a single parent working two jobs or a person rushing into a burning building to save others. However, sacrifice that is self to self has slightly different connotations. It is still self-sacrifice but with the caveat that we must first know ourselves to be able to sacrifice our self to self. This is self-sacrifice in the pursuit of understanding and knowledge about ourselves that we will use to help others grow and evolve. It is a sacrifice for the greater well-being of humanity and the Earth.

A sacrifice of self to self is usually one that others are unwilling to make—such as Óðinn's sacrifice of one of his eyes for wisdom—to drink daily of the well of knowledge, Mimir's well. What is important to note here is that Mimir's well symbolizes matter. Only by our immersion in the world of matter (nature), where both love and fear reside, are we able to achieve the experiences that provide us with knowledge and wisdom.

31 James Maffie, *Aztec Philosophy: Understanding a World in Motion* (University Press of Colorado, 2015) 30.

32 Beau Taplin, An Extraordinary Life

33 Joseph Campbell, *The Power of Myth* (Doubleday, 1988) 22.

34 Hawaiian meaning "foundation for seeking wisdom."

35 Paul Broadhurst, *Tintagel and the Arthurian Myths*, (Pendragon Partnership, 1996) 24.

36 Rev. Dr. JC Husfelt, *Do You Like Jesus – Not the Church?* (Snowy Owl, 2015) 154.

37 Maffie, *Aztec Philosophy*, 102.

38 David Fideler, *Jesus Christ, Sun of God: Ancient Cosmology and Early Christian Symbolism* (Quest Books, 1993) 134.

39 I've been in the presence of and witness to an archangel and the two assisting angels. My wife, Sherry, and twelve of our apprentices were witnesses to the same sacred visitation, which occurred on the night of the new moon on August 3, 1997, in the woods of Maine.

40 There is no greater external sign of the Holy Spirit of God than the morning star, the planet Venus, which symbolizes rebirth in Judaism. Even the historical geographical center of Judaism, Jerusalem, is connected with Venus. Its name "effectively means the place dedicated to Venus in its evening setting." [Christopher Knight and Robert Lomas, *Book of Hiram: Freemasonry, Venus, and the Secret Key to the Life of Jesus* (Barnes & Noble, 2005) 84.]

41 Arthur Edward Waite, *The Hidden Church of the Holy Graal* (Independently published, 2014) 13 - 14.

42 The morning star was seen as "God's eye," positioned between darkness (ignorance) and light (knowledge) but always the way-shower to understanding and wisdom. The great Lakota Black Elk spoke of the importance of the morning star as follows:

"Morning Star, there at the place where the sun comes up, you who have the wisdom which we seek, help us in cleansing ourselves and all the people, that our generations to come will have light as they walk the sacred path. You lead the dawn as it walks forth, and also the day which follows with its light which is knowledge. This you do for us and for all the people of the world, that they may see clearly in walking the **wakan**—holy—path, that they may know all that is holy, and that they may increase in a sacred manner[.]" (Ron Zellinger, "The Morning Star," *Akta Lakota Museum Cultural Center,*. http://aktalakota.stjo.org/site/News2?page=NewsArticle&id=8595)

[43] Campbell, *The Power of Myth*, 136.

[44] Elizabeth Van Buren, *Lord of the Flame*, 167.

[45] Iron Thunderhorse and Donn Le Vie, Jr., *Return of the Thunderbeings* (Bear & Company, 1990) 97, 99.

[46] Heyoka Merrifield, *Sacred Art Scared Earth* (Rain Bird Publishing, 1994) 95.

[47] These are eyes that are "fresh," non-judgmental and tolerant, that view the world with awe and excitement and recognize the oneness of the light and the dark of existence. Baby Eyes is one of the Three Pillars of Light of Divine Humanity. True Talk and Flower Heart are the other two pillars.

[48] *Those who believe in the infallibility of the Bible are blindly stuck in an elusive, dogmatic quagmire of mistranslation, misinterpretations, and misinformation.* – Rev. Dr. JC Husfelt (1997).

The Bible seemingly overrides common sense and experience. Add to this the realization that the Bible is a translated copy of words and teachings spoken ages ago. According to *Newsweek*, "No television preacher has ever read the Bible. Neither has any evangelical politician. Neither has the pope. . . . At best, we've all read a bad translation – a translation of translations of translations of hand-copied copies of copies of copies of copies, and on and on, hundreds of times."

"To demonstrate how a Translator's interpretation of a text can influence the readers understanding of the text, let us examine two passages from the New International Version. 'Let the land produce living creatures' Genesis 1:24, 'and the man became a living being' Genesis 2:7. From these passages, the reader could conclude that animals are classified as 'creatures' and humans as 'beings' (The KJV uses the word 'soul' here). When the Hebrew text is uncovered, we find that the above 'interpretation' would never have occurred as we find that the phrase 'living creature' in the first verse and the phrase 'living being' in the second verse are two different translations of the same Hebrew phrase 'nephesh chayah'. Because of the translator's opinion that there is a difference between men and animals, the translation of these verses reflects the translator's opinions. The reader, not knowing the Hebrew background to the passages, is forced to base his interpretation on the translator's personal opinion." (Husfelt, *Do You Like Jesus – Not the Church?*, 8, 240.)

[49] Even in the fiction of J.R.R. Tolkien we discover Venus, star of hope, as symbolized by Eärendel, half-elf (divine-angelic) and half human, as in this passage from J.R.R. Tolkien, *The Shaping of Middle-Earth: The Quenta, the Ambarkanta and the Annals (The History of Middle-Earth, Vol. 4)* (HarperCollins Publishers, 2002) 184:

"Hail Eärendel, star most radiant, messenger most fair! Hail thou bearer of light before the Sun and Moon, the looked-for that comest unawares, the longed-for that comest beyond hope! Hail thou splendour of the children of the world, thou slayer of the dark! Star of the sunset hail! Hail herald of the morn!"

[50] Cynthia Giles, *Russian Tarot of St. Petersburg* (U.S. Games Systems, Inc., 2003) 74.

[51] José Argüelles, *The Mayan Factor: Path Beyond Technology* (Bear & Company, 1987) 42.

[52] Daniel G. Brinton, M.D., *American Hero-Myths* (Start Classics, 2013) 29 - 30.

[53] Considering my soul vendetta against Christianity and my knowledge that it is based on the greatest lie ever told, it may seem strange that I would quote from a Catholic website, but considering the stranges times we are living in, perhaps it's not. This following is quoted from Stephen Beale, "Why Jesus is the Bright Morning Star," *Catholic Exchange*, October 10, 2016 (https://catholicexchange.com/jesus-bright-morning-star):

"**Before the sunrise**: The morning star, which is actually the planet Venus, derives its name from the fact that it appears before sunrise. Its appearance, therefore, heralds the coming of a new day while it is still dark.

"**Constant light**: Stars twinkle; planets, especially Venus, don't. The light of Christ never wavers, never fails.

"**Morning and evening**: Venus is not only a 'morning star' but also an 'evening star'. This makes it all the more fitting as a name for Christ, who is called the alpha and the omega and the beginning and the end in Revelation.

"**The Shepherd's Star**: The fact that Venus appears in both the evening and morning has also lent it its own nickname. Certainly, while Venus may not have had that name in the first century, a shepherd keeping watch over the flocks by night indeed might have been among the few in ancient Israel—other than insomniacs and military guards—to always glimpse this star in both its evening and morning appearances."

54 "All who follow the Buddha Way have read of that moment, seeing in the Buddha's pronouncement whatever registers in their own hearts. But for me, his spontaneous outcry on sight of the morning star was the first and perhaps most penetrating revelation of the deep ecology that permeates Buddhist life, for the Buddha's enlightenment was itself a realization that he, the star, and the whole of the earth were manifestations of one being. He saw that the surface of his skin was not the termination of self and that the 'I' for which he could no longer discern beginning or ending was as wide as the universe and as long as forever. The eye with which he looked upon the morning star was the one great organ of sight that awakens all our dawns." [Lin Jensen, *Deep Down Things: The Earth in Celebration and Dismay* (Wisdom Publications, 2010), via *Tricycle*, December 8, 2010, https://tricycle.org/trikedaily/sighting-morning-star/.]

55 This is not the Jungian concept of the shadow but the actual and physical reality of dualistic concepts, such as light and dark, or spirit and matter, which interpenetrate. The dualistic separation of light

and dark is the illusion, as our individual sense of reality (of separateness or duality) is an extension of the illusion of our basic core sense perceptions. Our eyes perceive separation between us and all things viewed. This constant reinforcement tricks us into thinking and believing that we are separate and an island unto ourselves.

Similarly, our personal symbolic light and dark are not separate, but interpenetrate to define our wholeness as individuals. Additionally, the two sides of our inner darkness also interpenetrate. There is no separate shadow, just a darkness that is both creative and destructive at the same time.

This concept of the dark within us is known as "the beast within." According to the Coptic Gospel of Thomas, Jesus said, "Blessed is the lion which the man eats, and the lion will become man, and cursed is the man whom the lion eats, and the lion will become man."

The Beast Within is explained fully in my book *Do You Like Jesus – Not the Church?*

56 Richard Andrews and Paul Schellenberger, *The Tomb of God: The Body of Jesus and the Solution to a 2,000-Year-Old Mystery* (Little Brown & Co., 1996) 398.

57 My book, *Do You Like Jesus – Not the Church?*, explains in detail the true message and the corruption of Christianity.

58 Kingdom does not imply or mean patriarchal. King is synonymous with queen. The usual analogy for the Divine is recognizable as operating on a vertical plane (an energetic norm descending or ascending) and male, even though the Divine, the All, the Absolute is neither male nor female. Thus, for convenience's sake and a terminology that most people will recognize, I use the term kingdom with the understanding that it is not patriarchal or one of male imagery. Its imagery may be considered stellar, as it is not one, solar (patriarchal), or the other, lunar (matriarchal), but both blended together as the seen and unseen universal cosmos.

59 The All, the Creator, the Unknown and the Uncreated, cannot be

identified or imagined in human terms, just in absolute terms, as it is the greatest mystery of all mysteries. I use the term God when referring to the Absolute, the All.

However, I am not referring to the concept of the Christian God—the Father, the Son, and the Holy Ghost—but to the Creator, the greatest Mystery of Mysteries, the Divine, the All, the Absolute, the Concealed and the Revealed, immanent yet transcendent and beyond human comprehension.

Thus, God, the One and Oneness of all, the Mystery of Mysteries, which is within us and outside of us, transcends our abilities even as divine human beings to comprehend the essence of what is the greatest mystery of all. God surpasses our dualistic view of reality and is neither male nor female but is the mystery of all that there is. God is love, not fear, immanent yet transcendent.

I believe that we are not made in the image of God or the Absolute, but we are, as are all other things of creation, a reflection of the original divine unity. For reasons beyond what any human mind may comprehend and in an act of creativity, the Absolute reflected itself – the Reflective Absolute. Instead of a substance, such as semen, it was the reflection of itself that then produced creation. Thus, the first divine pair, and thus plurality, resulted from the original emanation: $(1 + 1[\text{reflection}] = 2, 1[\text{reflection}] + 2 = 3)$. This concept of reflection is indicated in the first letter of the Jewish alphabet, aleph.

Thus God is immanent (reflection/many), yet transcendent (absoluteness/one).

60 Thunderhorse and Le Vie, *Return of the Thunderbeings*, 35.

61 The Antichrist would be a narcissist, an unhealthy egomaniac, a provocateur, and totally materialistic. It would be all about self, power, and money. No concept of "love thy neighbor," no unity; only a separation mentality. The Antichrist would be in a position of power where, through fear, he would influence, basically brainwash, people into following him even though their freedoms were

being eroded step-by-step. The Antichrist would play on people's fear and their need for a sense of safety and security. The Antichrist would be charismatic and a smooth talker who would speak about great things. He would be a master of deception.

[62] Husfelt, *Do You Like Jesus – Not the Church?*, 86 - 87.

[63] Ibid., 87.

[64] Marcus J. Borg, *Jesus: A New Vision: Spirit, Culture, and the Life of Discipleship* (HarperOne, 1991) 97.

[65] Ibid., 110.

[66] Universality of Divine Humanity: Throughout the past centuries, there have been few alternatives in the West to the institutionalized religions of Christianity, Judaism, and Islam. But now there is Divine Humanity, the original spiritual and religious philosophy of Jesus.

In addition, at various times there have been revivals of past religious traditions, such as Druidism during the Celtic Revival of the nineteenth and twentieth centuries. Over the past forty or so years, we have witnessed the establishment of neo-shamanism, neo-Druidism, modern heathenry, and modern paganism. These were birthed as alternatives to the three major Western religions as well as from people's opposition to the destruction of nature and the biosystem.

What is lacking in these alternatives is a universal, foundational spiritual or religious philosophy that would underlie practices such as modern heathenry and modern paganism. Divine Humanity provides this philosophy. There are no dogma, doctrines, or rules of practice connected with Divine Humanity. In other words, individuals and groups may conduct rituals and ceremonies in a manner they see and feel is effective and that matches their own belief systems. This includes the honoring of one's chosen gods, goddesses, nature spirits, and so forth.

Divine Humanity is not institutionalized or hierarchal. It believes in original divinity, not original sin. It is a green, ecological, and egalitarian philosophy and religion. It is all-inclusive. You do not have to pass a hierarchal gatekeeper to join, such as in the Christian church through baptism. There are no fees or donations required. All that is needed is the acceptance of Divine Humanity as your religion or philosophy and the willingness to awaken your spark or starlight within, as well as the additional acceptance of partnership with nature, a complete willingness to practice a Green Philosophy of equality, and to walk gently on the Earth with an open, loving, compassionate, and forgiving heart. These are asked of you with the realization that we are human as well as divine. We will make mistakes, get angry, and carry fear. Many times we need to forgive ourselves and others. But life is a journey of becoming, not a destination of finality.

[67] Laurette Séjourné, *Pensamiento y religión en el México antiguo* (Fondo de Cultura Economica, 1957) 112.

[68] As well as the divine nature of all that exists, seen and unseen.

[69] Joseph Campbell, *The Hero With A Thousand Faces*, p. 217

[70] The following is from my blog:

"Organic, denoting a relation between elements of something such that they fit together harmoniously as necessary parts of a whole. Of, relating to, or derived from living matter."

Divine Humanity is an organic religion. It is a natural religion, full of the experience of life from the awe of a sunrise to the first kiss of spring. The Earth is Divine Humanity's temple.

There is no doctrine, only experience with Divine Humanity. The religions that are based on texts or books are artificial. There is no beating heart to them, only guilt, doubt, and false hope. When a religion is based on a "sacred text – a book" and not on one's heart and personal experience of life and the mysteries of life, the only conclusion to be derived is that these religions are a stain and blight on humanity which permeates throughout the Earth affecting all living things.

Divine Humanity is not based on a sacred text. This allows personal freedom in establishing one's personal spiritual beliefs and practices drawn from the experience of life and nature. This is heart-based religion where we are in partnership with nature. A biosphere that is alive and conscious that extends throughout all of creation. This consciousness is divine consciousness (the sixth element), which permeates and connects all things together.

Within the totality of creation, there are six elements: earth, water, fire, air, space, and consciousness. Things that arise by dependent co-origination from the six elements fall into two categories: physical things and things of the mind. Physical things arise from the first five elements while mental things arise from the sixth element, consciousness. All six elements are mutually pervading. The first five elements wholly permeate the sixth, consciousness, and consciousness in turn wholly permeates the other five elements. In other words, physical thing and mental things interpenetrate without hindrance.

Consequently, all things have consciousness, not just humans, and will respond accordingly to our consciousness. This is the reason that humans' physical acts of pollution of the environment are not the totality of the problem. Nature and creatures are affected by the fear and anger of humans. Furthermore, humanity's mindset of separation, where humans are superior to all other things of the Earth, is caustic to nature and the environment. This is humanity's mind pollution. Instead of fear and separation, what nature needs is a nurturing spirit of unity, loving kindness flowing from our hearts, and our sincere gratitude for nature's beauty and its garden paradise. As we nurture nature, nature will nurture us.

Is there any proof to this theory of an all-pervading consciousness? There is according to new research from the Aerospace Institute of the University of Stuttgart in Germany. It supports the theory that water has memory (thus consciousness). "This theory was first proposed by the late French immunologist Dr. Jacques Benveniste in a controversial article published in 1988 in *Nature* as a way of explaining how homeopathy works." Think how this supports our theory on consciousness. "More than 70 percent of our planet is covered in water. The human body is made of 60 percent water; the brain, 70 percent; the lungs, nearly 90 percent. Our energies might be traveling out of our brains and bodies and into those of other living beings of all kinds through imprints on this magical substance. The oceans and rivers and rains might be transporting all manner of information throughout the world." Now, you may see the connection between humans' mind pollution and its effect on the Earth.

We may view this knowledge from a spiritual perspective. In the ageless sanctification rite of bathing, a person enters a river to submerge themselves three or four times in an attempt to access the Otherworld. However, entering into a river does not unto itself provide access to the Otherworld. It is the spirit song sung at the beginning of the ritual by a person of power, a shaman (in Jesus' time a chasid, a Jewish shaman) and his/her intention and strong mind that "opens" the river and provides the access to the Otherworld.

"Love thy neighbor as thyself."

This great teaching reflects our theory of divine consciousness. Love in its truest sense means unity or oneness. All other shades of love flow from this foundational meaning. As an example, sexual love is the unity of two humans, which may or may not include emotional love or oneness between the two. In other words, love your neighbor as yourself means there is no separation yourself and others. And love of self means unity of body, mind, emotion, and spirit.

We must realize that our divine consciousness underlies but blends with our dualistic consciousness, which makes the actual mindset and practice of this teaching difficult. The quest is to make this great teaching simple, a part of our daily consciousness, keeping in mind that our thoughts flow from our consciousness.

"The great interpreter of the Torah, Rabbi Hillel, was challenged to recite the entire Torah while standing on one foot. Hillel responded: 'Do not do anything to your neighbor that is hateful to you. This is the entire Torah. Go and learn.' And the greatest expositor of

Jewish law, Rabbi Akiba, taught that the central principle of Torah was, 'Love your neighbor as yourself.'"

According to Bernie Sanders, religion "essentially comes down to 'do unto others as you would like them to do unto you.' And what I have believed in my whole life (is) that we are in this together. . . . The truth is, at some level when you hurt, when your children hurt, I hurt. And when my kids hurt, you hurt."

The Key to the Kingdom—The Oneness of Self and Other

Today's cultural mantra is me, me, me! There is no consideration of other humans or the Earth and its creatures. It's all about me – a shallow and highly self-oriented and self-focused worldview. Recognizing this worldview and the unhealthy egos of people who are totally focused on themselves, the corporation marketing geniuses who are focused on maximizing their greed through the bottom line have subtly reinforced people's unhealthy egos through the names of their products. Think iPhone, iPad, and iTunes.

To the majority of people, life is nothing more than an obsessive, materialistic philosophy of consuming. In our so-called democracy, it's hard to believe, but people seem to be more focused and concerned about the style than about the substance of a political candidate's debate, even a presidential one. Wealth and external status rule the day. "But what would happen if someone refused to define himself or herself by his or her economic status? What if someone came along and insisted that there's nothing ultimately valuable in material progress? What if someone were to treat the getting and spending of money, neither with contempt, nor with respect, but with indifference?"

That someone was Jesus. The key to the kingdom was not to be found in external wealth and power. It was not to be uncovered in the rules and regulations of finite institutions. It was unearthed by discovering the oneness of self and others and following natural law. Accordingly, the secret to a peaceful and fulfilled life, one resulting in happiness and love, is to be found within our relationships to our own selves and to others, others including the world at large (animals, etc.). Love and forgiveness begin with self and then expand out to others. This was, and still is, the mystery of transformed consciousness – the mystery of our kingdom within and the mystery of self and other. When Jesus taught "love thy neighbor as thyself," he was referring to the metaphysical realization "that you and that other are one, that you are two aspects of the one life, and that your apparent separateness is but an effect of the way we experience forms under the conditions of space and time. Our true reality is in our identity and unity with all life." [Rev. Dr. JC Husfelt, "Ditch the Church – Become Organic and Natural." *Snowy Owl Speaks*, July 2, 2016, (http://www.snowyowlspeaks.info/?p=185.)]

71 "Those who know others are wise. Those who know themselves are enlightened."

"Know Thyself" is attributed to the Greek Philosopher Chilon of Sparta and was one of the maxims found inscribed in the Temple of Apollo at the ancient oracle site of Delphi, Greece. Knowing ourselves means recognizing, first and foremost, that we are Divine Human Beings. We are not sinful human beings but divine humans. Our divine spark, our indestructible seed of light, interpenetrates our humanness—body, mind and spirit. The Absolute interpenetrates the Relative.

This is the first step in knowing ourselves and realizing that each of us is a microcosm of the macrocosm. To awaken we must know ourselves and all other things—not only from our mind but also from our heart and our experience of life.

Original Divinity:

The immediate response that may pass through a person's mind to the religious philosophical principle of original divinity, that we are born with a divine, indestructible seed of light instead of original sin, takes the form of a question: "Why then do humans make war, kill, rape, and fly planes into buildings?"

The short answer is that the divine spark or seed has not been awakened. Knowing this and the realization that we are still humans with a body, mind, emotion and spirit and we will always have the choice of right-action, wrong action, a combination of both or inaction. In other words, even after we awaken our divineness, we will make human mistakes and possibly do actions that are not true and right. Knowing ourselves means that we will love and we will fear; we will struggle and we will overcome; we will suffer and we will have joy and happiness; we will live and we will die. This is knowing ourselves and then striving to become more divine with as little human wrong doing as possible.

Furthermore, natural law has not been awakened within the person's heart. Natural law is based on a belief in the inherent, natural, altruistic law of God that is found within each person. This natural law flows from the divinity within each individual but lies dormant until awakened by each person.

In other words, "in our deepest selves, we are divine. All living things are divine in their deepest selves. Now, that divine self may be hidden or covered over by hatred, envy, fear or other negative things. But, it is there nonetheless, and it is our 'true' and 'eternal' selves." (Husfelt, *Do You Like Jesus – Not the Church?*, 294).

72 "Jesus did not believe in original sin. He believed in original divinity, in purity, as each of us has the spark, the starlight of God, within us. We are born pure and 'born in love and not in sin. There is no love greater or holier than that of mother and child. There is nothing more sinless—baptized or not—than the child in the mother's arms. Woe unto him who dare offend one of these little ones, for of such is the kingdom of heaven.' [Ignatius Singer, *The Rival Philosophies of Jesus and of Paul* (Palala Press, 2016) 313 - 314.]

"Judaism does not believe in original sin. Thus there is no need for a savior in Judaism as there is in Christianity. God's natural, altruistic law, stated in Jeremiah 31:33 that 'it will be written on their hearts,' means that as soon as the soul, the breath and light of God, enters the body at birth, God's divine mandate of love and compassion is written on the heart. The logical conclusion would be that the little one is thus born in divinity and not in sin.

"Jesus was Jewish; as stated above, Judaism does not believe in the existence of original sin but of original purity.

"Divine Humanity believes that each and every person has an immortal spark within him or her—an indestructible seed of divine light, starlight, the divine immanence. This indestructible seed of divine light may be likened to a mustard seed within our hearts. This divine seed of immortality or spark, which sometimes may be referred to as the divine golden dew, constitutes the soul – an eternal spark in its essence, since it is a fragment of God, and immortal.

"This is our sacred self. This inner, indestructible seed of light that settles over and interpenetrates our DNA as divine golden dew." (Husfelt, *Do You Like Jesus – Not the Church?*, 65, 209 - 210.)

***

"The symbolism of dew, closely connected with that of rain by its very nature, is likewise related more especially to the giving of life; and this symbolism is common to numerous traditional forms – Hermetism, the Hebrew Kabbala, and to the Far Eastern tradition." [René Guénon, *Fundamental Symbols: The Universal Language of Sacred Science* (Quinta Essentia, 1995) 246.]

73 There are two different types of religion:

• Organized/Institutionalized Religion – a group or system of beliefs and practices, grounded in dogma and doctrine, which explain the mysteries (the sacred) or the transcendent aspects of creation. This type of religion may be based on a "holy book" (usually a literal scriptural theology) and may be termed exoteric, even though there may be an esoteric branch of the religion such as Judaism's Kabbalah or Islam's Sufism. Additionally, Organized/Institutionalized Religion is usually based on dogmatic theology and usually disavows mythmaking.

• Pure or Wisdom Religion/Spiritual Philosophy– a belief and/or system of beliefs and practices, absent of dogma and doctrine, which attempt to understand and explain the mysteries—un-seen, otherworldly, or natural (Earth-based) as well as sacred (heaven-based)—or, if you will, the immanent and transcendent aspects of life and creation. This understanding may take the form of myth-making. Pure Religion believes in the individual's ability to have a direct and personal (mystical/transpersonal) experience of the immanent and transcendent mysteries of heaven and Earth. This type of religion and spiritual philosophy is mythic, exoteric and esoteric. This is Divine Humanity.

74 "I believe in Spinoza's God, who reveals himself in the lawful harmony of the world," he told him, "not in a God who concerns himself with the fate and the doings of mankind." Albert Einstein

What that amounted to for Einstein, according to a 2006 paper, was a "cosmic religious feeling" that required no "anthropomorphic conception of God." He explained this view in the New York Times Magazine: "The religious geniuses of all ages have been distinguished by this kind of religious feeling, which knows no dogma and no God conceived in man's image; so that there can be no church whose central teachings are based on it. Hence it is precisely among the heretics of every age that we find men who were filled with this highest kind of religious feeling and were in many cases regarded by their contemporaries as atheists, sometimes also as saints. Looked at in this light, men like Democritus, Francis of Assisi, and Spinoza are closely akin to one another." (Brian Gallagher, "How Einstein Reconciled Religion to Science," Nautilus, June 10, 2019, https://getpocket.com/explore/item/how-einstein-reconciled-religion-to-science?utm_source=pocket-newtab.)

75 Our conscious mind is usually based on dualism, not a radical nondualistic consciousness. For the majority of people, their worldview is dualism – separation of the binaries such as male and female, spirit and matter, the brain's right hemisphere and the brain's left hemisphere. And politically, Democrat and Republican. Take a moment and ponder how this consciousness feeds the fires and flames of tribalism, sexism, and racism to name just a few resulting from a mindset of dualism.

Our Thoughts Affect Our Genes: We tend to think of our genetic heritage as a done deal. But, in fact, our genes are open to being influenced throughout our lifetime, both by what we do and by what we think, feel and believe. The new and growing field of epigenetics studies extra-cellular factors that influence genetic expression. While you may have heard that genes can be influenced by diet and exercise, many researchers are now exploring the ways that thoughts, feelings, and beliefs can exert the same epigenetic effect. It turns out that the chemicals catalyzed by our mental activity can interact with our genes in a powerful way. Much like the impacts of diet, exercise and environmental toxins, various thought patterns have been shown to turn certain genes "on" or "off."

Researcher Dawson Church, Ph.D., explores the relationship between thought and belief patterns and the expression of healing- or disease-related genes. "Your body reads your mind," Church says. "Science is discovering that while we may have a fixed set of genes in our chromosomes, which of those genes is active has a great deal to do with our subjective experiences, and how we process them."

As we think, we become; our body influences our mind and our mind influences our body. And our worldview and our thought processes are ruled by our foundational consciousness.

Our soul's DNA may affect our thoughts and patterns at various times during our life. Awakening will assist in activating our soul's DNA.

Growing Older May Make Us Smarter: Brain scientists used to be convinced that the main driver of brain aging was the loss of neurons, or brain-cell death. But new scanning technology has shown that most brains maintain most of their neurons over time. And, while some aspects of the aging process do involve losses—to memory, to reaction time—there are also some net gains.

What researches call a "neat trick" for net gain is named: "bilateralization." This involves using both the brain's right and left hemispheres at once. What the researchers don't realize is that this is the awakened consciousness of radical nonduality, the interpenetration or merging of both hemispheres. I refer to this state as a "strong mind."

When the two hemispheres of our brains are united in an inter-penetration of the logical and the intuitive, we experience reality not as separate from us but as a part of us and us as a part of it. This breaks down the barrier between our ordinary minds and our enlightened minds. The mirror of our minds will then reflect things in their true, original state.

There still may be dust on our mirrors (mind), but we will see clearer than those who remain stuck in a dualistic reality. When we realize that reality is not based on an either-or paradigm of dual-ism, we will finally discover a great peace within ourselves. There is great solace in knowing that we may be both enlightened as well as deluded. We do not have to be one or the other. We do not have to win or lose. This shift alone will transform us from self-centered beings into divine human beings that are participating in a journey of life and experience along with all other humans and all other creatures of the Earth.

Our minds become purer and calmer when we view and sense reality as united, not as a separate thing that may threaten our ego-tistical sense of safety and security. When we can see ourselves in all other things, not only other human beings, but animals, moths, trees, and so forth, we achieve a state of being that is peaceful, be-nevolent, compassionate, and empathic. This is something not just achievable in meditation, but more importantly, in every waking second of our lives.

One final point as we age, our minds/brains need to be challenged to seek new knowledge. We need to discover, to explore the far reaches. Not only do we need to far travel into the unknown, our minds need to seek what is not known. As it has been said, we need to "Boldly Go Where No One Has Gone Before." [Jon Spayde, "6 Surprising Things that Affect Your Brain, " *Care2*, (https://www.care2.com/greenliving/6-surprising-things-that-affect-your-brain.html)]

76 For the majority of people, dualism and duality are one and the

same. Even though at times I have used both terms interchangeability, they are the same and not the same: a paradox. Added to this paradoxical conundrum are the not-totally-solid definitions of the two. However, the definition of dualism is the more solid of the two. Dualism concerns opposition between two things, which causes separation such as in Christian theology: God in opposition or versus Satan, the Devil. With dualism, much of our time is spent denying the dark side of things as well as our own darkness. Ironically, this is the location of our creative self.

In dualism, there is no hope of reconciliation or the merging of the two things: Light and dark, heaven and hell, body and mind, men and women, spirit and matter. But common sense and nature open a window into the inaccurateness of dualism each and every day as the dark of night blends itself into the light of day. And the light of day blends itself into the dark of night.

On the other hand, duality recognizes the complementary aspects of things that our senses recognize as separate and opposite such as dark and light. Whereas dualism encourages and supports a battle between the dark and the light—good and evil—duality recognizes the complementary interaction of the light and the dark—spirit and matter—as forces that make up the whole of an existence that is held together and surrounded with another force, the unifying interpenetrating or blended force of creation – Oneness. This is the spiritual/religious philosophy of radical nonduality.

This then is the process of awakening to an indigenous consciousness of radical nonduality, our awakening as a plumed serpent. We proceed from a consciousness of dualism where all things are separate, composed of two diametrically opposed forces such as light and dark, to a realization of duality where we struggle with the knowledge of the complementary aspects of any two opposite polarities to a gradual knowing of integrative duality. This knowing allows us to achieve in our consciousness the union, merging, or blending of these opposites, a unifying of complementary polarities – a divine consciousness of radical nonduality.

This then is our sacred journey to become a Quetzalcóatl: We leave behind, detach from the soul-destroying and morally repugnant dualism reflected best by the paradigms of organized religion such as Christianity and Islam, then struggle to understand duality until finally through knowing ourselves, through self-sacrifice, and sacrifice self-to-self, our heart blossoms and becomes our face and our consciousness transforms into a state of being where there is no separation of things, just a union of opposites, Oneness, the blending of spirit and matter, fire and water: burning water: radical nonduality. (Rev. Dr. JC Husfelt, *Return of the Morning Star, Quetzalcóatl – Sixth Sun*, a book due to be published in 2020.)

[77] Reproductive Justice is the human right to maintain personal bodily autonomy, have children, not have children, and parent the children we have in safe and sustainable communities. It also includes the right to control birthing options, right to affordable health care, and the right to comprehensive sex education.

[78] Since there is no dogma or doctrine connected with the religious-philosophy of Divine Humanity, hopefully, after Sher and I pass-over, it will stay pure. A purity that has not happened with the message and teachings of Jesus or Muhammad:

"Like Christianity and Judaism, Islam would become, after the death of Muhammad, the Seal of the Prophets, opened to misinterpretation and extreme fundamentalism. This is not a criticism on Islam, merely a reflection of what happens to an ideal following the death of its leader. Women, for example, contrary to popular belief, were never required to veil themselves during the days of Muhammad. The decision was merely one of choice. Incidentally, women, under the laws of Muhammadism, did acquire rights for themselves, which they did not have before, including the right to inherit and run a business." [HRH Prince Michael of Albany and Walid Amine Salhab, *The Knights Templar of the Middle East, The Hidden History of the Islamic Origins of Freemasonry* (Red Wheel/Weiser LLC, 2006) 33.]

[79] Divine Humanity's foundational belief of radical nonduality

allows a person, a human being with the divine spark embedded within their heart, to express human short comings and dysfunctional behaviors. A freedom which allows a person to be authentic and not wear a false face. Even though awakened, with the divine fire brought to life, the person is still human and does not play the spiritual/religious/guru game of wearing a false-face of spirit perfection. These false-faced "leaders," supposedly spiritually and religiously superior to others, keep their dysfunctional behaviors in the "dark" which leads to harming others mentally, spiritually, and physically resulting in abhorrent actions such as child abuse.

[80] Referring to the fictional character Rocky Balboa, the protagonist in a series of eponymous boxing films.

[81] The Hebrew word for "spirit" also means "wind."

My nor'easter experience is a great allegory for the spiritual journey of awakening: Taking that first step; overcoming fear in facing the unknown; sacrifice; elemental purification; perseverance on the path even though the winds of conformity blow you to-and-fro; endurance in facing and confronting the obstacles of self, the past and the present; eventually the joy of feeling totally alive, and at long-last the merging of heaven and Earth within – with the realization that the journey continues on-and-on as we head home.

[82] David Freidel, Linda Schele, Joy Parker, *Maya Cosmos: Three Thousand Years on the Shaman's Path* (HarperCollins, 1993) 36 - 37.

[83] I was not in a fasting state. I was not meditating. I was not under the influence of a drug-induced trance. It was during the day, late afternoon, that I had my vision. Since Vince verified it was a true vision, it further proves the knowledge and ability of having a consciousness and awareness of radical nonduality. This was not a product or a subjective view of my mind but a visual reality of the Otherworld while awake and conscious in this world.

[84] Susan Milbrath, *Star Gods of the Maya: Astronomy in Art, Folklore, and Calendars (The Linda Schele Series in Maya and Pre-Columbian Studies)* (University of Texas Press, 1999) 177.

[85] Irene Nicholson, *Mexican and Central American Mythology* (Paul Hamlyn, 1967) 24.

[86] León-Portilla, *Aztec Thought and Culture*, 12.

[87] Huitzilopochtli, "Hummingbird of the South" or "Blue Hummingbird on the Left" was god of the sun and war, and considered the patron of the Aztec capital. He was also considered the brother of those other great Mesoamerican gods: Quetzalcóatl, Tezcatlipoca and Xipe Totec. He was always associated with the wizard or transforming shaman.

[88] Roberta H. Markman and Peter T. Markman, *Masks of the Spirit: Image and Metaphor in Mesoamerica* (University of California Press, 1994) 80.

[89] Even though intrigued, it was not until Christmas of 2017 that I discovered an explanatory commentary on this poem. One of my Christmas presents was Miguel León-Portilla book, *Aztec Thought and Culture – A Study of the Ancient Nahuatl Mind*. Studying his book, it became crystal clear in my heart and mind my connection to it:

LINE 1: The wise man: a light, a torch, a stout torch that does not smoke.

The "wise man" is the usual translation of the Nahuatl word *tlamatini*. The word is derived from the verb *mati*, "to know." The suffix *ni* gives it the substantive function, "he who knows" (Latin sapiens). The prefix *tla* before the verb form indicates that "things" or "something" is the direct object. So, etymologically considered, *tla-matini* means "he who knows things" or "he who knows something." The character of the *tlamatini* is here conveyed metaphorically by describing him as the light of a stout torch which illumines but does not smoke.

LINE 2: A perforated mirror, a mirror pierced on both sides. A mirror pierced on both sides: *tézcatl nécuc xapo*.

The allusion here is to the *tlachialoni*, a type of scepter with a pierced mirror at one end. This object was part of the equipment of certain gods, who used it to scrutinize the Earth and human affairs. Literally, as Sahagún notes, *tlachialoni* "means a lookout or observatory . . . because one observed or looked through it by means of a hole in the middle." Applied to the wise man, it conveys the idea that he is himself a medium of contemplation, "a concentrated or focused view of the world and things human."

LINE 3: His are the black and red ink, his are the illustrated manuscripts[.]

Here the wise man is described as the possessor of the codices and of the *Amoxtli*, the ancient Nahuatl books of paper made from the bark of the *amate* (wild fig tree) folded like a screen or an accordion. Only relatively few of these priceless manuscripts escaped destruction at the time of the Spanish conquest. The fact that important philosophical concepts were preserved in these codices is proved by the Codex Vaticanus A 3738, the first pages of which contain stylized drawings of the Aztec conception of the supreme principle, the directions of the universe, and so on.

LINE 4: He himself is writing and wisdom.

The Nahuatl expression used here, *Tlilli Tlapalli*, means, literally, that the wise man is black and red ink. But since these colors symbolize throughout Nahuatl mythology the presentation of and knowledge about things difficult to understand and about the hereafter, the obvious metaphorical implication is that the wise man possesses "writing and wisdom."

LINE 8: His is the handed-down wisdom; he teaches it; he follows the path of truth. His is the handed-down knowledge or wisdom.

This thought is expressed in Nahuatl by a single word, *machize*, derived from *machiztli*, with the suffix *e* indicating possession; thus "to him belongs." The compound loses the ending *tli* and becomes *machiz-e*. *Machize* is derived from the passive form of *mati*, "to know," which is macho, "to be known"; accordingly, it may be called a passive substantive, wisdom known, handed down from person to person by tradition. Its correlative form is *(tla)-matiliztli*, wisdom or knowledge in an active sense; that is, acquired knowledge. This gives some indication of the subtlety of Nahuatl thought and of the flexibility of the language which can concisely express such fine shades of meaning.

LINE 10: He makes wise the countenances of others; to them he gives a face (a personality); he leads them to develop it.

Three Nahuatl nouns of unsuspected depth enrich the meaning of this line: *teixtlamachtiani, teixcuitiani, teixtomani*. The word *tlamachtiani* means "he who teaches or communicates some-thing to someone else." The particle *ix* is an indefinite personal prefix indicating the receiver of the action of the verb or noun to which it is attached, "to the others." Consequently, *te-ix-tla-machtiani* denotes "he who teaches or communicates something to the countenances of others." The context shows that the "something" is wisdom, since the wise man has been described as "teacher of the truth," "the one who teaches truth."

The other two words, *te-ix-cuitiani*, "the one who makes others to take a face," and *te-ix-tomani*, "the one who makes others to develop a face," are even more interesting, for they reveal that the *tlamatini* functioned as a teacher and psychologist. In this passage, as well as in lines 11 and 12, the word *ixtli*, "face," whose root *ix* occurs in all three compound terms, carries a meaning strikingly similar to that of the Greek word prosopon, "face," not only in the anatomical sense but also in the metaphorical significance of personality. This figurative meaning of *ixtli* appears very often in the discussions and speeches of Sahagún's Indian informants and in many other Nahuatl documents.

LINE 14: He puts a mirror before others; he makes them prudent, cautious; he causes a face (a personality) to appear in them.

Here the *tlamatini* takes on the role of moralist. In the word *te-tezcaviani*, "he puts a mirror before others," the basic element is *tézcatl*, "mirror made of carved and polished stone," which, in Sahagún's words, "faithfully reproduced the face." From *tézcatl* is derived the verb *tezcavia*, which with the prefix *te* means "to place a mirror before others." The ending *ni* gives the term *te-tezca-via-ni* the substantive character, "he who places a mirror before others." The purpose of this action is then clarified: "to make them prudent and careful." Again there is a similarity to the ethical thought of Greece and India: man needs to have knowledge of himself, the *gnóthi seautón* or "Know thyself" of Socrates.

LINE 16: He applies his light to the world.

The Nahuatl conception of the world was designated by the term *cemanáhuac*, whose component parts are *cem*, "entirely," "completely," and *a-náhuac*, "that which is surrounded by water [like a ring]." The world was, then, "that which is entirely surrounded by water." This idea had a certain geographical confirmation in that the so-called Aztec Empire was bounded on the west by the Pacific and on the east by the Gulf of Mexico, the latter being a veritable Mare Ignotum beyond which remained only the mythological "place of Knowing," *Tlilantlapalan*. From the word *cemanáhuac* and the verb *tlavia*, "to illumine," "to apply a light," comes the composite "to apply a light to the world." This attributes to the *tlamatini* the nature of an investigator of the physical world.

LINE 17: He knows what is above us (and) in the region of the dead.

Here is another traditional aspect of the wise man: "he knows about that [which is] above us," *topan*, and below us, *mictlan*, "the region of the dead," that is, the hereafter.

The idiomatic complex *topan, mictlan* carries the meaning, "what is beyond our knowledge, what is in itself beyond experience." The Nahuatl mind formulated what we today would call a metaphysical order or noumenal world. Its counterpart is the world itself, *cemanáhuac*, "that which is entirely surrounded by water."

At other times, as has been noted, a contrast is made between what is "above us, the beyond," and "what is on the surface of the Earth (*tlaltícpac*)." The distinctness of this contrast and its frequent occurrence suggest strongly that, in their own way, the Nahuas had divined the duality or ambivalence of the world, a theme which has so deeply concerned Western European thought since pre-Socratic times. On the one hand, there is that which is visible, immanent, manifold, phenomenal, which for the Nahuas was "that which is upon the Earth," *tlaltícpac*; on the other, there is that which is permanent, metaphysical, transcendental, expressed in Nahuatl as *topan, mictlan*, "what is above us and below us, in the region of the dead."

LINE 20: Thanks to him the people humanize their will and receive a strict education.

Itech netlacaneco, "thanks to him, the people humanize their will"; such is the translation of the Nahuatl word *ne-tlaca-neco. Neco* is the passive voice of *nequi*, "he desires," "he is desired"; *thca* is the root of *tlácatl*, "man," "human being"; *ne* is an indefinite personal prefix. The combination of these elements, therefore, means "the people are loved as human beings," *ítech*, "thanks to him [the wise man]."

Another function of the *tlamatini*, then, is to teach the moral quality existing in "that which is human." In a sense, the text points to the existence of a "humanistic" thought among the Nahuas, for it seems to indicate that this "humanizing of the will" was one of the basic tenets of a Nahuatl education!

Summarizing what has been said concerning the whole text, it might be noted that the Nahuatl philosopher was symbolically described putting together the most meaningful aspects of his intrinsic nature: he throws light upon reality; he is a concentrated vision of the world; "his are the illustrated manuscripts"; "he himself is writing and wisdom." He is a teacher (*temachtiani*), "the road"; "his is the handed-down wisdom"; "he is the teacher of the truth and he does not cease to admonish." Moreover, he performs the duties of a psychologist (*teixcuitiani*), through whom "the faces of others look wise"; "he opens their ears . . . and is a master of teachers." That he also functions as a moralist (*tetezcahuiani*) becomes evident in these words: "He puts a mirror before others, he makes them prudent, cautious." Immediately after this, his interest in examining the physical world is discussed:

"*Cemanahuactlahuiani,*" "he attends to things, he applies his light to the world." One single sentence shows him to be a metaphysician, for he studies that which escapes our finite comprehension—"the region of the dead"—the hereafter. Finally, as though in summation of his qualities and in explanation of his principal goal, we are told that "thanks to him people humanize their will and receive a strict education." (León-Portilla, *Aztec Thought and Culture*, 11 - 16.)

90 During an interview with *The Washington Post* in 2016, Trump spoke about collecting rent from buildings his father owned in "dangerous" areas, like Coney Island, Brooklyn, and Cincinnati where he said he was "liable to get shot" if he came at the wrong time.

"You know when you collect rent—and you may have heard this—but you never stand in front of the door," Trump said. [Eli Rosenberg, "Trump said he would charge a gunman. Here's what he's actually done in the face of danger," *The Washington Post*, Feb. 26, 2018 (https://www.washingtonpost.com/news/the-fix/wp/2018/02/26/trump-said-he-would-charge-a-gunman-heres-what-hes-actually-done-in-the-face-of-danger/)]

91 This was the first time I had felt this sensation on the back of my neck and head. This turned out to be my body's response to extra-terrestrial and otherworldly beings and energies.

92 The Holy Grail is but a symbol for the sacred teaching of radical nonduality, – the interpenetration of spirit and matter. All things are divine with the spark, the starlight of God within them. In other words, the divine is within all things (seen and unseen), and all things are within the divine.

93 Anna Morduch, *The Sovereign Adventure: The Grail of Mankind* (James Clark, 1970) 11.

94 As it evolved, the twenty-two cards of the Tarot's Major Arcana incorporated the magical numbering process of the Hebrew al-

phabet. Beginning with Aleph (1) the Magician and completing with Tav (400) the twenty-second card – the World. Contrary to this numbering system, most present-day tarot systems utilize zero as their beginning card and call the zero card the Fool. In these systems, the last card, the World, is number twenty-one, not twenty-two. This is one of the indications of the mistake and wrongness of this numbering placement.

The Absolute or First Principle is the one, not a zero. A tarot system with zero as the beginning card is a dualistic system not a system of oneness. In addition, using zero as the beginning card results in the World card number twenty-one being assigned the sacred number 300. This is irrational. The sum of the digits in twenty-one, or two plus one is three. Three is the first prime number of the Father or the Absolute, it does not equate to the Relative, the Mother or the World, which carries a value of four, geometrically represented by the square or cube and philosophically by the concept of the "four winds."

However, if we begin our cards with one, the Magician, then the twenty-second or last card would be the World with a value of 400 from the sacred numbers of the Hebrew alphabet. Thus, the sum of digits is twenty-two or two plus two equals four. Interestingly, the number four carries hidden in itself the divine perfection of creation, the number ten. As we add the numbers leading to four, we obtain ten $(1+2+3+4=10)$. The World card also has a meaning revealed by the keywords of Consummation and New Beginnings.

If card twenty-two is the World, what then is the twenty-first card? It is the Fool card with the Hebrew letter Shin or Schin (300) with the keyword of the attainment of perfection for humanity. Schin as the fire of life or the inner spark is the awakened divine human being that now sees the world as the divine perfection of creation. The Fool card as an awakened divine human is symbolized by the Crown of the Magi, the Lotus Wreath and the Harp of God.

We eventually arrive through perseverance at the World card. This card represents the Oneness of self and life. But our journey is not yet complete as we continue being the fool but in a different way. We now have an awakening of reality and the oneness of life. This spurs us on to further adventures and awakening. And once again, we are the foolish one or the fool in other people's eyes as we strive on for the spiritual and not the material aspects of life ever seeking Divinehood (Feathered-Serpent-hood).

95 You might guess that I am not a fan of "superhero" movies.

96 *Kingdom of Heaven*, directed by Ridley Scott, 2005.

97 The archangel of the visitation that occurred in 1997 was Mikaël, known to most as the Archangel Michael. I had determined this through my research of the connection between myself and the archangel such as: "Michael was denominated by the Kabbalists and the Gnostics, "the Saviour," the angel of the Sun and angel of Light." [H. P. Blavatsky, *Isis Unveiled: Both Volumes – A Master-Key to the Mysteries of Ancient and Modern Science and Theology* (Pantianos Classics, 2017) 488.]

98 Bob Stewart, "The Grail as Bodily Vessel," *At the Table of the Grail*, John Matthews, editor (Routledge & Kegan Paul, 1984) 186.

99 This is a great way in which to visualize radical nonduality, the interpenetration or blending-merging, of our world and the Other-world.

100 At the time, we had no idea that we would be in Japan two years later where I participated in the first international *Bujinkan Tai Kai*, a gathering of martial artists. *Tai* means great and *kai* means sea – great sea.

101 Hamish Miller and Paul Broadhurst, *The Sun and the Serpent* (Pendragon Partnership, 1994) 13.

102 Exoteric/Esoteric Buddhism - Tendai esotericism (*Taimitsu*); Shingon esotericism (*Tōmitsu*).

103 This was years before my vision in 1993 when a voice from heaven declared me the Morning Star.

104 *Mikkyo* meditative techniques utilize all the faculties and ener-

gies of the human body-mind, focusing them on Buddhahood. The capacities to think, feel, perceive, know, and act are summed up in the three secrets (*sanmitsu*), the basis of esoteric practice, which are the all-pervading, enlighten activities of the Buddha's body, speech, and mind reflected in the individual. Quite simply, when one's three activities of body, speech, and mind unite with those of the Buddha, one becomes Buddha.

Mikkyo is based on the universality of the Dharma Body, the activity of which permeates all things. Its teaching is thus considered equally suitable for all people in all situations at all times. Based on the related concept that all phenomena are themselves manifestations of universal Buddhahood, *Mikkyo* uses any possible means to transform the "deluded" individual into a Buddha.

For the body, there are prescribed hand gestures called *mudras* (*ingei*), movements of the entire body, the smell of burning incense, and the taste of certain herbs. There are ritual implements to manipulate and sculpted and painted forms of art to contemplate. Such ritual art is an important element of practice. For speech, the practitioner recites prescribed invocations called *mantras* (shingon), as well as related verse prayers and chants. For the mind, there are visualizations (*kanso* or *kannen*) of deities and symbolic forms, involving colors, movements, thoughts, imagination, and feelings. [Taiko Yamasaki, *Shingon: Japanese Esoteric Buddhism* (Shambhala, 1998) 61-62.]

105 I am not motivated or burdened by guilt in this lifetime, but I would discover much later in life that I was carrying great guilt within my heart and soul from a previous lifetime.

106 Just as there is the astrological knowledge of your birth (the position of the planets at the time and place of your birth) there is also AstroCartography (the relationship of the planets at the time and place of your birth to the geography of the Earth). In other words, it identifies places on Earth at which planets occupied powerful positions at the moment of your birth. It wasn't until almost 2007 that I discovered Astro Cartography and its value. Kōyasan is the

location of Pluto on my IC at the time of my birth. Briefly, this is the place where "the ultimate battle of selfhood and identification is fought with family, the past, traditions, and roots of self, and a final, self-induced birth of a new identity is accomplished." Under the Pluto influence, "miracles can happen and Universal truth is seen and one can never again be able to live in the illusions in which most people exist. . . . a reality that totally changes life direction and perception." (AstroCartography booklet, Astro Numeric Service, Box 425-S, San Pablo, CA 94806)

The following October, this same influence became evident once again with the descending spirit exorcism at midnight in front of Kōbō Daishi's mausoleum.

107 In 1987, José Arguelles launched a word-of-mouth Harmonic Convergence campaign calling for 144,000 "Sun dancers" to gather near sacred sites at dawn on August 16 and 17 to "open the doors to the final 26 years of the 5,125-year Mayan Great Cycle," an era of unprecedented change and preparation for a new evolutionary cycle on Earth.

The Harmonic Convergence was celebrated worldwide by tens of thousands if not millions of people and marked the first-time human beings simultaneously coordinated their prayers, meditations, and ceremonies at sacred sites around the planet. Everyone from Shirley MacLaine to Timothy Leary to John Denver celebrated the event. Even talk show host Johnny Carson got his studio audience to "om" on behalf of the event. Many people reported significant shifts in consciousness and a reorientation in their life patterns.

The dates of the Harmonic Convergence were based on prophetic events beginning with Good Friday, 1519, when Hernán Cortés led the Spanish invasion of Mexico. This day on the Mexican sacred calendar marked the precise end of a fifty-two-year cycle. Since then, nine fifty-two-year cycles had elapsed, coming to a close on August 16, 1987. This also marked the last day of the nine hell cycles as prophesied by Mexican prophet Quetzalcóatl. It was a signal indicating that only twenty-five years remained before the end of the Mayan Great Cycle of History, which occurred on December 21, 2012. [Steve Beckow, "What was the Harmonic Convergence?" *Golden Age of Gaia*, August 9, 2017 (https://goldenageofgaia.com/2017/08/09/what-was-the-harmonic-convergence/).]

108 Robert Boissiere, *The Return of Pahana: A Hopi Myth* (Sigo Press, 1990) 60. Robert was a friend of ours, whom we met at a conference in Calgary. We had driven Mom and Vince Stogan to the gathering in the early 1990s.

109 The Good Friday Experiment was run by Walter N. Pahnke, a graduate student in theology at Harvard Divinity School, under the supervision of Timothy Leary and the Harvard Psilocybin Project. The goal was to see if in religiously predisposed subjects, psilocybin, the active principle in magic mushrooms, would act as a reliable entheogen (a chemical substance, typically of plant origin, that is ingested to produce a nonordinary state of consciousness for religious or spiritual purposes).

The experiment was conducted on Good Friday, 1962, at Boston University's Marsh Chapel. Prior to the Good Friday service, graduate-degree divinity student volunteers from the Boston area were randomly divided into two groups. In a double-blind experiment, half of the students received psilocybin, while a control group received a large dose of niacin. Niacin produces clear physiological changes and thus was used as a psychoactive placebo. In at least some cases, those who received the niacin initially believed they had received the psychoactive drug. ["The Good Friday Experiment," *Grow a Brain*, March 21, 2008 (http://growabrain.typepad.com/growabrain/2008/03/the-good-friday.html).]

110 Turquoise Reef Resorts brochure.

111 "Tulum Archaeological Site, Mexico," *Sacred Destinations* (http://www.sacred-destinations.com/mexico/tulum).

112 "The Descending God," *Best of Riviera Maya* (https://bestofrivieramaya.com/descending-god-tulum/).

113 Mexican archeologist and ethnologist best known for her study

of the civilizations of Teotihuacan and the Aztecs and her theories concerning the Mesoamerican culture hero, Quetzalcóatl.

114 It is interesting to note that the Aztec verb *temo* means both "to be born" and "to descend."

115 Guardians are usually referred to as totems or power animals. In our fast-paced, performance-oriented society, these Otherworldly energetic guardians have been trivialized in different ways, with one being the use of the term "power animals." A more appropriate name would be guardian spirit or "co-essence."

Co-essences may take many forms, even thunder and/or lightning. But many times the form is an animal. Whatever form, a co-essence is a powerful companion for us in our journey to awaken. These guardians may help us become closer to nature and its seemingly wild and untamed forces. We are never truly alone in our journey of life. Our guardians are our constant companions as well as our helpers. A hummingbird guardian may help us move faster on our feet, whereas a serpent guardian may help us internally release/shed our past that is inhibiting our happiness and growth in the present. A jaguar guardian may help us achieve a fearless state of mind, as well as give us the courage to face our symbolic death so that we may be reborn as a "person of power."

116 *Nagual* (*nahualli* or *nahual*) is commonly known as spirit guardian. "The word nahual derives from nahualli meaning both a form-changing shaman and the being into which a shaman transforms. The concept of a nahual has its roots in indigenous Mesoamerican notions of shamanic power and transformation. As a shaman possesses the power to transform him/herself into his nahual (say, a jaguar)[.]" (Maffie, *Aztec Philosophy*, 39.)

117 My tonal, birth guardian/co-essence, is not jaguar but snowy owl. Owls are spirit messengers representing prophecy, magic, silence, and forgotten knowledge. They are emblematic of a deep connection with wisdom and intuitive knowledge. The snowy owl has some extra, unique gifts, as it inhabits the realm of day. It has a special connection with the north direction (the same direction of

the visitation). Finally, the "snowy owl carries messages from the elders, and people with this bird as a totem will channel this wisdom in some way for the benefit of the world, usually in the form of the written word." [Lesley Morrison, *The Healing Wisdom of Birds: An Everyday Guide to Their Spiritual Songs & Symbolism* (Llewellyn Publications, 2011) 108.]

[118] John E. Staller and Brian Stross, *Lightning in the Andes and Mesoamerica: Pre-Columbian, Colonial, and Contemporary Perspectives* (Oxford University Press, 2013) 147.

[119] According to Joanne M. Spero of the University of Texas at Austin "It can be seen that the Kawak was a multidimensional concept. Kawak was (and still is) conceived of as a spirit of underworld caverns, the Lord of Earth and Water, and the guardian of the ancestors. He is considered to be an ancestor himself since he is called lak main (Chol), "our grandfather," tatik chawuk (Tzeltal), "our father lightning," and komam k'uh (Jacaltec), "our grandfather lightning." Because men petition for his powers in battle and Kawak symbols adorn their weapons, he is the patron of warriors. Lightning men, whose prototype was the ax-wielding GI (Yax Naab Chak) on codex-style pottery, derive their supernatural powers of good and evil from the kawak; as such he is the patron of witchcraft and curing." [Joanne M. Spero, "Beyond Rainstorms: The Kawak as an Ancestor, Warrior, and Patron of Witchcraft," *Sixth Palenque Round Table, 1986*, edited by Virginia M. Fields (P.A.R.I. Online Publications, La Sexta Mesa Redonda, 1991.)]

[120] According to a Yucatec account, "Chac is responsible for bringing rain, and four aspects of the god dwell in the 'trunk of heaven' in the eastern sky during the dry season. On June 2, they get their instructions from the archangel Saint Michael and they ride forth on four horses in four different directions. The descriptions suggest that these horses are different-colored clouds associated with different weather phenomena. The archangel may represent the fifth Chac, the one in the center who controls the clouds associated with the four Chacs."

Furthermore, "in the Postclassical Dresden Codex Venus pages, the planet is referred to as chac ek, 'great star.' This pattern of naming suggests a link between Chac and Venus, for the same term often refers to Venus in contemporary Maya accounts.

"Chac's title among the Maya is 'the Chac who makes brilliant the sky,' usually interpreted as an image of lightning, but also possibly an image of brilliant light. This would be an appropriate title for Venus, the brightest planet in the sky. Studies of Venus imagery suggest that 'the ultimate power over the rains is held by Venus,' and the northerly extreme of Venus coincided with the onset of the rainy season makes a strong case for linking the Evening Star aspect of Venus with rain-bringing and agricultural fertility. Chac may be linked with Venus in this aspect." (Milbrath, *Star Gods of the Maya: Astronomy in Art, Folklore, and Calendars*, 201 - 202.)

[121] The deity connected with *Quiáhuitl* is *Tonatiuh*—the solar god of the Fifth World, our present one.

[122] Staller and Stross, *Lightning in the Andes and Mesoamerica: Pre-Columbian, Colonial, and Contemporary Perspectives*, 133.

[123] Roberta H. Markman and Peter T. Markman, *Masks of the Spirit: Image and Metaphor in Mesoamerica* (University of California Press, 1994) 18.

[124] One of my innate abilities is keen depth perception.

[125] Markman and Markman, *Masks of the Spirit: Image and Metaphor in Mesoamerica*, 21.

[126] Most people believe that exorcism is the religious or spiritual practice of solely the expulsion of spiritual entities from a person. But there is another form of exorcism which is the descending of a spirit into a body, a blending of spirit and matter, a descending spirit exorcism. Historically, the only other person who has experienced this type of exorcism has been Jesus: the Spirit descending upon him like a dove. Mark 1:10 NKJV.

[127] This gives context to my experience of a fiery spirit descending into water. My body, as are all human bodies, is seven-eighths wa-

ter. "It can indeed be said that the one sure and inerrant key to the Bible is the simple concept of fire plunging into water, the fire being spiritual mind-power and water being the constituent element of physical bodies, as well as the symbol of matter. Soul (spirit) as fire, plunged down into body, as water, and therein had its baptism. In the Hebrew alphabet there were said to be three "mother letters," aleph (A), mem (M) and shin (SH). These ostensibly represent respectively the pre-creation stage (A), the middle stage of spirit's involvement in matter (M), and its final stage of glorious deification (SH), the symbol of fire. M is the symbol of water. Life emanates out of potential fire, is 'baptized' for evolutionary purposes in water, the symbol of matter, and returns to the source with fiery potentialities actualized by having "overcome" the powers in the water-matter. The Hebrew word for fire is *esh*, and spirit evolves its divine fire in man, *ish*. The divine fire in man made him the *ish*-man, and the divine man in tribal life of some nations was called the *shaman*." [Alvin Boyd Kuhn, Ph.D., *The Esoteric Structure of The Alphabet* (Martino Fine Books, 2015) 15, 16, 20.]

[128] Ibid., 20.

[129] Jay Sakashita, "Yakudoshi marks our peak year," *Honoluluadvertiser.com*, March 18, 2006, (http://the.honoluluadvertiser.com/article/2006/Mar/18/il/FP603180319.html).

[130] Kūkai, "Sokushin jôbutsû-gi," Zenshu, 1:56.

[131] Rachael Storm, *The Encyclopedia of Eastern Mythology*, (Southwater, 2018) 179.

[132] Allan G. Grapard, "Flying Mountains & Walkers of Emptiness: Sacred Space in Japanese Religions," *Kyoto Journal Issue 25*, 2011, 37.

[133] Cited by Gaston Renondeau, *Le Shugendo: Histoire, doctrine et rites des Yamabushi* (Paris: Imprimerie Nationale, 1965), 110-111.

[134] Name for the ancient Vedic fire ritual that is unique to Esoteric Buddhism.

[135] At the time I didn't realize that both Sherry and I have Alphard

as our Heliacal Rising Star; Alphard, The Heart of the Serpent, Hydra. Your Heliacal Rising Star is known as a Fixed Star and is determined by the time, date and location of your birth. The Rising Star is just one of many Fixed Stars that a person may have during each incarnation.

136 This "flower and song" (poetry) is dedicated to Kōyasan, Fudō Myō-ō, and the descending spirit exorcism.

137 Yamasaki, *Shingon: Japanese Esoteric Buddhism*, 30.

138 This is a very rare occurrence where a spirit descends into a human and they experience the interpenetration of spirit and matter; the Absolute and Relative of creation – true Oneness. This was the case with the dove (Venus) descending into Jesus.

139 Morton Smith, *Jesus the Magician: Charlatan or Son of God?* (Ulysses Press, 1998) 181.

140 Basically, *mudras* are various ways to use our hands including intertwining our fingers. The most commonly recognized religious *mudras* would be the Christian hands pressed together in prayer or the Islamic uplifted palms of the hands in reverence to Allah. Besides the prayer *mudra*, the next most commonly recognizable Christian *mudra* is depicted in many of the images of Jesus. This is the right arm held up with the forefinger and the middle finger raised straight up and the other two fingers curled under. Interestingly enough, this is referred to as the sword *mudra* in esoteric Buddhism. Frequently this *mudra* is used in energy work. Either the artists were practitioners of an esoteric form of Buddhism or Jesus was an esoteric teacher.

141 Bodhicitta is "Awakening Mind." Acalanātha (Fudō-Myō-ō) embodies the first quickening of the Bodhicitta. Fundamentally, awakening is "a way of collapsing the distance between mind and enlightened mind, and thus, abolishing the dualism that is itself the stuff of delusion." [Bernard Faure, *Visions of Power: Imagining Medieval Japanese Buddhism* (Princeton University Press, 2000) 16.]

142 When one is armed with this sensitivity (sixth sense), it is possi-

ble to perceive a changing environment or the essence of a personality at first meeting without any analytical preparation. [Mitsugi Saotome, *Aikido and the Harmony of Nature* (Shambhala, 1993) 92.]

143 At various times over the years since 1987, I have successfully utilized this secret teaching. Please see the section above titled "Pesky Snakes."

144 The advisory concerned the Shining Path guerilla movement in Peru.

145 On the trail, we never met any other hikers.

146 Douglas Sharon, *Wizard of the Four Winds, A Shaman's Story* (Free Press, 1978) 93.

147 During the late summer of 2000 C.E., a massive crane being used to film a beer commercial toppled over and damaged the *Intihuatana* stone. When I returned in 2007 with two of our apprentices, the stone was roped off as were most of the other sites. The funky hotel I'd stayed in was now a five-star resort and, where once there had been only a train station at the bottom of the mountain, there was a small town, a great sadness to my heart.

148 Conducting research for my forthcoming book, *Return of the Morning Star, Quetzalcóatl – Sixth Sun, Awakening to a New Consciousness*, I came across the following:

Chavin was not only the first high civilization of the Andes: it covered the widest area as well, probably extending right from the jungle to the sea—from the sources of the Amazon to the Pacific—and even the Pacific Islands. On the eastern slopes of the Cordilleras, in the Urubamba Valley and on the upper course of the Marãnao river, a temple fortress near Tantamayo probably belonged to the Chavin empire, and so did the colossal building on top of which the Incas erected their fortress of Machu Picchu. [Pierre Honoré, *In Search of Quetzalcóatl: The Mysterious Heritage of South American Civilization* (Adventures Unlimited Press, 2007) 171.]

149 *Mesa* symbolizes the duality of the worlds of man and nature, a veritable microcosmos duplicating the forces at work in the uni-

verse. Equilibrium is the key to Eduardo's entire system, when oneness with the cosmos is achieved and Eduardo becomes the manifest "center" by transcending the opposites at work in the cosmos and within his own being. (Sharon, *Wizard of the Four Winds, A Shaman's Story*, 62 - 140.)

150 According to Thomas Jefferson, Paul was the first corrupter of the doctrines of Jesus.

Saul (Paul of Tarsus), "the Spouter of Wickedness and Lies and the Distorter of the True Teachings of Jesus: From the Kerygmata Petrou, which originates from the Ebionites. In this account, the father of Christianity is described as 'an apostate of the Law,' the 'spouter of lies,' and 'the distorter of the true teachings of Jesus.' The events that occurred on the road to Damascus that resulted in Paul's 'miraculous' conversion are given very short shrift, and are simply described as 'dreams and illusions inspired by devils.' (Husfelt, *Do You Like Jesus – Not the Church?*, 26.)

151 Just as there is the astrological knowledge of your birth (the position the planets took at the time and place of your birth), there is also Astro Cartography (the relationship of the planets at the time and place of your birth to the geography of the Earth). In other words, it identifies places on Earth where planets occupied powerful positions at the moment of your birth. Machu Picchu is the location of Venus on my ascendant at the time of my birth. Briefly, this is the place where "men may . . . come to terms with the feminine parts of their personalities." (Astro Cartography booklet, Astro Numeric Service, Box 425-S, San Pablo, CA 94806)

152 It is interesting to note that "the Initiate into the mysteries of the '*Great Mother*' was always called the 'son' of the widow." My father had passed-over in 1984. As the only child, I was the "son of the widow." (Morduch, *The Sovereign Adventure: The Grail of Mankind*, 65.)

153 The Hermit is the ninth tarot card of the Major Arcana.

154 Arthur Lubow, "The Possessed," *The New York Times Maga-*

zine, June 24, 2007 (https://www.nytimes.com/2007/06/24/maga-zine/24MachuPicchu-t.html).

155 Carol Cumes and Rómulo Lizárraga Valencia, *Journey to Machu Picchu: Spiritual Wisdom from the Andes* (Llewellyn Publications, 1999) xi.

156 Like Vince Stogan (see the section titled "Spirit Dancing, Burn-ings and Bathings"), I'm loathe to call myself and Sher shamans. It seems that everyone calls themselves a shaman. Yes, we fit the crite-ria: we have been initiated and hold shamanic lineages; we heal; and we are the spiritual leaders of a community. We hold the medicine power of the two oldest ceremony's – burnings and bathings. We do not charge for healings or ceremonies. Our training and power come from first-hand or direct experience. We are shamans, medi-cine people, but we are not neo-shamans who receive their training through workshops. And then there is this… "The shaman is the man (woman) who *knows* and *remembers*…" [Joseph L. Henderson and Maud Oakes, *The Wisdom of the Serpent: The Myths of Death, Rebirth, and Resurrection* (Collier Books, 1963) 64.]

I feel a great disservice has been conducted by leading people down a path (based on of one's own lack of knowledge and power), where beating a drum and closing your eyes qualifies you to become a shaman or druid. The true and narrow path to becoming a person of power—whether that person is called shaman or mystic—is diffi-cult and takes years to achieve.

157 "The most effective shamans are those who have the natural ability to enter the trance state at will." [Philip Gardiner and Gary Osborn, *The Serpent Grail: The Truth Behind the Holy Grail, the Phi-losopher's Stone and the Elixir of Life* (Watkins, 2006) 19.] In other words, to access the Otherworld at will.

158 The unhealthy ego only considers "self" and "self-importance" as most important and as separate from all other things—an emphasis on the "I." The healthy ego views "self" as connected, or one, with all other things—the "I" in the "We" and the "We" in the "I."

159 Ancestral worship was important to most, if not all, indigenous people as it was to Anselmo's people: "The *Totil Me'il*, literally 'Fathers-Mothers,' also known as Ancestors, reside in the mountains above each community and watch over the lives of their children. . . . The Ancestors represent the first people who learned how to plant corn, praise their creator, and live as proper human beings." [Walter F., Jr. Morris and Jeffrey Jay Foxx, *Living Maya* (Harry N Abrams Inc., 1987) 153.]

160 Jesus was anointed by one Mary of Bethany – the Magdalene. In the Jewish faith, "both king and high priest were anointed and were thus a *meshiha*, a messiah." Messiah in Greek is Christ or Christos. Thus we end up with Jesus Christ and the term Christianity. Not Jesus the Anointed or Jesus the Christ, but Jesus Christ, —"a purely functional title distorted into a proper name."

The claim by Saul that Jesus was fully divine was a lie. But why the anointment? Could Jesus's anointment by the Magdalene have had a deeper meaning? Could it have been an acknowledgment of his unique humanness and role as prophet and messenger? And could it have been a statement of his divine mission and an outward sign of his divinity within – the divine spark? In addition, why was the anointing done by a woman and not by one of his male disciples? Could it have been a symbolization of the sacred marriage, which signified oneness?

Anointing with oil generally meant a person or object was "set aside" for divine service. This was a form of sanctification identifying a person as a priest or king – a messiah. This sanctifying practice extends back to the goddess tradition of the Near Eastern religions, where "anointing the head of the king with oil was a ritual performed by the heiress or royal priestess who represented the Goddess. In Greek, this rite was called the *hieros gamos* or 'Sacred Marriage.' The anointing of the head had erotic significance, the head being symbolic of the phallus 'anointed' by the woman for penetration during the physical consummation of marriage. . . . Through his union with the priestess, the king/consort received royal status, he became known as the 'Anointed One'— – in Hebrew, the 'Messiah.'" (Husfelt, *Do You Like Jesus – Not the Church?* 30 – 31.)

161 Usually, an assistant to the shaman pours the shots of posh, but since it was only the three of us, Anselmo did the pouring.

162 Morris and Foxx, *Living Maya*, 160.

163 Nicholas Mancall-Bitel, "Meet Pox: Whiskey, Rum and Mezcal's Mind-Altering Love Child," *Supercall*, August 11, 2017 (https://www.supercall.com/spirits/mexican-pox-mayan-liquor).

164 In August of 1987, I drove a few friends into Cancun for a night of clubbing. After a few hours, I was definitely over the legal limit for alcohol to drive. But three of the people decided to stay in Cancun, which left only one other person to drive besides me. And he was drunker than I was. As we were leaving the city limits and my friend was throwing up out the passenger's side window, we were pulled over by the Federales. As the officer walked up I got out of the car and approached him. I had my license in one pocket and the rest of my money in the other. Without waiting I put my license in his outstretched hand and within seconds, before any words were spoken, I grabbed it out of his hand and replaced it with all the money in my pocket, got back in the car and took off. How much money? To this day, I don't know. Was it the money or possibly my presence that resulted in us not being pursued or thrown in jail? I doubt you could get away with this today.

I am not justifying my behavior. It was not smart or the right thing to do to drive drunk. But I was not that drunk and in 1987 there were few if any cars on the road at that time of night heading south to Shangri La Caribe, outside of Playa del Carmen. We learn from our humanness. Each of us is divine as well as human. To truly awaken our divine spark, we need to experience our humanness as it blends with our divineness. This is one of the reasons for the abuse problems of the Catholic Church as the majority of priests didn't experience their dysfunctional dark side before they became priests. And they live the illusion of being God's mouthpiece and gatekeepers on Earth.

165 A weak mind has nothing to do with intelligence and is not equated to any level of intelligence.

166 This power I seldom use, unless necessary in circumstances such as this.

167 *Hunab Ku* means "The One God." This supposed ultimate deity of the Maya was an invention of the Spanish missionaries that was then hijacked by New Age authors who revived and popularized the concept of *Hunab Ku* in the 20th century.

Hunab Ku is not a pre-conquest Mayan deity. Before the Spanish conquest in the 16th century, no mention of *Hunab Ku* exists. Most anthropological experts and scholars have clearly defined *Hunab Ku* as a missionary invention.

If *Hunab-Ku* was a native deity of the Maya people then we would expect to see evidence of that in their codices (books of hieroglyphs). However, we find no evidence of *Hunab Ku* anywhere until the arrival of Franciscan Monks in the Yucatan.

Even though *Hunab Ku* is mentioned within the Book of *Chilam Balam*, scholars generally agree that *Hunab Ku* is the substituted name for the Christian god – an invention of the missionaries meant to convert Mayan people to Christianity.

"The first to hijack *Hunab Ku* was Mexican philosopher, Domingo Martinez Paredez, who presented *Hunab Ku* as evidence for Mayan Monotheism. Other men went further to hijack the idea of *Hunab Ku* based on Paredez's work. One very important man was Jose Arguelles.

"Jose Arguelles (1939-2011), was an American New Age author who is perhaps best known for his participation in the 2012 Apocalyptic Phenomenon. He is also responsible for made-up symbol that is said to represent the Supreme God or the One Being, which he popularized in his 1987 book 'The Mayan Factor.'" [Bethany Youngblood, "Hunab Ku: Were the Mayans Monotheistic?" *The Genius of Ancient Man*, March 6, 2015 (http://geniusofancientman.blogspot.com/2015/03/hunab-ku-were-mayans-monotheistic.html).]

The bottom line: *Hunab Ku*, the popular web image, and New Age beliefs are completely without foundation.

168 Markman and Markman, *Masks of the Spirit: Image and Metaphor in Mesoamerica*, 9.

169 The tribe largely can be found along the Negro River, which is a tributary of the mighty Amazon River and ultimately separates Colombia from Venezuela.

170 Nicholas J. Saunders, *People of the Jaguar: The Living Spirit of Ancient America* (Souvenir Press Ltd., 1991) 131.

171 One of the "tools" of the *h'men* is crystals.

172 Let me just say from my perspective of our morning "activities," doing authentic shamanic work and the experiences that come with it are not easy, may be dangerous, and sometimes very frightening. It is not the neo-shamanic nonsense of lying on a floor with a cloth over your face while someone beats a drum – easy, unauthentic, and non-frightening. How sad that people fall for this garbage or someone claiming to be a shaman or some guru who supposedly possesses knowledge from a four-thousand-year-old Toltec lineage. The Toltec civilization flourished in ancient central Mexico between the 10th and mid-12th centuries C.E., not four-thousand years ago.

173 Over the many years later, I recognized a pattern that I would begin bleeding after any intense or otherworldly experience. In my research, I found evidence that it is not unusual for a woman to experience bleeding in those situations.

174 In Maya mysticism, the jaguar is nocturnal and commonly an aspect of the moon.

175 Little did I suspect that decades later I would have an encounter with similar spirits in Iceland – the Hidden Ones.

176 Timothy Freke & Peter Gandy, *The Complete Guide to World Mysticism* (Piatkus, 1997) 15 -16.

177 With my firsthand experience during the Visitation, that stones actually "do" grow, we would modify the Hawaiian concept to

include the premise, that our stones within our bowl of light, our heart, enlarge through time. This make common sense as a wounding, such as spiritual, mental, and physical abuse, if not released would fester and grow larger overtime. This points up the fact, that it is essential, sooner than later, to deal with and release pass woundings. Could these unreleased stones, that grow over time, be a symbol for a mass of cancer cells?

178 Pali Jae Lee and Koko Willis, *Tales from the Night Rainbow* (Night Rainbow Publishing Co., 1990) 18-19.

179 Tiki is the more commonly recognized name for a carving of a Hawaiian god.

180 At the time, as a nine or ten year old, I didn't know the very small image was of the *Akua Ku*.

181 *Kū* ("rising upright") is guardian of the islands of Hawaii as well as the individual, family, and farming. He is also recognized as the god of war, fishing, power, canoe making, and the sunrise. He is the master martial god – the protector; his wife *Hina* ("leaning down") is the earth mother. To the Hawaiians, *Kū* represents the east, or the sun rising, which indicates morning. *Hina*, his wife represents the west, or the sun setting, which indicates evening. *Kū* and *Hina* are representative of the balance that is needed for a person's well-being. *Kū* symbolizes the external while *Hina* is symbolic of all that is internal. To the Polynesians who pre-dated the Hawaiian culture, *Kū* ('to penetrate darkness with light') was recognized as the morning star and his twin, his wife *Hina*, was the evening star.

182 Not my friend's real name. Kimo is used to keep his identity secret.

183 Usually refers to a white person.

184 God's natural altruistic law: "I will put my law within them, and I will write it on their hearts." (Jeremiah 31.33) Natural law is based on a belief in the inherent, natural, altruistic law of God that is found within the heart and mind of each person. It lies dormant until awakened. Once awakened, it will become each person's

nature, the world will be transformed through love, and Lost Eden will be revealed.

Thus, natural law is based on loving kindness and doing what is best for the well-being of others and all things of the Earth. It is not generated or codified by a society but is derived and flows from each and every person's natural, altruistic spirit.

Natural laws have their foundation in compassionate and loving actions between us and others.

Natural law may be likened to the concept of a "moral compass." A form of natural law is alluded to in the Declaration of Independence and is sometimes referred to as "natural rights." These concepts were championed by Thomas Jefferson, who used natural-rights ideas to justify declaring independence from England and justified the Revolutionary War by appealing to "the law of nature and Nature's God." (Husfelt, *Do You Like Jesus – Not the Church?*, 101.)

[185] Divine power – life force

[186] *Akua* (god/goddess/supernatural spirit) are the impersonal deities of the Hawaiian people. They may also be a Hawaiian's *aumakua* or guardian spirit. *Akua* exhibit not only divine traits and supernatural qualities, but much like Greek mythology, the Hawaiians' gods and goddesses express human frailties. *Akua* can also take different material forms such as an owl, shark, stone, a fireball or even an old woman, such as the form sometimes taken by *Pele* – the volcano goddess. *Kāne* is associated with sunlight.

[187] The official flower of the Big Island that originates from an evergreen tree of the myrtle family and is sacred to *Pele*, the volcano goddess, and *Laka*, the goddess of dance

[188] Ancestral guardians are of the Earth, and for some cultures, an indispensable part of life. These guardians are the spirits of the family lineage that protect and guide the people as well as form a sacred bond between the land and the people. Ancestral guardians provide a legacy of sacredness that guides the people to a oneness

of being with the Earth not separateness from the Earth. Ancestral guardians connect people to the land.

189 Hawaiian slang for brother but having a meaning of friend

190 http://www.systemiccoaching.com/huna_articles/mo%27oki-ni_heiau.htm

191 Ibid.

192 Goosebumps

193 Ellie Crowe and William Crowe, *Exploring Lost Hawai'i: Places of Power, History, Mystery and Magic* (Regent Music & Books, 2002) 4.

194 Spirit, ghost

195 Faure, *Visions of Power*, 192.

196 High priest

197 A prophet who brings a message and leads by example is known as an exemplary prophet. This was Jesus. He emphasized deeds over faith. By his personal example, he "showed the way" to the kingdom. This was not by faith but by deeds. His teachings were based on love (unity), not fear (separation). Through our deeds, we may perfect ourselves. There was no original sin. Accordingly, a priest, who might absolve sins, was unnecessary. Furthermore, there was no need for temple obedience as an ethical duty. It was one's deeds based on one's heart that mattered and led to the awakening of the kingdom. (Husfelt, *Do You like Jesus – Not the Church?*, 19.)

198 This knowledge I call "First Knowledge." Furthermore, the Egyptian hieroglyphic for the morning star has the literal meaning "divine knowledge."

199 Based on the extraordinary ontological opus of the physicist David Bohm, astrology is seen as a valid and sacred science.

"David Bohm's most significant contribution to science is his interpretation of the nature of physical reality, which is rooted in his theoretical investigations, especially quantum theory and relativity theory. Bohm postulates that the ultimate nature of physical reality is not a collection of separate objects (as it appears to us), but rather it is an undivided whole that is in perpetual dynamic flux. For Bohm, the insights of quantum mechanics and relativity theory point to a universe that is undivided and in which all parts 'merge and unite in one totality.' This undivided whole is not static but rather in a constant state of flow and change. . . .

"Bohm calls this flow the holomovement – holo, meaning holographic-like, and movement, suggesting dynamism and process. . . . In other words, the nature of reality is a single unbroken wholeness in flowing movement. So, everything is connected and everything is in dynamic flux. Now, in this term holomovement, holo refers to holographic structure, meaning that each part of the flow, in some way, contains the entire flow. . . . And the movement part of holomovement is that the whole flow is in a continual process of change.

"In analogy to holography but on a much grander scale, Bohm believes that each part of physical reality contains information about the whole. . . . Evidence for this kind of holographic structure in nature has emerged recently in the burgeoning field of chaos theory and its close cousin, fractal geometry. . . .

"Bohm proposes that the holomovement consists of two fundamental aspects: the explicate order and the implicate order. . . . What we call matter is merely an apparent manifestation of the explicate order of the holomovement. . . . In other words, the explicate order is the manifest realm; it is the physical space-time universe in which we live. This explicate order is the surface appearance of a much greater enfolded or implicate order, most of which is hidden. Thus, the implicate order is the unseen or the unmanifest realm.

"It's tempting, perhaps, to think of the explicate order as the primary reality, and the implicate order as a subtle, secondary reality. For Bohm, precisely the opposite is the case. The fundamental primary reality is the implicate order, and the explicate order is but a set of ripples on the surface of the implicate order. So that which we can see and feel and touch is merely the waves on the surface of reality, which is a vast ocean of implicate order.

"Contemporary physics and, indeed, most of science, deals with explicate orders and structures only, which is why physics has encountered such great difficulty in explaining a variety of phenomena that Bohm would say arise from the implicate order. . . .

"Another point that Bohm emphasized was that empty space is part of the wholeness – this unbroken flowing movement. Empty space is not just some giant vacuum through which matter moves, but rather, space and matter are intimately interconnected.

"In reference to the alchemical axiom of 'as above, so below,' the microcosm has all the elements, essentially of the macrocosm. It is important to emphasize that each part does contain the whole, not at a manifest level but at a process level.

"This all leads to a kind of metaphorical understanding of how astrology might work, and it works in a way that is not mechanistic. This is very important to understand. It's not that Pluto (planet) sends rays down to your brain, which acts as a radio receiver, picks them up, and goes and does Plutonic things. And it's not that Pluto is in you, in the sense that the physical Pluto is much too big to be contained in your physical body. It's that the process that's going on in Pluto is also going on in you. Literally. So, Pluto is literally contained in you, and in me, but at the process level, not at the manifest level.

"Astrology, in a sense, is a science of the order in meaning and of its interpenetration with the physical space-time universe. And this is where I think astrology is so profound. Because, in a sense, all of the esoteric sciences, such as the I Ching, Tarot and others, are sciences of the order of meaning. They are essentially models of the implicate order. But what is so profound about astrology is that, by virtue of its connection to planets and stars, it also precisely models the interpenetration between the invisible realms of meaning and the physical space-time universe.

So, what do I foresee, or perhaps pray for, for the future of science? Essentially, a grand synthesis of explicate and implicate sciences. Today's orthodox science would come to be seen as a partial science limited to the explicate order. It focuses on those manifest ripples we see all around us and mistakenly take for the whole of reality. Meanwhile, astrology and the other esoteric sciences are sciences of the implicate order, and rather than contradicting the physical sciences, astrology and physics are two aspects of a much greater whole. This will eventually lead to a grand synthesis of sacred and secular sciences into a much more profound science than we have today." [The preceding is excerpted from two sources: William Keepin, "The Lifework of David Bohm," *Vision Net*, (http://www.vision.net.au/~apaterson/science/david_bohm.htm); and William Keepin, "Astrology and the New Physics: Integrating Sacred and Secular Sciences," *The Mountain Astrologer*, Oct/Nov 2009.]

200 *The Mountain Astrologer*, Oct./Nov. 2008

201 "The Bundle Type: the Birth of the Hero, the Quest for Identity and Heritage, the Call to Adventure – Leo, Capricorn:

"It should come as no surprise that this type is the rarest of the group – only during a few days of any given year will all ten planets gather within one sector of the zodiac. I rarely encounter clients of this type. Whether there are actually fewer persons born under such a configuration, or if they simply tend to seek counseling less often, will have to be decided by further research. Nevertheless, the theme of individual uniqueness, of being somehow different and special, and the need to discover the meaning and purpose of this unique call to adventure form the backbone of the Bundle mythology. I have chosen the signs of Leo and Capricorn to represent this type because of the strongly focused, concentrated nature of their personalities, as well as their connection to the mythological themes of the search for a paternal heritage and legacy.

"Common to all the stories of hero births is the theme of dual parentage, where one of the parents is immortal. Either the hero is begotten of a Virgin Goddess, like Jesus and the Buddha, or the Divine Father mates with a mortal woman, as Zeus fathered Hercules and Perseus. This sense of an inner divinity mixed with the limitations of living in a mortal body creates the main challenge for these types.

"The mythology of Bundle types involves struggling to find ways to ground their immortality, energy, and talents within mortal form and earthly life – to discover both the divine within the human and the human within the divine. In short, they are personalizing their image of God as the Self, the inner guide. And to this inner guide they must put the quintessential hero's question, 'Why was I born rather than someone else? What is it that I was born to do that no one else can?' This awareness of being special is both a blessing and a curse, but it is the key to the synthesis of one's human and spiritual natures. This is a major part of what Jung called the individuation process, which is to get in touch with one's own unique essence, one's true calling. From this discovery springs a forward-moving impetus to action, a sense of individual destiny. We can see this process in the lives of both van Gogh and Igor Stravinsky, who struggled to bring forth unique and radical art forms that were ahead of their time.

"The motif of one parent being immortal is also tied symbolically to the idea of the second birth, the shamanic spiritual rebirth. As contrasted with the mortal birth from our biological parents, from whence comes our body, our name, and our social role, the birth of the individual hero from the unconscious is a victory of spirit over matter, of personal choice, risk, and adventure over the more mundane life of conformity to the collective expectations of society. In *The Origins and History of Consciousness*, Erich Neumann writes that this idea of a spiritual rebirth signifies 'the birth of the higher man . . . associated with conscious action, conscious knowledge, and conscious creation as distinct from the blind drive of unconscious forces.' This process is always bound up with a testing and strengthening of willpower and the ability to act independently, and, true to form, many of this type will find themselves frequently tested by difficult crises in life, a shamanic trial by fire through which they learn the lessons of courage, self-sufficiency, and the development of a strong will. In order to follow this inner calling, they will have to go against the wishes of family or loved ones, just as the hero Parsifal must disobey his mother's wishes in order to follow his knightly call to adventure.

"The sense of a dual parentage in this mythology will often produce an identity crisis in these individuals, such as in the myth of Chiron the centaur. One feels both divine and human, a mixed breed that doesn't feel at home among ordinary mortals. Thus, many Bundle types, even those who receive much attention early in life as a special or gifted child, often face difficulties in their social development, as they desire both to shine and to be accepted into the group. Again, to quote Neumann: 'He is a human being like the others, mortal and collective, yet at the same time he feels himself a stranger to the community. He discovers within himself something which, although it belongs to him, he can only describe it as strange, unusual, or godlike.'

"Also included within this mythology is the search for one's true origins or home, which usually takes the form of a search for the missing parent, the Divine One who holds the key to one's spiritual identity. Parsifal grows up without a father only to discover later that the wounded Grail King is indeed his grandfather or true spiritual father. This motif will frequently manifest in the lives of these people as a parent who is literally missing due to an early death or divorce. Or perhaps they are raised partially by their grandparents. The grandparents are a symbol of our spiritual origins and will many times play a pivotal role as the Divine Protectors or teachers.

"There are two main dangers that the Bundle person must face on the mythic journey. The first one is what Joseph Campbell termed 'the refusal of the Call,' when the person senses their inner destiny and knows in their heart what they must do, but, lacking the courage or belief in themselves, they back away from the challenge. This can cause inertia, depression, and even self-destructive behavior. In a sense, the mortal half is devaluing and repressing one's spirituality, and the buried energy of the divine side will often take its revenge in devastating ways.

"The other error is a sort of psychological hubris, whereby the person will ignore the human and earthly demands of their mortal side, and, much like Chiron, will suffer from a woundedness or split between their spiritual and physical lives. This problem may manifest itself through the body with serious injuries or ongoing health problems. Relationships, too, can be difficult for these types. Due to the clustering effect of the planets, there is usually a lack of aspects, particularly the opposition, which, far from being a bad aspect, actually helps us to gain more awareness and balance through relationships. What these types do often possess in abundance are conjunctions, indicating focused willpower and self-determination. Bundle types must avoid becoming too self-absorbed with their own personal adventure to the degree that they are oblivious to the other person's needs and feelings. (*The Mountain Astrologer*, Oct./ Nov. 1998, 107 – 110.)

202 My vision in 1993 predates the visitation in 1997.

203 What I found supported my identity as the morning star: my rising sign is in Libra at 12 degrees 05'. In the twelfth house, I have my moon at 8 degrees 51' Libra and Neptune at 7 degrees 10' Libra. In the first house, Mars is at 12 degrees 44' Libra, Venus at 21 degrees 32' Libra, Jupiter at 24 degrees 53' Libra, and the asteroids Chiron and Juno in Libra. Five planets and two asteroids all in Libra clustered around my Libra ascendant, and all ruled by Venus.

In addition, my moon is conjunct my ascendant, Neptune and Mars; Mars is conjunct my ascendant and Neptune; Neptune is conjunct my ascendant; and finally, Venus and Jupiter are in conjunction at only 3 degrees apart.

204 Nikolai Tolstoy, *The Quest for Merlin* (Little Brown & Co., 1988) 209.

205 The following is excerpted from: Ray Grasse, "Future Shock: Contemplating Uranus's Next Return

to Its Discovery Degree," *The Mountain Astrologer*, August/September 2017, bonus digital content; and Ray Grasse, "Decoding the Most Elevated Planet in the Horoscope," *The Mountain Astrologer*,

February/March 2018, 29.

"An elevated planet is the planet near or conjunct the Midheaven, or MC (Medium Coeli) – the zenith point of the horoscope. It is an important factor in understanding any chart and, in some cases, possibly the most important indicator. Any planet positioned above the horizon in the horoscope represents energies in your life that are more visible to those around you and comparatively more exposed to public view.

As the symbolic zenith of the chart, the MC can be considered as also representing the pinnacle of your life's direction, as something you are aspiring toward. You might think of it this way: Whereas the 1st house shows who you are, in terms of your everyday personality, the MC shows what you want to be – i.e., those qualities you feel ambitiously called upon to realize. There's a sense of achievement or sometimes even destiny involved with any planet located at this point.

"So, in natal horoscopes, what does Uranus, as ruler of the air sign Aquarius, signify? Uranus opposes the key Saturn principles of authority, age, tradition, and the status quo. Its position shows where and how we might seek to break the mold, tear up the rulebook, be radical, and feel awakened. It may also signify the rebel in us that riots against confining structures or feels compelled to incite group/social change. It can indicate what we find revolting . . . to the point where it's worth revolting/rebelling against!

"Our Uranus placement shows how we might feel like the outsider, the outcast – where and why we feel different. It's also where we have a perfect, complete vision ('Prometheus' means foresight) of what we—and life—could become.

"'Prometheus, with his gift of foresight, saw the potential of human consciousness,' explains Liz Greene. 'The fire he appropriates is solar; it is the divine spark of immortality, or awareness of the Self . . . the fire of imagination and vision, through which solar divinity and individual creativity make themselves known." She adds, tellingly,' He didn't give it to one special or chosen person; he gave it to all.'

(Liz Greene, *The Art of Stealing Fire*, CPA Press, 1996, p. 8)

"Uranus is not just associated with the rabble-rouser, deviant, or nonconformist. Its energy can be focused on the betterment of life and the fulfilment of potential. Paul Wright reminds us that technology, democracy, internationalism, common language, universalism, social amelioration, and evolution are key Uranian concepts. The planet 'breaks down divisive barriers, thus creating the conditions where what is separate can come together and move towards one end.' Wright argues that Uranus transcends generation, class, or nationality and that 'at a basic level Uranus and Aquarius are about the improvement of life, about the creating and sustaining of those conditions in which human potentiality can flower.'

Pauline Stone stresses the planet's link to the concepts of equality and brotherhood: 'Uranus helps us to accept each person as an individual and as our brother . . . It is representative of socialism in the non-political sense (Latin: socius = friend). This is an influence which eliminates prejudice and snobbery, allowing us to mix freely with all conditions of man. Through Uranus, we come to see the value and worth of that which is different. Thus, we come to realize that we are all in individuals yet at one with each other.' (Pauline Stone, *The Astrology of Karma*, The Aquarian Press, 1988, p. 72)

"The Divine Mind

"Liz Greene writes poetically of this awe-inspiring planet: 'To ancient peoples, the beauty and vastness of the star-studded vault of heaven revealed the awesome power and intelligence of an invisible creator god . . . [Uranus] is an ancient and awesome portrayal of the divine mind that conceived the idea of a universe before any universe was made.' (Liz Greene, *Mythic Astrology*, Fireside, 1994, p. 42)

She describes Uranus's gift as 'the capacity to envisage the whole before it is manifest.' Such awareness has been tapped into and received, rather than created. She continues, 'Some ancient systems of philosophy — such as Platonism and Stoicism, in which the cosmos is perceived as an interconnected, self-regulating system — bear the stamp of Uranian vision.

'Today, most branches of science investigate the material components of the universe with great thoroughness, but without that far-seeing awareness of an interconnected whole of which Uranus is the astrological symbol.' (Liz Greene, *Mythic Astrology*, Fireside, 1994, p. 43)

"Cordelia Mansall offers one reason that Uranus is considered the higher octave of Mercury: 'The initial step towards truth is perception. It is an altruistic, inventive type of intelligence that compels the true scientist to seek solutions and determine causes . . . It is the capacity to allow the intuition free rein to sift and sort information from the Collective Intelligence.' (Cordelia Mansall, *Discover Astrology*, The Aquarian Press, 1991, p. 85)

"Pauline Stone writes that the planet is 'based on wholistic [sic] rather than subjective reasoning,' and by breaking down the barriers of personal prejudice, it can provide access to the source of universal knowledge. She suggests that Uranus rules telepathy, extrasensory perception, and psychic expression. (Pauline Stone, *The Astrology of Karma*, The Aquarian Press, 1988, p. 71)

"Alan Leo named Uranus 'the awakener,' and Alan Oken considers Uranus 'the force for the awakening of higher consciousness . . . the planet which embodies the sixth sense. Its energy . . . is beginning to be felt personally by a growing number of people . . . Uranus symbolizes Man's liberation from the bondage of the personality and signifies the power which may be achieved through the collected energies of truly individualized souls working toward a conscious connection with the Source of Life.' (Alan Oken, *Alan Oken's Complete Astrology*, Ibis Press, 2006, pp. 216, 220)."

206 In my writings and books, I discuss the importance of natural law:

This is God's natural, altruistic law – the law of the kingdom. This natural law is based on a belief in the inherent, natural, altruistic law of God that is found within each person. This natural law flows from the divinity within each individual but lies dormant until awakened by each person. This is the true holy law of Moses, the basis for the teachings and the message of Jesus and a foundational belief of Divine Humanity.

Does natural law make null and void human-made laws? Not at all; human-made laws are as necessary as natural law. Just as the divine interpenetrates the human or the absolute interpenetrates the relative, natural law interpenetrates human law.

Natural law is an essential segment of an enlightened society and is based on doing what is best for the well-being of others and all things of the Earth. It is not generated by a society but is derived and flows from each person's natural, if awakened, altruistic spirit.

Human-made laws, on the other hand, are society-based and are focused on the probations of societal life in an attempt to control behavior. Many times, they are a necessary part of life. But they are not necessarily based on what is most beneficial for the well-being of life – the environment, the whole of humanity, and the Earth and its creatures.

There are international laws against torture. However, torture is still conducted through the manipulation of these laws. While there are laws against child abuse (thou shalt not), there are no laws that state that parents must be in their children's lives (adult children included) in a supportive way (thou shalt). There is nothing in the legal code stating that a divorce must not be so destructive, and revenge-filled that any children involved will be drastically affected in a harmful way.

While human laws are drawn up to protect the environment, they are not necessarily what is best for the environment. They do, however, tend to serve capitalist thugs, whether they are corporate elites or their paid-off political flunkies. Capitalist law is the law of the bottom line – profit by any means possible. In the capitalist world of market-based medicine, cures for diseases go unresearched and unrealized if there is no profit or not enough profit to be made. Natural law is the antithesis of this entire paradigm. (Husfelt, *Do*

You Like Jesus – Not the Church?, 199 – 200.)

207 Jamie Partridge, "Jupiter Trine Uranus 15 December 2019," *Astrology King*, April 3, 2018 (https://astrologyking.com/jupiter-trine-uranus).

208 The research for this last section, which begins with 'I am the Morning Star,' was done by me alone during the summer of 2009. From the time of my vision until the summer of 2009, I was not aware of the tremendous influence that the interplay of Saturn and Pluto with Neptune has on me as regards the ideal society, which is an integral part of our message.

209 Safran Rossi, "Waves Become Wings," *The Mountain Astrologer*, February/March 2018, 44.

210 Liz Greene, *The Astrological Neptune and the Quest for Redemption*, (Weiser Books, 2000) 444.

211 Eleanor Buckwalter, www.astrologyclub.org

212 John Major Jenkins, excerpt from "Tzolkin: Visionary Perspectives and Calendar Studies"

(1992, 1994) 270-272), (http://edj.net/mc2012/fap8.html).

213 Gary C. Daniels, *Mayan Calendar Prophecies: Predictions for 2012-2052* (Independently published, 2012) 24.

214 Philip Coppens, "2012: Odyssey of Time," *2012: Mayan Prophecy and the Shift of Ages* (http://philipcoppens.com/2012_art1.html).

215 There is a controversy concerning the beginning date of the "Great Cycle." Some will date it as beginning on August 11 and others will place the date as August 29.

216 Daniels, *Mayan Calendar Prophecies: Predictions for 2012-2052*, 25.

217 *Utne Reader*, March/April 1993, 30 – 32.

218 This "flower and song" (poetry) is dedicated to the wounded raven that hobbled by my window one wintry afternoon. "To know

the truth was to understand the hidden meanings of things through 'flower and song,' a power emanating from the deified heart." (León-Portilla, *Aztec Thought and Culture*, 182.)

[219] Norman Bancroft-Hunt and Werner Forman, *People of the Totem: The Indians of the Pacific Northwest* (Peter Bedrick Books, 1989) 76.

[220] Markman and Markman, *Masks of the Spirit: Image and Metaphor in Mesoamerica*, 106.

[221] Mircea Eliade was a Romanian historian of religion and philosopher.

[222] Markman and Markman, *Masks of the Spirit: Image and Metaphor in Mesoamerica*, 106.

[223] Vince's medicine practice of soul loss is similar to the Zinacanteco Maya shamans: "The contrast of good and evil is familiar to us. While the concept of two souls is not, this idea points to a fundamental and distinctive duality of spirit inherent to Maya reality. Zinacanteco Maya also have two souls, as do many other Tzotzil-speaking peoples of highland Chiapas. For them, one of these souls is invisible, destructible, and divided into thirteen parts. A scary accident, like a fall on a mountain path, can cause a person to lose a piece of this soul and come ill. Evil witches can also steal pieces of soul and sell them to the Earth Lord. Shaman seers can find the missing piece with proper preparation, the cooperation of the subject, and supernatural help and restore the human soul. Zinacantecos call this kind of soul *ch'ulel*, which has the same root as *ch'ul* or *k'ul*, a word used by ancient Maya scribes to describe 'holiness' and 'divinity.'

"Although subject to temporary damage, the *ch'ulel* is eternal. When a person dies, this soul hangs around the grave for some time, then becomes part of a pool of such souls in the care of the Father-Mothers, the ancestral gods who may decide to plant it again in the body of a newborn baby." (Freidel Schele, and Parker, *Maya Cosmos*, 181 – 182.)

224 "Nothing is older than water as an element of life and there is nothing more initial than its influence on the mind of man as an agent of destruction, of death, of an ending, the water of death being the natural antithesis to the breath of life.

"Water and Breath, in which baptismal regeneration finds its origin, are a symbolical representation of 'from out of the water into a new life,' or rebirth." [E. Valentia Straiton, *The Celestial Ship of the North* (Kessinger Publishing, LLC, 1992) 153.]

225 A Sufi saying

226 Michael Baigent, *The Jesus Papers: Exposing the Greatest Cover-Up in History* (HarperCollins, 2007) 214.

227 Since the nineteenth century, "important concepts of life were brought to the field of physiology such as homeostasis by Walter Cannon. . . . Dr. Canon realized the importance of balance between acid and alkaline in the body fluids, especially in the blood. . . . An acidic condition inhibits nerve action and an alkaline condition stimulates nerve action. One who has an alkaline blood condition can think and act (decide) well. On the other hand, one who has an acidic blood condition cannot think well or act quickly, clearly, or decisively. . . . For a long time, I searched for a quick way to change an acidic to an alkaline condition. Finally, I found one through religious rituals. Japanese Shinto religion strongly recommends performing the misogi ritual, in which one takes a cold water bath or shower in a river, waterfall, or the ocean." [Herman Aihara, *Acid and Alkaline* (George Ohsawa Macrobiotic Foundation, 1980) 1, 109.]

228 Edward B. Tylor, LL.D., F.R.S, *Primitive Culture, Volume II* (Dover Publications, 2016) 435.

229 Passion means anything that disturbs our mental tranquility such as anger and guilt.

230 Pao Chang, "How the Human Heart Functions as a Second Brain," *The Mind Unleashed*, Feb 19, 2016 (http://themindunleashed.org/2016/02/how-the-human-heart-functions-as-a-second-

brain-2.html).

231 Red ochre or red clay – iron oxide, has been universally utilized in ritual and ceremony as far back as 100,000 years ago. Symbolically, it represents life, blood, and rebirth. The earliest religious teachings of humans being formed out of the 'clay' of the Earth by a potter extends back to the predynastic Great Potter god of the Egyptians – *Khnemu* (*Khnum*) (to build, to unite). This ram-headed deity fashioned humans from the clay of the Nile and was connected with the annual inundation of the Nile and the resultant fertility.

Furthermore, "we are all familiar with the name 'Adam' as found in the book of Genesis, but what does it really mean? Let us begin by looking at its roots. This word/name is a child root derived from the parent דם meaning, 'blood'. By placing the letter א in front of the parent root, the child root אדם is formed and is related in meaning to דם (blood).

"By examining a few other words derived from the child root אדם we can see a common meaning in them all. The Hebrew word אדמה (*adamah*) is the feminine form of אדם meaning 'ground' (see Genesis 2:7). The word/name אדום (*edom*) means 'red'. Each of these words has the common meaning of 'red'. *Dam* is the 'red' blood, *adamah* is the 'red' ground, *edom* is the color 'red' and *adam* is the 'red' man. There is one other connection between '*adam*' and '*adamah*' as seen in Genesis 2:7, which states that 'the *adam*' was formed out of the '*adamah*'.

"In the ancient Hebrew world, a person's name was not simply an identifier but descriptive of one's character. As Adam was formed out of the ground, his name identifies his origins. [Jeff A. Benner, "Name of the Month – Adam," *Ancient Hebrew Research Center Biblical Hebrew E-Magazine*, March 2004 (http://www.ancient-hebrew.org/emagazine/001.html).]

232 Diamond Jenness, *The Faith of a Coast Salish Indian* (British Columbia Provincial Museum, 1955) 37.

233 "Katzie is a small Indian reserve on the Fraser River, some 25

miles from Vancouver. Its inhabitants, who number about fifty, belong to the Coast Salish tribe. The writer visited Katzie in February 1936, after spending several weeks among other Coast Salish communities on Vancouver Island. Nowhere did he find the religious beliefs of the Indians so well integrated, or their rites so clearly interpreted, as by Old Pierre, a Katzie man about 75 years of age who enjoyed a wide and honourable reputation as medicine man both on Vancouver Island and on the Mainland." (Jenness, *The Faith of a Coast Salish Indian*, 5.)

234 Jenness, *The Faith of a Coast Salish Indian*, 37.

235 Glauser and Kramarz-Bein, *Rittersagas: Übersetzung, Überlieferung, Transmission*, 119–131, 127 (https://www.academia. edu/10666162/Strengleikar_in_Iceland._2014._Rittersagas_%C3%9Cbersetzung_%C3%9Cberlieferung_Transmission_pp._119_131).

236 Graeme Fife, *Arthur the King* (BBC Consumer Publishing, 1990) 148.

237 Laurette Séjourné, *Burning Water: Thought and Religion in Ancient Mexico* (Shambhala, 1976) 99.

238 David Carrasco, *Religions of Mesoamerica* (Waveland Press, Inc, 2014) 61.

239 The Hebrew Shamayim (http://ccosmology.blogspot. com/2013/09/the-hebrew-shamayim.html).

240 John Opsopaus, *Guide to the Pythagorean Tarot* (Llewellyn Publications, 2001) 88.

241 James Maffie, "Aztec Philosophy: Teotl as Ultimate Reality and Root Metaphor," *Internet Encyclopedia of Philosophy* (http://www. iep.utm.edu/aztec).

242 Ibid.

243 Séjourné, *Burning Water: Thought and Religion in Ancient Mexico* 99.

244 Paolo da Floresta, "The Messages in Water," *Natural High Life*, Jan. 4, 2016 (https://paolodafloresta.wordpress.com/2016/01/04/the-messages-in-water).

245 Michael Green, *The Book of the Dragontooth: An Ancient Manuscript on the Secret History of the Dragon and the Unicorn* (Running Press, 1990) 38.

246 We had lived our entire lives on the East Coast until we relocated to the West Coast during the month of December 2001.

247 Fire and water: Oneness means that the world of physical phenomena is non-dual with the Divine Realm. One of the best ways to realize this philosophy is by working with the elements especially fire and water. Divine Humanity prescribes to six elements. Six is the first number of perfection. The world was created in six days: "Order involves numbers, and among numbers by the laws of nature, the most suitable to productivity is 6, for if we start with 1, it is the first perfect number, being equal to the product of its factors (i.e. 1 x 2 x 3) as well as made up of the sums of them (i.e. 1 + 2 + 3)." [F.H. Colson and G.H. Whitaker (trans), *Philo De Opificio Mundi, Vol. I* (Harvard University Press, 1929) p. 13.]

The six elements are earth, water, fire, air, space, and consciousness. Divine Humanity believes that all things of creation have consciousness, which interpenetrates the other five elements. These five elements are physical as well as metaphysical: i.e., water = water, emotions = water; fire = fire, spirit = fire; air = air, mind = air; earth = earth, body = earth.

Symbolically, fire represents the Absolute/Heaven while water corresponds to the Relative/Earth. Metaphorically, the blending of the opposites of fire and water results in harmony and a Oneness of Self. In Greek mythology, this concept corresponds to "Harmonia, which is usually translated as 'harmony,' but means any union in which the parts form a seamless whole while retaining their distinct identities. Harmonia is the daughter of sea-born Aphrodite and fiery Ares, whom Empedocles identified with Love and Strife, the two primary cosmic forces, which bring about all change in the universe. Pythagoras likewise said that cosmic Harmonia is born of the union of Love and Strife. She reconciles all oppositions." (Opsopaus, *Guide to the Pythagorean Tarot*, 88.)

There is a carved inscription at the Villa Palombara in Rome that reads: "He who knows how to burn by water and to wash by fire, makes Heaven out of Earth and precious Earth out of Heaven." In cryptic terms, this is a teaching of oneness – the interpenetration of Heaven and Earth. Most researchers will identify this statement as a theorem of alchemy during the Middle Ages. I would date it much further back in time, possibly as far back as thousands of years ago.

In the New Testament, we find the words: "baptize with the Holy Spirit and with Fire." We once again discover the veiled reference to oneness. But what does all this mean? How can we wash with fire and burn with water? What is it to be baptized with spirit and with fire? Again, Christian religious leaders, whether they be ministers, priests or bishops, answer these questions in theological terms, future-orientated events and/or faith issues. But how else could they answer these questions? If you have never seen or eaten an apple, how could you describe its form and color and its taste?

If you have never put your hands in fire and not have them burnt and never submerged yourself in a cold running stream and felt the icy-fire rushing through you, how would you even come close to understanding the hidden meanings of these veiled teachings? You wouldn't; all you could do is rely on faith and discursive linear thinking. Socrates put written words, supposedly God inspired or not, into proper perspective when he "compared written doctrines to pictures of animals which resemble life, but which when you question them can give you no replay." [W. Winwood Reade, *The Veil of Isis: Mysteries of the Druids* (Independently published, 2019) 64.]

There is no separation between the divine realm, the Otherworld, and the material realm, the Earth; they interpenetrate. The awareness of this interpenetration of the two realms is most evident near flowing waters such as mountain streams and rivers. It is here where the illusionary veil of separation may be dropped to reveal the Oneness of life through the process of bathing. The first time that we step into the stream to submerge, die and be reborn may be an apocalyptic experience that literally has the potentiality of being a volcanic implosion of our soul – an unveiling and purification of our heart/mind.

But for most of the time, our conscious focus and awareness are only on the material realm even though we exist in the divine realm as well. This is one of the reasons why Divine Humanity does not believe in sequestering ourselves away in so-called religious "cages," such as a monastery or the Vatican. This is an artificial and illusionary state of being, done more for power and control than personal transformation. It also provides a physical and visual form of legitimacy for their religious "badge" – authority. Add in the vestments and collars of Catholic priests and you have achieved a statement of separation from the masses and identified yourself as the mouthpiece of God.

The key to the gateway of the Kingdom of Heaven and the Realm of the Earth is to be found by fully participating in the totality of life by weeding our fields and sowing and harvesting the precious flowers and jewels of our earthly garden paradise. When we realize and keep in mind that all things have a consciousness, not just humans, and that the elements that compose life are metaphysical as well as physical, we gradually break down the illusion of separateness between ourselves and our garden paradise. This results in peacefulness, benevolentness, and compassion for all other things. The moth is you and you are the moth, the cat is you and you are the cat, the tree is you and you are the tree. I Am That . . .

This transformation of consciousness results in joy, happiness, and tranquility of the mind. We are no longer scared frightened children hiding, protecting and hoarding on our own personal island of fear against all things that are seemingly different and separate from us. Our island of fear dissolves and we realize the garden has always been there for us, where all things are one with each other.

However, we must be careful not to let five things interfere with this transformation of consciousness and the tranquility of our mind. These are desire, anger, ignorance, doubt and false views: desire is the attachment to materialistic and pleasant things; anger causes wrath and vengeance; ignorance, as well as pride and arrogance, leads us to feel superior to others and all other things; doubt cannot distinguish between delusion and enlightenment and cause and effect; false views believe in the doctrine and dogma of dualistic paradigms such as the Church.

248 Refers to the Norse creation myth of the blending of elemental fire, *Muspelheim,* and elemental ice, *Niflheim.*

249 D.H. Lawrence, *The Plumed Serpent* (Sovereign (electronic ed.), 2013).

250 Gerald Massey, *Ancient Egypt: The Light of the World, Vols. I and II* (El Bay, Zuu Books, 2011) 159.

251 There are people, with information only through books and workshops and without experience who will attempt to do spiritual ceremony and healing without the proper training and medicine power.

252 Please see the section above, "A Night with Peanut in Tulúm: The Ghosts of Tulúm."

253 Smith, *Jesus the Magician,* 169.

254 Saunders, *People of the Jaguar,* 71.

255 Permeating all of creation is a divine consciousness, a sacred power, a force. This force is the single, dynamic, sacred power or energy that is the unifying totality of all things – a universal life force. It's in constant movement, eternally self-generating and self-regenerating while encompassing and interpenetrating the whole cosmos. It is both immanent and at the same time transcendent. There is no distinction between the two. The Nahua (Aztecs) identified this force as *teotl.*

256 Maffie, *Aztec Philosophy,* 23.

257 "Dropping the stone" is a forgiveness process that is both manifest and visceral for healing our internal wounds. We have to identify the various woundings or "stones" within us. A few of these stones may indeed be boulders. To begin any healing, we need to choose a more recent "wounding," one that is not too large. We want to begin with a small stone, not a large boulder from our distant past. The boulders take time to release. This is the reasoning behind the need for patience and persistence. The following is the process of "dropping the stone":

Focus your intent on the forgiveness and the wounding (issue or emotion) you want to release.

Find a stone in nature and ask permission with your mind to use it. Then take the stone and sit with it alone (preferably in nature) and talk your feelings and emotions—cry, shout, yell, whatever it takes—into this stone. You may spend a few minutes doing this and then put the stone away in a special place. Or you may even carry it with you.

When you are ready to say more words of healing to the stone, repeat as often as necessary. This process may take hours, days, weeks, or months depending on the size of the stone. But when you feel ready to release, visit a stream, lake, or ocean. It can be at any time of the day, but dawn is the best symbolically.

Sit by the water's edge and relax. More words may need to be said and more tears shed. When you are ready, let go, forgive, and release – drop or toss the stone into the stream, lake, or ocean. As you let go of the stone, you are letting go of the stone, the wounding within, in your bowl of light. If you are unable to open your fingers and release the stone, it just means that you have more work to do on this wounding. Keep this stone, and take it back home again.

Repeat talking to your stone. When you feel you are ready again, revisit the stream, lake, or ocean and release. When you have forgiven and let go of this past wounding, sit by the water's edge and feel the lightness within you. Bless the experience and the place, give thanks, and leave an offering before you depart. Bless, thank, and love yourself for having the courage, wisdom, and love to forgive and let go.

258 Besides the prayer *mudra*, the next most commonly recognizable Christian *mudra* is depicted in many of the images of Jesus. This is the right arm held up with the forefinger or index finger and the middle finger raised up and the other two fingers curled under. Interestingly enough, this is very similar to the sword *mudra* in esoteric Buddhism. Frequently I use this mudra in energy work. The other *mudra* imagery is similar, but with the middle finger raised up and curled and the index finger raised up and not touching the middle finger. Even though the *mudra* of light is slightly different, as the middle finger is raised up and the index finger is slightly curled, it is too much of a consequence to deny the possibility that Jesus knew this *mudra* and used it in his spiritual practice.

Keep in mind these paintings occurred centuries after Jesus had passed-over and the knowledge of the exact hand/finger positions could vary slightly from the original.

259 Blavatsky, *Isis Unveiled: Both Volumes – A Master-Key to the Mysteries of Ancient and Modern Science and Theology*, 132.

260 If you are going to teach a Japanese martial art, you need to far travel to Japan and experience its essence. If you are a reenactor, you need to travel to the lands your persona is reenacting. Be authentic.

261 Lawrence, *The Plumed Serpent*, excerpt from Chapter XI, "Lords of the Day and Night." *The Plumed Serpent* is a 1926 novel set in Mexico during the Mexican Revolution.

262 Boissiéne, *The Return of Pahana*, 84.

263 Carrasco, *Religions of Mesoamerica*, 41.

264 Ibid., 41.

265 The first *chakra* is the Root *Chakra*. It is located at the base of the spine and deals with issues of security, basic needs, basic human survival, profane sex and inappropriate sexual activity, and one's

connection to the ancestors and the Earth (an unawakened first *chakra* views Earth/nature as hostile). This is the *chakra* of dualism.

266 Hugh Harleston, Jr., *Mayan Treasure: Space and Time Unified at Teotihuacan* (http://www.geocities.ws/harleston13/supplement.pdf) 14.

267 Bruce Scofield, "Quetzalcóatl and the Path to Culture," *Gnosis Magazine*, Spring 1995, 39.

268 Frank Waters, *Mexico Mystique: The Coming Sixth World of Consciousness* (Swallow Press, 1989) 126.

269 Séjourné, *Burning Water: Thought and Religion in Ancient Mexico*, 53.

270 Ibid., 84.

271 Ibid., 84.

272 Deborah Morrison and Arvind Singh, "The Plumed Serpent, Quetzalcóatl: A Symbol of Connectedness," *Nexus: A Neo Novel* (Manor House Publishing, 2006) (https://nexusnovel.wordpress.com/2006/09/19/the-plumed-serpent-quetzalcoatl-a-symbol-of-connectedness).

273 Belize Yucatec Maya – Facebook

274 Séjourné, *Burning Water: Thought and Religion in Ancient Mexico*, 53.

275 Lawrence, *The Plumed Serpent*, excerpt from Chapter XV, "The Written Hymns of Quetzalcóatl."

276 According to Laurette Séjourné in *Pensamiento y religión en el México antiguo*, the coyote (wolf dog) was the animal form of Quetzalcóatl. Additionally, Quetzalcóatl's precious twin was Xolotl (Venus as Evening Star) the dog-headed deity associated with lightning and death.

277 Concerning the mysterious dogs that disappeared, Quetzalcóatl's twin symbolizing Venus as the evening star is the dog-like deity, Xolotl, who accompanied Quetzalcóatl to the underworld to re-

cover the bones of humankind to birth the Fifth Sun. As such, "life in the Fifth Sun is created by Quetzalcóatl from bones and ashes of the previous population, which he was able to gather during a shaman-like journey to the underworld, the hidden world of the spirit entered only through a symbolic death to the world of nature. The shamanic nature of this creation is further suggested by the metaphoric reference to the belief that the life-force in the creatures of this Earth resides in the bones, the 'seeds' from which new life can grow." (Markman and Markman, *Masks of the Spirit: Image and Metaphor in Mesoamerica*, 111.)

Another interesting connection with Xolotl, "Bearer of the Dead," pertains to one of the medicine powers that Sher and I hold, which is "Feeding the Dead." This ceremonial medicine is explained in the section above titled "Spirit Dancing, Burnings, and Bathings."

[278] Neil Baldwin, *Legends of the Plumed Serpent: Biography of a Mexican God* (Public Affairs, 1998) 24.

[279] Ibid., 26.

[280] Hunbatz Men, *Secrets of Mayan Science/Religion* (Bear & Company, 1989) 84. Hunbatz was a friend of ours, whom we met at a conference in Calgary. We had driven Mom and Vince Stogan to the gathering in the early 1990s.

[281] Shelley M. White, "Heart-Based Consciousness: Using The Heart As An Organ Of Perception," *Collective Evolution*, April 10, 2015 (http://www.collective-evolution.com/2015/04/10/heart-based-con-sciousness-using-theheart-as-an-organ-of-perception/).

[282] More recently, it was discovered that the heart also secretes oxytocin, commonly referred to as the love or bonding hormone. (http://www.healthwithconfidence.com/heart-hormones.html)

[283] Diane Toomey, "Exploring How and Why Trees 'Talk' to Each Other," *Yale Environment 360*, September 1, 2016 (https://e360.yale.edu/features/exploring_how_and_why_trees_talk_to_each_other).

[284] Andreas Kornevall, "The Norse Legend of the World Tree—Yg-gdrasil," *Ancient Origins*, May 10, 2019 (http://www.ancient-ori-

gins.net/myths-legends-europe/norse-legend-world-tree-yggdrasil-002680).

285 Husfelt, *Return of a Green Philosophy: The Wisdom of Óðinn, the Power of Þórr, and Freyja's Power of Nature*, 77 – 78.

286 Erasmus of Rotterdam was a Dutch Christian Humanist.

287 This myth was written by one of the apprentice participants.

288 Jonathan Kendall, "The Thirteen Volatiles: Representation and Symbolism," *Universidad Nacional Autónoma de México, Instituto de Investigaciones Histórica* (http://www.historicas.unam.mx/publicaciones/revistas/nahuatl/pdf/ecn22/383.pdf).

289 The appearance, either physically or in in the dream state, of an animal or bird three times in a short period of time indicates a direct close connection with the animal or bird, possibly as a messenger or guide of the spirit world (Otherworld).

290 Susan Milbrath, *Star Gods of the Maya: Astronomy in Art, Folklore, and Calendars (The Linda Schele Series in Maya and Pre-Columbian Studies)* 94.

291 Referring to my tale in the section above titled: "Is That a Naked Man I See?"

292 Elizabeth Van Buren, *Refuge of the Apocalypse: Doorway into Other Dimensions* (The C.W. Daniel Company Ltd., 1986) 206.

293 "Numerous ancient documents, for example, attest that the disciples Jesus valued most were not the twelve male disciples we automatically think of, but his women devotees. These are the kinds of major surprises many conservative Christians are not eager to hear.

"Another shock these ancient manuscripts delivered was the extraordinary importance some groups of early Christians gave to the planets. In some of their texts, the signs of the zodiac are mentioned on nearly every page. There exists strong though highly controversial evidence that Jesus himself was acquainted with the power of astrology and that he taught his disciples ways of working with the stars[.]" (Linda Johnsen, "Jesus and the Stars: Nazarene

Astrology" *The Mountain Astrologer*, December 1998, 82.)

294 John the Baptist

295 David Wood, *Genisis: The First Book of Revelations* (UNKNO, 1986) 38.

296 Ibid., 39.

297 If we need to conduct a healing or empowerment on a person's head, we usually stand behind them with them seated or kneeling. With the anointing of the sacred oil over my head, Sher stood in front of me, whereas in most cases she would be behind me. At the time, we never considered why she was in front of me, instead of behind me. It was only years later that I discovered this knowledge:

"God in the Bible was never anointed as King, but neither was He ever crowned. Both of these would have seemed theologically offensive, surely to the prophetic mind. They would have indicated both that God's kingdom has a beginning and that someone stands over Him to pour the anointing oil, or behind Him to offer the crown." [Arthur Green, Keter, *The Crown of God in Early Jewish Mysticism* (Princeton University Press, 1997) 10 – 11.]

Since there is no first-hand knowledge on "how to anoint the head," it seems that the anointer, contrary to common sense, stands before the one being anointed, not behind them.

298 Due to a hereditary congenital disorder, both my hip joints were bone on bone by the age of fifty-two. This accident happened about nine months before my first hip replacement at the age of fifty-five in June 2001.

299 The Norse-Germanic concept of fate and destiny is based on a triple goddess (sisters) paradigm.

300 According to David Bohm, what appears to be random is, in fact, a result of the implicate order. In other words, "What appears to be random may, in fact, contain a hidden order. And unless your epistemological net is sufficiently fine, or sufficiently broad, you may miss that hidden order. Bohm called this order the implicate order."

(Keepin, "Astrology and the New Physics: Integrating Sacred and Secular Sciences," *The Mountain Astrologer*, Oct/Nov 2009, 39)

301 For Bohm, "the fundamental primary reality is the implicate (heavens) order, and the explicate (Earth) order is but a set of ripples on the surface of the implicate order. So, that which we can see and feel and touch is merely the waves on the surface of reality, which is a vast ocean of implicate order." (Ibid.)

302 This is in the introduction to my book: *Return of the Feathered Serpent – Shining Light of First Knowledge* (AuthorHouse, 2006). I wrote these words on the edge of the Caribbean during my last few days in Belize, 2004.

303 In this incarnation, my birth occurred on August 29, 1946.

304 Robin Heyworth, "Lamanai: The Jaguar Temple," *Uncovered History*, August 9, 2014 (https://uncoveredhistory.com/belize/lamanai/lamanai-the-jaguar-temple-n10-9).

305 Markman and Markman, *Masks of the Spirit: Image and Metaphor in Mesoamerica*, 17.

306 Christopher A. Matthew, *Beyond the Gates of Fire*, 61.

307 Ibid.

308 Herodotus (c. 484 – c. 425 BC) was an ancient Greek historian.

309 Diodorus Siculus or Diodorus of Sicily was an ancient Greek historian. He is known for writing the monumental universal history Bibliotheca historica, much of which survives, between 60 and 30 BCE.

310 Christopher A. Matthew, *Beyond the Gates of Fire*, 65.

311 Ibid, 68.

312 http://72.14.253.104/search?q=cache:PVdUzAG8XU8J:www.boredofstudies.org/courses/arts/history/ancient/1101256501_2004_Ancient_History_Notes_Renee.doc+greek+spartan+honor+loyalty+courage&hl=en&ct=clnk&cd=29&gl=us

[313] Christopher A. Matthew, *Beyond the Gates of Fire*, 71.

[314] Ibid, 185.

[315] Battle of Salamis, (480 BCE), battle in the Greco-Persian Wars in which a Greek fleet defeated much larger Persian naval forces in the straits at Salamis, between the island of Salamis and the Athenian port-city of Piraeus.

[316] Christopher A. Matthew, *Beyond the Gates of Fire*, 193.

[317] Ibid, 99.

[318] According to Paul Cartledge, Professor of Greek History and former Chairman of the Classics Faculty at Cambridge University, Leonidas was born in 540 B.C.E., which would have made him sixty at Thermopylae. This has also been conferred to me by my Greek friend from Delphi who has extensively researched the connection with Delphi to Thermopylae and the battle at the Hot Springs.

[319] My words that were engraved on a plaque as a 60th birthday gift from one of our journey apprentices.

[320] W.H.S. Jones (trans.), *Pausanias: Description of Greece* (Harvard University Press/Heinemann, 1933) *Book III*, 15:6.

[321] It refers to the process of the acknowledgment of fear, which is then "pressed down" only to be purged later on after battle. This is not the suppression or denial of fear where fear stays hidden but is still active within a person's behaviors, patterns of being and actions.

[322] Greek pre-Socratic philosopher

[323] Greek philosopher and mathematician

[324] Opsopaus, *Guide to the Pythagorean Tarot*, 88.

[325] The first *chakra* is the Root *Chakra*. It is located at the base of the spine and deals with issues of security, basic needs, basic human survival, profane sex and inappropriate sexual activity, and one's connection to the ancestors and the Earth (an un-awakened first *chakra* views Earth/nature as hostile). This is the *chakra* of dualism.

326 Dawn M. Shiley "Breed Profile: Getting to Know the Norwegian Forest Cat," *Cats Center Stage* (http://www.catscenterstage.com/breeds/norwegianforest-cat2.shtml).

327 Walter Burkert. *Greek Religion*, 323.

328 When reincarnation is not one of the beliefs of a religion then the metaphoric gates of hell are flung wide-open. The most vivid result of this is exemplified by the present-day Islamic jihad. Originally, jihad meant an "inner/internal struggle" that is necessary for humans to awaken their hearts. In its corruption, it is deemed an external struggle equated with a one-way ticket to paradise, even though you may have blown up innocents to achieve it.

329 Nancy B. Detweiler, "History of Astrology in Judaism & Christianity," *Way of Love Blog,* March 5, 2012 (https://pathwaytoascension.wordpress.com/2012/03/05/history-of-astrology-in-judaism-christianity).

330 Broadhurst, *Tintagel and the Arthurian Myths*, 99–100.

331 Rabbi David Wolpe, "Angels in Jewish Tradition," www.beliefnet.com, 4/22/2002.

332 M. Macleod Banks, *British Calendar Customs* (The Folklore Society, 1937) 94.

333 Malcolm Godwin, *Angels: An Endangered Species* (Simon & Schuster, 1990) 237.

334 Utilizing numerology, I took the August (8th month) 3, 1997 and added together the numbers: $8 + 3 + 1 + 9 + 9 + 7 = 37$, which is reduced to 10 $(3 + 7)$.

335 Elisabeth Haich, *Wisdom of the Tarot* (Aurora Press, 1983) 88.

336 Ibid., 89.

337 Characteristics or emanations.

338 "*Malkuth* means kingdom. It is associated with the realm of matter/Earth and relates to the physical world, the planets, and the solar system. It is important not to think of this *sephirah* as merely

'unspiritual,' for even though it is the emanation furthest from the divine source, it is still on the Tree of Life. As the receiving sphere of all the other *sephirot* above it, *Malkuth* gives tangible form to the other emanations. It is like the negative node of an electrical circuit. The divine energy comes down and finds its expression in this plane, and our purpose as human beings is to bring that energy back around the circuit again and up the Tree.

"In comparing with Eastern systems, *Malkuth* is a very similar archetypal idea to that of the *Muladhara chakra*. In this manner, *Malkuth* is again associated with the anus, although technically the *Muladhara* is located in the sacrum bone. In *Shakta tantra*, which is also associated with the Earth, this is the plane in which *karma* is expressed.

"Although *Malkuth* is seen as the lowest *sefirah* on the Tree of Life, it also contains within it the potential to reach the highest. This is exemplified in the *Hermetic* maxim 'as above, so below.'" (http://en.wikipedia.org/wiki/Malkuth.)

339 Haich, *Wisdom of the Tarot*, 89.

340 There is a Hopi prophecy connected with the Blue Star. This is the return of *Pahana* or "True White Brother."

341 "Daniel W. E. Green of the Harvard-Smithsonian Center for Astrophysics stated that the latest orbital calculations indicate that the Hale-Bopp comet last passed through the inner solar system about 4210 years ago. An Arutz-7 correspondent noted that according to the ancient Jewish text *Seder Olam Rabah*, the comet's previous appearance was approximately the same year that Noah began building the ark." "Signs in the Heavens" (http://www.catholicprophecy.info/signs.html).

342 "St. Nectan's Glen – A Mysterious History," *The Cornish Bird, A Blog about Cornwall's Hidden Places & Untold Stories* (https://cornishbirdblog.com/2018/11/18/st-nectans-glen-a-mysterious-history/?fbclid=IwAR3l-OnXMrjTSFDpinZGdVvLL1uks6B-RQQ4ErF-Cf3dybCs2IW14ryEGSiE).

343 I use the male identity for literary reasons and intrinsic identity, even though angels and archangels are neuter and neither male or female.

344 Miller and Broadhurst, *The Sun and the Serpent*, 32.

345 We would discover later that this is known as Merlin's ley line.

346 What apprentices call me.

347 Broadhurst, *Tintagel and the Arthurian Myths*, 52–53.

348 Ibid., 53.

349 Ibid., 180.

350 The spiral is one of the oldest spiritual symbols and reflects the inward and outward consciousness of the kingdom of God and the universal pattern of growth and evolution. Spirals are common in nature and the product of phi (φ), which is also called the golden section or the golden mean.

351 It is not necessary to state the name of my past life and my wife's as revealed by the visitation. The visitation along with our memoirs provides enough knowledge through our works and experiences for you to determine who we were.

352 This is a state of being or consciousness where the mind does not attach externally or internally to the sensory input, even though it is still a part of our consciousness, and we do not attach to the senses or the passions that arise from them. Passions are things that disturb the tranquility of our mind, such as fear.

Furthermore, this is the Japanese principle composed of two inter-penetrating concepts: immovable mind and no mind. Mastery is encoded within these two concepts, each with an ocean of meaning and understanding.

The highest level of body-mind skill is only attainable through a mind that is ever present with total sensory input (without mind chatter – no mind) but detached – a mind and heart that is ever flowing but does not attach and thus remains immovable.

Our eyes every day attach and judge with various emotions arising from this attachment and judgment. Our minds constantly chatter. Contrary to this, the highest level of martial or spiritual ability is to "see but not see" the other person or persons – no attachments, no judgments (i.e., win or lose, live or die). This is the "heart that sees," the Mesoamerican *Ollin* heart.

353 In one apprentice's words, "The rainstorm brought a lot of water as we know. The 'lean-to' really was not adequate to hold a lot of it off. The water running through the campsite and through the 'lean-to' was running over my foot. Not ankle high, but definitely covering toes. I did have concern about the electricity from the lightning going through the water to us."

354 *Lono* is lord of the east and the god of learning. "Lono in Hawaii is associated with cloud signs and the phenomena of storms. . . . In prayers to *Lono* the signs of the god are named as thunder, lightning, earthquake, the dark cloud, the rainbow, rain, and wind." [Martha Warren Beckwith, *Hawaiian Mythology* (University of Hawaii Press, 1970) 31.]

"In Hawaiian mythology, *Lono* is a fertility and music god who descended to Earth on a rainbow to marry *Laka*. In agricultural and planting traditions, *Lono* was identified with rain and food plants. He was one of the four gods (with *Ku*, *Kane*, and his twin brother *Kanaloa*) who existed before the world was created. *Lono* was also the god of peace. In his honor, the great annual festival of the *Makahiki* was held. During this period (from October through February), all unnecessary work and war was *kapu* (taboo).

"Some Hawaiians believed that Captain James Cook was *Lono* returned, and indeed this fact may have ultimately contributed to Captain Cook's death. There was a tradition that such a human manifestation of the god [*Lono*] had actually appeared, established games and then departed to '*Kahiki*,' promising to return." ["Ancient Hawaiian Tiki Gods! Hawaiian Mythology & Tiki God History," *MythicHawaii.com*, 2006 (http://www.mythichawaii.com/tiki-gods.htm).]

355 An individual's unique song of power; it is composed of vocalizations, not words, and only attained through rigorous spiritual and mental training. This leads to mastering the power of the "mindsong." The most powerful songs are the ones of long-dead shamans – this is the song that I carry.

356 "And they will say to the dwellers of this land, as they have heard, that you, *Yahweh,* are within these people who saw you, *Yahweh,* eye to eye, and your cloud stood over them and you walked before them in the pillar of cloud by day and in a pillar of fire by night." (Numbers 14:14).

357 "More than any other, the Archangel Michael is the angel of our time. Gabriel ruled the era from just before the birth of Jesus until the late 19th century, handing authority then to Michael, who rules the present era. He is the archangel of the twentieth century and the one who guides us into the 21st century and the New Age. He is our inspiration, our leader and he is here, above all, to remind us that we are spiritual beings.

"The Archangel Michael is often referred to as the Commander in Chief, Commander of the Heavenly Host, the Overlord or similar titles because the other archangels are linked to him and take their orders from him. Michael alone receives his orders directly from the Divine Source.

"In art, Michael is usually depicted carrying a sword or a spear—often both—and in armor. This, coupled with his many military-sounding titles, is puzzling for people who find it hard to reconcile such warlike imagery with the nature of a great archangel. To understand this, we need to look beyond the surface appearances to the deeper symbolism: Michael carries a sword in order to cut through ignorance. Sometimes he is shown subduing (not killing) a dragon with his spear, the dragon representing greed.

Somebody may be ignorant because they have never had the opportunity to discover the truth: for them, Michael and the angels have nothing but compassion. Compassion, though, can sometimes be vigorous. If we are ignorant because we are lazy, if we willfully ignore the knowledge that could guide us towards a more spiritual life, if we deliberately close our eyes to the evils going on around us because the knowledge is too uncomfortable, we may merit a little prod from Michael's sword!

"Michael's great battle, though, is against the forces of greed that are corrupting the world. Think about it for a moment: wars are fought, people-oppressed, populations go hungry, the Earth is polluted because of greed. The lust for land, oil, uranium, water, money or power lies at the root of so much that is wrong. Michael moves our hearts and minds to oppose the forces of greed." (*Kindred Spirit*, Issue 48, Autumn 1999, 19.)

358 Blavatsky, *Isis Unveiled: Both Volumes – A Master-Key to the Mysteries of Ancient and Modern Science and Theology,* 488.

359 A new moon and Virgo: "Even today, astrologers recognize that the sign of Virgo is the one which has reference to a messianic world ruler to be born from a virgin." [Ernest L. Martin, "Astronomy and the Birth of Jesus: Scripturally Connected by Mt. 24:30 and Rev. 12:1-2," *A Deeper Walk* (http://deeperwalk.lefora. com/2010/07/03/the-astronomical-sign-of-the-son-of-man/).]

"And there appeared a great wonder in heaven; a woman clothed with the sun, and the moon under her feet, and upon her head a crown of twelve stars[.]" [Revelations 12:1 (King James Version)].

"The essential factor in interpreting the symbol of Revelation 12:1 – 5 is the identification of the woman. . . . The woman in the first three verses is featured as being in heaven and both the Sun and the Moon are in association with her. . . . The important factor is the birth of the man-child and the woman's relationship with the heavenly signs while she is symbolically in heaven. (The first three verses of Revelation 12 shows the Sun clothing her, the Moon under her feet and the Twelve Stars on her head.) The 'birth' of the Messiah is associated with this heavenly spectacle. . . .

"Since the Sun and Moon are amidst or in line with the body of this woman, she could be, in a symbolic way, a constellation located within the normal paths of the Sun and Moon. The only sign of a woman which exists along the ecliptic (the track of the Sun in its journey through the stars) is that of Virgo the Virgin. She occupies, in body form, a space of about 50 degrees along the ecliptic. The head of the woman actually bridges some 10 degrees into the previous sign of Leo and her feet overlap about 10 degrees into the following sign of Libra, the Scales. In the period of Jesus's birth, the Sun entered in its annual course through the heavens into the head position of the woman about August 13 and exited from her feet about October 2. But the apostle John saw the scene when the Sun was 'clothing' or 'adorning' the woman. This surely indicates that the position of the Sun in the vision was located somewhere mid-bodied to the woman, between the neck and the knees. . . .

"The only time in the year that the Sun could be in a position to 'clothe' the celestial woman called Virgo (that is, to be mid-bodied to her, in the region where a pregnant woman carries a child) is when the Sun is located between about 150 and 170 degrees along the ecliptic. This 'clothing' of the woman by the Sun occurs for a 20-day period each year. This 20-degree spread could indicate the general time when Jesus was born. In 3 B.C.E., the Sun would have entered this celestial region about August 27 and exited from it about September 15. . . .

"This heavenly woman called Virgo is normally depicted as a virgin holding in her right hand a green branch and in her left hand a sprig of grain. In the Hebrew Zodiac, she at first (in the time of David) denoted Ruth who was gleaning in the fields of Boaz. She then later became the Virgin when the prophecy of Isaiah 7:14 was given in the time of King Hezekiah and the prophet Isaiah. This Virgin held in her left hand a sprig of grain. This was precisely where the bright star called Spica is found. Indeed, the chief star of the constellation Virgo is Spica.

"Bullinger, in his book *The Witness of the Stars* (29–34), said that the word 'Spica' has, through the Arabic, the meaning 'the branch' and that it symbolically refers to Jesus who was prophetically called 'the Branch' in Zechariah 3:8 and 6:12. And Bullinger (and Seiss in his book *The Gospel in the Stars*) maintains that this sign of Virgo designates the heavenly witness for the birth of the Messiah (Jesus).

"Jesus was born in early evening, and Revelation 12 shows it was a New Moon day.

"What New Moon could this have been? The answer is most amazing. It is almost too amazing! September 11, 3 B.C.E. was *Tishri One* on the Jewish calendar. To Jewish people, this would have been a very profound occasion indeed. *Tishri One* is none other than the Jewish New Year's Day (*Rosh ha-Shanah*, or as the Bible calls it, The Day of Trumpets, Leviticus 23:23–26). It was an important annual holy day of the Jews (but not one of the three annual festivals that required all Palestinian Jews to be in Jerusalem).

"What a significant day for the appearance of the Messiah to arrive on Earth from the Jewish point of view! And remarkably, no other day of the year could astronomically fit Revelation 12:1 – 3. The Apostle John is certainly showing forth an astronomical sign which answers precisely with the Jewish New Year Day. John would have realized the significance of this astronomical scene that he was describing." [Martin, "Astronomy and the Birth of Jesus: Scripturally Connected by Mt. 24:30 and Rev. 12:1–2," *A Deeper Walk* (http://deeperwalk.lefora.com/2010/07/03/the-astronomical-sign-of-the-son-of-man/).]

360 Rabbi Geoffrey W. Dennis, *The Encyclopedia of Jewish Myth, Magic and Mysticism* (Llewellyn Publications, 2016) 171.

361 Guénon, *Fundamental Symbols*, 161.

362 Malcolm Godwin, Angels, *An Endangered Species* (Simon & Schuster, 1999) 25.

363 Miller and Broadhurst, *The Sun and the Serpent*, 127.

364 James R. Lewis and Evelyn Dorothy Oliver, *Angels A to Z* (Visible Ink Press, 2008) 279.

365 Photo taken by Jim Kalnins.

366 Broadhurst, *Tintagel and the Arthurian Myths*. 191.

367 "Love is central to life. It is a binding force between a parent and their [sic] child and one divine human being to another divine human being. Love may be sexual, and possibly, emotional and physical intimacy.

"However, the foundational meaning and essence of Love is One-ness – unity.

"*Ahavah* means 'love' in Hebrew. The Jewish mystics remark on the affinity between the word *ahavah*, 'love,' and '*echad*,' one. The numerical value of their letters is the same: 13.

"Oneness, unity, is the aspiration of love, and love emerges from a perception of unity. This insight is also expressed in the *Shema*: its first line declares God's unity and ends with the word '*echad*.' Then follows the *mitzvah* to love God. Love comes out of a sense of God's unity pervading all things.

"There are three commands to love in the *Torah*; 'Love your neigh-bour as yourself' (Leviticus 19:18); 'Love the stranger as yourself' (Leviticus 19:34); and 'You shall love the Lord your God for all your heart, soul and strength' (Deuteronomy 6:4)." [Rabbi Julian Sinclair, "Ahavah, " *The JC.com*, October 28, 2008, (.https://www.thejc.com/judaism/jewish-words/ahavah-1.57740)]

368 One of the most devious methods of control that has ever been conceived is the Catholic Church's communion and its rite of con-firmation. Communion involves eating the wafer, symbolic of the body of Jesus, and drinking the wine, which is the blood of Jesus. During confirmation, little girls, all dressed in white, are Jesus's brides, and then, confirming their bodies, minds, and spirits to the church, they each eat the body and drink the blood of their groom.

Symbolic or real, it still affects the consciousness and subcon-sciousness of the blind participants. You are still eating the body and drinking the blood and, in the case of confirmation, marrying young supposed virgins to a dead person hanging on a cross. (Hus-felt, *Do You Like Jesus – Not the Church?*, 138.)

369 The following "Grace versus Compassion" is excerpted from my

book, *Do You Like Jesus – Not The Church?*

"Grace: a Christian theological term denoting divine gifts without which human salvation would be impossible.

"'Compassion comes from within us. Grace comes from outside us as divine gifts, but, of course, only for the believers.' – Rev. Dr. JC Husfelt.

"Christianity's concept of 'grace' is the child of the two Fs: faith and fear. Pure and simple, 'grace' is a paradigm of judgment flowing from a 'father-figure deity' – the Christian God. Grace is an absurd, immature religious concept that is supposed to help explain the mysterious events of life, which many times are tragic or unexplainable happenings. In reality, its prime purpose is to only keep the 'faithful' in line and in fear.

"Have you ever stood before a judge? I haven't, but I would have to think it is a little intimidating, with more than a touch of fear of the unknown thrown in. With 'grace' we have the ultimate 'judge and jury.' Taking this one step further, and based on the dogma of Christianity, your priest or minister is God's representative – a very subtle and slimy way to generate respect and a bit of fear, either consciously or subconsciously.

"Grace spreads a subconscious message of separation while scattering a veil of fear over a legitimate and, most importantly, religious concept – compassion. Think for a moment about a scenario where children are trapped in a burning building – some survive by being rescued, and others aren't rescued and perish. And we hear a statement from the mother of the children who were saved: 'By the grace of God, my children live.'

"How about the children who died? With 'grace' as your belief, it means that your children who died were judged 'not worthy' of life! How ludicrous a belief . . . but on the other hand, how dangerous a belief this is, as well as totally destructive, to a person's mind and sense of self – emotionally, mentally, and spiritually. . . .

"Ironically enough, but tellingly as well, Jesus didn't buy into a judgmental God who dispersed a 'grace' based on salvation-condemnatory criteria . . . Jesus's God was compassionate. When Jesus spoke, it was about the compassion of God as it flowed to all people and to all things of the Earth.

"Compassion and forgiveness were some of the basic principles that Jesus taught and practiced. Jesus did not teach 'grace' and never used the word 'grace.' He viewed compassion as a great, round mirror of the heart and mind that perceived self and others not as distinct but as merged identities. This was knowledge, wisdom, and the realities of life based on oneness, not an illusion of life centered on selective gifts from a 'Man-God.' Flowing from this oneness of reality, empathy emerges for us as a motivating force for proper deeds or right action.

"We must ask ourselves, then, why 'grace' is one of the pillars of Christianity. In my heart and mind, the answer is obvious: power and control. Since Jesus never used the word 'grace' or taught the 'way of a judgmental God,' we have another lie of the patriarchal church. (Husfelt, *Do You Like Jesus – Not The Church?*, 71 – 73.)

370 "State of Grace," *Catholic Dictionary, CatholicCulture.org* (https://www.catholicculture.org/culture/library/dictionary/index.cfm?id=36634).

371 Christopher D, Hudson, ed., *American Bible Society Presents Angels and Miracles: The Spiritual Realm and the World You Know* (Time Inc. Home Entertainment/ American Bible Society, 2009) 17.

372 Permeating all of creation is a divine consciousness, a sacred power, a force. This force is the single, dynamic, sacred power or energy that is the unifying totality of all things – a universal life force (we can think of this as something akin to electricity). It's in constant movement, eternally self-generating and self-regenerating while encompassing and interpenetrating the whole cosmos. The Nahua identified this force as teotl. "At the heart of Nahua philosophy stands the thesis that there exists a single, dynamic, vivifying, eternally self-generating and self-regenerating sacred power, energy or force: what the Nahuas called teotl." [Maffie, "Aztec Philosophy,"

Internet Encyclopedia of Philosophy (http://www.iep.utm.edu/aztec).]

373 Alexus McLeod, *Philosophy of the Ancient Maya: Lords of Time (Studies in Comparative Philosophy and Religion)* (Lexington Books, 2017) 162.

374 Maffie, *Aztec Philosophy*, 102.

375 Ibid., 103.

376 David A. Solté, "Quantum Shift 1997," The Mountain Astrologer, Feb/Mar 1997, 30.

377 Beatrix Murrell, "The Cosmic Plenum: Bohm's Gnosis: The Implicate Order," *Stoa del Sol* (http://www.bizcharts.com/stoa_del_sol/plenum/plenum_3.html).

378 Ibid.

379 Ibid.

380 Bohm's theory of the implicate order stresses that the cosmos is in a state of process. Bohm's cosmos is a "feedback" universe that continuously recycles forward into a greater mode of being and consciousness.

381 One of our apprentices, Jim Kalnins, took a picture of me during the day while we finished building the stone death spiral. No one saw what the camera picked up. The picture is not of pillars of light. It is an intense and immense light off to my left in the woods with two globes of light suspended above. The light has a shape almost like a sword in its center with golden rays coming off of it. It's been verified that it is not a reflection of the lens of the instant camera that took the picture.

382 These are adapted from the *Popol Vuh*: a Mayan document, an invaluable source of knowledge of ancient Mayan mythology and culture. [Douglas Gillette, *Shaman's Secret: The Lost Resurrection Teachings of the Ancient Maya* (Bantam, 1998) 108.]

383 Joseph Campbell, *The Mythic Image* (Princeton University Press,

1981) 182.

384 "Two lineages: There are two bloodlines. Every human being has not only an ancestral line of the Earth but also an angelic lineage of the heavens. Our earthly bloodline flows from our parents' ancestral lines, while our heavenly evolution stems from our previous incarnations.

"Each of us has two lineages. This is one of the reasons why there is emotional confusion surrounding the fetus and life. I have had people in their attempt to prove that the fetus is a living person state that their baby in the womb responded to various styles of music. Of course, there is an emotional attachment to the feelings of having life growing within you. Yes, it is alive, just as the heart of the mother is alive. Yet, it is not a soulful human being at this point in time. It is developing its earthly DNA lineage. It is a potential human being, as it has not as yet interpenetrated with its soulful heavenly lineage. This occurs at birth with the first breath of life, God's breath, and the descent of the heavenly DNA, the golden dew." (Husfelt, *Do You Like Jesus – Not the Church?*, 152.)

385 A line from William Shakespeare's play *Romeo and Juliet*.

386 "Green is the prime color of the world, and that from which its loveliness arises." – Pedro Calderon de la Barca.

Green is the color of nature. It symbolizes growth, harmony, fertility, revitalization, and rebirth. Green stimulates our pituitary gland. This is one of the reasons to spend quality time in nature and become one with it.

Green is the color of the Heart *Chakra* which connects us with the world around us. If your world is solely composed of materialistic thought processes and human-designed environments with little time spent in nature and no concern for the well-being of others, then your heart is asleep – symbolically hard and dead.

Green symbolizes prosperity, freshness, and progress.

387 I was identified as a prophet by my Hawaiian friend's spirit ancestor during the burning late afternoon before the vision and voice

from heaven.

388 Bill Ayres and Michael Steven Smith, "It Has Been 50 Years Since Che Guevara Was Murdered," *The Nation*, October 9, 2017 (https://www.thenation.com/article/it-has-been-50-years-since-che-guevara-was-murdered).

389 Paul Broadhurst, *The Secret Land, The Origins of Arthurian Legend and the Grail Quest* (Mythos, 2009) 76.

390 Ibid., 229.

391 Morduch, *The Sovereign Adventure: The Grail of Mankind,* 148 – 149.

392 It may also be a person's religion and spiritual belief.

393 Love in its pure meaning is unity or oneness.

394 Borg, *Jesus: A New Vision*, 35.

395 Ib Ravn, "Chapter 2: David Bohm on the Implicate Order in Ontology, Physics, Epistemology and Human Existence," *"Implicate Order" and the Good Life* (http://www.ibravn.dk/22126-impord-goodlife-2.htm).

396 "Jung appeared to be undecided in his own mind about the question of the ontological status of the archetypes . . . and this state of affairs has led to considerable controversy. But I believe that the ambiguity was necessitated by Jung's inability to scientifically reconcile his conviction that the archetypes are at once embodied structures and bear the imprint of the divine; that is, the archetypes are both structures within the human body and represent the domain of spirit. Jung's intention was clearly a unitary one, and yet his ontology seemed often to be dualistic, as well as persistently ambiguous, and was necessarily so because the science of his day could not envision a non-dualistic conception of spirit and matter.

"Jung's dualism is apparent in his distinction between the archetypes and the instincts which required for him a polarization of the psyche into those products derived from matter and those derived from spirit. He imagined the psyche as the intersection at the apex of two cones, one of spirit and the other of matter[.]" (Charles D. Laughlin, "Archetypes, Neurognosis and the Quantum Sea," *Journal of Scientific Exploration*, Vol. 10, No. 3, 1996, 375 - 400, http://www.scientificexploration.org/journal/jse_10_3_laughlin.pdf.)

397 Ravn, "Chapter 2: David Bohm on the Implicate Order in Ontology, Physics, Epistemology and Human Existence," *"Implicate Order" and the Good Life* (http://www.ibravn.dk/22126-impord-goodlife-2.htm).

398 Ibid.

399 Séjourné, *Burning Water: Thought and Religion in Ancient Mexico*, 157.

400 Court Stroud, "Dawn of the Sixth Sun: The Mayan Pope and Elders Visit the Big Apple," *HuffPost*, Oct. 12, 2012, updated Dec. 06, 2017 (https://www.huffingtonpost.com/court-stroud/dawn-of-the-sixth-sun-the-mayan-pope-and-elders-visit-the-big-apple_b_2007704.html).

401 David Day, *Tolkien's Ring* (Pavilion, 2012) 151.

402 Flower Heart—one of the three pillars of light of Divine Humanity—always expressing love from the heart and letting others, as well as ourselves, view the beauty and the divine perfection that is the true essence of our hearts. Smell is a powerful sense. With a Flower Heart, our fragrance is pure, sweet, and soothing to ourselves and others. The Flower Heart is also the Lily or Lotus Heart.

403 Waters, *Mexico Mystique*, 224.

404 Adapted from Elizabeth Van Buren's book the *Refuge of the Apocalypse: Doorway into Other Dimensions*, 330 – 331.

405 Literally, a "knower of things." According to Miguel León-Portilla, "a wise man appears as a guide, a person who points out the path to others." (León-Portilla, *Aztec Thought and Culture*, 22.)